AS

The Politics of
Empowerment

The Politics of Empowerment

ROBERT WEISSBERG

PRAEGER

Westport, Connecticut
London

Library of Congress Cataloging-in-Publication Data

Weissberg, Robert.
   The politics of empowerment / Robert Weissberg.
      p.   cm.
   Includes bibliographical references and index.
   ISBN 0–275–96426–4 (alk. paper)
   1. Social service—United States—Citizen participation.
   2. Community organization—United States—Citizen participation.
   3. Community power—United States.   4. Political participation—
   United States.   I. Title.
   HV91.W466   1999
   361.8'0973—dc21   98–38285

British Library Cataloguing in Publication Data is available.

Library of Congress Catalog Card Number: 98–38285
ISBN: 0–275–96426–4

First published in 1999

Praeger Publishers, 88 Post Road West, Westport, CT 06881
An imprint of Greenwood Publishing Group, Inc.

Printed in the United States of America

The paper used in this book complies with the
Permanent Paper Standard issued by the National
Information Standards Organization (Z39.48–1984).

10 9 8 7 6 5 4 3 2 1

Contents

Preface

The writing of *The Politics of Empowerment* was, not surprisingly, a learning experience. The project began almost casually, observing the term *empowerment* here and there and then coming to the conclusion that it was "everywhere." This was confirmed by some preliminary computer-assisted searches—merely typing in *empowerment* elicited thousands of entries in almost every imaginable social science field and then some. Perhaps "epidemic" might better describe this popularity. Such fashionableness quickly drew my curiosity and, ultimately, my suspicion. Had we discovered some remarkable yet unpublicized new cure for our aliments? Was empowerment the equivalent of antibiotics or other medical miraclelike cures for faulty education, poverty, racial antagonisms or whatever? Judged by the prodigious energy and enthusiasm being poured into empowering projects, it certainly seemed so. The chorus of praise singers was immense. Being naturally skeptical of heralded novelties, I concluded that an "outsider" inquiry might be useful. Perhaps my own (and eventually disappointing) personal experience as a hopelessly idealistic teenager easily infatuated with "instant cures" for formidable problems awakened this curiosity.

Initial expectations, admittedly, were not high. I reasoned that if all these projects were successful, their masterful accomplishments would have already reached me without having to dig deeply into obscure academic outlets in often oddly defined fields. After all, upgrading dismal inner-city schools is hardly the Manhattan Project, to be kept concealed lest the Evil Empire filch its secrets. On the other hand, those skilled at solving vexing problems need not be skilled publicists. Perhaps all these alluring cures, like some imminent hi-tech laboratory breakthrough, were merely on the edge of being mainstreamed. If that were true, then I could be the happy messenger, announcing to a wider audience that empowerment was the welcome answer to so many of our daunting dilemmas.

Alas, what I soon uncovered was hardly cause for celebration. As I became immersed in empowerment books and articles, as my trusty research assistant almost daily delivered boxes of fresh material to be (eventually) digested, I often could not believe what was unfolding. "Shoddiness" is a bit too kind, given the stakes involved. A more apt description might invoke one of those fraudulent "miracle diets" one step ahead of government regulators. Having just completed a book on tolerance, I was no stranger to scholarship substituting vacuous, though sincere, messages for hard fact. Nor would the existence of entire "scholarly industries" devoted to nonsense come as a major surprise. Nearly 30 years as an academic makes a complete shock on such matters unlikely. But, here, I believed, things would differ. Human lives are at stake—not some arcane academic dispute of marginal real-world consequences. Prattling on about the dimensionality of party identification is not to be compared to proscribing advice to educators overwhelmed by chaos. Human life should take precedence over crass academic vocationalism. Surely, I believed, responsibilities would be taken seriously—advice could not, of course, be guaranteed, but it should at least be sensible, factually based and feasible.

What emerged over the months of marching through this literature often verged on academic malpractice. Nostrum after nostrum would be paraded sans any decent evidence that it would improve conditions. In many instances, the flaws were immediately visible—for example, allowing academically deficient pupils to direct their own learning. What is one to say when an "expert" avers letting the seriously mentally ill run their own clinic? Can we really expect a slight-of-hand redefinition of "mentally ill" to heal street derelicts? Elsewhere I found a total disregard for the rules of evidence, even the idea that schemes have to be demonstrated as worthy. One educator even went so far as to assert that rationality was the enemy of empowerment.

Self-proclaimed authorities occasionally displayed a technical knowledge of their subject matter that was embarrassing. Apparently, one can certify oneself as an expert in the homeless problem without ever being aware of zoning laws or the real estate market. Credentials aside, much of this enterprise is profoundly anti-intellectual. In the case of African-American empowerment, a state of denial infects empowerment prophets—the same futile admonitions are ceaselessly announced despite their repeated failure. Again and again, the unsophisticated in distress are encouraged to launch crusades doomed to fail. One especially (and quite common) disturbing theme is conflating dependency with empowerment. Across multiple settings, the less fortunate are told that "real empowerment" means the capacity to effectively demand increased government benefits. Extortion and begging, not independence, are being counseled in empowerment's name.

I have occasionally made reference to this reprehensible advice given by academics, but it really deserves its own book. The phenomenon raises more than a few awkward questions. How is it possible that such clever people, blessed with so many resources, unencumbered to pursue truth, can effortlessly advance such atrocious guidance? Obviously, something is rotten in Denmark U. The explanations are, no doubt, plentiful, but if one had to be selected as the chief culprit, it must be the self-imposed ideological unanimity now gripping university life. Not only is one portion of the ideological spectrum—namely, the cultural Left—reproducing itself unhindered in many disciplines, but non–camp followers are cowered into silence. The ideologically blind citing the ideologically blind for fun and profit. As with the rabbit explosion in Australia, bereft of any forthright adversaries, it easily multiplies. After a point, ill-formed, half-baked ideas become "reasonable" if everyone seems to concur. That this "everyone" holds a Ph.D. only certifies this faulty consensus as authentic wisdom.

Disagreeing with this oft misleading party line risks far more than momentary intellectual rebuke. It was once said of success in Congress—"To get along, go along"—and this applies equally—if not more so—to academic life. To resist fashionable bandwagons, to criticize inept research too harshly, to favor "old-fashioned" remedies in place of ideologically laden gimmicks—these invite being ostracized, not a trivial condition in a setting where collegial recognition shapes one's professional advancement. The "game" is to be played by being agreeable, citing others profusely and favorably. As Chapter 7 elaborates, this "keeping quiet" is especially important on the sensitive topic of African-American politics. Here venturing into taboo territory may invite unpleasant confrontations and an undeserved reputation as an evil racist. I can speak to this point from firsthand experience. That human beings might suffer as a result of faulty scholarship is *never* at issue as research is dissected. Per chance the modern university's physical and social insulation from the "real world" permit such indifference painlessly. One can spend an entire lifetime spinning out horrendous counsel and never have to face a dissatisfied customer.

This enterprise is *not* directed to discrediting *all* empowerment as worthless snake oil dressed up in high-sounding academic verbiage. As we frequently note, our empowerment tour is selective, and much that we ignore is probably the real and highly commendable article. Our brief references to Robert Woodson's writings are disproportionate to its immense value— those who think empowerment may be worthy (and it is) are strongly advised to read further there. He makes the empowerment case superbly. When we speak of "empowerment" we largely limit ourselves to outcroppings in the academic literature plus the one recent grand political experiment—the federal government empowerment effort begun in 1993. Again, we are not anti-empowerment. We commend those who seek power over their lives by gaining new skills, conquering bad habits or imposing self-discipline. Nor do we admonish those citizens who seek to play a more active community role. The virtues of this type of empowerment are plain and hardly need documentation. Our focus is on the *extending* of empowerment, as directed by a small contingent of would-be advisers, to domains long judged inappropriate. We counsel limits on empowerment. To believe that empowerment is some universal elixir is to invite a most grievous mischief.

Finally, readers may detect a slight moral fervor infusing this project. This is correct. Down deep, my misdirected youthful "bleeding heart" instincts cannot be extinguished, though their form has shifted dramatically. My intention is to help, and this service should transcend ideology. The less fortunate are not convenient pawns in some grand political battle. And if one is unable to aid, one should not impede others. At a minimum, do no harm. This seemingly uncontestable axiom is routinely violated by many academics deceitfully preaching the gospel of empowerment: Advancing a veiled ideological agenda outranks helpfulness. In their eyes, for example, it is better to manipulate the homeless into demanding some amorphous first step toward socialism than actually to help those desperately in need. At times, political ventriloquism transpires: Advisers only need to coax the naïve that statism will offer an instant shortcut to riches. Political self-gratification (often coupled with careerism) trumps true benevolence, and the crime is covered up with high-sounding rhetoric and turgid academic jargon. If this is merely a matter of moral uncertainty, a confusion of what is useful and harmful, an incapacity to use objectively the techniques of social science, then they should forfeit their license to practice social engineering. Duplicitous counsel is more than bad scholarship; it is evil.

In writing *The Politics of Empowerment* I have benefited from the usual, though tiny, cast of supportive characters. Foremost is my trusted stealth research assistant, Charles DeWitt, who has relentlessly tracked down far more "stuff" than one person could possibly ever read over multiple lifetimes. The University of Illinois–Urbana library staff also deserves its customary gratitude for its ingenuity and civility. This book could not have been written without their help. The Earhart Foundation again graciously supplied funding to lighten my burden slightly. A special thanks goes to Erika Gilbert, who listened for untold hours to my endless kvetching and spontaneously provided her renowned advice absolutely free of charge. While others may read this book, she has lived it.

Lastly, given the controversial material that follows, let me acknowledge that these views are strictly my own.

The Politics of
Empowerment

1

Empowerment Everywhere

In the landscape of nostrums addressing contemporary problems, "empowerment" is ubiquitous (Safire 1990). This recourse applies whether impediments are personal—drug addiction, poverty, physical disability, sexual harassment, dismal academic performance—or involve more weighty difficulties, for example, uplifting entire ethnic/racial groups. Even the homeless, mentally ill alcoholic, we are told, will substantially improve his or her life by abandoning passivity and embracing emancipation. Narratives occasionally mimic religious revivallike "miracle cures"—a quadriplegic, mentally retarded cerebral palsy sufferer autonomously joining the advanced class and thriving, thanks to the empowerment gospel (Fetterman 1994; the story is, allegedly, true). That at least some people—schoolchildren, the ailing, the severely mentally impaired—prosper under benign domination is quickly discredited as out of touch with progress. "All Power to the People," the radical 1960s slogan, is now mainstreamed and glorified.

The size of this missionary chorus cannot be exaggerated. Business gurus advise employee empowerment as the assured path toward greater profitability and client satisfaction. Prestigious foundations such as Rockefeller and Ford bestow their blessings with financial generosity. Commerce embraces it—one travel agency offers an "Empowerment Cruise" departing from Miami, Florida, to Cozumel, Mexico, complete with gourmet food and Las Vegas–style gambling. A quick Yahoo website tour reveals some 167 organizations embodying empowerment doctrines: myriad health groups (mental disorders, sickle cell disease, families of children with Down's syndrome), endless sexual orientation societies (including cross-dressing), business assistance ventures galore, plus clubs for nearly every racial-ethnic segment of society, to mention merely the highlights of the highlights. It is also an intellectually inclusive, diverse bandwagon. Today's obsession, according to Barbara Levy Simon, has its philosophical roots in the ideas of John Locke, Karl Marx, Susan B. Anthony, Emma Goldman, Mahatma Ghandi, Mao Tse-tung, Franz Fannon, Martin Luther King, Malcolm X and Paulo Freire (Simon 1990).

A multitude of academic disciplines, from hardheaded economics to compassionate professors of social work and nursing, share this ardor. Between 1974 and 1986, PsycLit, the computerized listing of psychology journal articles, showed only 96 "empower" or "empowerment" entries; between 1987 and 1993 the comparable figure was 689 articles and 283 book chapters (Perkins and Zimmerman 1995). Applications are often quite original. A modern dance instructor argues that dance experiences bring empowerment and thus serve to promote world peace (Opels 1995). Another suggests that pathologies of inner-city youth might be solved if these youngsters were empowered—given enhanced control over their lives. That these troubled adolescents typically already enjoy extravagant freedom was ignored (Nessel 1988). The preoccupation is worldwide—problems as varied as political inequality and famine in South American, Africa, India and Asia, it is argued, are all susceptible to remediation via citizen self-determination. And, perhaps most surprisingly, the treatment draws endorsements across the political spectrum. Militant feminists and Marxists enthusiastically cheer its wondrous virtues, whereas conservatives invoke empowerment as the alternative to a failed, big-government welfare state. President George Bush, hardly an idealist, wished to make "empowerment" the centerpiece of domestic programs to assist citizens (DeParle and Appelbome 1991). House Speaker Newt Gingrich founded "National Empowerment TV" to promote conservatism. President Bill Clinton, ever attentive to popular moods, has enlisted federal funding to uplift and empower impoverished urbanites. During the 1996 presidential election, two prominent Republicans—vice-presidential candidate Jack Kemp and primary contender Steven Forbes—were both closely associated with Empower America, which preached capitalism to cure social and cultural ills.

This preoccupation runs deeper than a trendy passion for high-sounding verbiage. To be sure, some advocates unthinkingly voice "empowerment" as if it were a magical phrase capable of exorcising demons. Yet far more common are those citizens and professional experts who fervently believe that personal or collective capacitation, a "taking charge" of one's circumstances, can ameliorate our obstacles. One is reminded of an earlier era when zeal for religious piety and devotion appealed as the trustworthy route to regeneration. Today's Salvation Army, however, sings about seizing one's own destiny. From national civil rights groups to grassroots-based community action associations, organizations galore have enlisted into this modern rendering of progress. The quest also bestows money. Atlanta and

Detroit, among others, now enjoy entrepreneurial "empowerment zones," thanks to Washington's generosity. Urban planners today heed citizen involvement in their designs. Just as millions seek betterment via exercise and careful diet, tens of millions—whether militant gay activists demanding an AIDS (acquired immunodeficiency syndrome) cure or Christian fundamentalists seeking relief from secular education—are infatuated with this dogma.

With remarkably few exceptions, this doctrine goes unchallenged. For every voice raising even the slightest hesitancy, dozens wish to extend "the cure" to fresh terrain. To resist and express skepticism, it would seem, promotes servility and weakness. Surrendering to one's lowly fate, even if this brings contentment, is banished from the menu of nostrums. Assuredly, only if people would infuse their lives with the activist spirit, increase their communal participation and demand that their voices be heard, their lives—and society in general—would recuperate. When recalling all the warnings regarding unchecked power, modern advocates apparently suffer amnesia. Lord Acton's famous admonition "Power tends to corrupt and absolute power corrupts absolutely" has become obsolete. Similarly, Emerson's advice "You shall have joy, or you shall have power, said God; you shall not have both" would be judged out of touch with modern realities.

Unfortunately, as common for new-found medical miracles, claims and supporting hard evidence are flimsy. Faith often overpowers an unpleasant reality. If a particular scheme fails, it was only because the medication was improperly administered. The irony that relentless benign intervention to instill independence may only deepen dependency and despair escapes discussion. Failures become redefined into "successes" or ignored altogether. To hint that self-determination itself is suspect makes one a heretic. Nor are enthusiasts seemingly aware that a wonderful abstract idea preached to sympathetic choirs can prove troublesome in its implementation. In advertising language, prodigious "hype" may reside here. Worse, the antidote may ultimately be far worse than the initial disorder. These admonitions may well be social science quackery. Clearly, this new-fashioned fondness requires a careful scrutiny seldom rendered.

In this world of ever-more clamors for bestowing power to alleviate society's many ills, we are a self-appointed scholarly Federal Drug Administration (FDA). Our exploration ranges from the vast outcropping of scholarship trumpeting empowerment to massive government assistance schemes. The stakes are high here, for "empowerment" is truly an idea making a real-world difference. What was once merely a collection of abstract ideas espoused by idealistic social science professors and would-be activists is seeping out as a cherished civic religion among ordinary citizens seeking personal emancipation. Millions of African Americans, Hispanics, gays and others hold that their lot can be enhanced by gaining control of their schools, communities and lives more generally. Those groups, for example, Asian Americans and the elderly, that have not yet fully embraced this formula are told by self-appointed leaders that they, too, must join the self-enabling bandwagon, lest they risk falling behind. Often with minimal reflection or demonstrated effectiveness, this therapeutic solution has become a secular salvation. Acceptance is abundantly manifest in such enterprises as voter registration drives, energetic organizing and calls for guaranteed representation in relevant public policy decisions. All these particulars of seizing control reflect the general aim of empowerment. Much of the women's movement's agenda has likewise taken this particular trajectory.

Given that there are innumerable potential avenues to success, this choice is hardly trivial. What if, contrary to all the avowals, achieving power is *not* especially effective in securing economic gain, social acceptance or personal happiness? It cannot be assumed that since achieving control of one's life has brought satisfaction to some, it is universally applicable. Perhaps some lack the necessary abilities to pursue this quest proficiently. Worse, the time and energy spent on empowerment derails the search for more potent solutions. The unemployed might wisely resist the lures of empowerment and instead learn to drive a truck and join the Teamsters. Autonomy might be severely limited, but profitable employment would be steady. The personal costs of heeding bad advice may far exceed the awkwardness suffered by academics exposed as purveyors of ineffectual dogmas.

This admonition for securing control, if taken at full face value, is also deceptively radical and disruptive. Recall how post–World War I calls for national self-determination, a then wondrously idealistic slogan, have left a bitter legacy of enduring bloody ethnic strife. Its educational application, for example, is not necessarily akin to yet another pedagogical technique of bettering student performance, for example, replacing whole word spelling with phonics. Granting students authority over their own education alters the basic disciplinary relations and redefines knowledge content and the criterion for success. Ditto for granting destitute people political supremacy as the cure for their pauperism—empowerment extends far beyond familiar conventional elixirs such as modernized job training. Dabbling in this formula is seldom tinkering with technical details; when relentlessly pushed, the very contours of our social and political existence are altered.

A moral transformation similarly lies below the surface. To argue that people *ought* to pursue a superiority based upon control implicitly displaces other once-venerated virtues. Where is power now to be placed on our collective hierarchy of values? Whether admonitions on behalf of empowerment might be condemnations of obedience, duty, respect and similar traditional subservient qualities remains an unanswered question. The prospect of civic life mimicking a Hobbesian world of all against all, with domination being the supreme prize, hardly entices. Are families and communities merely arenas of competition? Imagine family life governed by appeals to Nietzsche or Machiavelli. No doubt, popular infatuation would cool if "revolutionary moral upheaval" were periodically inserted as a synonym.

Empowerment's penetration into our thinking is so deep that other menu options have become silently displaced. Though seldom articulated as such, the primary question is: empowerment versus some alternative. Surely it is nonsensical to insist prima facie that empowerment provides the sole or most effective solution to commonplace impediments. Such a contention is the equivalent of insinuating that since aspirin cures so many ills, it must cure nearly everything. Indeed, the historical menu overflows with choices, all of proven utility. Perhaps empowerment contributes, but only when combined with other endeavors. Like salt in a recipe, self-determination is an essential ingredient but only minutely. A plausible case can be made that religious devotion—a life of prayer, piety and conformity to holy strictures—is a legitimate pathway to happiness and whatever else empowerment advocates seek. Christianity spread widely preaching a doctrine of humility and faith, not domination. Indeed, obsession with religious "other worldliness" may deliver substantial economic rewards, although that is hardly the manifest intent. Economically successful religious sects abound—Hasidic Jews, Mormons, the Amish, for example—whose core beliefs celebrate their total *powerlessness* before the Almighty. Self-subjugation to overwhelming power is not, automatically, a recipe for misery and poverty. The connection between Calvinist predetermination of salvation—hardly a philosophy insisting upon worldly mastery—and temporal accomplishment is well known.

It is equally plausible that the concentration of power, not its diffusion, under certain conditions offers a pervasive and viable remedy for myriad problems. Giving everyone a "piece of the action" is an invitation to ruin. The appropriate model is the military or Catholic Church—a culture or organizational structure of innumerable, forever powerless subjects obedient to those at the top wielding far-reaching authority. On innumerable occasions, "top-down" authoritarianism has conquered the very obstacles now judged amenable to expansive empowerment. Antipoverty campaign recruits conceivably should seek to be worthy privates, not generals. Authoritarian Catholic schools have now been recognized for their academic successes without acceding hegemony to their pupils. Many a recovered alcoholic attributes his or her cure to faith in religious subservience. Surely successful American corporations did not achieve their towering achievements via worker control—the company was to be empowered, not the thousands of individual employees. And as a consequence of *surrendering* control, workers probably secured economic gain and personal happiness.

To anticipate a reoccurring theme, an intimate connection between who holds the reins of power and benefit bestowed is not axiomatic. Over 200 years ago, William Godwin warned that "Power is not happiness." There is certainly no logical conjunction, and the empirical link remains to be proven: History offers endless tales of all-powerful rulers commanding cataclysms upon themselves. The bond between young children and their parents easily exemplifies the power-wisdom disconnection. Plainly, to empower youngsters in education, recreation, nutrition and similar consequential matters solicits disaster. Even as children mature, success likely accrues to those who surrender choices to wiser adults. More broadly, to empower those lacking required competence is senseless. Are ignorant students to direct their teachers in the pursuit of learning? Witness the innumerable former African colonies gaining political autonomy only to collapse into direr poverty and cruel violence. Surely we must acknowledge severe limits on the cure's scope; a guarantee against disappointment is specious.

The guidance of *dependency*—as we have hinted—is often far more worthwhile. Professional relationships—those between lawyer and client, for instance—are paradigmatic exemplars of where the quest for control ensures inefficaciousness. Recall the old adage that a self-representing lawyer has a fool for a client. Do we really want patients directing their doctors? Must schoolteachers flatter pupils' foolish desires? This lure may be an especially bad, though understandably enticing, bargain for those lacking wisdom. Why assume that the poor can prosper if they gain economic control? The quest for personal control may simply glorify indulgent ignorance. Escaping poverty or drug addiction might instead lie in closely following the wishes of prudent heads. Perhaps empowerment should be reserved only for those demonstrating superior competency.

The Politics of Empowerment explores our infatuation as an all-purpose panacea. Ours is a skeptical stance, not an outright, one-sided attack. Deep down, a moral concern infuses our review. We are worried that the prescription is often dispensed all too easily to people scarcely able to evaluate its potency. That it is eagerly embraced by intended beneficiaries—often at the expense of older remedies—places an enormous responsibility on those singing its praises. This is especially true since many advocates—whether professors of social work or community organizers—are personally distant from the consequences of this admonition. They suffer not if their advisees aimlessly pursue blind alleys seeking relief. If this treatment were instead a potentially dangerous chemical or diet pill, not a social science nostrum, the need for closer scrutiny would be obvious. Skeptics such as ourselves would be praised for their devotion to public health, not castigated for sabotaging progress or encouraging a dangerous dependency.

Equally pertinent, those about to be seduced by this lure may not wish a society defined by power relationships. This "cure" may not be fully grasped. Young women may want to view marriage as the beginning of family life, not as a contest of wills. What reward is to be secured by convincing women that raising children intrinsically debilitates by removing them from the power-infused economic marketplace? Is this "everything is empowerment" philosophy to serve as a sharp-edged scalpel to expose morality and custom as mere subterfuges in winning control? Who benefits when the legal code is convincingly portrayed as "mere" cover for the amoral exercise of force? And if this exposé were accepted as authentic, would life improve? These are daunting questions typically left hidden in exhortations.

Our examination explores at length the meaning of *empowerment* as utilized across disparate academic and professional fields. This is a critical task, for the term's growing popularity encourages an ever-expanding definition that, eventually, may well render usage virtually meaningless. Worse, if it means everything to everybody, it then, ultimately, means nothing other than, perhaps, a rhetorical device for disguising the absence of content. It is conceivable, for example, that *empowerment* has evolved into little more than a synonym for personal competence in familiar situations. Thus, for a high school student to be "empowered" merely signifies mastery of appropriate skills, for instance, reading or mathematics. Similarly, empowering women, according to certain denotations, implies nothing more than, say, acquiring suitable proficiency in financial matters or signing up for "assertiveness training." Empowerment, thus grasped, is but pouring old wine into new bottles and passing it off as a new-found miracle cure.

Or, in contrast, empowerment might be defined as the acquisition of ascendancy. A turning of tables is implied—those once subjugated now command. This would be its most radical expression. Newly empowered elementary and high school students now control their schools. If this is the implication, then teachers and administrators must suffer a corresponding diminishment in their capability since the total power—as it is usually understood—can only be divided, not enhanced. Empowerment might also be construed—much less radically—as encouraging self-expression solely for the intrinsic rewards of this action. There is no implication that these views carry weight. The voicing itself as a gesture engenders the empowerment. If this is what is meant, it is hard to imagine empowerment being an effective solution to intractable problems.

Or perhaps empowerment is a redistribution of hegemony so that more people have power than previously. This is analogous to economic leveling. In the instance of empowering students and teachers, a modicum of power from, say, school boards or government might be surrendered. Similarly, workers now make choices once reserved for bosses. This practice, alas, constitutes little more than the familiar decentralization dressed up as high-sounding self-determination. A far more intriguing version, not mere decentralization, treats empowerment as enhancing the grand total of societal power; *everyone* gains. This might be analogous to improving the performance of an automobile engine. Just how this situation of no losers and universal benefits is supposed to be accomplished is hardly self-evident.

Yet another alternative conceives power to be essentially psychological in character: Empowerment is wholly a mental state—one just "feels" powerful—regardless of exterior conditions. "I feel empowered; therefore I am empowered" articulates this view succinctly. This reformulation easily squares the circle since everybody within a school (and elsewhere) can now painlessly experience its advantage. Costs are slight and painless—everyone need only be convinced that, indeed, they really *are* powerful and that this euphoric condition is beyond demonstration. Conceptually, empowerment resembles self-defined exalted states: heightened self-esteem, self-confidence or happiness. Thus conceived, what is enjoyed by one is independent of what exists in others. Relieved of being a zero-sum contest, the propagation opportunities are boundless.

The line demarcating real-world empowerment and its purely psychological embodiment can be deceptively complex. Imagine, for example, that a few people decide to empower themselves and thus organize. An energetic-sounding name is selected, everyone wins prestigious elected group offices, funds are raised and aggressive proclamations are issued regarding forthcoming potent action. Enthusiastic well-attended marches and rallies draw favorable publicity. Predictably, group members experience a rush of empowerment and can, honestly, point to concrete accomplishments—a newsletter, a swelling membership, mass media notoriety and similar activity. Yet not only is this effort without results beyond itself, but concern for genuine impact is lacking. The entire venture mimics "playacting" empowerment, not securing intended results. Nevertheless, the *feeling* of empowerment—and varied visible signs—is authentic. Is this the genuine article?

Pushed further, such "playacting" offers only the pleasurable illusion of empowerment and might be better described as *de*powerment. Specifically, this quest for psychological fulfillment provides a hospitable, even enjoyable, detour from accomplishment. Participating in a distant sideshow is falsely equated with being a player in the main event. Instead of seeking influence amidst the multitude, group members instead dominate a peripheral organization composed entirely of fellow believers. Engagement in larger activities, for example, joining a conventional political party, might even be eschewed as a corrupting dilution of group power. The accomplishments—whether publications or parades—are more akin to therapeutic, self-centered exercises than actions to influence protagonists. Ironically, as feelings of empowerment rise, genuine influence may well diminish. From the perspective of group enemies, this infatuation with isolated, nonconsequential empowerment is especially welcome. After all, better to have opponents off by themselves playacting than infiltrating entities where key decisions are made.

The very opposite situation is equally imaginable: People possess momentous sway while constantly feeling helpless. Indeed, such circumstances are especially common given that most political action, especially given the immense network of interest group politics, is performed on behalf of people lacking direct involvement or even knowledge. An apathetic union member, for example, may well feel unprotected confronting economic and political forces beyond immediate control, yet his or her modest monthly dues support an organization of appreciable clout. No doubt, many elected officials impute notable power to citizens who judge themselves nearly impotent. This imputation may in fact drive these officials as if "powerless" citizens were truly all powerful and ever watchful. It is not unusual to find those occupying positions of great authority pleading that they are paralyzed with regard to ostensibly lowly subordinates who truly run things. Yet these subordinates as individuals feel powerless.

A closely related topic is the precise rewards to be bestowed by empowerment. If empowerment is the medicine for the troubling disorder, what comprises the healthy condition? Again, our review pushes beyond simple platitudes and statements whose veracity owes more to heartfelt conviction than evidence. Are newly empowered people supposed to be forever complacent, or is the quest insatiable? Are wealth and prestige the authentic prizes? Perhaps the enrichment is broadly collective in character—society as a whole is improved if its constituent elements singularly gain in self-mastery. In game theory language, empowerment is a positive-sum, not zero-sum, contest. Conceivably, moreover, the quest for self-determination —more so than its actual final obtainment—may generate most of the promised rewards. This is not an unfamiliar paradox: The earning of fortunes may grant greater satisfaction than mere possession. Perhaps only a modest pot of gold resides at the end of the empowerment rainbow, but it is uplifting to chase it.

Interwoven throughout these glowing intonations is an underlying association with democracy. For some, democracy and empowerment are two sides of the same coin. In fact, one of contemporary empowerment's ancestors is the philosophy of participatory democracy—authentic democracy requires that all citizens control the institutions that shape their lives, from government to school boards. Nevertheless, this easy linking obscures a multitude of thorny dilemmas. History surely informs us that suddenly empowered people need not act democratically: stories of enraged mobs violently taking matters into their own hands without regard for democracy are familiar. To quote Edmund Burke, "The greater the power, the more dangerous the abuse." Power can corrupt as well as ennoble, and a reasonable case can be made that the former is far more prevalent than the latter.

More troublesome is the inherent contradiction between empowerment (understood as accumulating power) and notions of democracy insisting upon the diffusion of power. It is arguable that a free, democratic society requires ample measures of interdependency. Madison's vision of a government hobbled by separation of powers, checks and balances and dispersion of power across independent governing bodies (federalism) remains relevant to contemporary democracy. The missives of the *Federalist Papers* still should command our attention: Angels do not govern, and when men enjoy unchecked power, they will surely usurp the rights of others. Relentless empowerment thus, ironically, may provide the seeds of tyranny; democracy may reside in interdependency: nobody having much power but everyone seeking it without success.

On a more practical level, stretching empowerment might yield gridlock, not betterment. Instead of cooperation among mutually dependent individuals or groups, society degenerates into diminutive competing feudal baronies. Thus understood, the promotion of autonomy yields stalemate. Imagine, for instance, a city in which quarreling groups all empower themselves to dominate nearby schools. Unfortunately, matters demanding system-wide coordination—school financing, student assignments, standardization of graduation requirements, teacher qualifications and similar choices—may become unwieldy. With dozens of extra veto groups, each jealously guarding turf, even simple decisions now require tedious negotiation. The cost of neighborhood power may well be communal collapse. Pushed to a reductio ad absurdum implication, imagine conducting a school in which everyone, including students, was all empowered. Learning would cease.

And what does the empirical research on empowerment depict? Do those mobilizing to gain leverage in civic life enjoy payoffs commensurate with their investments? Are African Americans as a group, for example, better off as a result of their quest for community control of schools or high elective office? Do people plagued by unfortunate circumstances find their lives mended by following the empowerment prescription? Or, on the other hand, is the lure of empowerment merely in its claimed *potential* for rectification? In a situation where empowerment is conceived of in psychological terms, is achievement of any consequence beyond the euphoria? These are critical yet all-too-often avoided questions that we shall confront squarely in subsequent chapters, but we can say that this answer is hardly unequivocal.

An especially perplexing problem concerns unraveling complex cause and effect relationships deeply embedded in the dogma of empowerment. Might empowerment's benefits also be the prior condition of securing mastery? Or is this entire relationship impossibly complex? For example, it is often asserted that group advancement requires political activism—if one wants good schools, jobs, quality health care or any other reward of modern society, a group's agenda must be forcefully pushed. Yet it is equally arguable that the flow of causality works the opposite way: It is first necessary to achieve affluence privately before political stratagems make sense. To wit, the prosperous can easily pursue politics far more effectively than the poor. Relentless grassroots activism cannot gain the unskilled prestigious employment. Empowerment is not an unmoved mover.

Questions also lurk here regarding assessing empowerment's alleged benefits. Perhaps claims regarding what is to be improved remain beyond scientific proof—the liturgy of taking control more closely resembles a faith than a proven recipe. As in the religious promise of eternal life, empowerment's payoff may reside in some ever-distant future, a first step in a never-to-be-completed journey. Oscar Levant once said that happiness is never experienced; it is merely remembered. Perhaps empowerment is likewise never experienced but always just beyond reach. Or, as when the sorcerer's spell fails to bring expected effects, facile excuses about the disruptive evil intent of others are quickly invoked. This is easily facilitated by the complexities of modern social science. The results of the empowerment ingredient may be hopelessly ambiguous, and accepting one version of reality is largely a matter of taste. For example, if the average income of blacks rose along with greater voting participation, can we say that voting instigated this rise? Any number of alternative and contradictory assessments are possible, all plausible according to social science. A firm conclusion may be inaccessible or even unwanted to those who cherish their faith uncontaminated with reality.

Even if empowerment is wondrous remedy often depicted, this scarcely means that it is easily teachable. Tutoring this gospel is hardly equivalent to instructing about, say, safe sex or healthy diets. Imparting a willingness to act independently, to challenge the status quo against formidable odds or to acquire arcane skills is far easier said than done. The inability of schools to impart learning offers a depressing parallel. What might instead be conveyed is empowerment's superficial vocabulary or an appreciation of its trumpeted virtues without corresponding mastery. Or those newly empowered might pursue this path only if prodded. Like schoolchildren under a teacher's watchful eye, these converts behave themselves only when watched. When guiding experts withdraw, habits of subjugation quickly return. There is also an irony here: The notion of experts training people to be empowered invokes the image of the traditional hierarchical teacher-pupil relationship. Is it possible to instill empowerment by telling those in inferior positions how to be empowered?

This infatuation with an uncertain gospel also draws our attention. Why do so many within diverse professions and across a wide political spectrum embrace it? Can we safely assume that this allure resides in demonstrated efficaciousness? Perhaps but unlikely. It is equally conceivable that this is mere fashion—calls for empowerment are fundamentally indistinguishable from, say, infatuations with Italian chic or big-budget action films. The clamoring is but climbing on a trendy political bandwagon. More personal motives are also possible. Surely those who ply the trade of electoral politics stand to gain from insisting that potential adherents become more vigorous in their electoral commitment in contrast to, say, improving their private spheres. A social service professional is hardly a disinterested bystander when instigating clients to empower themselves by demanding more state-supplied welfare services.

A subterranean ideological agenda also lurks. Recall that empowerment draws favorable attention from both radicals and conservatives and all points in between. Needless to say, the immediate objects of empowerment cannot be the same. Why, then, this common passion? Are militant feminists and Newt Gingrich both on the same wavelength when dreaming of civic perfection? More to the point, might empowerment schemes be little more than thinly disguised calls for unappetizing ideological programs carefully shielded from public view? This view is given credence by how empowerment is selectively dispensed. Thus, for example, rather than insist that difficult, traditional subjects be removed from public schools because of the culture they convey, it is far more convenient to argue that children should decide their own studies. That is, empower students so they can "decide" whether to read John Milton or Mickey Mouse. Similarly, rather than lobby for expanding government welfare services, instead labor on behalf of empowering those who will boisterously demand such services. Empowerment is thus political subterfuge: Promote a problematic civic program by disguising it in high-sounding rhetoric.

PLAN OF THIS BOOK

Our empowerment expedition will be extensive, drawing materials from sundry scholarly and real-world fields. Chapter 2 explores several troublesome issues underlying those effortless admonitions on behalf of greater mastery. "Taking charge" is far easier advised than done, and much of this counsel is either simplistic or deceptive. Chapter 3 delves into empowerment's divergent meanings as we proceed across the political spectrum. What precisely is "empowerment" to all these diverse entities besides a useful slogan to rally the troops? Here we dwell briefly on intellectual roots, inclinations as diverse as the 1960s "Black Power" movement to more esoteric scholarly concerns far removed from daily politics. Chapters 4 and 5 examine the application of empowerment schemes as a therapy for personal afflictions (including poverty) and as a means of improving educational performance. In both instances, empowerment is presented as a remedy far superior to previous undertakings. We ask a simple question: Is the lure of empowerment justified?

Chapter 6 looks at the federal government's venture into community empowerment. Once again, as during the Great Society era, Washington has become involved, bestowing millions of dollars in assistance plus tax law modification to jump-start local economic development, both urban and rural. Whether this ambitious "top-down" bureaucratic-administered enterprise can inculcate grassroots betterment is an intriguing question. Explicitly political empowerment via electoral mobilization, especially as embraced by African-Americans, will be explored in Chapter 7. When African American leaders hail voter registration drives, greater neighborhood control and proportionality in the distribution of elected offices, it is this empowerment vision that guides. It is also a burgeoning movement as other ethnic groups—notably Hispanics and Asians—plus women and gays join the empowerment refrain. Inquiry begins at an abstract, theoretical level, particularly the conflict between this vision and our constitutional system. We shall also contend that this "political solution" is far more difficult than imagined; it may even be impossible under existent conditions. The empirical side of the ledger will also be probed—the alleged improvement derived from participation. Is it the case, for example, that electing African-American mayors or a black-dominated city council substantially benefits blacks? This question is far more complex than it appears.

We conclude by drawing together several themes pertaining to empowerment's worthiness. We commence with a frank and multifaceted assessment of the empowerment enterprise. On balance, is all the infatuation plus the prodigious commitment justified? Are we assembling techniques to remediate problems that have long baffled society? Our journey will also peek below the surface to ask about infatuation's source. Is this yet another fad sweeping through the Ivory Tower, bestowing rewards independent of betterment? Why all the sincere preaching on behalf of uncertain remedies in comparison to alternatives with proven track records? The record here may well raise some disturbing possibilities regarding the true nature of this advocacy.

Our conclusion peeks into the future regarding this alleged "miracle cure." It will not be an optimistic assessment. It is not that empowerment is faulty; under proper, and quite limited, conditions, it can be truly wondrous. Rather, much of what is being passed off these days is counterfeit, often the very opposite of independence. More than deception is involved, however. All the alluring empowerment rhetoric may well obscure traditional cures that *really* work. It is this substitution of real medicine by a placebo that is so disturbing. Our Doctors of Empowerment have taken on an enormous responsibility, and as we shall see, they have largely empowered themselves, not those they claim to assist.

2

Empowerment and Its Problems

The across-the-ideological-spectrum infatuation with empowerment must, evidently, disguise a multitude of distinct prescriptions. If empowerment is to be more than a faddish slogan, some prodigious disentangling obviously must be done. Here we delve deeper into this broadly popular term. We commence with formal definitions of *empowerment* and show that this facile dictionarylike consensus leaves noteworthy dilemmas unresolved. Indeed, empowerment's rhetorical usefulness might, ironically, require superficiality. This exploration of half-hidden vexatiousness will certainly strike empowerment fans as excessively negative. Celebrating passivity is hardly the intent, however. We are skeptical regarding all enthusiasms—including empowerment—promoting marvels. Because empowerment thrives largely as a promise, attributing miraculous capabilities is painless. This is expected: Heralded untried remedies always outperform today's cures. Unfortunately, denial and obliviousness may haunt future implementations. Better to uncover flaws in the abstract now than ruin lives with misguided efforts.

UNRAVELING EMPOWERMENT

In a contest for concepts pretending clarity while yet obscuring untold uncertainties, empowerment might easily win. A deceptive consensus exists. Consider the meaning of *power*. The *Oxford English Dictionary*, unabridged second edition (*OED II*), offers several relevant meanings, all sensible and commonplace:

Ability to do or effect something or anything.

Ability to act or affect something strongly; physical or mental strength; might; vigour, energy; force of character; telling force, effect.

Authority given or committed; hence, sometimes, liberty or permission to act.

Legal ability, capacity, or authority to act; esp. delegated authority; authorization, commission, faculty; spec. legal authority vested in a person or persons in a particular capacity.

Possession of control or command over others; dominion, rule; government, domination, sway, command; control, influence, authority.

Plainly put, possessing "power" means a capacity to impose one's will or achieve a position of superiority. This might be accomplished, variously, via physical exertion (as in moving an object), by virtue of legal position (as a policeman has power) or as a result of one's persuasive skills. Applied by social scientists, however, it is a relational concept—the power of one person (or group) over another. Lifting heavy weights lies outside discussions of empowerment. The power of A involves getting B to do something B would not otherwise do, or securing something similarly coveted by B. Thus, to say "whites have more power than blacks" could mean, among other things, that whites can control blacks or acquire more successfully what is collectively preferred: wealth, status and so on.

"To empower" or "to be empowered" then becomes the acquiring of power. This definition, it should be noted, implies nothing about enhanced psychological states of those gaining power or other rewards. The powerful, definitionally, need not be any happier or be especially successful. What power produces is entirely an empirical determination. Being able to command may prove an unwelcome burden. "To empower" according to the *OED II*:

To invest legally or formally with power or authority; to authorize, license.

To impart or bestow power to an end or for a purpose; to enable, permit.

To gain or assume power over.

Finally, to conclude our dictionary tour, *empowerment* means:

The action of empowering; the state of being empowered.

This dictionary understanding—a person (or group) gaining control to secure advantage—infuses the empowerment literature, regardless of ideological inclination. A brief and unsystematic sampling confirms this perspective.

It [empowerment] is inextricably linked to both the ability and opportunity to make decisions and to act for oneself. Thus, empowerment is egalitarian in nature, stressing the competence and right of people to take charge of their own destinies. (Staples 1990)

Empowerment is viewed as a process: the mechanism by which people, organizations and communities gain mastery over their lives. (Rappaport 1984)

Empowerment is generally understood as interventions and policies intended to enhance the degree of control vulnerable individuals exercise over their lives. (Prilleltensky 1994)

Empowerment is a process by which people, organizations and communities gain mastery over issues of concerns to them. (Zimmerman 1995)

[Empowerment] . . . is a continuous process that enables people to understand, upgrade and use their capacity to better control and gain power over their own lives. It provides people with choices and the ability to choose, as well as to gain more control over resources they need to improve their condition. (Schuftan 1996)

Empowerment may be conceptualized, then, as the ability of community organizations to reward or punish community targets, control what gets talked about in public debate, and shape how residents and public officials think about their community. (Speer and Hughey 1996)

By empowerment I mean the all around capacity, resources and information and knowledge, self-confidence, skills, understanding. Organization, and formal rights people can use to determine individually and collectively what happens to them. (Levins 1995)

This parade of research-based definitions could be endlessly extended, but the common element is evident: Those empowered can orchestrate their lives and control the world around them.[1] Terms such as *autonomy*, *independence* and *mastery* are also implied. Conceptual differences concern emphasis and detail, for example, how this transformation is to be accomplished or particular resources required. Moreover, regardless of ideology, exaltations focus on assisting the less fortunate (or "oppressed" in some analyses). Empowering the wealthy or already influential is off the agenda. It is tacitly assumed that the privileged—unless, perhaps, they suffer debilitating conditions such as mental illness—already possess sufficient power, and adding more cannot benefit either them personally or society more generally. The quest for empowerment thus entails expanding the power of the hapless: the indigent, the homeless, disadvantaged minorities, the disabled, the oppressed and whoever else cannot dictate their fate. The paradigmatic scenario portrays an impoverished woman trapped in shabby public housing who, expertly advised, organizes neighbors to rectify the deplorable situation. Eventually, now more self-confident and skilled, she creates a thriving small business, thereby lifting herself and friends out of lifelong poverty. She becomes healthier, wealthier and wiser, thanks to empowerment.

Thusly presented, this message is seductive. Who could counsel passivity for the disadvantaged facing calamity? Nor does old-fashioned paternalism have much charm today. Challenging empowerment would seem tantamount to condemning competence. Unfortunately, the remedy's lure disguises innumerable formidable underlying conceptual problems and unsettled assumptions. To be sure, not every analysis is riddled with defects, but this diverse literature, when taken together, leaves vexing issues unresolved. Additionally, schemes often labeled "empowerment" only superficially resemble the authentic item. These difficulties are akin to flaws in a building's structural steel—the edifice appears imposing, yet hidden are debacles waiting to happen. Such invisible pitfalls are easily escaped, provided empowerment remains but a glittering, inspirational slogan. Perhaps skirting troublesome dilemmas is predictable. Impassioned promoters seldom invite nay-saying Devil's advocates to their celebrations. Nevertheless, these perplexities are quite real and, like injurious side effects of otherwise worthy medication, they can make matters worse.

EMPOWERMENT'S DESIRABILITY

A never-challenged theme informing empowerment's promotion is its desirability among intended beneficiaries. Longing to control one's life, apparently, exists as a biological drive, perhaps akin to craving food. Implementation, it follows, merely entails instructing predisposed students. Hesitation is to be overcome with kindly persuasion. That people might wish others to govern evidently escapes notice. Similarly, expressing desire for control is fully believed, even where no prior experience with autonomy exists.

This is grossly unrealistic. Contrary evidence on the inbred nature of the "control one's life" inclination abounds. Paternalism has long been popular among *all* relationship parties. Millions freely join religious orders, the military, authoritarian companies promising almost unthinking, pervasive obedience. Voluntary surrender in personal relationships—the dutiful spouse, servile employee or submissive child—is commonplace. Nor is subordination a patent sign of duplicitous "oppression." Given a choice between achieving mastery over one's environment versus surrendering to fate or luck, many painlessly opt for the latter. Perhaps fatalism, not the desire for self-determination, defines the human spirit.

The enticement of independence may be far more seductive abstractly, not in practice, especially when costs are obscured. Fulfilling self-determination's obligations can be burdensome. Endless TV watching is often far more comfortable than learning necessary skills. Nor are innumerable meetings, educational activities and risking dislocation always welcome. Nevertheless, at least to the supporters of empowerment, the idea of people willingly avoiding control is a far distant and disbelieved defect.

A rational case exists against these sweeping enticements for self-determination. The venerable division of labor principle and law of comparative advantage might well dictate dependency—one *gains* by surrendering control over vast territory. While one can "take charge" of tax preparation or health care, prudence advises turning these arcane tasks to experts rather than meddle. Control here occurs only over the acceptability of the final outcome, not managing details. Helplessness has its rewards; freed from preparing one's taxes, one can earn more money. Amateurs insisting on self-doctoring may well invite catastrophe despite the joys of empowerment.

The potential "downside" of empowerment is demonstrated in a *Wall Street Journal* story on employee empowerment at a South Bend, Indiana, metal forging factory (Aeppel 1997, A1, A14). This small forge provides a textbook case of awarding employees expansive control. Hours and overtime are on the self-reporting honor system. Each employee learns multiple jobs and enjoys considerable autonomous discretion. Small coworker teams freely discuss problems ranging from fixing broken equipment to handling faltering colleagues. Workers, not distant management, decide quality control. The traditional intrusive, ever-watchful boss has been replaced by the in-the-background "vision supervisor." Hiring is shared among those already employed. Even disciplinary action is performed in face-to-face workers' groups. To make the egalitarian point unmistakable, all plant employees (including front office personnel) wear identical blue uniforms.

Nevertheless, the facility is hardly the anticipated workers' paradise. Turnover—about 10 percent annually—is high among the company's 155 factories, especially considering the intense scrutiny given prospective employees, and the generous pay. Some turnover reflects the work's difficult physical nature, but this open, democratic, egalitarian style hardly pleases everybody. Certain employees still prefer the traditional passive boss-is-the-boss system in contrast to group-based decisions. Others find the added responsibility too stressful and uncertain. For them, the cut-and-dried 8:00 to 5:00 job is more attractive. Workers will occasionally ignore small tasks if this smacks of spying (for example, reporting dirty personal lockers). Overall, at least at this single factory, empowerment works reasonably well, but it is not for everybody.

Avoiding autonomy need not be judged a failing. Even those proficient at controlling their destinies might still choose otherwise. The ability to control is but one of multiple objectives on life's menu. Some crave status; others need excitement and pleasure. To be sure, places do exist in which the quest for domination is all-pervasive, and one's existence is devoted to its achievement. Yet such a preoccupation is hardly universal, and of greater importance, this pursuit need not be a moral imperative. In the Indian caste system, for example, dutiful acceptance of a lowly station is unequivocally recognized as part of a grand design in which today's passivity secures future reward. The wise may covet much without adding self-determination to the list.

Finally, and most ironically, caution is advised regarding those preaching the gospel of autonomy. Campaigns for self-determination may artfully disguise co-optation schemes. After all, leaders may resist their would-be followers becoming *too* self-reliant. Intervention to help, even if the aim is self-rule, often brings the very opposite effect, a fact known to those volunteering liberation slogans. As one overview of proffered assistance noted, "Research on recipients reactions to aid suggests that, indeed, good intention may be the paving stones on the road to hell. Despite the benevolence of donors, their attempts to improve the lot of unfortunate others may leave those others feeling out of control, incompetent, and incapable of overcoming their present or future problems" (Coats, Renzaglia and Embree 1983, 253). What separates the engendering of helplessness from independence is a devilishly perplexing problem, dependent on innumerable factors ranging from the morality of the assistance to how the assistance is perceived. Unfortunately, as subsequent chapters will show, such intricacies are rarely scrutinized regardless of sincerity of commitment to autonomy. Merely to proclaim the goal of empowerment is usually—and falsely—taken as proof of expertise in navigating this dilemma.

INDIVIDUAL VERSUS COLLECTIVE EMPOWERMENT

Explications of empowerment typically speak of both individuals and groups (e.g., a neighborhood association or racial entity). Usage is customarily casually interchangeable—what holds for one pertains to the other, and no contradiction exists to empower both simultaneously. At least theoretically, collective empowerment typically comprises one-by-one accumulation of power: To empower women as a class, for example, necessitates empowering each woman individually. The more empowered women, the greater the power of women collectively. Yet the difference between empowering people and empowering collections of people does surface. One researcher even suggests a terminological distinction between these two levels, calling individual empowerment "psychological empowerment," or PE, in distinction to community empowerment (Zimmerman 1995).

Individual and collective control are not interchangeable—enhancing one need not promote the other. They might well vary independently. It is easy to imagine a small community inhabited by self-confident, empowered citizens shaping all local matters, although as a town they are exceedingly vulnerable to uncontrollable outside forces. People may effectively band together and conquer their personal problems, but this need not cumulate to a society-wide solution. It has been implied, for example, that the empowerment success of self-help groups such as Alcoholics Anonymous may simultaneously hurt their sobriety cause by undermining more encompassing remedial efforts for those outside these small groups (Riessman and Bey 1992).

More important, within an organization seeking a common goal, these two versions of empowerment can well be *inherently contradictory*. This underlying potential conflict is seldom frankly acknowledged, let alone engaged. Staples (1990) is an exception who offers the scenario of "Rosie Potential," a welfare recipient leading a successful tenant association within her public housing complex. In this communal role, she both gains the personal benefits—for example, planning skills—and assists her neighbors. But now flush with success, Rosie enters a medical technician training program. Here again, she thrives, becomes further empowered as a person and soon escapes welfare. Alas, her communal work suffers, and deprived of their dynamic leader, the once-powerful tenants' association falters.

The most common collision between individual self-determination and collective empowerment probably occurs in small organizations. Here what amplifies individual power may well subvert collective accomplishment, and vice versa. In her overview of feminist group failures, Riger (1984) singles out this individual versus group tension as a leading culprit. In the group's inclusion of everyone in decisions, endless discourse may dominate group life, often overshadowing achieving goals. With everybody adding their two cents and nobody's input totally rejected, outcomes veer toward incoherent compromises. Meanwhile, by treating all contributions as equally valid, genuine expertise is disregarded. Choices, according to Riger, frequently reflect friendship bonds and a reluctance to injure the emotionally vulnerable. Eventually, sustaining a "happy group" of equals often substitutes for the organization's original purpose; taking action becomes secondary if not disruptive. Competent members who still pursue initial goals become frustrated by this therapeutic, "we are all equally powerful" environment and depart.[2]

Is this individual versus collective empowerment conflict resolvable? Staples (1990) briefly wrestles with the contradiction, all the while insisting, "Groups as well as individuals must be empowered in order to change the social structure" (36–37). Boyce (1993) poses the dilemma as one of efficiency versus empowerment and, to solve this tension for public health decisions, offers an exceedingly detailed, technical formula of popular input and expert recommendation. Perhaps the most thoughtful theoretical resolution is offered by Speer and Hughey (1995). Here individual-level empowerment, definitionally, "is represented through the individual actions that contribute to developing an organization's social power (a process) and changes within individuals that result from working in an organization to develop social power (and outcomes)" (736). Moreover, this participation is guided by democratic procedures. In short, personal empowerment flows not from personal attainment but from collective fulfillment. And because organization members shape decisions democratically, each gets a "piece" of this overall capacitation. At least in principle, a "win-win" situation occurs: Individually and collectively empowerment is enhanced.

Unfortunately for those seeking to remedy both personal and aggregate maladies, this tension may be nearly intractable. The clever balancing act offered by Speer and Hughey (1995) is, after all, hypothetical. Its applicability remains unknown. No guarantee exists that organizations that sustain this balancing will prove more efficacious than those favoring one direction over another. Neglect by researchers of this dilemma might better be described as irresponsible though convenient denial, not ignoring a minor technical glitch. The potential conflicts between these two versions are hardly obscure and regularly surface.

An equally serious problem facing this integration of personal and aggregate empowerment is the proclivity for oligarchy among democratic organizations. In his classic study of European socialist parties, Robert Michels coined the phrase "Iron Law of Oligarchy" (Michels 1915). That is, despite democratic procedures, power inevitably flows toward those who daily run the organization. It is the logic of governance, not malice, that corrupts democracy. Rank and file gradually defer to more knowledgeable leaders and, ultimately, merely reaffirm prepackaged decisions. More harmful, the organization may exclusively serve leadership aims regardless of initial member objectives. Activity is misdirected to keeping leaders in power and handsomely rewarding them. While this "Iron Law" is most applicable to large bureaucratic entities, even small grassroots participatory-oriented groups may succumb to it (see, e.g., Green 1985).

At the other extreme is the predicament of excessive participation. The cliché "Too many chiefs and not enough Indians" pointedly captures the difficulty of sustaining organizational effectiveness when everyone seeks input. Organizational efficiency—group empowerment—*requires* that followers outnumber leaders. Accomplishment may also require professional leadership, and experts cannot be expected to incorporate every rank-and-file suggestion. Moreover, without fixed procedures and binding rules, organizations become disparate individuals drifting toward their idiosyncratic paths. Everyone cannot improvise; somebody must possess final say. Recall the overemphasis of consensus building within feminist groups depicted by Riger (1984). To be sure, leaders may occasionally solicit subordinate opinion, delegate discretionary authority and otherwise involve underlings, but attentiveness does not equal empowerment. Lowly army privates enjoy power, so to define *empowerment* as possessing *some* power definitionally makes everyone "empowered." When facing tough choices, for example, entering combat, this "empowerment" vanishes. If a modicum of power constituted "empowerment," preaching the cause is pointless since the empowerment campaign is already won.

Pushed further, the empowerment of subordinates eventually detracts from overall effectiveness. Soliciting divergent views requires time and energy. Collective empowerment, particularly when rapid action is necessary, may have to be paid for with depowering centralization. Tales of organizations falling into disarray as everyone is "off doing their own thing" are commonplace. The history of American Marxism well illustrates the disarray when everybody can "empower" themselves through endless breakaway factions, all with their own names announcing slightly different dogmas. As Marxists holding "power" multiply, the movement itself deteriorates into squabbling camps. The real beneficiary, of course, in this Marxist proliferation is capitalism. Similar conflicts have perplexed labor unions, civil rights organizations, women's organizations, various antiwar efforts, the environmental movement and virtually every other recent mass-based political cause. Individual empowerment when pushed to extremes *subverts* group attainment.

This tension between individual accomplishment and group advancement offers a further ironic twist. As individual opportunities multiply, the lure of group defections grows proportionately. Consider, for example, a talented, ambitious African American today versus 50 years ago. In the 1940s with personal economic opportunities gravely constrained, supporting group advancement made excellent sense. No amount of personal exertion would open doors closed simply due to one's race. Aggregate and personal advancement were deeply intertwined. Today, however, the likelihood of success is possibly greater via personal strategies. Despite unfinished business, unashamed individualism is far better investment. Why fret organizational survival if victory can be accomplished on one's own?

If this paradox is escapable, practical solutions remain undiscovered. Theoretically, one could imagine everyone enjoyed genuine empowerment but in distinctive, nonoverlapping realms. Given ten organizations, each with ten authentically empowered leaders, every follower could simultaneously be a leader in one of the ten organizations. The circle is thus squared: An individual serves as a private one place and as a general elsewhere. Or the dutiful passive clerical worker returns home to be dynamic neighborhood organizer, while the obedient follower here is the potent business entrepreneur downtown.

No doubt, assuming copious relevant skills and inclinations, this arrangement is feasible. It would undoubtedly prove satisfactory for many who would now possess at least one field of domination. Organizational effectiveness would coexist with universal self-determination. Nevertheless, given society's size and complexity, such "empowerment opportunities" would surely be modest, for example, controlling a menagerie of household pets. Yet though this scaled-down accommodation may be widely welcomed, it is not what empowerment theorists imagine. Their agenda demands far grander objectives. Directing the local stamp club is insufficient, regardless of gratification. The real arenas, at least for these prophets, are fundamental societal relationships. Squaring this circle is far more demanding.

THE EQUALITY OF EMPOWERMENTS

Typically embedded in empowerment prescriptions are two important assumptions. First, the remedy is applicable, broadly, to all aspects of one's life: family, job, fraternal groups, the immediate neighborhood, local community and even one's country. Second, within each domain, empowerment applies to matters of consequence: wealth, safety, access to health care, human dignity, self-actualization and similar serious affairs. This is particularly true for winning empowerment for one's racial or ethnic groups. Additionally, the more radical conceptions envision it as a totality, not a choice of domains. Ideally, one is to gain mastery in everything from family relations to shaping momentous matters of state.

Needless to say, however, ever-expanding conquest is unobtainable for nearly everyone. A Herculean uplifting beyond human capacity would be necessary. Grim reality imposes choices; even the commanding autocrat may feel helpless in certain personal matters. The day provides only so many hours, our energy is finite, not every necessary skill is masterable and nonempowerment matters surely need periodic attention. The inevitable question, then, is deciding among competing calls. Is, for example, tackling neighborhood crime more compelling than, say, stopping scurrilous treatment of one's religious group? Does one invest long hours improving working conditions if this exertion neglects family decisions? Although it is easy to sidestep these onerous choices calling for "everywhere on all matters of importance," choosings are inescapable.

What principles should guide potential power engagement options? Several are immediately evident. Recall that empowerment advocates insist on the primacy of basic political and economic arrangements. Once these are mastered, details will follow. Hence, for an African American in a repressive, racist political system, genuine betterment occurs only when the political order itself is altered. To focus on secondary matters—for example, the observance of a holiday honoring Martin Luther King, Jr.—wastefully distracts. Even if successful, the latter endeavor is but an illusionary gain. In a nutshell, empowerment requires careful analysis of underlying socioeconomic forces, and action should concentrate accordingly.

Alternatively, calculations regarding success may guide strategies. Faced with innumerable options, minimized risk is superior to pie-in-the-sky grand crusades. Small victories yield more empowerment than disastrous battles for unobtainable exalted objectives. Driving away vandals represents a wiser decision than laboring to replace an unfair economic system despite the latter's more fundamental character. Or, to suggest a third calculation method, engagement choices may merely reflect the subjective psychological satisfaction. If daily personal safety is more valuable psychologically than economic power, strategies should seek that goal. Conceivably, one might acquire adeptness in purely personal matters—improved basketball skills. Empowerment, thus understood, becomes not some utilitarian greatest good for the greatest number enterprise but instead a more selfish greatest good for the particular person.

A paradox, seldom appreciated, frames this discussion when counselors prescribe the worthy objectives of self-determination. It is assumed, often explicitly, that to transform the hapless means adherence to expert guidance on aims. Our paradigmatic impoverished public housing resident will be wisely tutored on controlling the "objectively fundamental." The menu offers only the initial possibility listed above—matters of grave consequence. The lesson plan will commence with the person's miserable condition ("consciousness raising") and then move to reconstructing particulars— laws, mobilization strategies, acquiring resources and so on. That this poor person may seek enhancement beyond the expert's agenda is inconceivable, if not reprehensible, to the scholarly experts. Yet if autonomy is to mean anything, it surely means that the person empowered decides worthy pursuits. This poor person may be required to hear contrary arguments, we may even plead that he or she heed this sagacious advice, but the final choice cannot be dictated. Insisting otherwise corrupts the core idea of self-determination.

Acknowledging "inexpert" autonomy exposes troublesome issues easily evaded in today's glib theorizing. What if our poverty-stricken person embraces consumerism—relentless material acquisition? The evils depicted by self-designated experts—a pervasive society-wide repressive ideology, an inequitable economic system, disparagement of one's culture and structurally biased political arrangements—are subordinated to pursuing "good deals" on designer clothing or exotic electronic gadgets. He or she thus becomes a "power" within the marketplace: deciding where to shop, badgering clerks, haggling prices and otherwise imposing his or her will.[3] A nearby neighbor similarly shuns outside expert counsel and empowers himself by artfully engaging in hedonistic indulgence. A third adroitly devotes himself to a noisy high-powered car and with great exhilaration illegally races it while skillfully escaping the police. All are triumphant in their pursuits, reaping all the wondrous benefits claimed by empowerment disciples. If informed about the "objective" nature of their helplessness facing oppressive sociopolitical conditions, they profess sincere indifference. Perhaps these "unempowered" souls might instead tell empowerment theorists that shopping, hedonism and fast cars constitute the "real" path to aggrandizing power.

This counterexample is hardly peculiar or intended to belittle outside expertise. Incalculable self-determination opportunities always abound. A parallel, perhaps, can be made with vitamins—source is far less important than adequacy, and vitamins are everywhere. We cannot assume that popular selection obeys the menu recommended by academic champions. In fact, many expert-endorsed choices are likely to be ignored by people more attuned to daily pleasures. Mass-market publications directed at African Americans even argue that wise consumer choice is one form of black empowerment (Graves 1996). Perhaps the heroic remedies favored by academic theorists are impractical, and ordinary folk have wiser heads. Not everyone, regardless of effort, can take charge of their job or organize block associations. For the great mass, more humdrum activities, consumerism or sports, for example, may be the only feasible outlets guaranteeing mastery. Measured psychologically—self-confidence, self-perception—an "empowered shopper" might indeed be indistinguishable from an "empowered political activist." And given their respective odds of securing their objectives, who can say that the self-indulgent shopper/hedonist/hot-rodder is misdirected toward personal fulfillment?

Experts typically reject this egalitarian "all empowerments are equal if they feel equivalent." For them, "allowing" empowerment via frivolous activities reinforces the status quo by cloaking misery. If thousands of workers assemble to cheer their victorious World Series team instead of seizing economic control, this is but "bread and circuses" empowerment. Deplorable but reversible circumstances are ignored, thanks to what Marxists label "false consciousness." Nevertheless, in the final analysis, what authorizes distant experts to direct ordinary people's goals? Surely this is not a granted right or a jurisdiction justified by past accomplishment. To repeat, such experts surely can plead their case (and vice versa), but to insist that our destitute public housing resident surrender his or her 75-channel TV (which affords a satisfying degree of command via the remote) in favor of creating a tenants' group is presumptuous.

OBJECTIVE AND SUBJECTIVE EMPOWERMENT

Proponents of mobilizing people to gain control understand that this requires both psychological transformations and modifying material circumstances. Action rests on positive expectations, but psychology must also be validated by genuine accomplishment. While both ingredients coexist in this recipe, the prescribed proportions are uncertain. And how are these two unlikely attributes interconnected? For example, is the psychological condition a prerequisite for the acquisition of necessary material resources? Or is a sense of mastery merely the outcome of securing authentic material power? Perhaps the relationship is iterative. Further infusing this analysis is the role of perceptions. Are perceptions of being empowered unquestionably "real" insofar as people believe them to be genuine?

This balancing of external objective factors with inner psychological beliefs is, abstractly, unclouded. "All are related to empowerment" is the common nebulous answer, and this satisfies provided inquiry ceases. Matters grow murkier, however, when power's real-world complexities surface, and implementation will undoubtedly exacerbate this tension. The first quandary concerns ultimate purpose. If empowerment cures a disorder, what constitutes "health"? Is the medication successful if the patient "feels" empowered, or must this redress be certified by specified exterior circumstances? Conversely, might the all-powerful sovereign "legitimately" feel helpless? This is not an abstract hypothetical dilemma, and answers profoundly shape the entire enterprise.

Empowerment advocates typically equivocate on the ultimate centrality of this inner sense of empowerment—whether it is the final triumphant product of one's efforts or the preliminary step. The easiest resolution argues on behalf of equal relevance (e.g., Kieffer 1984, 30; Parsons 1991, 10–13; Rappaport 1984, 3). Those in the Marxist tradition, in contrast, argue for the primacy of objective reality—the discernable distribution of tangible power. Others, however, favor greater "inner empowerment." Julian Rappaport, a leading practitioner, writes, "The cognitions, motivations, and personality changes experienced by those who gain a sense of control may be the essence of empowerment" (Rappaport 1985, 15). The self-esteem movement virtually enshrines psychological potency as the ultimate goal. Not only will a heightened sense of self-mastery cure problems such as perplexing welfare and drug abuse, but—at least according to some—it is now central to democracy's very existence (Cruikshank 1993). Feminist writers particularly stress psychological dividends as intrinsically meritorious. Faver (1994), for example, argues that even unsuccessful social action can bring empowerment if it is consciousness-raising action. One might lose, but at least one tried, and that it more important than passivity.

A more ambitious "internal" definition of betterment promotes resisting dominating societal norms and standards. Here self-determination initially eschews material gain, for example, decent housing, though this might eventually follow. More central is attaining control of internalized cultural or group identity. Rather than being labeled by society at large, one self-defines, and this becomes the most crucial of all control actions. Consider a simple example. Imagine a culture that demeaned one's very actuality— its ideals regarding "good" or "normal" where unobtainable. The culture might, for instance, idealize being blond and blue-eyed. For many Hispanics, Asians and African Americans, this standard is forever unreachable, regardless of diligence. The dominant culture thus permanently consigns one to inferiority. A daily glance in the mirror reveals "failure."

The only answer, at least initially, must come from within. As Sanchez and Garriga (1995) put it, "The ability to define one's own reality and to set out to enhance those 'pictures' of that reality, is one of the true indications of being in control and having power" (9). Collins (1990, Ch. 5) similarly bids black women to empower themselves to overthrow the negative and debilitating self-images imposed by an oppressive society. According to Collins, it is this "inner" rejection of an oppressing white culture—for example, seeing a black woman merely as "a welfare mother"—that permits black women to sustain their sense of self-worth even under horrendous conditions. In her words, "the act of insisting on Black female self-definition validates Black women's power as human subjects" (Collins 1990, 107). Here mastery begins by finding reaffirmation among friends and artistic expression, particularly the blues and black women's literature. Williams and Wright (1992) echo a similar sentiment: "[E]mpowerment requires that African-Americans redefine themselves with the context of their history and culture, and not in relation to Euro-centric frameworks" (24). Thus, those dominant white cultural judgments of "deficiency"—for example, illegitimacy—must be rejected.

Empowerment for personal redefinition is most notable in school curriculums reaffirming diverse cultural inclinations and physical traits. Here empowerment means to reaffirm one's existence. To continue our example, being blond and blue-eyed would cease to be the sole standard. All eye and hair colors become commensurate, and Hispanics, African Americans and others are no longer automatically inferior. Indeed, this effort to empower students via enhanced self-definitions has become hugely popular, far extended to validate just about every trait previously judged inferior (see, e.g., Weissberg 1998, Ch. 8). Blacks campaigning against negative mass media stereotypes, since such images subvert African Americans' self-worth, is another familiar example. What is key here is that empowerment's aim is internal, the enhanced sense of self, not securing palpable rewards.

Thusly depicted, this goal seems defensible. After all, tangible ends such as jobs are measured by the standard of psychological satisfaction, so improved self-definition is hardly a profoundly unique aim. If attending vast gatherings stimulates accomplishment, a feeling of belonging to a swelling historical force, or inspires renewed personal vigor, is this not empowerment? Such an imposing display of unity, moreover, sends a convincing message to the outside world, further confirming momentousness. One might thus speak of different types of empowerment—those quests aimed at concrete objectives such as better day-care facilities or more subjective, psychological pursuits, for example, a feeling of ethnic pride. And since the empowerment process, by definition, reflects personal choice, all forms are valid.

The difficulty here is not in the abstract principles but in the opportunities for counterfeit, self-indulgent therapy. Accomplishing something real, overcoming real obstacles with real struggle, can hardly be compared to transforming one's thinking and stopping at that. Altered beliefs may be prerequisite to action, but self-determination cannot be gained via self-hypnosis. If subjective reality becomes the sole benchmark, delusion is the recommended prescription. Manipulating perceptions is, after all, far easier than tangible accomplishment and, for that reason, may well "crowd out" more exacting endeavors. Patricia Hill Collins (1990), for example, spends 238 pages exhorting black women to empower themselves by modifying their thinking, yet she never offers a single specific recommendation on what should follow. If pushed, this "inner empowerment" undermines the genuine commodity. Defenseless people in dire situations may well convince themselves that they nevertheless possess prodigious mystical powers unintelligible to outsiders. Why not seek empowerment via alcohol or drugs? It is far easier than confronting harsh reality.

This quest often betrays a proclivity closer to therapy. Witness the growing popularity of self-esteem enhancement as a substitution for genuine education. That is, one learns to think of oneself as "good at math" as opposed to in fact excelling at mathematics. Students easily pass lenient tests, receive awards for minimum proficiency and are otherwise beguiled to a false ability. With repetition, it may well be internalized as authentic. Indeed, numerous studies show that less academically proficient students often grossly exaggerate their competency despite clear contrary evidence— they are "empowered" but only in their private world (see, e.g., Levin 1997, 75–77). In a nutshell, pseudo-empowerment triumphs. Unfortunately, such misdirected, psychologically intensive solutions extend well beyond the classroom. A sense of power can be deceitfully achieved by rewriting history to exaggerate group accomplishments or even insisting on worthiness sans supporting evidence (Lefkowitz 1996). Deficiencies and shortcomings are now dismissed as irrelevant to shelter self-respect. Entire university curriculums do little more than confirm the wisdom of preexisting highly flattering knowledge. This trickery is comparable to a would-be dieter rigging the scale "to show" weight loss.

This pseudo-empowerment may be undetectable, artfully mimicking the real item. And who can disagree, given the autonomy that inheres in empowerment? Campaigns for tangible goals may well subtly transform themselves into self-satisfaction bereft of worldly accomplishment. Recall the conflict between individual and collective power—groups gravitate toward gratifying talk and abandon deeds altogether. Empowerment exists only as a "feeling," not in results. Huge efforts may be undertaken for inconsequential "symbolic benefits." Rather than improving the education of one's ethnic group—a prerequisite to economic advancement—activists instead focus on renaming the school after a group hero or insist that certain holidays be celebrated. Similarly, genuine political power may be disdained in favor of misleading yet enjoyable appearances—fancy titles, handsome offices, attentive assistants but no real power. It is not too much of an exaggeration to liken such "in-your-head" empowerment to the "high" experienced by drug users.

As pseudo-power may disguise helplessness, the opposite is also true. Imposing appearances may hide futility. Thus, to mount a campaign to acquire the prerogatives of position may well expend effort to acquire a territory of unsatisfactory value. To a lowly employee, the boss may be an unchecked tyrant. He or she can hire, fire, assign tasks, set rules, determine pay and otherwise rule subordinates. No wonder, then, that employees may believe that to share power with the boss, even become a boss themselves, would yield wondrous results. At a minimum, they would no longer fear arbitrary orders, job uncertainty or unfair assignments.

Perceptions, however, can mislead. Feeling inferior does not necessary mean that those above easily command. If roles were suddenly reversed, nothing substantial might change. For one, the immediate boss is just one cog in a long chain of supervision. Although superiors can appear omniscient, they may be mere pawns in meeting responsibilities dictated by top executives, shareholders, government officials, market forces and the competition. Laying off workers may resemble ultimate control, but in reality it may be predetermined by uncontrollable economic forces.

Managers may similarly feel impotent despite seeming godlike power over individual employees. Suppose, for whatever reason, in a certain locality and at a given wage, all recruits are slightly dishonest. This is just a fact of life beyond anybody's influence. No amount of persuasion, economic incentive or supervision curtails petty theft. Only replacing one conniving worker with another, and perhaps making adjustments in wages and prices to cover losses, is possible. As workers come and go, as one disliked security scheme after the next is implemented, employees undoubtedly feel powerless.[4] Yet superiors share the exact sentiment. And if power were shared, all may now share in this futility.

This is a general problem infusing empowerment. It is easy to overestimate the authority of those in commanding positions. Seizing control over one's workplace or neighborhood only shifts the battlegrounds. When tenants gain control over their housing, they may discover that motivating unionized maintenance workers is exasperating. But that is a snap compared to controlling unruly children or convincing recalcitrant bankers to refinance loans. And if this were not daunting enough, how about satisfying the multiple impossible-to-enforce bureaucratic rules made by distant officials? And repairing cranky elevators lacking available spare parts? The promise of empowerment may well be largely empty.

POWER TO DEFEAT WHAT?

When theorists discuss power, they speak of relationships. Enhanced empowerment conceivably bestows intrinsic satisfaction, but attainment itself—save self-delusion—cannot be obtained singularly or in isolation. The process inherently involves competition, a somebody to be vanquished. The golfer who endlessly practices "to empower" knows that matches bring the true trial. A habitual loser is hardly authentically capacitated regardless of progress in practice. To focus exclusively on one party's superiority offers a woefully incomplete picture. It would be as if one observed practicing golfers and, on the basis of form, confidence and success in rehearsal, declared the upcoming match's winner.

Prescriptions offer familiar practical resources lists: personal self-confidence, organizational skills, a keen understanding of the situation, adequate time and money, adroit alliances, cultivating leadership and facility with communications. A rough parallel exists with getting oneself physically fit: increasing endurance, building muscle strength, etc. The key issue, however, is not what resources are abstractly necessary but what the task at hand demands. Battles are not won by stockpiling advantages and heartfelt cheerleading. In other words, how does one's effort match up with the enemy? Years spent improving one's golf game may provide immense personal satisfaction, but this empowerment will likely fail competing against Tiger Woods.

A deeper moral quandary also lies in assessing success likelihoods. Empowerment promoters bare an inescapable responsibility to advise wisely. To encourage the hapless to "pick the wrong fight" is not cost free. Nor does indicating a rare triumph make risky mismatches any more commendable. Realism is a prerequisite prior to advising impoverished public housing tenants to resist entrenched bureaucrats. Constant disappointment hardly builds self-esteem or provides any other benefit, so efforts should be feasible. A cost-benefit calculus should also be applied—outlays should reasonably relate to probable outcomes. Why, for example, expend months forcing officials to clean up a neighborhood playground just once? After all, more profitable allocations of time may be available, to wit, taking a McDonald's job. Provoking unwinnable attacks easily breeds despair and, eventually, ingrained apathy. To counsel welfare recipients to combat huge odds is hardly risky; this is less true for those serving as foot soldiers.

In embracing this alluring remedy, the opposition's strength is often ignored or depreciated. The clamor for grassroots activism routinely has a romantic flavor, visions of multinational corporations and evil government bureaucracies being subjugated by hoards of energized Lilliputian groups (e.g., see Pilisuk, McAllister and Rothman 1996). Underestimating obstacles even occurs over more modest aims. A typical neglect example is Speer and Hughey's investigation of two midwestern organizations (1996). Organization members were carefully quizzed about multiple matters: personal familiarity, group interactions, organizational involvement, the motivation for participation, member assessments of group influence, among myriad other details. Their agendas focused on rolling back increased public transportation fares, sale of foreclosed properties to low-income people and the enforcement of drug and prostitution laws. It was assumed that these tasks were within the group's competence.

Compared to all possibilities, these objectives are seemingly obtainable. Yet they are formidable problems long perplexing similar communities. There also may be difficult-to-change legal requirements easily skipped over in the midst of battle. Victories are often temporary or very partial. In gaining cheaper public transportation, a "solution" may invisibly exchange one burden for another—artificially low fares might reduce service, increase municipal borrowing (and thus, ultimately, higher taxes) or necessitate reduced equipment maintenance. Transportation officials may also be legally bound by labor contracts, federally imposed safety standards, and multiple binding financial obligations. Vigorously attacking "drug houses" invites civil liberties abuses or cosmetically shifting the problem's location and reducing police enforcement in equally needy localities. Generously awarding foreclosed homes to the indigent might only shift ruinous mortgage defaults to the future. Local officials may also be legally obligated to sell foreclosed property to the highest bidder, not the poorest bidder, despite contrary opinion.

Our argument is not that this agenda is hopeless—it is not. Nor are we suggesting trifling aims be pursued. Rather, the entire analysis here disregards "the enemy" in assessing the matchup. Critical elements in the equation—city finances, the drug culture's tenacity, scarce municipal resources, the criminal code and housing economic—lie beyond scrutiny in this study. The "wish list" is never challenged in the rush for empowerment. Perhaps solutions are available: What about fleeing the mess entirely?[5] It is also a static battle analysis. It is assumed that the opposition—city officials, drug dealers and prostitutes—will passively await their defeat from energized citizens. Conceivably, these "enemies" are simultaneously empowering themselves to meet the forthcoming challenge. A strategy that worked yesterday may flounder tomorrow. Only a detailed battle investigation, as one might analyze a continuing military campaign, can predict the outcome. The stockpile of resources is but one small piece of the picture.

This tendency to underappreciate, even disregard, the enemy is commonplace in this literature.[6] It often seems that success, even when involving profound social change, merely entails confident thinking and pooled resourcefulness. Strident calls for popular self-determination mimic the illfated 1212 Children's Crusade when 30,000 beguiled European youngsters marched on the Holy Land (most died en route or were sold into slavery). That today's "victory" may be a long-term catastrophe is never contemplated. Pay raises or enhanced benefits may ultimately push jobs overseas to cheaper localities. A clinic coerced into accepting paupers may reduce the workforce, heighten workloads, outsource services and replace people with machines.[7] Prospective employers may fear locating in areas with a reputation of cantankerous citizen groups prone to suits and disruption.

Forcing cities to provide "free" expensive health care could bring municipal bankruptcy, a disaster for the poor. In many instances, these possible defeats are well beyond those whose infatuation with "victory" clouds all reason.

Especially troubling are immoderate agendas. An apparent disinclination often exists to assess carefully just what is obtainable for ordinary people in conventional circumstances. Empowerment slides into a technique to conquer the world and, eventually, a prescription for failure. Consider a sampling of such exalted objectives:

[Empowerment] promotes fair and equitable distribution of resources and burdens in society. . . . [T]he unequal distribution of wealth and power in society severely restricts access to services, education and employment. Consequently, empowerment calls for the interventions designed to rectify this imbalance of opportunity wherever it exists. (Prilleltensky 1994)

Empowerment is a viable challenge to the increasingly hollow formal democracy being trumpeted as a model of capitalist governance. . . . Broad empowerment must be the cornerstone of a revolutionary [anticapitalist] society. (Levins 1995)

Any theory that does not adequately conceptualize issues of social justice and fairness and the forces opposing these elements of a quality world—for example, racism, discrimination, economic exploitation, abuse and misuse of political power, and destructive United States foreign policy—cannot honestly hold itself out as providing people with relevant and empowering strategies to "control" the complex sociopolitical and economic forces in which oppressed people find themselves embedded. (Sanchez and Garriga 1995)

We use the term *empowerment* to connote a spectrum of political activity ranging from acts of individual resistance to mass political mobilizations that challenge the basic power relations of our society. (Morgan and Bookman 1988; italics in original)

Environmentalists, feminists, neighborhood and civil rights activists are also vital to this struggle [empowerment], especially as they join hands with workers in forging a coalition around issues of common interest. . . . Similarly, workers, feminists, neighborhood and civil rights groups stand to gain by collaborating on such issues as housing, education, child care, health benefits, and the minimum wage. (Bachrach and Botwinick 1992)

Empowerment is to improve the conditions of one's own life *and* the conditions of other lives, especially those lives limited by discrimination and social injustice. (Irwin 1996, italics in original)

These are not well-focused admonishments for enhanced personal competence. The troublesome inclination toward grandiose agendas is compounded by an underappreciation of the immense difficulties in political conflict. The old cliché "Fools rush in where angels fear to tread" may be applicable. At times, those advising "take charge of your life and community" appear to believe that self-determination can be accomplished as if one followed bicycle assembly instructions. That is, one lays out all the pieces, gets the proper tools and proceeds step by step until neighborhood crime is eliminated or sexism vanquished. That even "minor" difficulties— maintaining today's public housing—baffles experts scarcely seems to bother those counseling others. Reflect on what one prominent expert advises: "Individuals may also need to develop a critical awareness of their environment, including an understanding of causal agents in order to effectively interact in the settings that are important to them" (Zimmerman 1995, 589). A former president of the American Planning Association similarly instructs, "Planners are helping their customers become their own planners by teaching them networking, conflict resolution, consensus building, and the political decision-making process" (McClendon 1993, 147).

Far easier said than done, and libraries seldom proffer these insights in necessary detail. If such simple-to-follow cures actually worked, we would have achieved paradise centuries ago. It is bizarre to argue that poorly educated, chronically unemployed people can grasp the intricate factors shaping their lives, let alone adeptly apply these lessons. It might be far more efficacious to simply instruct on the necessities for gainful employment, not preach self-discovery of a bewildering environment. To expect dutiful housewives to become apt students of feminist theories of oppression asks too much. Moreover, if the endless scholarly debates are any harbinger, a roomful of experts will surely diverge on proposals. Worse, and this point cannot be overemphasized, judging from the success rates of past endeavors to uplift society, the expert advice may well be untrustworthy.[8] After all, what public housing tenants' groups are now to battle via empowerment was once state-of-the-art social science recommendation.

Perhaps nowhere is this expert guidance more troublesome than its stress on direct-action localism. Reviewing these admonitions intimates that nearly all of one's misfortune can be ameliorated via grassroots "taking charge" among fellow sufferers. That growing proportions of society's problems originate in national or international events, many of which are immensely technical, is rarely admitted. A similar disinterest applies to recognizing that many forces shaping modern society are beyond *anybody's* power.[9] The empowerment solution can become a Procrustean bed in which all difficulties are made amenable to energetic local initiatives. From bad schools to unsafe neighborhoods, from unemployment to government neglect of the homeless, just organize and press the correct, convenient buttons. Even the alleged principal disorders of modern society—economic inequality, racism, sexism and so on—begin with small groups of people altering their thinking. Looking to distant levers of power and wisely counseling abandoning personalized empowerment-based solutions are off the agenda.[10] Unfortunately, especially where legal or economic authority resides outside the community, local agitation may detract from a solution. In the case of ineffective schools, for example, community pressure may be misdirected if the problem derives from inept state or national policy. Here a more intelligent strategy is dutiful support for an interest group over which each local person has but scant influence.

The seemingly endless need for close-support expertise raises yet another irony in the quest for self-determination. Those who need uplifting the most are, in all likelihood, the identical people possessing the least requisite capacity. If our impoverished public housing resident could unravel his or her troubled situation and act accordingly, he or she would have long since departed. It is ignorance, often coupled with an incapacity to use knowledge when adroitly provided, that accounts for difficulties in the first place. That those most in need may be incapable of utilizing expert advice is an awkward, all too often disregarded, fact. Moreover, to provide constant intrusive direction encourages dependency, not autonomy.

Yet the identical newfound competence secured by those already empowered may be applied far more efficiently. And this gain may ultimately be paid for by those at the bottom of the heap. A wealthy, capable neighborhood group can easily "take charge" when a local garbage dump is proposed; they will likely secure its location elsewhere, probably closer to poorer neighborhoods. Meanwhile, poorer, less-well-educated residents— even if energized by the call to empowerment—are more likely to feel overwhelmed. In a showdown between these two "empowered" groups, victory will go to the more initially capable. As is said in seeking bank loans, the rich are more likely to get more. The society-wide infusion of self-determination prescriptions may ultimately only exacerbate have and have-not differences. Surely we cannot prohibit those with power from seeking even more.

COMPETENT EMPOWERMENT

Empowerment advocates often resemble military strategists depicting a forthcoming struggle in which the helpless rise up to secure their proper place. Some "generals" are modest in their designs—victory in a housing project—while others endeavor to transform society itself, but they all share certain inclinations. Much time is spent delineating weapons and tactics, denouncing the enemy and inspiring the troops. Enticing futuristic visions are announced, and reports hint of modest victories nearly achieved. That these "generals" typically occupy prestigious academic posts and have long labored in empowerment theory provides, it would seem, confident inspiration.

Yet to compare these enablement crusaders with a mighty army about to vanquish a feeble foe grossly exaggerates. Previous discussions have hinted at a pitfall potentially impeding this conquest, namely, the questionable expertise of self-proclaimed experts. Put bluntly, what makes professors of psychology, urban planning, social work, women's studies or educational policy so clever in their nonacademic advice? Does their expertise permit them to command poor people how to prosper? This is a perplexing question, yet demonstrations of fitting expertise are a glaring omission in this call to arms. Adequacy is easily assumed, even for the most daunting tasks. When debates over guidance giving surface, the discussion centers on the ethics of social scientists slipping into advocacy (with the answer always being yes to crossing over). Ultimately, of course, this inquest can only be answered by the results, not prior speculation. Nevertheless, much suggests caution in obeying commands from these "generals."

The incentive structure for professorial advocates and those who might actually do the empowering are quite distinct, even contradictory. To secure an academic reputation demands visible scholarly proficiency. One publishes in professional journals, edits books, participates in conferences and draws the approval of professional peers via frequent citations. These skills are highly specialized and necessitate considerable abstract analytic ability, mastery of the erudite style and sensitivity to shifting disciplinary trends. One communicates only to other professionals through disciplinary jargon while heeding precise research conventions. And requirements may vary substantially, depending on one's academic field and publication outlets.

This scholarly realm diverges enormously from the circumstances of those requiring enablement. Plainly, academic career advancement offers slight training for uplifting the downtrodden. Brilliant conceptual frameworks may prove absolutely irrelevant among the depressed homeless or chronically underemployed poor women. Ideas that bedazzle fellow academics may puzzle the less sophisticated. More central, few incentives propel academics to align prescriptions with "outside" reality. For one, it may be impossible for academics to bridge this awareness gap, even if he or she lived in public housing temporarily or volunteered at a homeless shelter. Frequent slum visits will surely yield insights, but only superficial ones if middle-class comforts await at day's end. Advice books about the less fortunate are almost never written by the less fortunate—they are penned by fellow academicians.

Second, amassing detailed insight into troubled people has only limited worth in academic circles. A smattering usually suffices. The university's currency is published scholarship, not time-consuming encounters to cement rapport with teenage welfare mothers. Being an "activist" in the academy means writing about activism, not surviving full-time among those to be uplifted. Finally, providing faulty advice many be a disaster for recipients, but no professorial careers suffer. One hardly risks tenure by using empowerment to subvert teachers' authority when these teachers are trying to help "at-risk" students (see Gruber and Trickett [1987] for an example of ill-advised academic "assistance"). Aiding the disadvantaged is unlike coaching the university's football team. A losing record in the latter will surely bring dismissal; not so if one ineptly coaches welfare recipients.

By contrast, those actually performing the "dirty work" of empowerment may be ill-suited to offer persuasive opinions to professionals. This is even largely true for middle-class practitioners in the field without access to respectable academic publications. It is not that they are ill-informed—the opposite is probably true. Rather, these sage observations and advice are unlikely to infuse the "empowerment literature." By academic standards, their counsel is too impressionistic, unsystematic or poorly articulated to be publishable. Their familiarity with the reigning disciplinary vocabulary is probably minimal. Those with a knack for pushing public housing tenants to attend meetings promptly will seldom evince talent for crafting arcane theoretical treatises. "Real-world" assets—proven trustworthiness, facility with street language, a reputation for toughness, physical courage—typically count for little among academic experts and their careers. Predictably, those who "cross over" from one domain to another, figures like the legendary Saul Alinsky, are exceedingly rare. Indeed, a contemporary empowerment-oriented academic—Marvin Olasky (a professor of journalism)—who has spent prodigious time actually working with the downtrodden seems to have escaped notice in most scholarly outlets.

Establishing bone fide expertise is not straightforward. Measured by the usual standards of professional certification, namely, a detailed technical knowledge of a narrow subject, most academic empowerment experts would probably fail. Professors of psychology, social work and others advising empowerment seldom evidence relevant practical knowledge in their empowerment scholarship. One writer when depicting the necessary skills for successful empowerment contended that counsel consisted of "a set of interventions that encourages clients to find their own answers to their own questions while making their way in a difficult world" (Evans 1992, 143). Perhaps it is assumed that having mastered their arduous academic specialty, they can now competently venture forth virtually everywhere. Recall how vital circumstantial details, for example, municipal legal obligations, typically fall outside the scope of analysis. Tasks disheartening experts—cracking down on prostitutes—are glibly accepted as readily feasible. Conceivably, empowerment advisers might be licensed, as one accredits doctors. Thus, for example, prior to a social psychologist advising the homeless, he or she must pass a examination covering building codes, legal regulations regarding involuntary confinement, the economics of housing and similar elaborate pertinent subjects.[11] And if things go badly, the expert might be sued for malpractice. How else might those seeking guidance be assured that they might receive sound counsel?

Another troublesome, unexamined matter concerns who can expertly advise. The empowerment "industry" is highly multidisciplinary, and unlike medical specialties, no professionally imposed division of labor exists. Involvement reflects the expert's choosing, not demonstrated competence. Interventions often reflect nearby opportunities, not a match between the problem and expertise. Given disciplinary divergences in remedies, choice of "doctor" is hardly trivial. Recommendations will fluctuate by academic specialty—urban planners may counsel the homeless quite differently from social workers. Jurisdictional and substantive disputes will surely arise. Advisers automatically assume that professional colleagues are qualified to consult across multiple surroundings. In other words, when a psychologist writes about women needing low-cost health care, it will be the psychologists who will point the way to mastery. One is unlikely to hear: "This is too perplexing for me; perhaps we should call a health care administrator."

The contrast between preaching empowerment versus offering counsel on other weighty matters is sharp. A certified specialist is available for those wanting their taxes prepared, teeth fixed, eyesight corrected or disease cured. Even automobile mechanics and morticians are now certified. When confronting choices about one's entire life, even altering basic political structures, qualification is merely self-proclaimed. This uncertainty of knowledge is particularly troubling for the less sophisticated, the very people most dependent on the aptitude of others. Which of all the many Doctors of Empowerment is most knowledgeable? Which one possesses the necessary human touch? As in early primitive medicine and today's psychic hotlines, anybody who claims a knack for advising can freely solicit business.

A final point concerning competency concerns funding sources. Funding for empowerment mobilization in recent decades has oftentimes originated from nonprofit foundations and church-related groups (Rabinowitz 1990). Unlike past arrangements in labor unions or local political machines, benefactor and recipient now live in totally sequestered worlds. The opportunities for misdirection and outright foolishness from this disjunctive funding arrangement abound. In many instances, distant foundation or charity experts, not those directly affected, decide appropriate goals and procedures (see, e.g., Hall 1995, Ch. 2). These missives for uplifting may reflect restrictive tax law requirements, current philanthropic fads (today a passion for "innovative" action) or patron doctrines, not genuine needs. No doubt, moreover, given donor group legal guidelines, empowerment projects may be circumscribed, lest the IRS revoke tax-exempt status. A shortsightedness is also encouraged, given that generosity must be frequently replenished, and it is thus the donor's wishes that must be carefully obeyed. The arrangement that places a premium on grant-getting skills only loosely relates to internal organizational requirements.

EMPOWERMENT AND THE "GOOD SOCIETY"

A bedrock, barely articulated, premise informing empowerment gospel is that societal improvement inevitably follows. Only rarely is there any hint that empowerment may turn out poorly (one such exception is Riger 1993). Why else the strident commitment? The broadening of power is also considered intimately connected to democracy and, at least among some, a defining element of democracy. Wondrous appreciation transcends ideology, though, predictably, detailed notions of betterment vary across the political spectrum. On the Left, a self-determining citizenry will impose economic equality, subdue elitism, secure social justice and enhance participation. To be empowered are the familiar recipients of liberal ameliorative policy: African Americans, Hispanics, the poor, the homeless, the handicapped, AIDS sufferers, women and gays. Wittig (1996) talks of empowering grassroots organizations as a means of attacking "the root causes of social problems." The Right, though less well represented in this literature, shares this hopefulness. The enticing prediction is of people freed from bumbling, intrusive centralized bureaucratic control. Thus liberated, society thrives. People now skillfully do for themselves what was once ineptly done elsewhere. Schools become effective, communities safer, health care improves, taxes decline, welfare dwindles and the entrepreneurial spirit explodes.

Every social problem, it is said, was born a reform, and empowerment may conceivably induce its own calamity. Housing experts intended to provide cheap, well-constructed, affordable housing when today's violence-prone, drug-infested public housing was initially constructed. No iron logic connects the empowerment of those previously enfeebled and peaceful democratic outcomes. The shifting possessions of power are inherently neutral—power is equally suitable for good or evil.[12] Freshly empowered citizens might just as well create a fledging Nazi Party as mobilize for justice. One could well imagine the Klu Klux Klan embracing this heady prescription, setting up workshops and writing action manuals to advance bigotry. No ideological identity check guards empowerment's door.

Nor does the "empowerment will allow communities to improve themselves" argument protect against disaster. What is "good" for a self-determining community is often a matter of dispute; "improvement" for some may entail tragedy for others. Racial segregation and discrimination were once "obviously" wholesome for the community. Only after many southern towns were "depowered" were these practices ended. Our exemplary pitiable public housing tenants may decide by majority vote that since drug traffic is unstoppable, "the community" should reap its financial rewards. Self-appointed "experts" may even declare that drug dealing is government tolerated and thus de facto "legal." Residents arm and capture this business for themselves. Now these once-destitute people own splendid mansions, thanks to taking charge, and with all resistance gone, addiction soars. It is they, not outsiders, who decide prices, selling sites and merchandise. True empowerment. Indeed, vicious criminal organizations, often employing analogous tactics celebrated by empowerment theorists, have long been a common form of communal control. If the Mafia were described without mentioning its activities exactly, one might well depict a model community organization.

Leaving aside inherent neutrality, several strong arguments suggest a riskiness for democracy. Substantially shifting fresh power to the long deprived and promoting its easy use need not bring promised prizes. Most evidently, empowering the once-apathetic commonly exacerbates conflict, often unnecessarily, without much being gained. Tranquillity is replaced by escalating strife and heated emotion as all sides become convinced that progress means overpowering the enemy. The outlines of this transformation can already been seen in the proliferation of litigation, demonstrations, voting registration drives and other mechanisms of communal empowerment. The problem is not the activity per se but the risk of its escalating beyond democratic rules of the game. If democratically taking economic control of neighborhood schools fails, perhaps some physical intimidation is necessary. If that is unsuccessful, try arson. The passion for self-termination, as is evidenced throughout the world, is an appetite difficult to contain once instigated. This is especially troublesome for democracy if such cravings are rooted in long-smoldering ethnic or racial disputes.[13] Empowerment merely rekindles long-dormant antagonisms.

Some self-determination fans cherish this heightened conflict, appreciating its vital democratic health and essential tool for rectifying injustice. No doubt, partial truth resides in this charitable portrayal. Nevertheless, envisioning society as an incessant battlefield over domination collides with civil society. No guarantees exist that relentless vying for advantage enhances the common good. Goodies may be contentiously redistributed but not necessarily increased. For one group to "win" jobs via mobilization may mean unemployment for an equal number elsewhere. Empowerment skill may not necessarily foretell superior job performance. More broadly, depriving "haves" to enrich the "have-nots" via squabbling is not the definition of social justice. One person's gain may be another's loss, not a victory for society. Getting the prostitutes out of one neighborhood only relocates them elsewhere.

The momentary triumphs should not obscure the losses that empowerment will surely bring. Ceaseless empowerment wars may detract from other activities promising satisfaction and betterment. Our destitute tenants might eschew getting organized and selfishly attend night school and dutifully learn a dull, blue-collar trade requiring subordination. Society need not resemble the World War I engagements in which millions were hurled into bloody futile battles for "power." At some point, one's station in life, even if less than desired, must be accepted as permanent or at least not worth additional conflict. Some fatalism is often quite realistic and certainly an ingrained human trait. Not every problem or misfortune is curable.

Considerable evidence also strongly hints that suddenly empowering society's have-nots may unleash forces detrimental to democracy. The Pollyannaish vision of the forthcoming egalitarian participatory democracy may be a mirage. This is especially likely once attached empowerment advisers, all undoubtedly defenders of democracy, withdraw their guidance. The less-well-educated disproportionately reject democratic principles—for example, the right of unpopular speakers to express themselves—and are more willing to impose authoritarian solutions to troubling problems. There is also less willingness to accept the compromises and uncertainties that inevitably accompany democratic give-and-take (e.g., McClosky and Brill 1983; Mueller 1988). Imparting such ideal values to those of limited intellectual ability is no easy task, although it might be accomplished.

Moreover, many of the traits commonly associated with those awaiting empowerment, for example, an inclination toward violence, traditional hierarchical social relationships, are hardly compatible with the promised egalitarian democracy envisioned by devotees. Left to their own devices, the path toward self-determination of the once-dispossessed may be strewn with riots, looting, arson, terrorism and other violent antidemocratic acts. To believe that the once-oppressed, now enlightened, will now gratefully adopt tumultuous but peaceful give-and-take of liberal democratic ideology is probably a romantic illusion, not a probable outcome.

More important than predicting possibilities is the sorry historical record. When those seeking empowerment enter the political arena, their participation often reveals an authoritarian, if not violent, character. And this tendency affects nearly all groups. Even those sympathetic to the plight of African Americans would not depict the Black Panthers as a peaceful democratic group, yet much of its rhetoric and public relations activity mimicked the self-determination prescription. Ditto for the Klan and similar white supremacist groups who speak only "of controlling their own destinies." Is the burgeoning militia movement an exemplar of taking control of one's life? After all, many of its members are disaffected, relatively poor citizens who feel a powerful need to reassert control over their lives. Can Louis Farrakhan's Nation of Islam, which embraces the self-determination agenda, be classified as "democratic"? Is the only difference between a rural white militia and a newly empowered urban tenants' group the presence of guiding academics at the latter? And what should happen if counselors departed? Tactics might well take an entirely different and worse direction.

Scanning American history surely illustrates poorer, estranged people empowering themselves via movements tinged with hatred and disorder. The Klan and the militia movement are but the tip of the proverbial iceberg.

Lipset and Raab (1970) offer a virtual catalog of such groups, drawing extensive (though not exclusive) working-class support: the Know-Nothing Party, American Protective Association, the Black Legion, Defenders of the Christian Faith, Silver Shirts, National Union for Social Justice (the Father Charles Coughlin organization), the Huey Long campaign, the Christian Crusade and untold others attracting the disempowered. The myriad off-shoots of Nazism and similar white supremacist groups that seem to peri-odically erupt onto our political landscape can likewise be appended (Thayer 1968). Although all had their peculiar agendas regarding the gain-ing of influence, none displayed a predilection for liberal democracy. The overseas record—working-class fascism in Germany, Italy, Spain, France and Argentina—only confirms this dismal assessment. No doubt, much of today's bloody strife in the Balkans and Africa has an element of "empow-erment" embedded within it. Hitler did, after all, temporarily empower millions.

A search for counterexamples comes up largely empty. If the mainte-nance of an open, constitutional society were the primary goal, conserving power in the hands of the already empowered is a safer bet. At most, power granted to unsophisticated outsiders should be constrained, for example, being able to vote but not being permitted to define election rules. And, to impede recklessness, change should be made cumbersome, with a bias to-ward compromise.[14] Bringing the once-excluded into "the game" may well modify the game more than it reforms the new arrivals.

To argue that our new store of knowledge now permits a democratic transformation of these fresh arrivals is questionable. To insist on one path—peaceful democracy—violates the autonomy principle central to the very meaning of self-determination. Paramilitary violence might well be the ticket to success in unique situations. A far greater obstacle is the tenacity of deeply ingrained cultural dispositions. The venerable cliché "More ed-ucation to educate for democracy" is highly questionable guidance. Academic-style lectures on democratic virtue will hardly convince those enamored of naked force. A capacity for debate, compromise, obedience to "petty" rules and restraint are not to be instantly conveyed in a few workshops. If billions of dollars and extensive educational effort cannot reverse welfare dependency, that a few professors and social workers con-vert their clients to the advantages of slow-moving, often exasperating de-mocracy seems unlikely.

DISINGENUOUS PSEUDO-EMPOWERMENT

Empowerment advocates typically speak as if they are providing a wor-thy, straightforward, uncontroversial service not unlike proffering technical expertise on public health. Nevertheless, such claims may mislead; ultimate beneficiaries are not those to be guided. Intervention camouflages a far-reaching political agenda. As H. L. Mencken put it, "The urge to save humanity is almost always a false-face for the urge to rule it." This is especially likely if advisees are scarcely in positions to make their own informed judgments. Similarity of language disguises divergent purposes. Do not confuse the genuine article—helping people overcome their plight—with the pernicious fake mimicking benign facilitation.

Return again to our hypothetical public housing tenant organizing to secure improved living conditions. Conventional advice would be to learn skills, pool resources, develop plans and so on. But ambitious assertiveness may be pushed beyond grappling effectively with life's obstacles. Tenants may be told that progress can only come from political action, for example, making housing administrators stand for election. Furthermore, present municipal financial commitments are insufficient and, as a matter of inalienable right, must be doubled without raising rents. Advisers then encourage boycotts, litigation, petition drives, coalitions with fringe political sects and similar escalations. If this strategy fails, expand the fight to demand direct housing subsidies or furniture allowances. Perhaps meetings will be disrupted or public officials harassed by angry protestors. The rhetoric shifts from narrow, reachable personal goals to vague admonitions for "economic justice." The process is now moving beyond acquiring control over one's immediate living environment. The germ of an anti–status quo movement is being fashioned.

Such duplicitous manipulation is well illustrated in one project involving poor, politically uninformed minority homeless women living in a shelter (Lee 1991). To inspire the quest for empowerment, the group leader (a professor of social work) explained that while the Department of Defense received 52¢ of every budget dollar, money allocated housing was less than 2¢ on the dollar. Although this is a blatantly inappropriate comparison, this "less than 2¢" theme nevertheless inflamed the women, and they soon "spontaneously" took to denouncing "rich white men," "the millionaires" and "the big companies." A revolutionary spirit was fashioned out of misinformation fed to desperate women. How this newfound "knowledge" proved useful other than, perhaps, satisfy the social worker adviser's political agenda is inconceivable.

Particularly if "reformist" remedies flounder (a likely outcome), the slide into yet more unruly solutions is tempting. A version of the gambler's fallacy ensues: If one loses with small efforts, double up and, eventually, one will triumph. Given frustratingly slow progress, attention turns to more "fundamental" barriers, the distribution of political and economic power, claims on wealth and evil society itself. Tenants are now tutored that their true enemy is market capitalism. An entirely novel conceptual apparatus, perhaps one stressing the primacy of class, race and gender conflict, will be superimposed. The agenda expands toward redistributing income, guaranteed employment and multiple universal entitlements (Belcher and Hegar

1991). People who one sought simple services now speak of "deconstructing the vocabulary of oppression" (see, e.g., Morgan 1988). The quest has transformed itself significantly, yet the superficial phraseology remains unchanged. Social upheaval or even revolution might be a more apt description.

To appreciate the underlying political displacement, reverse the ideological drift. In response to city official complaints regarding contentious public housing tenants, conservative professors are enlisted to advise. They recommend that housing administrators be given extralegal carte blanche power to evict troublemakers, that permanent records be kept to deprive malcontents of government benefits and that persistent "agitation" be criminalized. If that fails, fence in the housing, issue identity cards and establish a permanent 7:00 P.M. to midnight curfew. Empowering administrators, one might say. Predictably, howls of outrage would ensue from today's empowerment espousers. These conservative experts would be castigated as "police state agents," tools of the entrenched elite, even fascists. Clearly, at least for those who link empowerment with social upheaval, assistance is inherently one-sided; only those at the bottom must be helped—and then only in a leftward ideological direction. "Right-wing empowerment" would be labeled a fraud.

Academic political meddling is not the issue. This occurs endlessly and properly. No objection could be offered if, for example, housing experts were summoned to improve security. This request addresses a problem judged worthy by everyone (save, perhaps, criminals). Ditto for being invited by all parties to teach empowerment understood as instructing tenants how to better manage their activities, for example, creating a neighborhood crime watch. It is a far different matter when self-selecting intervention has no relationship with authorized public policy and, in fact, seeks to subvert it. No standing societal admonition declares, "Present unequal power relationships are wrong. It is the duty of all citizens—especially professors and similar self-designated experts—to intervene to correct this injustice, preferably by reshaping society itself." Imagine the outrage if an oddball artist collective spontaneously decided that city hall was ugly and, since some city workers detested the dreariness, one night covertly repainted the building bright orange.

Not all empowerment prescriptions are the genuine article. Nor are proscribed humdrum cures the equivalent of sage public health advice; much depends. Often far grander schemes remain hidden. Calls for empowerment frequently are thinly veiled clamors for aggrandizing the liberal state. In one plan to assist poor black women with mental illness, the solution (in part) entailed government-paid minimal incomes, universal health care, low-income housing, more government training programs, child care benefits for working women, plus extending other top-down ameliorative programs (Gibbs and Fuery 1994). The underlying tension between self-mastery and colossal government was never broached.

Proposed remedies may go well beyond a refurbished Great Society. "Cures" may be subversive of the established order, not just fixing up a deteriorating neighborhood. What might Morgan and Bookman (1988), two widely cited researchers on empowering women, have in mind when they declare:

For the women whose lives form the subject of this book, empowerment is rarely experienced as upward mobility or personal advancement. Rather, "feeling powerful" is constrained for them by the ways in which their gender, as well as their race and class, limit their access to economic resources and political power. For these women, empowerment begins when they change their ideas about the causes of their powerlessness, when they recognize the systematic forces that oppress them, and when they act to change the conditions of their lives. (4)

Clearly, aiding the destitute is not the overriding objective. Picking up new skills counts little in this ambitious design. The enduring inferiority of these women is assumed unless a more profound transformation occurs: a new consciousness regarding the "systemic forces" of oppression. The troops receive training for a more profound struggle, not a local skirmish. Only when fundamental social and economic relationships are overthrown can success come. And as the authors state elsewhere, this transformation even reaches down to altering family relationships (8). Empowerment thus is re-created into a sweeping radical political movement. The Highlander Folk School, a popular empowerment "academy" founded in 1932, typifies this radical interpretation. Its ambitious "empowerment" agenda calls for the uprooting of class domination, race domination, gender domination, capitalism and similar evils, all of which are deeply woven into our social fabric (Morris 1991).[15] Surely few would argue that we now live in a state of perfection and that nothing need be done, but this attack on "root causes" is nothing but a call to revolution.

Let us be clear: Nothing prohibits nonviolent revolutionary activity in the United States. A counterrevolutionary tract is not our purpose. We merely insist upon honest labeling. Demanding the overthrow of capitalism, a drastic redistribution of wealth, fundamental changes in relationships between men and women, the full acceptance of homosexuality as valid sexuality, a foreign policy of passivity and similar radical endeavors misleads. Additionally, the historical record makes it absolutely clear that overthrowing capitalism is no guarantee of worker empowerment, women's self-determination or similar betterments. These vague, lofty promises are also without proof. Labeling such schemes "empowerment" is disingenuous, akin to calling violence merely "nontraditional communication."

Needless to say, the prospects of radical devotees of empowerment winning are zero. It is hard to imagine public housing tenants, revolutionary consciousness fully raised, storming city hall and announcing the People's Republic of Chicago. The argument is not a caution about insidious radicals about to grab power. Would-be revolutions have every right to keep on trying. Our concern is preserving a term from corruption, not reigning in would-be subversives. The message here is that "empowerment" mobilizations may well be disguised conscription for tasks other than personal self-determination.[16] In this seditious vision, pubic housing tenants are not to be assisted to secure control over their lives. More accurately, they are to be the clueless conscripted foot soldiers in a much larger war. And, if perchance they won, the outcome might well prove disastrous if the past predicts the future.

CONCLUSIONS

Discrediting empowerment is not our goal. No hidden agenda lurks counseling passive fatalism to the hapless. Nor do we recommend unthinking obedience to some more competent, paternal elite. Empowerment, we believe, has its advantages, but these benefits do not certify a universal elixir, a miracle drug for every imaginable human predicament. We suggest a realistic caution too often neglected when new remedies entice the well-intentioned frustrated by past defeats. Counseling improvement is a serious responsibility. Being unrealistic or misdirecting is especially consequential for those most in need. What, then, might we advise those who recommend empowerment?

Most evidently, empowerment disciples must acknowledge that this hardly exhausts the remediable menu. Some of the powerless might reject mastery over their circumstances. The real question is empowerment versus something else. Forcing hospitals to provide low-cost health care via demonstrations is not the sole path to improving health. Coercion in personal well-being or strict direction toward affluence are feasible alternatives. Unfortunately, alternatives are seldom debated, and as a result, the enterprise is redefined into tactics within empowerment. That less self-determination, diminished autonomy and more forceful direction may prove more effective is glibly dismissed. Such "authoritarian" counsel is not only judged ineffective but tacitly deemed "immoral," to boot. Perhaps this single-mindedness reflects an underlying liberal political ideology celebrating the efficacy of grassroots activism. Maybe the old adage "If all you have is a hammer, everything looks like a nail" applies here. The initial question should be, "What can help?" not "How best to empower?"

The obstacles inherent in popular mobilization strategies are often neglected. The vision of demonstrators agitating heroic victories can become a romantic fixation. Momentary passions easily obscure the formidability of tasks. Large bureaucracies are not easily conquered by angry protestors unacquainted with arcane policy details. Today's triumph can be quietly reversed months later when the advisers have departed and apathy returns. Intimidating companies to provide jobs may be paid for by shifting future employment expansion to more tranquil places. Let us not confuse winning an occasional clash with the war itself.

The necessary technical knowledge to prevail is likewise disdained. Being a distinguished professor of psychology hardly certifies expertise on municipal government. Arming the troops with attractive slogans and teaching them rudimentary organization are inadequate against entrenched, resourceful enemies. Most notably, the role of full-time professionals is too easily forgotten in the rush to maximize involvement. The labor union is the alternative model: A few highly empowered officials negotiate benefits for a largely passive clientele. Hiring well-paid professionals intimately acquainted with local housing codes may do more to help the homeless than well-publicized rallies punctuated with stirring rhetoric. We do not need any more children's crusades.

Finally, the preaching of personal mastery may be disingenuous, more a sweeping campaign to subvert the status quo. Familiar vocabulary may disguise deceptive repackaging. Worse, intended beneficiaries are little more than misled pawns. Such manipulative endeavors will only disappoint, even if nominally successful. In other instances the quest becomes therapy. Goals and strategies reflect what is personally satisfying, not what is pertinent. Making history is replaced by the rewriting of chronicles to instill group pride. Self-gratification trumps confronting unpleasant but essential choices. Advice is given not because it is demonstrably effective but because it conforms to academic standards regarding publication. Organizations become settings whose de facto goal is endless discussion and high-sounding but empty pronouncements. It is not that such transforming activities are improper—therapy and revolution are perfectly legal. More germane, if empowerment is the objective, then it is empowerment that should be pursued. As in making consumer choices, one should be aware of one's purchase.

NOTES

1. Our sampling only highlights these nuances; complexities abound when we proceed beyond general definitions. Indeed, much of the empowerment literature constitutes little more than scholastic quibbling over deeper or "real" meaning. That this contentious uncertainty remains unabated suggests caution in waiting for dramatic results. For a sampling of this definitional variety, see Dunst, Trivette and Lapoint (1992).

2. A revealing story is told by Morgan (1988) of a women's group attempting to reopen a closed health clinic. When a taxpayers lawsuit was filed by the group, an ultimately influential weapon, the technical complexity alienated many women

and caused an exodus. Discussions regarding the suit became "boring," reminding would-be activists of school. No doubt, adding other pertinent but complex material might have well destroyed this empowerment group despite the material's worthiness.

3. The consumerism versus "real" empowerment need not be a contradiction. Frank Riessman, a radical empowerment adherent, sees consumerism as a precursor of political self-determination. As he put it, "The choosing dimension is the forerunning of the empowerment orientation. Empowerment obviously is more than choosing at the marketplace and more than the power of choice alone. But the underlying feelings and the skills associated with choosing form an important base, which together with other dimensions serve to stimulate an increase in empowerment" (Riessman 1986, 56).

4. An intriguing irony exists here. Workers and others who are evidently incompetent may, in effect, exercise considerable power since it is pointless to push them. The lazy, dishonest, bumbling employee thus escapes difficult tasks. After a few bad experiences, bosses disregard such employees and select more capable ones. Indeed, it is entirely possible that for those at the very bottom learned incompetence, even helplessness, helps resist exploitation.

5. This "running away" option may sound cowardly and seems to have escaped the empowerment menu of valid solutions. Nevertheless, it is not only valid, but historically it has proven quite effective. Persecuted religious groups, for example, the Mormons and the Amish, solved their problems by fleeing, not fighting hopeless causes.

6. Proposed solutions to the problems plaguing the black community in particular reek of naïveté. It is almost as if the deeply felt desire for miracles overpowers grim reality. One missive—authored by three academics at reputable universities— suggests that the solution to the crack cocaine problem in public housing projects is to take down the license plate numbers of drive-through buyers and search their cars. They simultaneously reject intrusive police intervention. Only can only imagine the ruthless reaction of drug dealers to this unarmed citizen vigilantism. Other community empowerment measures suggested are equally foolish or, if successful, would merely move the drug trafficking a few blocks (Bowser, Thompson and Fullilove 1990).

7. These commonplace business practices apparently escape notice when tales of empowerment are told. Sacks (1988), for example, recounts how lowly hospital workers organized to gain better salaries and working conditions in a hospital. Her analysis details this empowering process minutely, but it never seems to occur to her that higher wages might eventually translate into fewer workers. This inattention to mundane business economics seems typical in the rush to laud grassroots activism.

8. Indeed, the popularity of the empowerment approach among social scientists seems at least partially a consequence of past failures in tackling the identical problems. Yet to assert that "bottom-up" approaches will outperform past discredited "top-down" remedies is disingenuous if the old experts are now to guide this "new" client-centered strategy. Unfortunately, this lurking and awkward contradiction seems to escaped the notice of empowerment converts (see, e.g., McClendon 1993).

9. One might even speculate that the sudden interest in empowerment partially flows from the expanding uncontrollability of political and economic forces. The

unrelenting spread of technology, the globalization of markets, the fluidity of capital and several other transnational forces are beyond the power of any one person, corporation or even government. Fluctuations in the value of the dollar, for example, may have more to do with local employment than militant job campaigns. Hence, the idea of empowering workers to help keep their tasks from being automated or sent elsewhere is quixotic.

10. This local grassroots fetish lingers even when the primacy of global forces is frankly admitted. Pilisuk, McAllister and Rothman (1996) offer one possibility out of this conflict: the idea of "global grassroots organizing." Clearly, the possibility of thousands of separate groups coordinating their efforts to uplift the poor seems like a long shot.

11. It could also be argued that a comprehensive certification review would inquire into the empowerer's personal life. After all, if one cannot empower oneself, how is he or she to guide others?

12. Empowerment discussions routinely stress power as an end in itself, not a means (e.g., Mondros and Wilson 1994, 2). Older warnings regarding the inherent evil of power seem forgotten or discounted. One can only speculate why this highly questionable assumption goes unchallenged. Perhaps experts believe that their control of events is so strong that newly empowered people are incapable of evil. Or their optimistic vision of human beings excludes any notion of depravity.

13. This apparently has been the situation is several urban, predominantly African-American neighborhoods. Talk of "economic empowerment" quickly becomes an attack on local businesses owned by Koreans, Indians, Jews and other nonblacks. Confrontations often escalate, moving from demonstrations to boycotts to violence, even firebombings. Needless to say, empowerment advocates do not defend violence, but once the genie is out of the bottle, control may be difficult.

14. Such a scheme, of course, is exactly what underlies the U.S. constitutional order. The Founders full well realized the risks of permitting ordinary citizens a direct say in government and devised our system of checks and balances as a means of combating impulsiveness. Architecturally, American politics is not designed to promote citizen empowerment.

15. This overthrow of these dangerous "isms" is commonplace in the radical incarnations of empowerment, yet the precise way this is to be accomplished is never spelled out. It would not take much for this impulse to become totalitarian if most ordinary citizens would resist this attack on social customs and economic arrangements.

16. For decades the Communist Party U.S.A. used a strategy of temporarily latching on to causes to disguise its true subversive aims and advance Marxism. As conditions permitted, communists defended blacks, rural whites, workers trying to join unions, farmers and whoever else seemed like a "good cause" for the moment. It was all opportunistic, and campaigns would shift with the party line. There was never any long-term commitment or genuine concern. We mention this to suggest that promises to help the less fortunate may not always be authentic.

3

Visions of Empowerment

Empowerment exhortations seemingly appear everywhere. Unfortunately, common terminology may well disguise quite distinct designs. Here we dig deeper into this ubiquitous fascination, shifting our focus from general issues to specific proclivities. Given this proliferation—literally thousands— disentanglement is daunting. Common vocabulary typically hides substantial differences and quarreling sects, all mutating over time. Deeply buried assumptions must also be articulated. Espousers commonly preach to the choir, making it unnecessary to say "what everybody already knows." Full implications of admonitions are seldom pushed; prescriptions are often little more than slogans, not proven conclusions. Finally, an enterprise of this type requires picking and choosing among advocates. Not every voice can be heard. This is deceptively complex, for influence may not be reflected in the published literature, our window to the subject. Our characterization is thus less a definitive treatise than a broad outline of dissimilar movements to correct society via "empowerment."

We single out five major viewpoints: African-American political action, community psychology, militant feminism, participatory democracy and anti–big government conservative empowerment. Each possesses an evolved history and extensive followings. No doubt, other versions and innumerable variations abound, but these five seem rooted in some articulated theoretical framework.

AFRICAN-AMERICAN EMPOWERMENT

Few groups appreciate empowerment more than African Americans. Such concern is, of course, predictable, given their historical political exclusion. Over 50 years ago, prominent unionist and black civil rights leader A. Phillip Randolph spoke to the National Negro Congress: "True liberation can be acquired and maintained only when the Negro people possess power; and power is the product and flower of organization . . . of the masses." Some 30 years later, Malcolm X similarly expressed power's efficacy in achieving black objectives: "Power in defense of freedom is greater than power in behalf of tyranny and oppression."

The "Black Power" movement of the 1960s and 1970s foretold today's quest for self-determination. This expression masked disparate positions, from peaceful compromise to violent revolution, but the belief that African Americans' progress depended upon controlling their own destiny was central (McCartney 1992, Ch. 7). Although the revolutionary component has virtually vanished, this control impulse remains vital. The phrase "black empowerment" has replaced "Black Power" and is regularly—almost ritualistically—invoked in rallies and demonstrations.

Differences in nuance aside, a consensus on the term's meaning prevails. According to Lawrence J. Hanks:

The black empowerment process, then, has, in theory, three measurable phases: (1) blacks holding office in proportion to their numbers in the population; (2) the enactment of public policies favorable to the black community; and (3) the rise in the socioeconomic status of the black community. (1987, xi)

Green and Wilson concur:

We envisage black empowerment not as an attempt by black to monopolize or exploit power but rather as a process through which they will come to share power alongside other groups and partake as equal partners in decision making. A prerequisite to empowerment therefore must be the development of strategies to force state power to become more accountable and responsive to black. A demonstrated willingness by the state to accommodate itself to blacks' quest for increased access to power and justice would inevitably lead to improved quality of life for all citizens of the state. (1989, xii)

And according to Keiser (1993):

Empowerment is a process by which a minority group or representatives of that minority group gain a greater ability to influence political outcomes in favor of the minority group. [Empowerment] can be measured by analyzing the minority group's success in capturing important offices, instituting policies that are high on the group's agenda and meet resistance from established groups, [and] securing miscellaneous benefits that other groups also desire. (p. 85)

The resources necessary for implementation are hardly esoteric. Hanks (1987, 111), for example, lists economic development, providing services, political mobilization, political education, resolving conflict and managing fear. Other analyses offer creating alliances, securing a favorable electoral system, enlisting the help of black churches, formulating programs with mass appeal, skilled use of litigation and similar pressure-oriented strategies. Resources are usually built around gaining elected office. A typical scenario has blacks uniting to elect a black mayor, who, in turn, rewards supporters with jobs or civic improvements such as neighborhood day care centers. In a nutshell, empowerment means mustering group pressure—votes especially, demonstrations and boycotts, if necessary—to secure benefits.

This understanding diverges from other self-determination conceptions. Most plain is its unequivocal political character, especially the stress on voting. In 1957 Martin Luther King spoke, "Give us the ballot and we will help bring this nation to a new society based on justice and dedicated to peace" (quoted in Hamilton 1982). This electoral infatuation remains impregnable. Self-determination and its rewards require mastery of government, securing formal positions to decide public policy. Indeed, analyses of black empowerment often explicitly defined blacks to be more highly empowered if they can elect black officials (Bobo and Gilliam 1990; Parker 1990, Ch. 1).[1] Capturing the political arena is the supreme victory.

Implicitly rejected are more private pathways to comparable aims, alternatives such as economic self-help organizations, philanthropy, individual spiritual fulfillment or, like various religious sects, withdrawal from the mainstream. Booker T. Washington's prescription of diligently yet quietly moving up the economic ladder apart from aggressive politics is thoroughly rejected. African-American empowerment does not exclude the worthiness of personal attainment, but this occurs exclusively in a collective racial context. For example, enhanced education both is a prerequisite to further empowerment (a resource) and is advanced via empowerment (a benefit). Even religion—churches and faith—are integral to politics: Ministers contribute organizational leadership, whereas creed provides courage against resistance. To talk about religion in championing empowerment subordinates salvation to worldly accomplishment.

A sharply polarized vision of societal conflict abounds. On one side, blacks are long excluded from power and, as a consequence, suffer hardships as diverse as impaired health and inferior schooling. Helplessness in the face of enormous obstacles is axiomatic (see, e.g., Solomon 1976, Ch. 1). In opposition, whites traditionally monopolize power and, predictably, will not concede anything unless forced. When challenged, dominant whites tenaciously resist and defend their privilege with everything from police brutality to more subtle devices such as biased electoral rules (see, e.g., Hanks 1987, Ch. 2). All other divisive cleavages—social class, region, age—are subordinate. To deny race's enduring centrality or to preach color-blindness subverts the quest for empowerment. Thus understood, political conflict resembles two armies—one black, one white—battling for hegemony with the outcome decided by marshaling troops and resources. A truce will come only after blacks have gained parity with whites, especially economic equality.

Less obvious is the unexpressed belief that *only* government—principally Washington—can supply sought ends. Proposals thus routinely insist upon multiple government bureaucratic programs to assist people comprehensively (see, e.g., Gibbs and Furey 1994). Government "holds" what is desirable: jobs, health care, safety, educational proficiency, decent housing or social standing. Economic gains are especially central. In fact, it sometimes appears that *only* via the securing of political influence can blacks advance economically (see, e.g., Jennings 1992, esp. Ch. 1). Constraining political force as a matter of prudent principle or acknowledging bureaucratic incompetence is silently off the agenda.[2] Apparently, there is no dread of power being abused or breeding corruption—constraining government can only impede black empowerment. At core, this is statism.

Officialdom's proficient remedial capacity is dogma; claims of insufficiency are mere excuses. The 1960s expression "If the government can send a man to the moon, they surely can fix the ghetto's problems" captures this optimism perfectly. Empowerment means coercing reluctant officials into bestowing benefits under their decree or capturing command centers outright. If educational mastery is sought, the "correct" strategy is to mobilize and seize control. Choices regarding building new schools, altering the curriculum or installing classroom computers are mere tactics and largely secondary (see, e.g., Hatton 1977). That government—regardless of who rules—can notably improve education, not merely provide resources, is presupposed, an uncontestable article of faith. Even when government fails, for example, school busing does not raise test scores, trust in government's potency remains unchallenged.[3] Tactics, not the core strategy itself, might be refined. The spotlight might now focus on tougher enforcement of laws or greater spending, not the empowerment strategy.

That political action is the wellspring of progress is, of course, arguable. Especially troublesome is the presupposition that government can satisfy demands. In principle, *anything* can be sought from public officials. Wish lists can range from curing medical afflictions to ending pollution. As in Santa Claus letters, only imagination constrains. Yet as the modest record in solving perplexities proclaims, officialdom is not omnipotent (see, e.g., Murray 1984). No amount of protesting, voter mobilization or threatening rhetoric may correct intractable problems, or at least in conformity with democracy and financial prudence. To redouble empowerment efforts may be futile for motivating indifferent pupils, putting the unqualified to work or disbanding violent street gangs.

The image of two monolithic racial groups locked in conflict is similarly overdrawn. Innumerable whites clearly sympathize with blacks, including many pubic officials. Momentous civil rights laws were enacted by nearly all-white legislatures and enforced by white judges and bureaucrats. By the same token, to insist that all blacks follow some racial party line is unrealistic. Nor might elected black officials—typically an empowerment indicator—be sympathetic to commonly perceived black interests. This polarized perspective may, ironically, lead to ineffectiveness, not enhanced control. Expelling whites from black organizations on behalf of "black unity" may diminish organization efficiency. Insisting upon racial cohesion solely "because this is the path to empowerment" invites needless discord. African Americans, as with all people, are subject to cross-cutting cleavages: What is desirable for middle-class blacks may be harmful to the poor, black women may disagree with black men and black teenagers may resist generous Social Security payments to their grandparents.

This polarized portrayal also ignores how a permanent numerical minority achieves decisive power in a democracy governed by majority rule. We are not Syria or Iraq where small ethnic or religious cliques can brutally dominate. African Americans may empower themselves in a city, for example, Detroit or Atlanta, but the city will always be subordinate to the "uncapturable" state and national government. Even when "capturing" a city, our characteristic fragmentation of power—regardless of one's race—forever imposes constraints. A black mayor combining with an all-black city council and all-black bureaucracy will surely discover objectives outside their grasp. Critical policy domains are controlled by distant "white legislatures." And future elections may suddenly reverse this gain, as happened in Chicago, New York, Philadelphia and elsewhere. Whites, and white-controlled businesses, may simply flee, leaving blacks bereft necessary tax revenue. Coalitions with other groups are possible, as in the "Rainbow Coalition," but this inevitably requires compromises. Dreams of empowerment may thus be unrealistic, an irreclaimable ideal detracting from the more obtainable. Invoking the language of cooperation, coalitions and influence, rather than promising Utopian power, may be wiser.

This politically based empowerment model is hardly pointless. The civil rights movement record, especially its legislative accomplishments, is substantial. The topic is not one of success versus failure; the question is whether this grand strategy can deliver the ambitious results desired, even if African Americans dominate politically. Manipulating government levers may, for example, racially integrate schools or eliminate offensive textbook material, but this attainment cannot be extended ever onward to more arduous tasks. A successful voter registration drive may ensure that municipal facilities are more equitably distributed, but building convenient clinics does not guarantee residents will live healthy lives, which, after all, is the ultimate objective. Political coercion may be an essential ingredient for group advancement, but it may be inadequate by itself.

This mobilization and benefits linkage is an empirical one, not an article of faith. This fusing of group progress with a unified assault on the bastions of civic power is, after all, a theory, not a law of physics. Its incessant reaffirmation may yield momentary psychological benefits, but the results exist independently of heartfelt belief. At a minimum, the connection between securing authority and its rewards are exceeding complex. Surely black political control of cities such as Gary, Indiana and East St. Louis, Illinois, have brought minuscule transformation. The question remains open.

Finally, a colossal irony infuses this empowerment formula. Reduced to its essentials, blacks are merely asking white-dominated government to remedy their misfortune. This is even true for using black votes to gain political office. To wit, if past electoral efforts fail to deliver the rewards, the courts, Congress and Department of Justice—all white dominated—are pressured to alter the system to encourage more black registered voters or better translate black votes into black victories. Eventually, blacks will attain power but not until whites have redrawn the districts or abolished an allegedly biased electoral system. To be sure, whites may be culpable in this calamity, and the request may be highly vigorous, but the pressuring is essentially a beseeching for relief. And when structures are captured, it is up to whites to supply the necessary tax funds required for black betterment. Empowerment advocacy disguises a fundamental black dependency.

The never-expressed postulate is that *only whites in positions of power can supply what blacks want.* Power here more closely resembles a temporary gift, for it may eventually be withdrawn. For a group of agitated African Americans to demand that white school officials give black youngsters a better education tacitly acknowledges black weakness. That is, they cannot raise the needed money, design a curriculum or guarantee superior performance. If this could be performed autonomously—true empowerment—why pressure whites? And if blacks were "given" a separate black-controlled school by whites, this largess may end if imposed conditions are not satisfied. Black power, then, endures at the pleasure of whites. The example of Congress giving substantial self-government to Washington, DC, and then abrogating this grant when black leaders financially mismanaged the city illustrates this possibility.

Black empowerment need not require this dependency. Alternative forms of "black empowerment" are quite feasible. The quest for self-determination does not irreversibly lead to demands for government intervention. History and contemporary politics offer a multitude of alternatives. Some self-sufficiency remains possible even within a complex interdependent modern society. Rather than attempt to coerce white officials into supplying better housing, residents themselves might upgrade their accommodations. If white city officials deny adequate police protection, security is available privately. Indeed, nearly every objective of the empowerment rhetoric is obtainable outside of government intervention. Religious groups as unlike as Catholics and Orthodox Jews have eschewed state help in promoting church-affiliated schools. Asians often make business loans to each other instead of pressuring government to coerce banks. The Amish and Mormons have private welfare systems. Among blacks themselves, Louis Farrakhan's Nation of Islam exemplifies this tradition of empowerment via self-reliance apart from government beneficence.

COMMUNITY PSYCHOLOGY EMPOWERMENT

Compared to other empowerment plans, the community psychology movement is less prominent. That it is largely an academic, nonconfrontational enterprise unaligned with any particular ethnic or racial grievance group no doubt explains this obscurity. Nevertheless, it would be mistaken to confuse peacefulness with political insignificance. Its impact lies primarily in influencing thousands of university-trained professionals entering the "helping professions"—social work, psychology, urban planning, education or public health. These professionals leave school carrying a creed about a virtuous society and their own alleviative role that may well affect millions.

Like other empowerment inclinations, it emerged in the turbulent 1960s (Rappaport 1977, Ch. 1). Psychologists intervening to assist the troubled long predates the 1960s, of course. The 1960s, however, profoundly altered how this historic aim was to be accomplished. Responding to tumultuous events, a portion of the psychology profession adopted a wholly novel mission statement. Older, traditional notions of assistance assumed (1) potential clients would individually (usually voluntarily) seek professional help, (2) clients would be aided via therapies to modify their thinking or behavior and (3) this therapeutic intervention would guide clients toward dominant cultural values. Thus, for example, a guilt-driven homosexual seeks out a psychiatrist who delves into a disturbed childhood to instill heterosexuality. The overriding goal was aligning the unconventional into reputed normalcy.

For the forerunners of community psychology, this traditional understanding with its stress on paternalistic assistance was severely challenged beginning in the mid-1960s. The emergence of the militant black civil rights movement was particularly central. Now African Americans were no longer content to remain passively subservient, to "fit in" with the lowly station socially assigned to them. This campaign for equality abruptly pushed to the surface certain structural features of American society—notably endemic discrimination, institutional racism and deeply ingrained legal bias—making the conventional path of painstaking self-help dubious. After all, how could blacks become educated if racist schools refused admittance or provided inferior facilities? Nor could prodigious personal effort acquire better housing if exclusionary residential policies were enforced. Conventional person-to-person counseling of frustrated blacks (or whites, for that matter) could hardly suffice.

Paralleling this political awareness was a keener and more encompassing appreciation that misfortune need not be personally caused (Rappaport 1977, Ch. 5). One book, William Ryan's *Blaming the Victim* (1971), encapsulated this view succinctly and achieved enormous popularity. Innumerable social scientists now believed that "the system," not individual "flaws," necessitated transformation. Fixing a few personal predicaments was futile if society itself was deeply defective. Structural constraints on black Americans were only the beginning. When children could not read after endless schooling, the educational system, not the students, was responsible. If mothers failed to feed their children, blame the lack of decent jobs, not indifferent mothers. Moreover, and equally important, recognition grew that "bad" behavior was society's interpretation, not the behavior's intrinsic nature. Deviancy was, accordingly, merely a label imposed by a society intent on marginalization. A child born to an unwed mother was thus no less worthy even if castigated as "illegitimate." In sum, individual ameliorative therapy must give way to transforming the context of a person's life.

Along with this reconceptualization of human misery came multiple tangible changes. The elimination of distress once thought to be intractable—poverty, illiteracy, hunger, unemployment, faulty health care, and dilapidated housing—now became top federal government priorities. States and localities also joined this ameliorative quest. Suddenly, millions were poured into numberless undertakings nearly everywhere. Especially consequential, programs often legally required local citizen participation. If new housing was to be constructed or day care centers built, bureaucrats would be obliged to assemble citizen consultation groups. The right of "community participation" quickly entered collective consciousness. In turn, multiplying federal programs coupled with expanding higher education greatly swelled the "helping professions." These advisers entered the workforce to be the lieutenants leading once-troubled citizens to better, happier lives.

By the late 1970s this exalted federal government–led transformation of society—the "Great Society"—was in retreat. Many programs had vanished or were reduced sharply; enthusiasm for direct citizen involvement cooled noticeably. Varied social scientists were also rethinking the worthiness of removing all blame from the disadvantaged. A few scholars, for example, Charles Murray (1984) brand the entire 1960s reconstruction experience a colossal failure. Nevertheless, underlying intellectual premises of this transformation effort continued to mature among academics under the self-designated label of community psychology. As animals evolved over eons to adapt to sparser conditions, ambitions were downsized. The giant 1960s million-dollar "top-down" programs were to be supplanted by modest, manageable, "bottom-up" interventions (Swift 1984). The battle cry no longer was for massive infusions of funds to abolish all poverty or to rebuild the cities. And, notably, the "one size fits all" vision of pushing everyone into middle-class respectability was junked. Community psychology is not about restoring the Great Society.

Community psychology interprets empowerment not simply as group control; it commences with an expansive philosophical concept of a "good society." Unlike black empowerment, no firm policy agenda dictates. In principle, society is not war of all against all; everyone, even the economically privileged, can benefit from expanding control. Three broad propositions define this conception (Rappaport 1977, Ch. 1). First, everybody enjoys the right to be different without risking material or psychological sanctions. The claim to autonomy is fundamental. The traditional idea of a unique, superior social standard—generally white middle-class values—to which everyone adjusts is explicitly rejected. Helping professionals therefore possess no obligation "to cure" those repudiating the dominant culture. Replacing unforgiving conventionality is cultural relativity: the inherent equality of distinctive cultural values. Regarding families, for example, comparable alternatives replace a singular definition—one can have gay parent families, extended families of disparate relatives or single-parent families. All are "families," though of different sorts.

Second, resources cannot be allocated solely according to the dominant criterion of competence. Simply tolerating differences is insufficient; nonconformists must not be deprived of health care, education, housing, welfare and similar benefits essential to a proper life. This is a matter of right (Knitzer 1980). To continue with alternative definitions of family, neither single parents nor their offspring should be stigmatized or denied benefits merely on the basis of this condition. Eventually, moreover, abolishing the single gauge of competence will deliver greater resource equality. The privileged will no longer enjoy a near monopoly of wealth while the disabled, the elderly and members of minority groups remain destitute. A parallel leveling out will also occur in social prominence—the homeless, the mentally ill, those embracing "alternative lifestyles," immigrants, those with distinct sexual orientations, the misfigured and others judged unconventional and outside "the mainstream" will all be equally affirmed. This transformation will not only assist the once marginalized but construct a better, more diverse society generally.

Third, it is the professionally trained helping agent's responsibility, utilizing psychology, to bring equanimity through nonviolent methods (Rappaport 1977, Ch. 2). This assistance must be collaborative, not imposed. In a word, the enterprise is ecological—fashioning harmony among the diverging components of society. And since the goal is the alteration of existing structures and norms to achieve great equality, not individual therapy, this intervention requires shifting power. There is no pretext of "professional neutrality," though the conventional labels of "liberal" and "conservative" are rejected as irrelevant. The community psychologist is not akin to the boxing referee enforcing rules evenhandedly. An in-the-ring coach obligated to keep the decision a draw by aiding the underdog is more accurate. The client need not seek assistance; rather, the community psychologist might initiate the intervention. The "repair-the-defect" model is replaced by creating equality and harmony amidst differences.

How is this empowerment concretely actualized? Again, this perspective diverges fundamentally from other conceptions, notably black and feminist self-determination with their sweeping emphasis on capturing centralized political power. The path is more modest, more locally oriented, and entails both internal psychological change and winning control of community institutions of consequence. Examples offered (Rappaport 1977, Ch. 5) included neighborhood schools, local policing, health care and comparable decision-making entities amenable to local direction. In education, parents would impose accountability to achieve desired outcomes by insisting schools compete for students. Those educational institutions that satisfied parents and students with their curriculums, administrative styles, nonacademic activities and whatever else they could devise would flourish. Parents, not some distant bureaucracy, hold the decisive power. Local community members not only gain the tangible benefit of improved education, but their internal sense of mastery—psychological empowerment—is similarly enhanced. Each component—educational gain and sense of control—is integral. After all, the identical educational results can be achieved "top down," but accomplishing this objective on one's own both deeply satisfies and inspires further mastery.

The intervention cannot resemble police daily responding to 911 calls. The more enduring objective is building on community strengths to eliminate the disorder's deeper sources (Rappaport 1977, Ch. 5). Without addressing persisting conditions apart from momentary individual troubles, the remediation process is both never-ending and, ultimately, futile. A conspicuous example is the pervasive racism faced by African Americans. Chronic joblessness, juvenile delinquency and drug addiction are but symptoms. Intervention must anticipate and then attack the malady of racism rather than launch a piecemeal, one-person-at-a-time counseling program.

To continue our education illustration, consider the problem of academically underperforming black students. A traditional approach may recommend individual tutoring to overcome deficiencies and dispatch experts to schools. The community psychology effort, however, concentrates on the milieu that lies at the heart of the quandary and seeks enduring, systematic solutions. Instead, remediation efforts might reform schools citywide. At the behest of parents and local leaders, now fully appreciating the problem's magnitude, the curriculum might be reshaped to instill greater awareness of black historical attainment, a sense of black cultural pride and skills to resist negative stereotypes. At parental urging, schools might also hire successful blacks to demonstrate education's dividends. Local businesses may join this communal effort by rewarding academic achievement with part-time after-school jobs. All of these possibilities, it should be noted, are not top-down imposed but develop within the community itself. No doubt, innumerable solutions exist, and trial and error are necessary. Collective democratic problem solving replaces bureaucratic paternalism. The upshot, hopefully, will be an invigorated community in which school problems are addressed broadly.

This, then, is the essence of community psychology's empowerment stratagem. While it frankly acknowledges itself as a social movement, capturing government is not its aim (Rappaport 1985). It lacks the rhetoric of grand transformation, it eschews ideological labels and seeks harmony. Improvement arrives one small project at a time, as invited scientifically trained experts assist people to gain increased mastery over their lives.

As one reflects on this empowerment, a humane, and quite traditional, impulse of aiding "the little guy" against "the big guy" emanates. The early twentieth-century Progressives battling the exploitation of the poor by craven capitalism might be judged spiritual ancestors. Today's community psychologist merely champions the contemporary downtrodden—welfare recipients, abused minimum wage workers, the homeless and untold other have-nots. In a sense, empowering the defenseless is not all that different from traditional charity efforts. What is distinctive is the focus on teaching autonomy and self-determination, not paternalistically dispensing Christmas turkeys.

This flattering comparison misleads. What sharply separates the community psychology movement from past reform efforts is inattention to moral guidelines. The present incarnation cannot answer the question "Empowerment for what?" This emptiness (or perhaps outright avoidance) is particularly displayed in an essay entitled "Criteria for Excellence" (Shadish 1990) that seemingly takes on this question. But, alas, the title is deceptive. Rather than dwell on empowerment's aims, certainly a worthy issue, the argument is redirected to excellence of research in community intervention. Only technique, not substance, matters. We are thus told that "good" analyses are explicit in their theorizing, monitor the consequences of intervention, elucidate embedded values and clarify how knowledge is constructed. Nothing is said about ultimate substantive objectives. The closest end value alluded to is some vague "social change."

This indifference flows directly from cultural relativism—the receiving of all values as equally worthy. Guidance can only apply to the "how," not the "what." Allegedly, within the limits of tranquil democracy, all ends are indistinguishable. When experts talk of "improved lives," they are silent regarding "improvement" (see, e.g., Zimmerman 1995). A pauper becoming more adept at begging might be "improvement." To insist otherwise, to interject substantive content into goals, constitutes judgmentalism and thus violates the movement's core mission.

Past betterment campaigns always asserted an unmistakable moral purpose. Intervention was not a vague enhancement scheme; it was intended to encourage an explicit end, ordinarily in harmony with what today are labeled "bourgeois values." Here, too, the purpose was empowerment, though of a special sort. Nineteenth-century religious reformers, for example, typically exalted religious devotion, abstinence from alcohol, sexual restraint, family obligations and steady employment. Through such discipline, it was believed, prosperity and happiness would surely follow, even to the poorest of the poor. Empowerment proceeded from self-control, piety and conformity, and this was the only true path. The helping agent kept his or her charge on the straight and narrow, not changed society or celebrated uniqueness.

We cannot rehash the debate over applying bourgeois values to today's misfortunes. The issue concerns the consequences of promoting prescriptions sans boundaries. After all, almost any self-indulgent scheme can be advanced as "helping" the less fortunate. Likewise, the survival of almost anything enhances diversity. Outside of violating criminal law, what lies beyond facilitation? Might some situation occur in which the community psychologist confides, "That's a truly stupid idea, and you will be regretful if you proceed, so I will not assist"? Is there any obligation to restrain fools? Or do heartfelt admonitions breach the sacred principle of cultural relativity? If disaster ensues, are those offering guidance absolved since "they were merely following orders"?

Expert empowerment advice lacking controlling standards invites calamity. There can be no guarantee that enhanced power will be employed wisely. The sorry record of popular foibles, especially among the less sophisticated, is undeniable. Recall Chapter 2's warning about antidemocratic movements springing from popular empowerment. Again contemplate educational problems within the African-American community. Suppose that black parents and youngsters insist that the "cure" for their ills is schools automatically passing everyone regardless of performance. They believe, erroneously, that schoolwork is useless and prefer bogus rewards. Money allocated to remedial programs, moreover, should be given directly to the students themselves. The community goal, then, becomes abolishing tests and spending guidelines imposed by hostile downtown bureaucrats. Are the techniques of empowerment to be employed for that purpose? If successful, this gutting of educational content will surely bring economic disaster and further dependency regardless of all the bestowed psychological dividends.

More generally, successful empowerment may well promote the servility it seeks to alleviate. The analogy with a parent who repeatedly rescues an errant child from misfortune is appropriate. Eventually the youngster learns that poor decision making is harmless, and thus no impetus exists for permanent reform. Interventions are not cures but momentary "fixes" until the next misadventure. Inattention to health, sloth, laziness in school and similar personal deficiencies will all be "taken care of" by eventually acquiring power. That is, announce that "none of this is my fault" and then invite the clever expert and together coerce government to provide free medical care or automatic diplomas.[4] And feel good about one's mighty accomplishment, to boot. As for black empowerment, utilizing "empowerment" to gain government benefits may obscure deeper dependency. One is hardly independent if autonomy depends on a psychologist conveniently available for rescue operations.[5]

These difficulties emerge when examining an actual empowerment illustration certified as successful (O'Sullivan, Waugh and Espeland 1984). This involved the Yavapai Indians living at Fort McDowell, Arizona. For decades, the federal government proposed to build a dam at the intersection of the Verde and Salt rivers whose purpose was flood control, effective water management and the creation of recreational facilities. This plan enjoyed widespread support, especially from business and agriculture in the Phoenix area. From an engineering perspective, it was also a highly cost-effective solution to numerous problems. Unfortunately for the Yavapai Indians, this dam would require their relocation and surrender of land prized for its religious and historical significance. The government had offered generous financial compensation for the territory plus promises of employment in a marina to be constructed. Nevertheless, despite all material allures and pleas, the Yavapai refused to budge.

Ultimately, after years of conflict, the federal government substituted an alternative plan, and the Yavapai kept their land. Their arsenal of empowerment techniques, mostly guided by outside allies, included litigation, skilled use of national environmental regulations (the land was a bald eagle habitat), well-publicized demonstrations, creating alliances with church groups and emotional appeals to save Indian culture. Matters were also greatly helped by a study that predicted a plethora of ensuing social pathologies—family disruption (violence and divorce), higher mortality rates, growing alcoholism and drug use, decline in satisfaction with life, increased unemployment, a weakening of communal involvement and undermining of tribal authority—if relocation occurred: in short, a classic case of the once-helpless, thanks to astute intervention, resisting domination from rapacious, powerful outsiders.

The successful empowerment was, predictably, celebrated by the assisting participant-observers. A model was portrayed of what people can do only if ingeniously empowered. Yet another side of the story remains untold, and the lessons are less inspiring. First, this is not a tale of clashing abstract "good" versus "evil." During this protracted debate over dam construction, Phoenix experienced three major floods. None would have occurred had the dam been constructed. Water management was also necessary to promote area-wide economic growth, a benefit for untold poor people. This was not a cost-free rescue. A purely utilitarian analysis might dictate empowering the other side. The generous financial settlement given to the Indians might also have enhanced lives and strengthened Indian culture, not debilitated it.

Second, the application of "empowerment" may be a misnomer. The government, exercising the power of eminent domain, could have acquired the Indian land at any time (and still can). The Yavapai Indians simply made themselves a bothersome nuisance to authorities. Nor could this annoyance value have been brought about without multiple non-Indian allies and a legal system facilitating time-consuming litigation. Rather than evict the Indians and risk adverse publicity, Washington officials took the easier path and implemented a costly alternative. Millions of distant taxpayers involuntarily absorbed this munificence. The Yavapai remain as vulnerable as ever, regardless of their newfound sense of self-determination. A few minor legal or political changes occurring elsewhere would radically undermine past advantages. In leaner times government might not be so generous. Benevolence in the face of modest discomfort should not be confused with an alteration of authority.

Finally, does this community psychology case study illustrate the actualization of a "better society"? It does not. That judgment would require a standard, and none is supplied. Amorphous notions of "diversity" and "equality" are useless in their specific applications. Nobody suggested exterminating the Yavapai, and their well-compensated relocation did not irrevocably foretell cultural extinction, so diversity was not necessarily to be diminished. If enhanced economic equality were the goal, Washington's ample settlement should have been accepted, for it would have instantly ended Indian poverty.

Only possible winners and losers can be totaled up. Clearly victorious are most but not all Yavapai (a minority preferred the cash buyout) and local environmentalists. Winners also include those receiving psychic gratification from preventing possible personal disaster for the relocated Indians. On the ledger's other side are a more numerous assembly of varied business interests (including ordinary citizens) and Phoenix residents confronting increased flooding risk. There are also some Yavapai who have involuntarily foregone considerable wealth. One group—most Indians and their allies—have increased their sense of self-determination, whereas a much larger number now feel less powerful.

The only unambiguous lesson is: Things are now different, thanks to empowerment. Such indistinctness is hardly atypical in such endeavors. This determination only barely pertains to material costs-benefits of this unique example. Of fundamentally greater bearing is the inherent and willful absence of judgmental standards. This is an intractable dilemma. A cultural relativism with minimal exceptions, for example, nonviolence, as axiomatic, automatically foregoes verdicts that partake of designations like "good," "improved," "enhanced" or whatever else suggests underlying evaluative criteria. Empowerment as is understood in community psychology, outside of some transfer of power, can only make life different, not better. From this perspective, no distinction applies between helping people achieve illiteracy versus literacy. To invoke prosperity or happiness is to return to the pernicious "one size fits all" standard. Empowerment intervention merely enables people to choose their self-defined destiny. Every underdog is as worthy of assistance as any other underdog. If one were to impose more conventional evaluative standards, for example, utilitarianism, a strong case can certainly be made that society is collectively worse off after empowering the Yavapai Indians.

The upshot of abandoning evaluative criteria is authorizing nearly any project imaginable. This freedom to roam about seeking intervention opportunities is openly recognized (see, e.g., Knitzer 1980). Only the most minimal guidelines now apply: Intervention must be consistent with peaceful democracy and empower those of lesser power. Given that nearly every sentiment, sect or assemblage is, in some sense, powerless in confronting today's harsh reality, the menu of invitations is expansive. The dogma of community psychology grants a license to meddle endlessly. Everywhere, no doubt, are circumstances that can be rectified via redistributing power. Surely there are things desired, from personal luxuries to government group entitlements to naked domination. And who is to pronounce that these appetites should not be facilitated? Each expert freely indulges his or her own values. This facilitation is especially appropriate on behalf of those coveting the unconventional. Regardless of one's sexuality, morality or novel lifestyle, the claims on empowerment cannot be contravened. To contend otherwise, to argue that society must possess a consensus on core values, is to commit the sin of holding everyone to the identical standard.

When pushed to its logical conclusions, community empowerment subverts civil society. It consciously rescues the ostracized from assimilation or suppression. Society rests on standards of conduct, a code of do's and don'ts, and community psychologists labor to block the enforcement of these moral strictures. If homeless alcoholics occupy the local park to create "a community" and officials wish to disband it, experts might empower these homeless to resist and demand government aid to sustain their "valid lifestyle." If, by chance, empowerment counselors are repulsed by the filth and disorder, they, too, are guilty of nefarious judgmentalism. This destruction civility in the name of empowerment is hardly hypothetical. Much of what in the 1960s appeared as liberating people from the oppressive norms of conventionality now is understood as dangerous folly. Surely we have paid a terrible price when we empowered youngsters to resist custom regarding illegitimacy, sexual restraint, drug use, respect for parental authority and similar "old-fashioned" virtues. Perhaps most disturbing, this unfortunate turn of events is intrinsic to a vision of social change that eschews any standards of morality.

FEMINIST EMPOWERMENT

Like black demands for self-determination, feminist empowerment enjoys the public limelight. Thousands of disparate women's groups seek its rewards, whether electing U.S. senators or improving day care facilities. Perhaps owing to this popularity, disentangling "feminist empowerment" is perplexing. The phrase often disguises several interrelated causes—empowerment for black women, women of color (itself often ill-defined), working-class women and Third World women, plus women more universally (see, e.g., Black 1989, Ch. 1). It occasionally takes on sexual connotations as autonomy is melded with lesbianism or promiscuity. Moreover, "feminism" is hardly coterminous with women generally securing power. Indeed, politically active women can reject the "feminist" label, whereas self-proclaimed feminists diverge on doctrine. Almost constant ideological turmoil similarly poses obstacles—notions embraced in the 1960s ("women's liberation") have mutated relentlessly and will, undoubtedly, continue to mature. Finally, advocates typically define themselves primarily as scholar-activists, not philosophers. Key terms, for example, *justice*, that infuse rhetoric receive minimal delineation. Nevertheless, uncertainties aside, several major themes of feminist empowerment are clear.

Feminist empowerment immediately diverges from other interpretations of "power." Recall that power's accepted connotations implied coercive capacity—person A can force person B regardless of B's inclination. This coercive element figured prominently in black empowerment and was implied in community psychology. At core, it is a zero-sum, disputatious construction of conflict: The resisting enemy must be conquered. Among feminist writers, however, "power over" is replaced by "power to." As Sarah Hoagland (1986) put it: "Power over is a matter of dominance, forcing others, bending them to our will. . . . It is the power of control. . . . Power-from-within, on the other hand, is a matter of centering and remaining steady in our environment as how we direct our energy" (p. 7).

This conceptualization deeply shapes women's empowerment. The objective thus becomes self-mastery, enhanced competence and autonomy, not defeating one's opponents. One might, for example, become empowered via literary expression celebrating women's history if this inspires confidence. Culture, more than day-to-day jockeying for advantage, looms large. Again, the contrast with black empowerment is sharp—women are not to turn the tables on men as African Americans long to reverse their subordinate relationships with whites. It is a matter of creating an encompassing existence rooted in feminist values, for example, cooperation, tenderness and sharing. For women to insist upon ascendancy, even if such dominion profited women, contradicts feminist empowerment, for it tacitly accepts the masculine hierarchical political model (Deutchman 1991). Authentic feminist action must reflect sharing of power, an openness to participation and a rejection of formalism (Lips 1981).

Equally central is an all-encompassing definition of "the political." Traditionally, and this applies generally within empowerment conceptions, a gulf divides personal and civic life. Although occasionally fuzzy and disputed, the principle is undeniable. Our notion of limited government recognizes areas beyond political authority. Empowerment may entail personal transformations, for example, acquiring skills, but the objects of power reside in the public realm—policies, recognition, offices and so on. Feminist empowerment rejects this dichotomy. As Sprague (1988) confidently asserts, " 'The Personal is Political' has been the banner of the contemporary women's movement" (p. 159). Indeed, according to one writer, to insist on this public versus private distinction is to depoliticize politics (Ackelsberg 1988). Empowerment is thus about *everything* in society.

The implications here are deceptively profound. Government action as it affects women, itself a robust list of possibilities, merely constitutes the beginning. Also included are policies seemingly irrelevant to women as women, for example, local zoning rules, for these shape creating nontraditional families (Sprague 1988). That is, a family comprising two lesbians and their children would not be permitted if zoning laws used standard heterosexual language to define "family." Employment and social relationships, even friendship, likewise fully fall under empowerment's jurisdiction. Finally, matters traditionally considered largely private—courtship, sexual conduct, marriage, procreation, child rearing, housework and divorce—are also appended to the agenda. Even sexually related stereotypes—women as emotional and men as stoic, for example—are political, for they impact on power (Ackelsberg 1988). An empowered women must therefore recognize being subordinated by government, her employer, social clubs, acquaintances and family.

This change goes well beyond reforming legal rules and regulations; in the language of feminism, the solution lies in overthrowing patriarchy. Dominating "maleness" (hegemonic masculinity) itself is the culprit. Consider, for example, the physical abuse of women by men. The traditional recourse involves passing laws, stiffer penalties for violators or education. Even if such state action diminished abuse, this is not the path recommended by feminist empowerment. More vital is altering the basic societal milieu breeding violence. Transformations might, for instance, address mothers-children relationships, marriage expectations, women's own role construction and how law enforcement officials discern antiwomen violence. Even religious doctrines must be altered, given that they reinforce male domination by portraying deities as males. Empowerment means permanent emancipation from a society steeped in violence, not harsher punishment of offenders. Legal protection is but a small step.

As with black empowerment, the equality struggle is polarized along a unitary dimension: male and female. In today's exploiting world, women are a community of oppressed, and men are—regardless of standing—a community of oppressors. It is axiomatic that one's gender irrevocably defines a far-ranging and universally agreed-upon political agenda. Although crosscutting divisions are admitted, especially class and ethnic frictions, these are judged temporary distractions. The goal is a united movement transcending economic or social position. Women who might demur are considered misguided, suffering "false consciousness," perhaps seduced by trifling concessions. The possibility that at least some men are allies or that most men are not antiwomen seldom surfaces. That men have supplied monumental victories for women's groups, for example, the right to abortion, is celebrated as a triumph for women, not a testament to the power of alliances with men.

Again paralleling black empowerment's claim of imposed subservience, women's dependency is asserted to be purposeful, not benignly accidental, freely preferred or biologically "natural." Proof of this discrimination is witnessed in income gaps or the humble status assigned female-dominated occupations. Men, consciously or unconsciously, *want* to subordinate women, and this is ceaselessly accomplished at every opportunity (Brehm 1988; Stacey and Price 1981, Ch. 8).[6] Women are *assigned* to undesirable tasks such as child rearing and lowly clerical positions. Political apathy is not a sign of contentment but a result of consciously being denied power (Almeleh et al. 1993).

Convention is but a mechanism for ensuring impotence. Such subordination is, moreover, deceitfully presented as inevitable and beneficial to both sexes. Young boys, for example, are taught domination through physically aggressive sports, whereas young girls are pushed into passive recreation. Books, meanwhile, portray men as dynamic leaders and women as dutiful helpers in nursing or motherhood. The economy itself arbitrarily rests on values awarding men the advantage while penalizing women (for instance, prizing ruthlessness while demeaning compassion). Even emotions associated with women—as empathy for the underdog—are less esteemed than "manly" sentiments. Indeed, so powerful is the patriarchal indoctrination that most women succumb to it, internalize this inferiority as equality or accept it without a struggle.

Given the multifront character of this oppression, its intrusion into the very essence of our culture, pursuing empowerment is boundless.[7] Electing a female mayor or registering more women to vote is inadequate, although these are worthy efforts; society itself must be refurbished top to bottom. The endeavor begins with women's self-examination, reflection and study to surmount blinders imposed by a society ruled by hegemonic masculinity.

Faver (1994) is typical when she announces that "personal change and social transformation are inextricably linked" (p. 124). Women must rediscover their true nature and through feminist literature share their common experiences (Bystydzienski 1992). Democratic, decentralized, inclusive grassroots activism everywhere pervades feminist values and is the path toward betterment. To embrace traditional interest group politics over less formal networking invites corrupting cooptation (Ackelsberg 1988).

Politically, women must unite to protest subjugation at home and in the workplace, gain control over neighborhood organizations, nurture a sense of community and overthrow a worldview based on force, hierarchy, inequality, competition, aggression and similar masculine ideal. Laws that promote gender inequality, for example, equal pay for equal work and edicts against sexual harassment, must also be pursued. Vulnerable women—single mothers, divorced women, those at risk from domestic abuse—require protection and support. The educational system must not make young girls feel less worthy or incapable. Some would add the antipornography campaigns to this agenda insofar as pornography helps to sustain female inferiority by degrading women sexually.

In this collision of perspectives, men are not to be vanquished as one army might destroy another; rather, it is their destructive, oppressive, often menacing value system that must be overthrown. The victory of feminist empowerment is but a movement on behalf of a more humane, peaceful and compassionate society for everybody, men included. In a phrase, America is to be "feminized." It will be, hopefully, a world without violence or hate, a workplace of greater equality and heightened kindness for the less fortunate. Respect for differences will replace the stigmatization of uniqueness, and a sharing of responsibility via widespread participation will render top-down authoritarianism a dim memory. Among the more radical feminists, it will also be a world of stricter environmental protection, the cessation of militarism, the demise of racism and homophobia, the collapse of market capitalism, plus untold other benefits (Faver 1994).

As with all other empowerment visions, alluring elements abound. Surely a more peaceful, kinder world is enticing. Yet a chasm separates rhetoric and reality, and more important, this conception of politics invites risk. The most conspicuous problem concerns the feminist discernment of social conflict. Recall that it divides society into two camps—kind, compassionate, egalitarian women and aggressive, dominating men. As a battle cry to mobilize the troops, this polarized notion is seductive, but as a theoretical foundation, it is an invitation to debilitating confusion. Far more is involved than mere distortion of complexity, though this flaw is hardly trivial.[8]

Most evidently, what if this polarized oppressive portrait is mistaken? To empower women—that is, to allow them to exist according to what feminists see as their "true nature"—is therefore a hopeless cause since liberation recipients disdain it. Voluntary oppression is, furthermore, non-sensical. Conceivably, many women, possibly a majority, *prefer* being wives, homemakers, mothers or secretaries. Perhaps nursing is more appealing than being a medical doctor. Only radical feminists, not all women, judge their status as "inferior." And if a woman sincerely inclines to be "inferior," pushing her elsewhere hardly constitutes "empowerment." Is an unhappy but richly compensated female corporate CEO (chief executive officer) authentically empowered if she would rather be housebound raising children? Scarcely, if we take empowerment as meaning self-determination.

Accept momentarily that this sharply drawn depiction of oppression is accurate. The next question is whether it is socially created or biologically determined. Or maybe some bewildering blend of both nature and nurture dependent on myriad factors. This daunting issue escapes serious attention in feminist writings, but it applies directly and inescapably to empowerment. If we assume, as is reasonable, that man's "dangerous" masculinity (proclivity toward violence, domination) is substantially biologically ingrained, how is feminism to preponderate without the forced subjugation of men? That is, since men's instincts cannot be remediated through education or exhortation, how is control possible? What fate awaits millions of men ever anxious to boss around women, make war and otherwise brutalize society? It might even be contended that men are incapable of being "authentic feminists" since they cannot truly experience womanhood (see, e.g., Klein 1984, Ch. 1). Overcoming biology does not conjure up mental pictures of a kind, gentle society. Might men, like domesticated animals, be bred to enhance feminine traits? Might hormone treatments or even castration suppress aggressiveness? How about police-state measures, for example, a secret informer network, to prevent men from "getting out of hand"? These are hardly appetizing solutions for a free society.

Nor do serious problems vanish by accepting gender roles as 100 percent socially constructed. Extensive resocialization is hardly less complicated than biological engineering. There is certainly no surefire formula for feminizing men, and devising this recipe may exceed our scientific capacity. Witness the failures of comparable transformation efforts directed at curing chronic welfare dependency, ending drug addiction, combating teenage pregnancies or inspiring academic motivation. Equally relevant, expecting most men to embrace this new self-definition voluntarily is impractical. Imagine the resistance, for example, if male children are forbidden to play rough-and-tumble sports, hectored to emphasize emotional openness, punished for competitiveness or denied access to action movies. How might such a reeducation program be imposed? No doubt, success would require a coercive effort making the Stalinist transformation of the Soviet Union look comparatively benign.

Less obvious, but just as reasonable as presupposing sex-related trait malleability, is the masculinization of women. Indeed, this is far more credible than the reverse. To wit, as women assume positions of authority, as they acquire economic leverage and enjoy ever-widening lifestyle options, they adopt characteristic male traits. It is a matter of reinforcing successful behavior. Women discover, for example, that self-centered selfishness, not subordination to the friendship group, brings success. Moving up the corporate ladder and other male-dominated professions, moreover, demands ruthlessness, a taste for bad-tempered conflict and masking emotion. Personal relations likewise gravitate to the manly model—the pursuit of "sex objects" supplants affection, and men are coerced into unpleasant domestic chores. This possibility has not gone unnoticed by feminists. Brehm (1988) discusses the "Margaret Thatcher syndrome" in which prominent women succeed by being confrontational, uncompromising, independent, and hard driving, all the while being traditional, dutiful wives. Such women abound in today's world and may provide attractive role models to young girls. Ironically, women become empowered by mimicking men.

If these obstacles were overcome—highly improbable—there still remains the formidable obstacle of unifying women, a category divided by enormously heterogeneous aims. Recall that feminist empowerment aspires beyond becoming yet one more politically active "women's group." Securing a handful of favorable laws, no matter how commendable, is merely a first step, not final victory. It is the uniting of women and transforming society that constitute the grand prize. This goal is probably forever unobtainable. The discord among women, frankly acknowledged among feminist writers, can hardly be papered over with high-sounding rhetoric. Middle-class white women often disagree with poor black women on salient issues—taxes, education, health care or crime. There are, no doubt, similar animosities deriving from differences of age, sexual orientation, ethnicity, education and whatever else separates people. Disputes on deeper cultural values, for example, illegitimacy, divorce, sexuality and religion, are similarly endemic. Many women also reject abortion on demand, a litmus test, nonnegotiable issue for nearly all feminists. Assembling a grand coalition may be a romantic illusion, far easier said than accomplished.

Predictably, then, a huge rift separates theorizing and actual outcomes. Faced with insurmountable obstacles, the effort predictably turns inward, directed toward relishing psychological rewards, not tangible benefits.[9] Recall Chapter 2's discussion about organizations nominally committed to empowerment mutating into discussion groups driven by self-gratification. Debate in which everyone has their uncontested input painlessly substitutes for arduous action. Real-world dilemmas are escaped by writing turgid theoretical treatises directed at the faithful, rehashing comfortable ground. Empowerment, the gaining of capacity to impose change, is informally redefined into consciousness raising, an alleged first step on a journey often lacking a second step. In a sense, the goal's very enormity is its own worst enemy: Rather than reach for what can be grasped, an overreach breeds exasperated futility.

Such futility may, however, possess a bright side: It insulates traditional limited government from subversion via the "personal is the political" doctrine. Failure of feminist empowerment means a continuance of shielding private actions from state intervention. Surprisingly, this might bode well for feminists, even providing a degree of self-determination. Politicizing the personal is a two-edged sword—it also authorizes men to ubiquitously impose their allegedly harmful values on women. Just a women may insist that men be raised to be more feminine, men can insist that all girls undergo marine-style boot camp to rid them of sissy inclinations. And in a battle of views, it is hardly certain that the feminist ideal will reign supreme.

More important, sustaining this bulwark permits a true diversity of choice. Provided personal relationships are generally "off limits" to government edict, men inclined toward the feminist ideal—sharing housework, for instance—are free to do so, and vice versa. Feminists can be feminists, and macho men can be macho men within legal limits. Women offended by masculine proclivities can, for the most part, simply avoid them. If people wish to politicize friendship, they can, provided they act only individually. Child rearing, entertainment, sports, sexuality and the like remain "personal decisions," not matters to be decided by officialdom. Mothers will not be told, for example, to teach young boys nurturing cooperation, not rambunctious conflict. It is even possible to establish entire communities or academic departments dedicated to feminist empowerment without transforming unwilling males.

Moreover, even when the goals are modest, the gains of feminist empowerment are deceptively slender. Consider one case study offered as an exemplary model—efforts during the early 1980s to use the "equal pay for equal work" doctrine to secure pay raises for largely women unionized clerical workers at the University of Washington (Almeleh et al. 1993). After a lengthy battle involving lawsuits, negotiation and direct political action, the lowest-paid clerks did receive a raise. Just as important for empowerment activists, however, these female workers, even those not benefiting financially, acquired a newfound pride and heightened self-esteem. At least for activists, this victory provided a transforming experience, proof of what women can accomplish when united. Yet as was true in our Yavapai Indians example, such progress is far removed from the genuine self-determination article. Indeed, judged from another angle, it has scarcely anything to do with self-determination and autonomy.

Most notably, the salary raise was granted by a largely male legislature, albeit pressured by female activists. Had these male legislators said no, the clerical workers would have gone home empty-handed. Again, this is more "the power" to annoy (especially given the easy replacement of office help) than securing autonomously one's own desert. Alternatively, the women could have quit and become independent contractors to supply these clerical services. They remained hourly employees in a hierarchical setting, however, not bosses. Furthermore, the "equal pay for equal work" movement eventually collapsed despite these early minor successes and the enormous effort expenditures.

The entire outcome, moreover, rested a "male" cultural context, although this was never acknowledged. Judges, administrators and union officials did not casually network, appraising every viewpoint equally meritorious, incorporating every divergent voice, and then decide according to some impromptu sense of compassionate fairness. Instead, they paid homage to a demanding abstraction called "the law," and once that was interpreted, they dutifully and bureaucratically followed it regardless of their personal feelings. More than an illustration of feminist empowerment, the entire incident exemplified traditional contentious union-management conflict despite the surrounding feminist oratory. The game was played under rules provided by the patriarchy, and these were never altered.

The parallel with the Yavapai Indians is clear. These clerks remain as vulnerable as ever despite their elation. What the state bestows, it can reclaim, although it is highly improbable that they will rescind a contracted pay hike. Responses are more indirect. A university, like any business, can trim labor costs by reducing hours, altering benefits, not replacing departures, increasing workloads or—most likely—replacing people with machines. If clerks earn "too much," invest in computers, faster copiers or other alternatives to bloated payrolls. Some tasks might be dropped altogether if costs become excessive or reassigned to better-paid, more efficient employees. Pushing wages above market value, as many an unemployed manufacturing worker will attest, offers an empty triumph. Whether this downsizing transpired is not, alas, part of the story, but it should be included if empowerment if to be assessed accurately.

More generally, while a single example cannot capture the full landscape of feminist empowerment, it does nevertheless reflect a prevalent theme—in practice, empowerment entails *getting things from government or businesses* (see, e.g., Morgan and Bookman 1988). The menu may be considerable—from obtaining health care clinics to improving schools—and tactics may vary, but the formula remains immutable. Pressuring the powerful, not independence, is the game. This is not to argue that these benefits are inconsequential. They may, in fact, be significant. But this does not alter the relationship's character—one party beseeches the other for discretionary relief. The scenario is one of demanding more pay for the same work, not learning new skills to get a promotion. Becoming an entrepreneur is even further off the agenda. In this sense, feminist empowerment parallels black empowerment in accepting state bountifulness and believing that "power" is the ability to extract these prizes.

What might society resemble if the fondest feminist empowerment dreams came to pass? Would it be, as promised, some Utopian pastoral planet of peace and happiness? Peeking into the future is always risky, but no guarantee exists of measureless improvement. Today's prosperity undoubtedly rests on "male" traits—hierarchy, competition, toughness, coldhearted calculation, avarice and so on. A modern economy run according to feminist values is difficult to imagine. And will wars disappear? Again, there can be no assurance. Some of our era's most belligerent political leaders—Margaret Thatcher, Golda Meir, Indira Gandhi—were women. It is entirely reasonable that if many women assumed leadership positions (including the corporate world), masculine traits would dominate.

Lastly, politicizing the personal invites totalitarianism. This is especially probable if empowerment weakens family life, as it well might, given feminist veneration of life outside of household drudgery and parenthood (Klein 1984, Ch. 3). With family ties undermined, social pathologies soar, and government easily assumes by necessity an in loco parentis guardianship of its subjects. Witness some ghettos where children go largely unsupervised. State-administered family life is only the beginning. The state's full bureaucratic power, authorized by the personal is the political, can now intrude everywhere. This intrusion will become more energetic as transformation efforts come up short, a likely event given the task's enormity. There can be no privacy, no escape and no alternatives. Child-rearing codes may run for hundreds of pages, as would the regulations governing sexual relationships. The present-day complexities and ambiguities with sexual harassment are but a harbinger to come. The only alternative to state-imposed conformity is to leave society altogether.

PARTICIPATORY DEMOCRACY

Thus far empowerment visions all blend scholarship with activism. Indeed, theoretical foundations and mobilizing oratory are sometimes inseparable. By contrast, participatory democracy is almost entirely an academic enterprise. Such was not always the case—throughout the 1960s this creed galvanized innumerable groups to insist upon participation everywhere. From university students insisting upon self-defined curriculums to inner-city communities demanding control over police, this philosophy was ascendant. "Power to the people" became a cliché. With matters more calm, these passions have faded, mutating into grand scholarly theorizing. Nevertheless, they remain relevant; hibernation may be a more apt description. As with community psychology, influence predominantly flows through students absorbing these lessons of the "good society." Particularly among idealists seeking community amidst modern society, the call remains alluring.

At the center of this conception lies a distinctive, unconventional appreciation of democracy. This radical understanding promises both the benefits of empowerment while scripting its attainment. Rejected are today's commonplace conceptions, what might be called liberal or elitist theories. These discards underscore the accountability of elected leaders and the protection of freedoms via the enforcement of rights. They generally stress process, not content. How policy is made, not what policy does (beyond not trespassing upon certain rights) is critical. The proscribed citizen role is also constrained, typically not much beyond voting. The representation of interests, not daily participation, is supreme (Pateman 1970, Ch. 1). Furthermore, particularly when standard democratic conceptions are blended with capitalism, government economic intervention is fettered. While it may regulate select features of commerce, for example, workplace safety, most decisions remain with business managers or owners.

To replace this bounded "democracy," the notion of "participatory democracy" is advanced. It is especially applicable to workplace choices, but it pertains equally to all organizations within society—universities, churches, unions, professional organizations and even private clubs. Simply put, all business employees (or students or groups members), from the lowest to the highest, along with community representatives participate equally in agenda setting and policy making. Decentralization and involvement of ordinary citizens are fundamental (Cook and Morgan 1971). Although this may seem a novel idea, it has flourished for centuries, infusing myriad political causes (Kramer 1972, Ch. 2). All choices applying to all of one's existence are subject to democratic resolution (Kramer 1972, Ch. 3). Rather than being power's object, or possessing just petty control, one becomes empowered ubiquitously. A person might thus help decide his or her job hours, local policing policy, school curriculums, and similar life-impacting policies. This expansive notion of politics and the feminist "the personal is the political" doctrine are not dissimilar. Traditional democracy is to be refurbished fundamentally.

The alleged benefits of this transformation are multitudinous. Participation offers practical protection of personal interests, a mechanism for ensuring fairness and communal welfare. Corporations, now needing workforce and nearby resident assent, might thus be compelled to pay fair wages and not pollute the environment; schools, dependent on parental acquiesence, more closely fill student needs. Citizen participation also enhances organizational performance. Surely, for example, university students would receive a better education if they themselves shaped educational policy.

Of more enduring consequence is transforming citizens themselves. Empowerment, the taking control of one's circumstances, uplifts and ennobles. Whereas traditional democracy presupposes a citizenry of circumscribed capacity, participatory democracy recognizes democracy as a technique of civic improvement. Energetic participation would, as one writer (Davis 1964) expressed it, help in "the education of an entire people to the point where their intellectual, emotional and moral capacities have reached their full potential and they are joined, freely and actively in a genuine community" (p. 40). According to its advocates, the wisest of policies cannot regenerate if imposed top-down—it is involvement, in and of itself, that elevates.

A parallel invigoration will be bestowed upon politics more generally (Bachrach and Botwinick 1992, Ch.1; Cook and Morgan 1971). With heightened self-governance, society's rampant political alienation dissipates. Everyone, even those historically excluded such as African Americans, now feels communally integrated. The democratic process, no longer marred by apathy, indifference and cynicism, regenerates. As ordinary people acquire political experience, public debate improves. Welfare, drug abuse, faulty education and crime problems that have long perplexed government hobbled by fragmented power will be unraveled by empowered citizens (Bachrach and Botwinick 1992, Ch. 9). Coldhearted, distant bureaucracies can no longer dictate clumsy policy to their helpless subjects. Indeed, as participatory democracy gains momentum, bureaucratic structures will wither away, replaced by citizen activists. In a phrase, the body politic will gain health.

Prosperity will likewise flow (Bachrach and Botwinick 1992, Ch. 9). Taxes will decline with the demise of inefficient government projects and subsidies to politically well-connected industries such as the saving and loan industry. Billions are to be saved from resolving welfare and crime problems; budget deficits and trade gaps will similarly shrink. Most important, the disadvantaged will enjoy a new economic security plus better wages. Productivity climbs as workers and managers cooperate. Flexibility and decentralization replace rigid hierarchies, while once-indifferent workers are now energized. Citizen empowerment combined with a revitalized labor movement further counterweights corporate selfishness. The days of companies suddenly shutting plants, drastically downsizing the workforce, exploiting wage earners or sending American jobs overseas will cease.

Although this vision may initially appear universalistic, its aim is narrower. Not everyone profits equally: Empowerment must adjust basic power distribution. Specifically, those below are to gain at the expense of those above. Democratization, in the words of Bachrach and Botwinick, "is to create political space for the underclasses to acquire voice and a more empowered sense of community involvement, thereby enabling them to compete more effectively with the upper classes in all arenas of politics. . . . Expanded and newly created participatory counterstructures are therefore essential if the subordinate classes are to develop sufficient social consciousness and political skill to effectively articulate and defend their interests" (13). Empowerment flattens drastically the socioeconomic pyramid. Transforming workplace conditions is merely the point of attack in a bigger war. Corporate hegemony, in particular, is to be overturned.

Who might benefit from this metamorphosis? Those "at the bottom" are surprisingly heterogeneous: workers (possibly including middle-class professionals toiling for a wage), environmentalists, students, feminists, plus neighborhood and civil rights activists. In sum, a grand coalition of almost everyone, save top corporate management and the very affluent. What unites such people is, supposedly, their potential commitment to participatory democracy and their subordinate wage-earner status. Having much to gain and little to lose by acquiring greater mastery, they will surely transcend differences. Policy domains attracting activists are similarly nearly all-encompassing, ranging from child care to the minimum wage (Bachrach and Botwinick 1992, Ch. 1).

And what will bring this empowerment about? Predictably given the enormity of the task, detailed plans are sparse. Even when discussed widely during the 1960s, concrete manifestations concerned little more than food cooperatives and neighborhood associations. European workers councils, a system of uncertain U.S. applicability, were often idealized (Kramer 1972, Chs. 4 and 5). Today, in lieu of concrete stratagems are innumerable exhortations on why participatory democracy is an enticing blueprint personally and collectively. It is hoped, we can assume, that ceaseless propaganda coupled with ongoing economic upheaval will win popular acceptance. When faced with declining standards of living and growing government incapacity, citizens will welcome this nostrum (Bachrach and Botwinick 1992, Ch. 9). Moreover, participatory democracy will—presumably—prevail against competing panaceas such as fascism. It is intellectual argument, not voter mobilization or disruptive threat, that will triumph. Surprisingly, a dim view is taken of the various worker participation programs recently enacted within American industry. Affording workers influence over production is not the genuine article. Such programs, it is maintained, are quite constrained and, more fundamentally, are merely devices for spurring productivity, not authentic control mechanisms. Similarly, employee-owned firms apparently bestow none of the control originally anticipated (Bachrach and Botwinick 1992, Ch. 5).

As with all schemes promising future near-Utopias, this exhortation is easily picked apart. No doubt, dozens of solid reasons exist why it will fail. The 1960s optimistic experiments of citizen control disappointed. Cataloging the inherent difficulties of galvanizing millions to abandon nonpolitical pursuits in favor of unabated activism would fill a volume. Ditto for sustaining alliances among people otherwise profoundly divided. Will citizens levy taxes on themselves or make other unpleasant choices?[10] The picture painted of the American economy, the alarmist account of perpetual crisis and despair, the plan's impetus, is surely overdrawn. If collapse of capitalism is a precondition, participatory democracy may be a long time in coming. Yet empowerment via massive participation remains ever attractive despite all these noteworthy obstacles. An interesting paradox seemingly prevails: Its very idealism and its often wrongheaded rejection of unpleasant reality also help to explain its enduring attraction. Grim realism is over-powered by starry-eyed hope.

Rather than again rehearse obvious "it will not come to pass" arguments, consider instead possible success. Suppose that millions did gain empow-erment by actively participating in the choices that shaped their lives. Un-fortunately, the rosy picture painted by participatory democracy advocates is but one alternative. Just as likely is a scenario of endless civil strife as newly energized citizens now make political encounters a full-time job. Choices obscurely enacted by public officials now drag on endlessly as com-munity group after group insists on self-governance. "Community activist" will become a respected job category. Tranquillity collapses into acrimony of confrontation, demonstration, threats and litigation. Especially as clash-ing factions gain sophistication, final resolution may grow impossible. No sooner does victory seem immanent than the battle is reopened afresh. Chaos or gridlock on a vast scale, not democratic invigoration, will likely prevail.

Worse, as conflicts expand, as frustration builds, as novice troops join the fray, sustaining a peaceful democratic give-and-take becomes more strenuous. The lessons of calm democratic governance are hardly auto-matically learned via involvement. This is but hope, not fact. Recall the path taken by 1960s student demonstrations: Early peaceful, almost festive, rallies soon escalated to violent, tear gas–laden police confrontations. A similar patterns plagued the black civil rights movement as the nonviolence of Martin Luther King, Jr., was replaced by Black Panther militarism and rioting. The lure of capturing public jobs and money may be irresistible and inspire violence. The weakening of top-down state control may well make it impossible to contain contentious escalating disputes. Imagine local school policy being "made" by thousands of angry blacks and whites quar-reling over the curriculum or personnel.

A comparable problem concerns the necessary aptitude. America cannot be likened to a romanticized fifth-century Athens or colonial New England. Governance everywhere is exceedingly complex, often dependent on ex-pertise baffling citizens. Just as involvement hardly begets democratic in-clinations, we cannot infer that it builds competence. It is preposterous that amateur community activists can "decide" a city's financial borrowing or mass transportation. The limits of time and cognitive capacity are not easily surmounted. Faced with such daunting complexity, in dozens of domains, ordinary citizens may well defer to authorities after perfunctory consulta-tion. Participatory democracy will degenerate into ritual, a public cere-mony, not unlike today's stockholders' meetings whereby a tiny percentage of "owners" dutifully approve management-made decisions.

Finally, the participation-power linkage cuts both ways. Historically, cit-izen electoral engagement has often *enhanced* state control over its population, not the reverse (Ginsberg 1982). After all, without receiving a voice, citizens might resist taxes or disobey the law. Employee participation in industry frequently shares this intent—permitting workers choices on details builds loyalty and enthusiasm far more cheaply than pay increases. The process is one of cooptation, not bestowing self-determination. The possibilities for manipulation, surreptitiously manufacturing a top-down consensus, are endless. The tale of the better-educated middle-class people "taking over" organizations ostensibly set up for the poor is a familiar one (Kramer 1972, Ch. 6). "Spontaneous" decisions may well reflect how alternatives are posed, the arguments offered, what information is supplied and the rules for deciding. No doubt, under the guise of "empowering those at the bottom," superiors may further enhance domination. In short, such "empowerment" deceives.

CONSERVATIVE EMPOWERMENT

Though the preceding theories occasionally eschew ideological categorization, in varying degrees they all represent the spectrum's left side. Most notably, leveling inequalities, the hallmark tenet of the left, was the antidote for modern society's plagues. Typical of radical political schemes, an infatuation existed for remolding human psychology—empowerment constructs a "new person." Differences were largely tactical—blacks, for example, favored elections, and feminists emphasized self-transformation, while community psychology trusted expert scientific counsel. All advocates, no doubt, sincerely believe that their transforming nostrums will restore health to a troubled civic life.

Conservative empowerment, despite the ideological distance, shares similar though far more modest reformist impulse. Regardless of its endorsement by prominent Republicans (for example, Newt Gingrich and Jack Kemp), it partakes elements of its most radical namesakes. Divergences surface in implementation, its scope and how government is to be managed. Like participatory democracy, conservative empowerment takes dead aim at rampant "gigantism": measureless, heavy-handed bureaucracy, monumental yet largely ineffectual government and often bewildering economic complexity. Such bigness estranges citizens, leaving them dispirited regarding democracy. Touring many modern cities displays this pernicious malady—deteriorating, life-threatening Soviet-style public housing projects occupied by listless tenants, army-like police departments impotent to keep streets safe, impersonal public assistance agencies overwhelmed by misery, handsome freshly built schools ineptly teaching indifferent pupils, and so on and on. Nor have billions of dollars or government-supplied expertise helped.

The solution is not, however, returning to the pre–New Deal days. This draconian measure is both politically unfeasible and would leave millions needlessly adrift. Furthermore, at least in some domains, national defense, managing the economy, bigness are considered assets. Government's functions are to be curtailed, but this is no exalted romantic revolutionary manifesto for unreachable self-sufficiency. In the words of Joyce and Schambra (1996, 29), "the restoration of civil society will require nothing less than a determined, long-term effort to reverse the gravitation of power and authority upward to the national government and to sent that authority back to local government and civil institutions." How, then, is alienating massiveness to be diminished while preserving all of big government's vital benefits?

The key lies in strengthening "mediating" structures: "those institutions standing between the individual in his private life and the large institutions of public life" (Berger and Neuhaus 1996, 158). It is through participation in these that today's psychologically detached citizens gains self-determination and re-integrate the fabric of community life. Potential mediating structures abound, but among the most central are the neighborhood, family, church and voluntary organizations. These link individuals and the huge, distant institutions now dictating public life. One's block association or Masonic Lodge provides the rewards of direct democracy and facilitates coping with civic discontents. In sharp contrast to other, more ambitious empowerment agendas, society is to be pragmatically reinvigorated piecemeal, not systematically transformed into heaven on earth. Nor is there, as with black empowerment, the expectation that empowerment bestows tangible benefits. Officialdom is neither to be decimated or strengthened in revolutionary service; it is to be complemented to enhance civil society by people acting autonomously and efficiently. An institutional balance is sought between the highly statist theories of feminists and black empowerment and the near Utopian communalism of participatory democracy.

This understanding has a pluralistic appreciation of cultural differences without embracing the sweeping relativism of community psychology. Indeed, the invigoration of mediating structures will vitalize unique communities risking immersion in homogeneous mass culture. Like community psychology, the emphasis is on small and uncommon. The empowered community is composed, for example, of flourishing ethnic organizations, esoteric hobby clubs, music guilds, social fraternities and well-attended affinity groups of all sorts. Local politics may be made in a plethora of neighborhood clubhouses. It is also a noncoercive pluralism insofar as there are no "bad" inclinations within the limits of the law; the Marxist book club is perfectly welcome. Membership is voluntary—nobody will be required to join anything, even if participation would benefit everyone. If teenagers play "Rambo" in the hills or feminists form a women's collective, no problem.

Conservative empowerment's remedy follows along two paths. First, the damage caused by the national government's injurious intrusion into civic life must be halted and reversed. Building lively mediating structures is not an original, untested scheme. In fact, such robustness is normal. For centuries, mediating structures thrived and accomplished tasks now mismanaged by government clerks. Most still remain vital today, although in some locals—particularly among the poor—they have wilted altogether. As one must act to prevent environmental destruction before the cause is unsalvageable, Washington's cumbersome hand must be restrained before it destroys civic life.

The top-down centralized debilitation of mediating structures has, alas, been imposed with noble intentions, often celebrated as "enlightened." The assault list is immense, and we can highlight only a few. In school policy, for example, the courts and bureaucrats have consistently prevented teachers and administrators from maintaining the discipline essential to learning (Horowitz 1996). Let a principal suspend "too many" students, and he or she might attract a bevy of "student rights" organizations threatening litigation and charges of racial or ethnic "insensitivity," inattention to disability, absence of due process or arbitrariness. Federal judges themselves have periodically taken over local schools with dreadful consequences (Roberts and Stratton 1997, Ch. 5). Meanwhile, teachers are routinely ignored when demanding physical safety. Add the weakening of neighborhood schools through endless busing to achieve racial integration despite the uncertain educational benefits.

If alcoholic vagrants expropriate public space formerly the site of neighborhood gatherings, courts protect them, redefining parks and streets as "affordable housing." Nor can these community-minded residents defend "their turf" if Washington bureaucrats locate homeless shelters in their midst. A similar enervation occurs in public housing projects when tenants attempt to eject troublemakers. Courts will surely "protect" these drug dealers and gun-toting criminals as exercising "personal freedom" (Horowitz 1996). Meanwhile, once effective private philanthropic organizations, increasingly dependent on government largess, now tailor activities to funding requirements and abandon original missions (Lenkowsky 1996). When charities steep their efforts in religion, this must cease as a condition of government funding, regardless of effectiveness (Olasky 1996).

The empowerment strategy's second element is stronger utilization of existing mediating structures. It is a government and citizens cooperative effort, not merely a "get-involved" exhortation. Historically, the Homestead Act and the Land Grant College Act are the exemplars (Toppings 1982). Government facilitates—provides incentives, perhaps minimal funding and enabling legislation—but does not control. The burgeoning school voucher movement notably illustrates this possibility. Here parents—not education bureaucracies—control educational funds and freely select schools reflecting their preferences. Competition for pupils enhances educational attainment, whereas the necessity for choice motivates parents toward engagement. Additional government enticements include more generous tax deductions for charity or lowering the financial burden of raising children. On a grander scale are several in-place government programs providing business incentives for firms to locate in high unemployment areas. In 1993, for example, Washington established rural empowerment zones and enterprise communities eligible to receive a variety of financial and technical assistance to spur economic development (http://www.ezon.gov). Overseeing this program was the Community Empowerment Board headed by Vice President Al Gore.

Particularly successful examples of this type of empowerment are the projects run by the National Center for Neighborhood Enterprise (NCNE), headed by Robert L. Woodson, Sr.[11] The NCNE, presently in 38 states, works exclusively in poor inner-city areas and has achieved far greater success with "problem populations" afflicted with drugs, violence, illegitimacy and crime than comparable federally administered programs (Woodson 1996). Several features of this effort distinguish it from comparable top-down assistance ventures. For one, it relies heavily on local residents, many of whom once suffered the same disabilities as intended beneficiaries. Outside authorities are not "parachuted in" for brief sojourns. Such indigenous counselors know "the locals" and family networks, essential ingredients in achieving enduring results. Nor are they easily taken in by deceptions. Former alcoholics recognize, for example, the tricks of the trade in manipulating welfare programs to obtain booze. Local facilitators also serve as inspirations and instill hope. The stress on making one's own choices, taking responsibility and not effortlessly blaming "the system" for one's misfortune is fundamental. People, not society, need uplifting.

No simplistic miracle cures or grand theories of justice are proclaimed. Demonstrations or threats by the impoverished soliciting empowerment are off the menu. Empowerment comes from attaining self-mastery of traditional skills, moving up economically to modest respectability. By middle-class standards, accomplishments are slender, and society in general may scarcely notice. But for beneficiaries, the difference is enormous. Success may derive from savvy heart-to-heart talks—"tough love"—plus dispensing modest visible material rewards, for example, a nicer room at a shelter, to addicts taking small steps toward progress. If improvement continues, leaders can assist with local employment. Fix-up campaigns are popular. In one situation a neighborhood was able to buy nearby crack houses for the unpaid taxes and make them rentable, using their own labor and donated supplies. Advancement is often painfully slow and daunting, yet the payoffs eventually mount. Such upbeat tales are commonplace, fortunately, and reflect a multitude of unique circumstances. They add up to people learning to control their lives by making distressing situations bearable if not pleasant.

There is a resemblance here to traditional charity whereby assistance is given personally to coax recipients toward a more productive, satisfying life. The exalted refurbishing of society is not on the agenda, save promoting innumerable modest improvements. Accomplishment means a nicer apartment, a job, a more tranquil nearby park. From its perspective, teaching public housing residents carpentry outshines soliciting votes with promises of invented jobs. Better to clean up litter than rally for bountiful welfare benefits. This is hardly a formula attracting notoriety. It remains invisible in the academic literature, perhaps owing to its pedestrian character. It embraces America's traditional virtues—hard work, sobriety, community involvement, obeying the law and respectability. Absent is all the cant of mobilizing the poor to transform America by ending hegemonic domination.

Given past accomplishment and modesty of aims, this empowerment hardly appears as pie in the sky. It rests on proven methods—the task is to extend what is already there, not invent novelties. Once government's heavy hand is lightened, the mediating structures will again thrive. Its advocates already claim substantial success, and no doubt, it will continue to gain momentum if Americans return to appreciate small-scale self-reliance. The real issue, then, is whether this nostrum can be dramatically extended under conditions quite different from simpler times. A danger lurks of romanticizing the past, envisioning today's public housing as small nineteenth-century villages. The venerable mixture of little groups of friends and neighbors working together to roll back crime, family disorganization, inept schooling, urban decay and many of the other maladies of modern life might be an illusion. Conquering giant education bureaucracies may not be so easy. Devotees may still yet succumb to the lure of government generosity. Successes may only slow down pernicious trends, not reverse the flow. For every five uplifted via empowerment, ten may sink into despair as a result of conditions well beyond local control. In sum, its effectiveness remains to be tested.

CONCLUSION

Our exploration has been a lengthy one, and many territories remain unexplored. These endeavors reveal a curious paradox. On the one hand, each empowerment enterprise, as weighed by all the published literature, seems impressive. Yet despite this abundance, the pictures offered are woefully incomplete. Our section-by-section critiques expose serious limitations, seldom drawing attention, let alone resolution. Discussions are typically more intent on preaching or condemning enemies than unraveling

thorny dilemmas. Recall, for example, how black and feminist empowerment devotees conveniently skip over government limitations in supplying
their aims despite demonstrated ineffectiveness. Community psychologists
pass on the troubling implications of cultural relativism. Devotees of participatory democracy seem to venerate the power of good argument to
surmount an unpleasant reality. Conservatives seem incapable of questioning self-interest as a source of guidance.

These sins of omission undoubtedly flow from intellectual inbreeding.
Theorists comfortably sermonize to true believers so arguable assertions
easily go unchallenged. Skeptics are apparently not invited to the convocations. Common vocabulary also disguises narrowness, a self-absorbency.
Feminists, for example, ignore community psychology, whereas optimistic
black activists apparently have no inkling of the troubled historical legacy
of community control. Perhaps conservative empowerment devotees would
benefit from examining participatory democracy's disorderly past before
raising up the innate desire for autonomy as dogma. The scholarly edifice
grows ever larger but without corresponding advancement. Since these remedies are to be practiced in the real world, such blemishes are hardly cost
free. To enlist thousands into a cause built on defective dogma differs drastically from faulty literary interpretations.

Equally troubling is an inattention to prescription liabilities. Perusing
empowerment resembles visiting a health store stocked with endless "guaranteed" cures. Not only is this "guarantee" of dubious value, but the "injurious side effects" portion of the label is, alas, obscured. Those to be
capacitated are seductively told they dwell in a risk-free world. Particularly
absent is alertness to opportunity costs—benefits foregone when this option
is pursued. It is often easily supposed that if a restorative might assist, it is
worth chasing, no matter how slender the payoff. Confessing that ceaseless
electioneering or consciousness raising might hinder more worthwhile endeavors is, unfortunately, taboo. That the quest for self-mastery may make
life *worse* is even more unthinkable. "Social change" sans hard-nosed assessment of risk has transformed itself into gospel.

Finally, the pervading optimism is curious given the paucity of success
stories. Progress, we are forever reminded, is inevitable; experts will soon
unlock the secrets. To identify problems commences relief. To accept one's
fate thus proclaims unacceptable defeat. Rather than advance only margin-
ally, reach for the sky. Middle-class feminists, for example, cannot relent
until male hegemony is vanquished. Meanwhile, of course, the poor are
told that empowerment will bring the material benefits currently enjoyed
by affluent feminists. All the considerable rewards of the status quo, from
political freedom to material abundance, are insufficient and subject to empowerment perfection. Is this quest endless? Are the appetites insatiable?
This is not to argue that such optimism is fraudulent; rather, it is all a
matter of unquestioned creed, not a proven reality.

NOTES

1. To appreciate this extreme emphasis on capturing power centers, apart from merely securing influence, consider "Jewish empowerment." Although Jews may be overrepresented among political officeholders, Jews seldom live in cities with Jewish mayors and typically direct their political efforts to electing non-Jews. Yet it is undoubtedly true that Jews as a group exercise disproportionate clout in U.S. politics. Clearly, this "holding of office" centered definition of empowerment is appropriate solely for African Americans.

2. Even more stridently rejected is the idea that government intervention only makes matters worse. Government intrusion is deemed inherently constructive, and national intrusion is preferable to guidance from state or local officials. The legacy of inept social engineering is thus a failure of details rather than any limitation of energetic big government.

3. A critical, but seldom noted, distinction in evaluating empowerment success is public versus private rhetoric. For example, a program of empowering a community to raise educational attainment may fail as measured by academic criteria, but it may be a resounding achievement in terms of providing well-paying jobs to unemployable incompetents. This might be the underlying aim, but it was never said publicly. This is no small problem, given the frequency of disguised agendas.

4. The larger issue that informs this discussion is, of course, individual versus systemic culpability. Regardless of how one might ultimately apportion out blame for human misery, it is clear that matters are seldom black or white. This is especially true in a society with multiple opportunities. And as the lessons of the last few decades make evident, "blaming the system" is hardly relief even when containing substantial truth. For the community psychology to insist, as a matter of dogma, that a person's predicament is wholly due to exterior conditions probably does far more harm than good.

5. Our assessment of "empowerment" among the Yavapai applies more generally, obviously. To suggest that groups of poor citizens actually gain "power" against government may be more an exercise in semantics. Such groups derive their momentary influence by their willingness to make trouble, but if the amount of trouble becomes excessive, there is no question of who ultimately prevails—the government. Moreover, as was true in this illustration, this power typically depends on the willingness of more sophisticated outsider assistance, assistance that could suddenly vanish.

6. The reasons offered for this misogyny are revealing. Brehm (1988) advances several, including men's fear of sex, the awesomeness of women's bodies (since they can bleed without external interference) and the fact that women give birth. Suppression of women also makes men feel better about themselves, thus increasing their self-esteem. None of this apparently rests on empirical research and, more important, cannot explain the wide variation among male views regarding women. This ingenuity in escaping the possibility of biological explanations is not unique. Another review suggested that women's inferiority is imposed because women's sexuality makes them too powerful. This scarcely exhausts the possibilities (see, e.g., Stacey and Price 1981, Ch. 2).

7. Feminist empowerment need not, logically, be expansive. A wholly different

approach would be to narrow the focus to empowerment within the family. By devoting themselves as wives and mothers, women could create a powerful extrapolitical matriarchy. Public life would thus only nominally be male dominated. Behind the scenes, women would exercise real power.

8. A further notable inaccuracy concerns the alleged powerlessness of women. To reach this exaggerated conclusion requires discarding substantial evidence, notably their votes, organizational involvement, financial resources and the enduring cooperation of males in commanding positions. Again, to speculate a bit, rhetoric useful for galvanizing supporters has been raised up to the level of dogma. It is debatable whether a strategy of political self-depreciation yields tangible benefits.

9. This inward turn also may help explain the infatuation with the "personal is the political" doctrine. With the big prizes beyond reach, attention then turns to the close at hand: family, friends, the workplace, or the neighborhood. Redefinition of politics escapes innumerable failures. This infatuation with politicizing personal relationships was not always the case. One major analysis of the women's movement during the 1970s explicitly defined feminism in terms of conventional pluralistic political action (Gelb and Palley 1982). It was even argued that further success would come from employing conventional political tactics such as alliances and incrementalism (Ch. 8).

10. The financial burdens of self-government are totally absent from theoretical consideration. It is tacitly assumed that people will levy taxes upon themselves, an argument often refuted by the defeat of tax referendums. Interestingly, in one example of successful neighborhood empowerment (Kotler 1971), it was the federal government that largely financed this experiment. Such fiscal reliance hardly suggests true self-determination.

11. A similar empowerment organization is the Empowerment Network Foundation. Here, too, the emphasis is on small-scale projects, particularly the training of public housing residents in skills to make them more employable. In common with the NCNE, funding is almost entirely private.

4

Uplifting the Needy

The urge to assist the less fortunate is surely a virtue, and charity is as ancient as the Old Testament. Deut. 15:11 proclaims, "[F]or the poor shall never cease out of the land; therefore I command thee, saying, thou shall open thine hand wide unto thy brother." Yet while the principle is sacrosanct, implementation is devilishly demanding. How is one to befriend? The most worthy assistance, on occasion, may be cold indifference. The Hebrew Talmud (Kethuboth, 67b) implores, "The man who refuses to live within his means, but seeks to be supported by charity, must not be helped." Indeed, careful restraint in rushing to aid the destitute long characterized American public charity (Olasky 1992, Ch. 1). The menu of profitable prescriptions is boundless and, alas, seldom straightforward. Not everything is effortlessly reducible to feeding a starving person. The most tight-fisted skinflint rightly insists that he or she is as authentically charitable as the most generous welfare state supporters. Desire to help implies nothing about what is to be done.

Empowerment in all of its distinct promulgations occupies but a paltry portion of the prescriptive menu. Mother Teresa and others famous for ministering to the less fortunate hardly spoke its vocabulary. In fact, empowerment's underlying premise—the needy must dictate their own destinies—stands well apart from our ameliorative legacy. Traditional remedies ordinarily interpret misfortune as prima facie proof of personal inadequacy. Sage superintendence, not autonomy, composes helpfulness. A heavy burden of proof thus falls on those advancing self-determination's novelty, for its record is undemonstrated. Empowerment must not only correct, but it must outshine proven alternatives while being cost-effective and consistent with democracy. That alleged ministration concerns desperate people mired in calamity makes this proof all that more pressing.

Inquiry into this new-sprung panacea proceeds as follows. First, we explore theoretical suppositions informing this prescription for personal adversity. The academic side of this movement (including professionals attuned to the academy) is our focus, not the more familiar idiosyncratic self-help impulse. This academic theorizing constitutes the bulk of empowerment rhapsodizing and is taken seriously, for without plausible theoretical justifications, this cure is an empty assurance. Why might we a priori expect the gaining of mastery over one's environment to secure individual improvement across multiple impairments? To reiterate, it is *personal* advancement of the misfortunate, not one's group or society more generally. Our review is skeptical; we expect sound theory and concrete proof, not mere hope.

Such justification can take many forms. The connection may be logical— power to control means gaining what one covets, so to enhance power is to achieve what is advantageous. Empowerment, ipso facto, enhances life. Or this linkage between control and betterment may reflect convincing empirical research—power, like other success prerequisites (money, prestige, etc.), demonstrably secures benefits. It is also conceivable that admonitions lack any underlying cogent reasoning and constitute a jumbled yet fervent exasperation reflecting past failures. As with the ill staring at sure death, desperation invites hope in the unfamiliar and unproven.

Examples of research in health improvement (broadly defined), ending poverty and reducing homelessness are then examined. Our focus will be on those enterprises that self-consciously, occasionally stridently, embrace empowerment trappings rather than endeavors merely interpretable as consistent with self-determination. As we shall see, this literature is remarkably thin in concrete examples despite the multiple well-voiced claims. Nevertheless, if empowerment is to be taken seriously, these exemplars deserve closer attention. The question is simply whether devotees have proven their case. This is, alas, deceptively complicated. Enabling schemes may have manifold—even shifting—goals. After all, poverty can be "solved" both by increasing wealth or, as has more often been the case traditionally, helping the destitute psychologically accept their dismal lot. And even wealth may not bring contentment, the nostrum's assumed ultimate purpose.

EMPOWERMENT AND PERSONAL BETTERMENT: THEORY

Previous chapters traced innumerable ambiguities coupled with contradictions and vagueness when empowerment disciples pleaded their cases. These conceptual inadequacies hardly vanish as we draw nearer theoretical exegesis. Perusing essay after essay portraying enhanced capacity as the universalistic curative reveals an unwillingness to grapple openly with pivotal assumptions. "Theory" is sometimes buried under an avalanche of jargon. One social worker limned her theoretical foundation as "practice theory [sic] that encompasses the knowledge of individual adaptive potentials, mutual and group processes and dynamics, and large scale and structural change, with special attention to concepts of empowerment on the personal, interpersonal and socio-economic political levels" (Lee 1991, 12). The efficacy of this instrument is, apparently, so matter-of-factly consensual gospel that teasing out explicit justification seems superfluous. Indeed, one paean implies that scientific rationality itself conspires *against* self-determination (Irwin 1996, Ch. 2). To exaggerate only slightly, it would be as if builders enthusiastically sought to construct a skyscraper disdaining blueprints or engineering knowledge. What, then, drives legions of reformers to link greater autonomous determination with personal betterment?

One popular argument fuses enhanced mastery or proficiency with empowerment. The task is for the dependent to gain ascendancy over obstacles, whether promoting careers or conquering a psychological debility. As one educator put it, "I am using the term empowerment to refer to the process through which students learn to critically appropriate knowledge existing outside their immediate experience in order to broaden their understanding of themselves, the world, and the possibility of transforming the taken-for-granted assumptions about the way we live" (McLaren 1989, 186).[1] In prosaic language, empowerment means adequate knowledge, commensurate competence. The oft-heard appeals to poor blacks to uplift themselves into prosperity by building on indigenous skills likewise exemplifies this "harness your ability" understanding (e.g., Loury 1987). The facilitator at a respectful distance provides overall guidance plus the resources—money, legal advice, etc.—necessary for fruition.

Thus deciphered, the empowerment-improvement nexus is virtually definitional—not empirical—in nature. "Success" is de facto conjoined with "empowerment" as in "an empowered person is somebody who has accomplished his or her aim." Try imagining in this context someone enabled who, nevertheless, failed. "Failed empowerment" is oxymoronic. A poor person desirous of riches who becomes well-to-do is thus, tautologically, truly capacitated, for he or she has mastered the economic challenge.

This interpretation is scarcely novel; the tangible prescription—become accomplished—is vacuous and is indistinguishable from exhortations to "be something worthy" or "take charge of your life." Cheerleading is commendable, but its merit hardly requires unique terminology. The real assignment is how *precisely* to secure victory. For a pauper seeking riches, all the vague pleading will come to naught without explicit—even forceful—guidance. Perhaps instead of repeating "empowerment" as poverty's cure, the missive should admonish frugality, punctuality, education and similar prosaic advice. Perhaps this amorphous infatuation betrays ignorance of useful specifics or a disdain for the conventional. To be sure, if detailed advice were given and heeded, and wealth secured, this process constitutes nothing more than humdrum "education" reclothed into something more fashionable.

A more superficially sophisticated theoretical justification anchors itself in self-interest. To this proficiency element are added uniquely defined personal goals. As one social worker put it: "Accepting the client's definition of the problem is an important element of an empowering intervention. . . . This technique also places the client in the position of power and control over the helping relationship" (Gutierrez 1990, 151). Recall feminist invitations for women to escape the lures of conventional and enervating stereotypes and to seek their special singular destinies. These need not be the socially desirable objectives customarily assumed by helpful outsiders. A freshly empowered feminist, for example, might quit her executive post and instead seek a career as a rock singer if this is truly desired.

The tacit logic is as follows. People inherently know (or can grasp through consciousness raising) their self-interest. These ends are incontestably worthy. The pursuit of one's own goals, no different than in selfish capitalism, will unleash enormous, newfound energy. Unfortunately, this release of dynamism is often blocked by innumerable factors, everything from bureaucratic inertia to racism. With obstacles removed, behavior becomes zestfully motivated by internal forces—greed, status—not the beseeching of experts. Fervid inner fire replaces (assumed) ineffectual external expectations, and goals are soon satisfied. Public housing tenants vandalizing their buildings, for example, will surely be more prudent if granted ownership. Now, goes the reasoning, maintenance efforts are financially lucrative, and assuredly everyone wants to be better off financially.

Counselors merely facilitate by removing roadblocks. This is clearly the modus operandi of community psychology and more radical invocations (see, e.g., Belcher and Hegar 1991). Conservative exhortations are similarly rooted in unlocking naked opportunism. A particular charm here is the veneration of personal autonomy, the underlying essence of empowerment. Although ends might be debated and vigorously promoted by experts, they cannot be imposed; the authority to choose one's lot is sacred. Self-determination, understood in this context, is value neutral and exclusively instrumental; it differs from the first "theory" in the centrality it affords egoism. No one value, for example, prosperity, is assumed a priori. Society becomes a grand "game" now—often thanks to empowerment intervention—played among equals where all compete to satisfy egotistical needs and desires.

As a rhetorical device, such egoism is unmatched. Yet as a justification for selecting one prescriptive remedy over worthy competitors, it quickly evaporates. Recall past warning on the mischievous impact of cultural relativism. The logic is far more a slogan—a glorification of hedonistic indulgence—than a device relevant to laborious deeds necessary to uplift. What is the sympathetic expert to say when a client intones "empower me to be affluent without working"? To demur violates the principle of autonomy. There is almost a magical quality about empowerment rhetoric in this context: Empowerment invocation, like voicing some occult incantation, promises instant escape from drudgery. It is patently obvious, moreover, that no society qua society could survive all indulgences. Are criminals to be uplifted into superior criminals? And surely there are those—children, the deranged—unsuited to make choices. For empowerers to argue that they are merely helping people nonjudgmentally attain what they want foretells a disaster in which the ultimate outcome will be mayhem, not accomplishment.

To reiterate a theme requiring constant repeating, would-be recipients of empowerment assistance are frequently those whose inept decision making has consigned them to distress. To wit, if homeless substance abusers *were* able to choose wisely, their current predicament would cease. Hence, to cater to their desires may well compound their infirmity. And it cannot be assumed, as is common, that the needy can *ever* achieve independence. A more worthy strategy might be to insist that their appetites are improper and conduct must be painfully contrary to unsuitable desire. Dependency on wiser heads, not independence, is the best refuge. Remember the warning of Chapter 2 regarding what can happen when the powerless are abruptly given control—mayhem, not betterment, may ensue.

A third possible, and more empirically anchored, linkage between empowerment and personal improvement centers on a psychological sense of control. This is both a broad outlook and a collection of multiple, overlapping, more detailed, research-based psychological theories (Zimmerman [1995] delineates these intertwined concepts). Our review can only highlight. One literature centers on people's estimation of control over their lives as empowerment's impetus (see Lefcourt 1966, 1972 for an overview). This perspective roughly sorts people into two types. Some believe that they themselves dictate their fate (a condition technically deemed "internal" since the locus of determination resides within). For "internals" life is generally self-understood as mastering challenges, and critically, this belief translates into behavior. Among traits relevant to proficiency, internals are inclined to acquire new information, are bettered attuned to their environments, are academically superior, adapt more successfully to fluid conditions and handle failure more adroitly (Lefcourt 1972). In contrast are "externals": those attributing their destiny to luck, predestination, machinations of unreachable others and similar unmanageable forces. When confronted with a challenge, externals easily surrender, feel overwhelmed or otherwise behave passively. Psychologically, externals usually lack self-confidence and feel inferior while prone to high-risk, low-reward behavior. Particularly relevant is the oft-documented correlation between control location and worldly success; being internal breeds empowerment, and empowerment brings tangible accomplishment.

The prescription requires people to feel that they, not others, are in charge. In conventional language, this is the precept of internalizing personal responsibility. The poor person must feel that their personal action—showing up for work promptly, for example—not a rescue by outside forces or winning the lottery, will bring rewards. Feelings of despair, helplessness and alienation are to be replaced by self-confidence in one's own ability.

This acquisition of inner control–related beliefs has other theoretical relatives. The most famous, undoubtedly, revolves around "self-esteem." Here having a positive self-image, a sense of self-worth, is a precondition for the energy necessary for accomplishment. While internal versus external personality type theory stressed beliefs about efficacy, here the emphasis is on internal *affective* states. It is this emotion-laden self-definition that, supposedly, instigates the quest toward mastery. After all, how is one to pursue schooling successfully if, for example, one presumes oneself (falsely, it is assumed) to be intellectually worthless or an unsavory group member? Enabling fundamentally begins with self-transformation; facilitators (teachers, community activists) are to reverse debilitating internal psychological conditions. Invigorated self-esteem "jump-starts" the march toward accomplishment.

This infatuation with enhanced self-esteem infuses legions of today's educational effort aimed at uplifting the disadvantaged. Multicultural education, especially as directed toward women, African Americans and Hispanics, deeply embraces this logic. These groups (among others) are shortchanged by society, and a major culprit of this inequality, goes the argument, is that society at large inculcates all too easily absorbed negative stereotypes. Indeed, one proposed solution for combating AIDS among African Americans frames the prescription almost entirely in terms of dropping negative stereotypes of American black sexuality and awarding greater respect to positive African self-images (Stevenson 1994; similar advice regarding AIDS also has been offered to women—Highsmith 1997). Debilitation is both external—discriminatory laws, for example—and internal—negative self-perception. For instance, young blacks are kept unaware of black success in "white" fields like science and business. A self-fulfilling prophesy is thus created whereby expectations of failure generate yet more inadequacy. Why even try if "everyone" frankly believes exertion to be pointless? The capacitating path is to reverse this self-depreciation and cultivate positive achievement expectations.

Yet another self-transformation theory favors the term *self-efficacy*: "people's beliefs in their capacity to mobilize the motivation, cognitive resources, and courses of action needed to exercise control over given events"

(Ozer and Bandura 1990). Supposedly, self-efficacy translates into noteworthy behavior. Those lacking a well-developed sense of self-efficacy may avoid surmountable challenges, they likely shun potentially useful situations and they might be needlessly overcome with injurious anxiety. On the other hand, where self-efficacy sense is stronger, accomplishment efforts will be more vigorous and persistent. Skills will also be more effectively translated into action (Ozer and Bandura 1990). To believe in one's effectiveness is a precondition for real power. Extrapolating to empowerment is straightforward: The enhancement of self-efficacy will encourage those behaviors that bring the bountiful rewards craved by everyone.

Whether genuine empowerment, not mere wishful thinking fantasy, via modification of self-perception and belief can be taught is a complicated and momentous empirical question. Some experts believe it can be instructed and take that datum as an unquestioned starting point (especially Bandura 1986, 422–449). Nevertheless, convincing evidence on the alleged benefits derived from transformation exercises are hardly self-evident. Laboratory experiments with college students are not automatically generalizable to troubled populations. The debate is not whether being "internal" or having self-confidence enhances performance, particularly among the underperforming who have the potential competence. That much is well documented. The question is whether "manufactured" mental states, conditions that did not exist "naturally," among those with insufficient capacity, possess the identical potency. One extensive overview of research (Skinner 1995, Ch. 12) suggests that objective conditions (talent, the environment) *cannot* be overcome via manipulation of beliefs. Put differently, assuming that these internal transformations are teachable, how much upgrading can these "lessons" bestow? Going from a "D" in mathematics to a "C−" is progress, but this remains a long way from "A"-level work. If empowerment via jump-starting one's belief in mastery were a potent prescription drug, it would undoubtedly still be under review in small clinical trials, given the paucity of confirming documentation.

Furthermore, the direction of causality here is quite tangled, possibly forever indiscernible. This perplexing dilemma is, alas, often brushed aside in the rush to uplift, yet it is of the utmost importance. To chart intimate associations between beliefs in success and favorable outcomes is *not* to prove that real-world accomplishment begins with psychological refurbishment. The *reverse* flow is, obviously, just as plausible if not more so: Achievement builds self-confidence. Internals are that way as a *consequence* of surmounting obstacles. In fact, this cause-and-effect relationship might be highly iterative—some inner psychological state might initially inspire accomplishment, and then this success encourages yet more self-confidence, producing yet more feelings of competence. But the independent utility of boosted self-confidence apart from any observable action might be slight.

To convince those justifiably plagued by feelings of inadequacy that they are rightfully competent surely invites disappointment, even anger.

A quite different type of underlying theorizing connecting empowerment with overcoming individual predicaments stresses political change as the medication. Two versions of this "politics as cure" theory are prevalent—one relatively narrow, the other more sweeping. The first, more restrained version, centers on *control* of strictly political institutions—elected positions, bureaucracies, courts and so on—and political mobilization as a precondition for bestowing betterment. The ill-fated will be uplifted when, thanks to empowerment, valuable public resources—education, welfare, police protection, housing—are redirected. The political institutions and the attendant economic foundations are left intact; one set of participants and/ or policies merely replaces another, and this shift brings betterment. The aim is not revolution but a redistribution of society's prizes.

The familiar spectacle of community activists instigating citizen pressure to close a toxic waste dump or supply a day care program exemplifies this mechanism.[2] African Americans often favor this supposition when invoking community empowerment. One demands, government responds; to remain silent is to be helpless. LaVeist (1992, 1993) implicitly affirms this cosmology when he examines the relationship between black local political attainment, that is, black control of political offices, and black infant mortality rates. It is assumed, though never directly demonstrated, that political "muscle" translates into superior services. To wit, black-dominated cities devote greater resources to inadequate education and comparable problems that disproportionally ravage African Americans. LaVeist's hypothesis is confirmed. A variant is advocacy training as empowerment. It is assumed that the powerful possess what is needed to correct the misfortune of the powerless. The trick, then, is to extract it. In one study aptly named "Empowering People with Physical Disabilities Through Advocacy Training Skills" the disadvantaged are sensitized on procuring superior services by exerting pressure (Balcazar et al. 1990). They succeed. In a nutshell, the desire for advancement coupled with achieving political power can yield improved lives.

A second, and far more ambitious, politics-based theoretical linkage, one common to the feminist and egalitarian notions of empowerment depicted in Chapter 3, stresses the broader structure of society—the laws and power distributions—in shaping personal outcomes. Here individual misfortunes such as homelessness or chronic health problems are "built in" to the very gist of society. The needy are not "troubled" or "deficient"; they merely suffer maltreatment. In fact, those once characterized as wretched are now portrayed as "oppressed." In this grand scheme, a smattering of election victories only begins a protracted campaign to alter society fundamentally. Inadequate shelter, it is asserted, flows from capitalistic banking practices discouraging investment in affordable housing and economic exploitation of the vulnerable. Necessary is the transformation of foundational structures—the economy, political decision making, the status hierarchy and social relationships. This vision is quite radical, not merely demanding black or Hispanic local political control. Customized ameliorative person-to-person charitylike remedies are irrelevant. Concentrating on a single person's unique misfortune, whether this is a lack of skill or a poor self-image, only *subverts* reform by detracting from the calamity's deeper sources; one should not learn to cope with a bad system.

This "genuine empowerment means changing the system" is surely alluring for those feeling overwhelmed and frustrated by the limits of individual action. Yet, less obviously, it is a double-edged sword for headway. Imagine a young mother on welfare advised: "Your plight is entirely due to society's racism, sexism and adherence to capitalism; only a sweeping upheaval can improve your distress." A perfectly reasonable response would be to sink deeper in feelings of helplessness. Now, alas, the obstacles are absolutely crushing and would, even under ideal circumstances, require decades to overthrow. Even if several thousands of these "victims" combined, these monstrous conditions remain daunting. "Blaming the system" may be comforting therapy, but it is a formula hardly useful to counsel, to daily hunger or to imminent eviction.

These politics-based ameliorative conceptualizations, even those calling for wholesale change, resemble a more conventional depiction of politics called pluralism—groups battling over benefits within a democratic framework. Empowerment, regardless of scope, is but the pursuit of self-interest, typically economic gain. Only the invitation for the once-excluded, notably minorities and women, to play the game more vigorously is new. It is assumed that power, in and of itself, is sufficient to deliver the desired change. If only one commands high political office or the banks, this authority over levers and buttons will cure everything from homelessness to AIDS. That some problems remain unamenable to political solutions is seldom, if ever, confronted. Guiding experts are imbued with vast knowledge to assist the downtrodden much like a coach would help a novice athlete against formidable foes.

A difficult issue embedded in this enterprising conceptualization is the role assigned to outside facilitators. Recall our caution from Chapter 2: Depictions of "empowerment" via mobilizing political strength may well disguise cooptation or even manipulation. For the sick to obtain better health care or the homeless to gain shelter need not require any political triumphs, let alone "fundamental" political change or egalitarianism. Relief via politics is but a single choice on a measureless menu. Hectoring the wealthy to fulfill their traditional paternalistic charity obligations could bestow identical material benefits. Moreover, given that empowerment definitionally means a substantial degree of personal autonomy in ends, for these experts to thrust the unsophisticated toward venturesome political projects is hardly authentic empowerment. After all, the typical poverty-stricken person is unlikely to independently attempt to revamp minimum wage laws, let alone overthrow capitalism to relieve their misery. Such sweeping objectives undoubtedly reflect leftist academic agendas. Even if the indigent did fleetingly consider themselves oppressed by the class structure, they will likely disdain such grandiose solutions. Truly left to their own inclinations they might well pursue more prosaic alternatives, for instance, moving in with relatives. Remember our warning from Chapter 2 about how troubled people can be conscripted into ideological movements not of their own making.

Clearly, empowerment nostrums claiming to uplift troubled individuals hardly rest on scientific laws. Many—perhaps most—schemes are nearly bereft of explicit, systematic conceptual foundations. Where justifications are more forthcoming, lacuna abound. At most, bits and pieces of hard evidence are conjoined with hardy measures of trusting plausibility. We are told, for example, that self-confident people are inclined to gain the rewards of empowerment, but this does not certify that the hapless can be exhorted into self-sufficiency. Similarly, demonstrating that the affluent are disproportionately politically active is not solid evidence that prosperity's path goes through capturing civic position. Contradictory arguments also plague this collection of "theory." For example, some devotees stress teaching their clients that their plight lies in "the system" and counsel against "blaming the victim." Yet other empowerment scholars, sometimes within the identical inclination, insist that empowerment requires that people internalize control over their own destinies.[3] How are we to venerate a hardheaded reality-testing skill while tolerating contrived "facts" to flatter self-esteem? If political movements will bring forth bountifulness, why diligently sharpen talents?

Nor are these theories pitted against alternative contrivances to test relative effectiveness. Empowerment, it would seem, is implicitly advanced against the apathy option (and passivity itself is never judged a feasible choice) or some unknown obviously inferior competitor. This differs from the customary scientific practice of assessing one theory's utility against rivals. Equally pertinent, the aligning of designs with maladies is haphazard. One practitioner may prescribe increases in self-esteem for a difficulty; another favors a political solution for the same deficiency. Choices apparently reflect taste, not analysis. Imagine if modern medicine took this approach—physicians dispensing their pet drugs regardless of the disease. Yet theoretical insufficiency aside, the true test is results. After all, weak theorizing need not preclude worldly success—favorable outcomes may occur for reasons unknown to those preaching empowerment doctrines. The proof is in the pudding.

EMPOWERMENT AND PERSONAL BETTERMENT: PRACTICE

Improving Health

The pathways toward improved health are multitudinous, and most are irrelevant to empowerment. Regardless of one's personal capacity, diseases are now escaped thanks to improved sanitation, food purity standards, prohibiting dangerous substances, professionally trained doctors, inexpensive plenteous food and effective medicine. Modern society's overall prosperity also contributes insofar as abundance facilitates well-being. Even helpless, disadvantaged citizens enjoys vitality unknown a century ago solely by existing in a community that, for instance, purifies its drinking water, pasteurizes milk, requires refrigeration of food and can afford technologically adept hospitals. This top-down, imposed healthiness, no doubt, explains most of our advancement. Indeed, as health professionals often lament, outside of uncontrollable genetic disorders, many illness antecedents—smoking, alcoholism, obesity, inactivity, disinterest in prevention—must be *pursued*.

Moreover, even conceding serious health shortfalls, individual self-determination is not the sole regimen. Paternalism, empowerment's opposite, can surely assist the ill, and this stratagem has long been popular. Inspiring citizens to "play doctor" is foolish; autonomy and health are not intimately connected. Those who, for example, insist on drunkenness or addiction can be committed involuntarily; medication can be forcibly administered and unhealthy behaviors criminalized. The Chinese once rid themselves of narcotics not by empowering citizens but by executing addicts. Democracies have traditionally coerced their citizens toward improved health—compulsory childhood vaccinations, obligatory automobile seatbelts and airbags, confinement and mandatory treatment for contagious disease carriers and health certificates for those contemplating marriage. Bribery and threats can also promote healthful behavior—for example, lower insurance rates for nonsmokers or stigmatizing overeaters. Paternalistic charity in which the helpless are condescendingly assisted remains as viable as ever. To contend that empowerment is *essential* to the substantial advancement of health ignores reality; it is only one of many options.

Furthermore, not everyone seeks ever more wellness, particularly at the margin. Riskiness is not guaranteed suicide. People may self-consciously and reasonably forgo slight improvements in favor of momentary enjoyment—smoking, overeating—or allocate money that might be spent on health to other requirements, even worthy ones such as education. What some deem "unhealthy" may well be a deeply cherished cultural trait, for example, a sedentary lifestyle or eating fat-laden foods. And if empowerment means unquestioned autonomy, who can say that self-inflected indisposition is wrong?[4] Equating imperfect health with powerlessness is mistaken. A self-reliant person may have the capacity to get regular checkups but may choose otherwise. Indeed, executing this option is far more consistent with the ideals of self-determination than coercing the ill into treatment programs.

Nevertheless, several general hypotheses link heightened fitness risk to helplessness. One emphasizes the material aspects of the environment. Most notably, a connection exists between poorer health and being at the bottom economic rungs of society or membership in low-status racial or ethnic groups. Writing in the prestigious *Journal of the American Medical Association*, Braithwaite and Lythcott (1989) intone, "Poverty of the spirit and of resources remains *the* antecedent risk factor of preventable disease" (282; italics in the original). Explanations of this nexus abound: The poor typically cannot afford superior care, they are discriminated against in the distribution of medical resources (e.g., clinic locations), they receive treatment from inept novice practitioners or their particular afflictions are ignored in research. Other accounts center on education—the poor are uninformed about ailments, are less capable of seeking assistance and may be unnecessarily suspicious of health care professionals. Unwise health habits themselves contribute to poverty. Steady gainful employment may be nearly unreachable for those bedeviled by illness or inclined toward risky habits or incapacitating indulgences.

Less tangible factors conjoin being empowered and enjoying superior well-being. Psychology is critical, not mere access to care facilities or other material resources. For example, U.S. and Swedish studies show that workers in higher-stress employment lacking control over their tasks suffer disproportionate heart disease, even after taking contributing factors such as smoking and obesity into account (cited in Wallerstein 1992; more generally, see O'Leary 1985). Stress conjoined with powerlessness, not stress per se, is the culprit. Similarly, nursing home residents evince better health when participating in choices shaping their medical treatments. More generally, those who feel "in charge" of their situations have greater feelings of mastery, typically enjoy greater health (Wallerstein 1992). These psychological factors can strongly combine with material circumstances. To wit, poor black women not only may lack access to quality doctors, but the burdens of coping with a troublesome environment—crime, a disruptive family life, dilapidated housing—make physical and mental illness endemic (Gibbs and Fuery 1994).

These helplessness and health links take on greater urgency as traditional top-down, technologically based techniques falter in assisting "at-risk" populations. Extending public health or commissioning more doctors can help only to a point. Advancement requires people to possess the wherewithal to make themselves healthier, not inventing yet one more miracle drug. The potential intervention targets are plentiful. Minority inner-city residents, prone to despair and alienation, often suffer innumerable illnesses (including addiction and violence), although cures are readily available elsewhere, often at minimal cost. Isolated rural populations plus many of the elderly suffer a similar fate—the problem is not technological but bringing relief to the indigent. Empowerment thus becomes a catalyst to engage the ill with the rewards of modern medicine. As John L. McKnight put it, "Our research indicates that it is impossible to produce health among the powerless. It is possible to allow health by transferring tools, authority, budgets and income to those with the malady of powerlessness" (McKnight 1985, 38). In sum, power, not insistent expertise, is the prescription.

How is this empowerment to be concretely achieved? One especially prevalent strategy draws deeply on the writings of Brazilian educator Paulo Freire, a successful organizer of literacy programs for Brazilian slum dwellers. His oft-cited work constitutes a popular blueprint for enablement, informing dozens of field projects, and deserves closer attention. Freire contends that traditional education is not value neutral, particularly for the poor who are inevitably socially and economically subservient. Instructing the poor to improve their diets, for example, confirms them in a familiar situation: powerlessness. This passivity-breeding condition will surely fail and is thus the crux of the problem. Education is to be human liberation: Pupils are not empty vessels passively receiving knowledge but creators of enlightenment. Dialogues are to replace monologues. Effective instruction must have a participatory orientation engendering a capacity for critical thinking. The social and economic roots of their plight must be grasped. Eventually, teacher and pupil become co-investigators to interpret their communal adversities and formulate collective social action agendas.

This engagement, this fresh awareness of surrounding oppression, inspires beliefs of capacity to change. This radical stance calls for challenging traditional hierarchies and received knowledge. In the case of health specifically, "the goals of the health promotion program must be carefully examined to determine whether it subtly fosters dependence and powerlessness, or whether it enables participants to be decision makers and assume responsibility for their own programs and curriculums" (Wallerstein 1992, 204). Armed with this newfound awareness of how forces conspire to subordinate people, assisted by experts attentive to their co-equal pupils' wants, action toward betterment will now transpire.

Does this program work? More specifically, are those who receive this instruction healthier than before? This is a stern but inescapable standard. Consider a few exemplars. The Adolescent Social Action Program (ASAP) is intended to address health problems among low-income, high-risk students in a multiethnic New Mexico community (Wallerstein 1993; Wallerstein and Bernstein 1988). This project, sponsored by the University of New Mexico School of Medicine, organized small groups of teenage volunteers to converse with patients and their families in hospitals as well as visit substance abusers in county detention centers and others experiencing troubles. This personal contact is supplemented by talks with sundry medical professionals. Student volunteers learn, among other things, coping and communication skills, how to personalize the consequences of unhealthy behavior, peer communication ability and how to analyze various media and social policies (e.g., how liquor is sold in New Mexico).

According to project practitioners, this endeavor differs substantially from superficially similar programs designed to scare at-risk teenagers by, say, visiting hospital emergency rooms to witness drunk driving aftermaths. The key difference is the emphasis on the youngsters' "feelings, their world view, and their solutions to the problems they face in their communities" (Wallerstein 1993, 223). These teenagers are not merely objects to be intimidated; they are equals in seeking deeper understanding. Moreover, these volunteers are being inspired to become school and community leaders, address younger pupils and discuss (assisted with videos) their experiences with teenagers outside the school. In one videotaped role-playing episode a frank discussion transpires with liquor store owners, police paramedics, ex-addicts and others about local community problems. Untold hours are spend conversing with addicts and their families. Critical thinking about these terrible conditions is drawn to the surface by expert facilitators. The aim is to analyze the surrounding environment. Finally, students are asked, How can you serve? What changes should be implemented? Which strategies might be pursued?

Only the slightest trace of demonstrated accomplishment informs this project—not a single before-and-after statistical comparison of addiction; not even anecdotal tales of going straight. Where assessment is attempted, it wholly concerns *attitudes*. Even self-reports of change focused on new-found attentiveness to risk, not discernable action (Wallerstein and Bernstein 1988). Heightened consciousness, not behavioral change, is the great victory. The project's apparent aim is psychological transformation; the tangible benefit of improved health being totally assumed. As Wallerstein expressed it. ". . . [A] Freirian-community inspired community education or development program would incorporate a philosophy of personal and social transformation with people who often experience societal inequalities, cultural conflicts or powerlessness" (Wallerstein 1993, 225). This infatuation with attitudes is not preordained. Data abound from police reports, liquor sales and similar "hard" sources.

Three further brief points are worth noting. First, the project's intrinsic design, the absence of measurement of noncontestable, demonstrable effects, makes rigorous assessment *impossible*. The empowerment hypothesis can never be rejected because failure (or success) cannot be measured precisely. One might speculate that this obvious methodological weakness betrays a more overriding concern with "stirring up" discontent than truly eliminating the pathologies. Second, all these participants are *volunteers*. The most needy are, probably, unwilling to join preventive programs. No evidence is given of reaching out to those most in danger, and we cannot assume that the nostrum would be any more (or less) successful. Third, the opportunity costs are never assessed. The utility of this multiyear project is *never* compared to a reasonable alternative, for example, tougher police enforcement of drug and alcohol laws. The undertaking's cost must have been substantial, given all the professional medical personnel participation, yet is treated as "free." This is not to assert that all the effort was wasteful; rather, the empowerment claim is not even seriously scrutinized, let alone confirmed.

This sort of mentality is hardly atypical. A similar Freire-based approach informs two well-funded health-related empowerment projects executed with poor people outside the United States. The first was organized in rural Peru in the mid-1980s and sought to involve semiliterate peasant women in health and family planning programs (Wang and Burris 1994). Coloring books were distributed depicting familiar village situations, including its unpleasant side (violence, alcoholism). These line drawings guided group discussions, including some of the social and economic forces shaping communal life. As the pictures were colored in (individually and in groups), village and personal wellness–related issues were discussed with facilitators. When the women finished the coloring books, the last page awarded them a diploma.

Women completing this exercise expressed satisfaction with their feat. Self-confidence increased, and a few entered a literacy program. In some communities women even continued to meet and talk after the intervention program formally ended. Perhaps most important, inspired by their discussions, women took action: They worked to bring health care closer and assist those women suffering from domestic violence. Yet and this is the bottom line, no evidence is presented regarding enhanced health. It is not even clear whether soliciting resources succeeded. What is presented is a story of impoverished women coloring, discussing pictures and then awakening to shortcomings in community resources. Needless to say, measuring improved health—even health utilization—is eminently straightforward.

A further example concerns rural Chinese women empowered to better their reproductive health (Wang and Burris 1994). Here the vehicle was the photo novella—a collection of amateur photographs depicting everyday village scenes. According to these outside experts, "Photo novellas envisions a self-defined space that would diverge from depictions by outsiders superimposed on a culturally charged background. The women's own words represent their own lives as they see them and speak about them" (Wang and Burris 1994, 180). Sixty-two peasant women in 50 villages received free cameras, film was shipped off for development and the resultant snapshots focused group deliberation. These candid photos, according to the plan, allowed the women to proffer their side of the story and present a documentary record of their lives and obstacles to higher officials (the women were also paid for their efforts). Typical images showed toddlers accompanying their mothers in fields or caring for their siblings.

Again, this empowerment rendering is but coaxing the disadvantaged to voice dissatisfactions. "Agitation" might be a more appropriate term. No demonstration of improved well-being is offered, and given the research design, this proof is unobtainable. Ironically, this "empowerment" de facto means appealing to higher authorities for relief, not independent action. Health is to be enhanced not by correcting one's diet or engaging in exercise; the benefits of wellness are to be handed down from above, thanks to clamor inspired by Ford Foundation–funded academics (the Chinese project sponsor). These outside facilitators are, frankly, more akin to lawyers coaching pleaders than instructors encouraging independence.

Other empowerment projects resemble Freire-based enterprises despite differences in theoretical nomenclature. Fawcett and his associates recount an extensive, well-funded undertaking in three Kansas communities to combat teenage substance abuse (Fawcett et al. 1995). Enhancing the community's empowerment capacity was the overall objective. This involved enlisting numerous civic leaders plus professionals from health care, community development and the behavioral sciences. Coalitions assessed available resources and identified potential barriers to success. Frequent town meetings, small group discussions and several surveys supplied pertinent information. No interest was excluded—meetings were organized in places as disparate as public housing projects and military bases. Several feasible interventions were deliberated—extended hours for recreational programs, peer assistance programs, for example—and these were reviewed by divergent people embodying a wide expanse of experiences and values. Various undertakings soon came forth to meet local conditions (a one-day health fair, a Saturday school for youths and so on). Programs were also established to enlist students to assist.

Progress was gauged by measures taken to combat drug abuse. Over time, accomplishments such as a local radio station banning songs glamorizing drugs or training ministers in substance abuse prevention rose substantially. These were closely monitored by staff members. Between January 1993, when the project commenced, to early 1995, the number of varied community empowerment projects another had risen from zero to about 25 (Fawcett et al. 1995, 691). Yet, to recite a familiar motif, actual substance abuse levels remained beyond investigation. Prevention *effort* was, definitionally, taken as *the* successful outcome. Raging communal drug epidemics would have escaped observation given study design. Empowerment was exclusively hypothetical potential. Finally, the oft-repeated axiom of heeding the client's desires was never debated or followed. The project's aim was imposed sans any discussion of ultimate purpose. Perhaps these Kansas adolescents coveted drug addiction.

This empowerment rhetoric to depict a disguised top-down remediation program is hardly unique. Let us be clear on what is being done. Imposed aims, even if deceptively stated, may be absolutely, incontestably laudable. Fraud may even be occasionally necessary. We surely cannot argue that adolescents should be asked about their cravings, and if drug addiction is the answer, facilitators should assist this goal. The point concerns the labeling of such deception as "empowerment." After all, falsely steeping the imposition as "self-determined" may ultimately be exposed, angering those being manipulated. Forthright paternalism may be more advantageous in achieving aims.

This clash between experts "bringing" health and people's autonomous ideas regarding their well-being are well illustrated in an extensive rural Georgia intervention program (Jenkins 1991). The quandary is improving well-being among those with restricted access to modern medicine—especially the poor, the elderly and physically isolated—in areas undergoing economic dislocation. Given that doctors and hospitals rarely flock to these rural counties, the solution, quite reasonably, is for residents to exhibit greater initiative and self-reliance. This is certainly the rhetoric that infuses the enterprise. We are informed that "[c]ommunity wellness programs teach people, step by step, to identify problems, consider alternatives, and plan solutions. The advantage of this self-help approach is that citizens determine what is to be done, and in the process they learn both how to achieve a specific task and how to accomplish future goals" (Jenkins 1991, 396). In short, the classic empowerment formula.

To this exhortation of self-determination is joined an extensive, generously funded bureaucratic apparatus to enhance health. Largely through the Georgia Cooperative Extension Service, varied services are offered. There are workshops for stress reduction, programs to reduce heart disease risk (including convenient free cholesterol and blood pressure screening), periodic public health fairs to dispense advice and counseling, resource guides prepared and distributed, enhanced training for rescue workers regarding farm accidents, plus efforts to recruit health professionals to these rural areas. Local meetings involving all community segments, from local fraternal organizations to medical practitioners, are also frequently scheduled. A county-based Community Wellness Council oversees planning and implementation. Data on both community needs and outcomes are constantly gathered and dispatched to the state for analysis. A 650-page manual covered this multitude of programs and complex relationships.

Yet the announced vision may cloak the more conventional noblesse oblige mentality. The supremacy of expertise is laid bare when local desires collide with professional opinion. In one instance, vital statistics revealed that the major health problems in a county were cardiovascular diseases, cancer and motor vehicle accidents. Local surveys, on the other hand, acknowledged some of these problems but also identified alcohol-drug abuse, AIDS, teenage pregnancy and health care cost as pressing problems. Rather than accede to client agenda definitions, the issue was forwarded to the local Wellness Council for further consultation. In another case, public meeting participants expressed concern over teenage pregnancy. But since experts decided that this topic had "racial overtones," it was dropped from the agenda. More generally, it is difficult to imagine how these unsophisticated Georgians can impose their definitions of "good health" if outside specialists disagree. This obedience may be wondrous for health, but it does not speak to the virtues of empowerment. Claims to the contrary, the terminology of empowerment masks a benign, well-intentioned co-optation.[5]

A further example of utilizing empowerment language to impose a rather conventional medical regimen is Feste and Anderson's (1995) recommendation of patient autonomy to manage chronic diabetes. This is a serious, life-threatening disease requiring constant, careful attention to diet and medication. Feste and Anderson disagree with the established medical approach emphasizing medication and technology designed to limit patient autonomy. For them, successful management "requires that patients be able to make choices that will help them achieve their personal and health-related goals" (140). More specifically, diabetes suffers "are helped to examine and clarify the emotional, social, cognitive, and spiritual components of their lives as they relate to decisions that they must make about their health" (140).

Health professionals can only facilitate, not impose, the unfolding of this wellness giving self-mastery. Expert-supplied contrivances include educational books and videotapes plus organizing self-help groups in which patients can define their support needs and elicit comfort from fellow plight suffers. Patients are encouraged to question their personal philosophy and lifetime dreams in the context of their impaired situation. Nurses and doctors may also step outside their narrow professional roles and share their personal feelings with clients. Other empowering behaviors include modifying one's language so as to encourage the making of choices and using stories—even biblical tales—as a means of discovering one's unique inner strength.

Unfortunately, despite the allure of this "take charge of your own cure" admonition, the evidence on its efficacy is nonexistent. It may perform wonders, but oration aside, we cannot tell. And once again, determining benefits scientifically would not be especially baffling if the study were properly designed. Moreover, all the celebration of empowerment obscures a profound ethical dilemma in the doctor-patient relationship. Both by law and by their Hippocratic Oath, doctors must take every possible measure to ensure patient improvement. This may be daunting, but the responsible cannot be disowned. Let us not confuse a degree of negotiated latitude with self-determination. A patient insisting upon autonomy cannot command medical professionals to obey. In fact, the very idea of self-determination in a well-delineated medical matter such as diabetes may be illusionary. A diabetes sufferer rejecting established therapeutic procedure would surely be scolded or coaxed into compliance. For a medical practitioner to recommend that those in need should be encouraged "to play doctor" is surely disingenuous if not irresponsible.

Braithwaite and his associates present similar empowerment "triumphs" for health care though the particular vocabulary varies somewhat (Braithwaite, Bianchi and Taylor 1994). Here the focus is on modifying the community environment as the path toward enhanced individual wellness. The root causes of debility, it is argued, flow from poor agency service, lack of service or discrimination. Change must come from the community itself, given that those who control society are scarcely interested in those below. Improved health thus requires community mobilization, and this is to be accomplished in a program entitled Community Organization and Development (COD) that will increase "healthy lifestyle behavior, [increase] total years of productive life, and [decrease] morbidity and excess deaths in communities of colour" (408).

The COD approach proclaims the usual elements of empowerment: "self-determination, shared decision-making, bottoms-up planning, community problem solving, cultural relevance, a debunking the blaming of victims syndrome" (408). Success will come, the authors contend, when those at risk identify their own problems and formulate their own cures. Techniques emphasize the collection of data from the community itself via using key informants, focus groups, analysis of existing records and so on. Understanding community needs in the local context is critical. And in addition to the amelioration of disorders, this COD plan will further the emergence of indigenous leadership, spill over into other quality-of-life issues—promoting social justice, literacy, improved housing, recreation and education. Most fundamentally, the goal is to organize the community to reduce physical disease risk factors and promote freedom from disease.

Several ongoing COD interventions are reviewed. A Hartford, Connecticut, program involves two housing projects occupied primarily by African Americans and Puerto Ricans. Among the programs organized were a community health fair, a household health survey and a campaign against rodent infestations. Eventually, this informal COD group was incorporated as a nonprofit organization and sought municipal grants and other handouts for a local health clinic. A similar endeavor of community forums, observations and planning workshops was instigated in Atlanta, Georgia, although here the collection of information highlighted drug abuse awareness.

The most ambitious projects were then conducted in three communities (two suburban, one inner-city) under a W. K. Kellogg Foundation grant.

The approach "was conceptualized as a system change and paradigm shift model for facilitating collaboration for health programming wherein the community residents have a dominant voice in all major decision points" (410). Participants included two local health departments, a school of public health and a medical school. Over a many-months period, community leaders were identified and interviewed and coalitions created with the appropriate by-laws, memorandums of understanding and articles of incorporation to delineate roles and responsibilities. Considerable effort was spent getting to know the community—even driving through it during the night and conducting informal interviews. Informal social events were also scrutinized for clues on how to assist. This huge volume of information on needs and resources then was utilized to plan health programs.

And what emerged from this extensive enterprise? The account is by now all too familiar. In the case of the last and most ambitious well-funded empowerment intervention, the researchers discovered that smoking, drug abuse and the disproportionate placement of African-American children in "developmentally delayed" classrooms were community-perceived problems. How remarkable. And while health outreach efforts often transpired, no evidence is presented on their impact. None. In fact, stripping away the rhetoric, these efforts resemble the prosaic wellness efforts long practiced by bureaucratic health organizations, for example, antismoking campaigns. Nor was there any concrete evidence of ordinary people shaping policy— everything was seemingly "sold" to those to be uplifted. Finally, and confirming the idée fixe of black empowerment, all action is ultimately directed to extracting money from above. Citizens are empowered not for independence but to be more forceful and skilled in enticing government generosity.

Our final excursion into empowered health enhancement involves mental illness, particularly its more debilitating forms. The exemplar examined here is unusual in its attention to theoretical issues and relentless, wide-ranging pursuit of information (McLean 1995). Equally atypical is its balance and open-mindedness—almost clinical detachment—regarding the efficacy of self-determination as a cure. While it is impossible to say whether the results are typical, it is clear that if the empowerment's benefits were to be discerned accurately, they would have been revealed here.

The backdrop to this account is the energetic movement within the mental health profession, reinforced by government edicts plus alliances of user-family associations, to empower patients. Indeed, the theme of the mentally ill playing a vital role in their cure, even having full access to their records, has now become a project of the World Health Organization (Bertolote 1993) On its face, this "take charge of one's fate" idea seems eminently attractive. Nevertheless, the aim, predictably, is often ambiguous and contentious in concrete application. In some instances, this entailed giving therapy recipients a (undefined) greater voice in their treatment. Patients are thus akin to consumers who might legitimately dispute services received or their cost. A quite opposite understanding sees the mentally ill as empowered to escape professional assistance altogether—gaining normalcy independently or by selecting among nontraditional remedies. This may, of course, conflict with laws regarding the institutionalization of those judged dangerous or the practice of fraudulent medicine. Empowerment in this mental illness context also receives a political flavor—a coalition of patients and professionals organizing to secure more plentiful resources. The terms might also mean obtaining greater community acceptance of psychiatric disability or escaping one's stigma of mental illness. This hardly exhausts the conceptual possibilities. In principle, all are valid interpretations, although, as the case study makes clear, acrimonious contradictions are unavoidable.

The study sought to determine whether an outpatient mental health affiliate explicitly committed to empowerment could deliver its promise. This facility was the "Quad," a storefront "drop-in" resource center in a small urban setting, nominally administered by a large, bureaucratically run state mental health agency. The Quad's explicit mission included encouraging client empowerment by developing their independence and skills while simultaneously advocating the cause of the mentally ill. The day-to-day assistance provided was typical of such facilities—the gamut from intensive therapy to group work and, informally, a place to socialize. The Quad was popular, especially among those lacking an alternative. Users generally suffered severe mental disorders; most had one or more times been institutionalized, and because of their debilities, regular employment was nearly unattainable. Significantly, both chief administrators during the study period had also experienced severe mental illness.

Data on the Quad's performance were collected by far-ranging interviews of both leaders and 24 patients over a nearly two-year period. This was supplemented by direct observations and discussions with professionals familiar with the Quad's operation. Notable effort was extended to obtain information from those initially reluctant to be forthcoming. Patients represented a mix of backgrounds and varied in awareness of mental health issues and satisfaction with clinic service (most were dissatisfied). Hardly anyone saw the Quad as relevant to empowerment; it was largely perceived as a comfortable milieu in an otherwise unwelcome community. Indeed, the term *empowerment* was virtually foreign despite the Quad's explicit rhetoric, and when the researcher defined the term, only about a quarter said that the facility encouraged it. A sizable gap clearly separated official policy and what transpired daily.

The factors conspiring against the clinic's empowering functions were many, and some, no doubt, are beyond remediation. The initial coordinator was an M.D. unemployable elsewhere, owing to his mental illness. His time was largely spent away from the Quad, drumming up community support or advocating the mental health agenda. While his absence might have assisted organizationally, it, alas, necessitated a formalized "by-the-rulebook" atmosphere within the clinic. Volunteers of moderate capacity often filled in during the director's absence. His distancing from daily chores was seen as aloof and "elitist," and following numerous complaints, he was dismissed. The director's unfamiliarity with the language and theories of empowerment, preferring instead the technical vocabulary of psychiatry, also proved a major handicap to some critics.

His replacement, also a mental illness sufferer, was a near opposite. Initially, she infused the clinic with tremendous energy, lifting client spirits, and spread abundant "motherly" warmth and affection. She also campaigned tirelessly for patients' rights, increased funding and eliminating the stigma of mental illness. The physical setting changed for the better, and the empowerment mission was invigorated. Utilization and patron satisfaction soared. This honeymoon, alas, proved misleading. When the new director was physically absent, the atmosphere quickly reverted to passivity; people complained of emotional dependence on the new leader and feeling directionless, regardless of her self-sufficiency exhortations. Equally important, discontentment grew regarding her alleged overdirective personality and intolerance toward disagreement. Ironically, patients soon united to oppose this "empowering" coordinator, especially her plan to abolish the clinic's "drop-in" feature, its most popular aspect. Matters quickly escalated to heated confrontations between coordinator and patients. Eventually, after a near-total boycott of the Quad, the coordinator—the person infatuated with empowerment—grudgingly acceded to patient demands. Within a few months, this once-popular administrator was dismissed.

The insights from this troubled application of empowerment theory transcend a single psychiatric setting. Most evidently, it may be unwise to speak of "empowerment" in a climate of multiple, and often conflicting, obligations. This is endemic for democracies and, surely, commendable. Compromise and accommodation may be more relevant; some empowerment aims must be sacrificed on behalf of others. A thriving agency need not mean masterful clients. All the participants—from distant state agencies to mentally ill street people needing a hangout—have distinctive needs, and all lack sovereignty. What is commendable for one may be harmful for another; funding agencies need explicit budgets, whereas administrators require flexibility to satisfy ever-changing needs. A financially responsible administrator may be judged "too rigid" by community groups suddenly enamored of fresh crusades. A favorite patient program may collide with public expectations and thus bring reduced funding. To insist upon privileged user or agency self-determination under these circumstances is impractical.

A second lesson concerns the dilemma of professional expertise. Recall that the first coordinator, an M.D., was faulted for his "professional" vocabulary and leadership style. Yet the clinic's official purpose is to *medically* assist, not provide a cheerful clubhouse. Similarly, the second coordinator justified her disliked actions on formal mission statements and her proven competence. Especially given the grave mental disturbances affecting Quad users, do we—to invoke an old phrase—"want the inmates running the asylum?" Surely the public can demand that tax dollars go to intended therapeutic use, even if cures are imperfect. What if the Quad habitues insisted that all the funds be spent on electronic games? Would this be empowerment? Limits on indulgences are hardly impositions when stipulations are applied to those barely able to manage their lives.[6]

Overall, this tale cautions us against the facile prescription of self-determination. It is all too easy in such circumstances to blame insufficient funding, poor leadership, insincerity, an unsympathetic community or accidents of fate. Perhaps impediments beyond management will always bedevil. Yet, at least in this Quad setting, for empowerment to work as intended innumerable things must go right—and go right nearly all the time. Administrators must both be professional bureaucrats and expertly sensitive to fluid, complex human needs. Funding agencies must willingly reinterpret periodically their legal mandates to please clients who experience extreme difficulty surviving life's mundane challenges. Taxpayers must acquiesce to hazy demands made by advocates who may change jobs tomorrow. Meanwhile, friends and family of the mentally ill must also feel in control of a difficult situation. Such multifarious accomplishments, let alone curing the seriously mentally ill, are hardly simple.

HOMELESSNESS AND POVERTY

Uplifting the homeless and the poor has perplexed both policy makers and private citizens for decades, perhaps for centuries. The quandary is both elementary and devilishly unfathomable. Obviously, our astronomical wealth permits us to grant the less fortunate housing or guaranteed incomes. And, some have suggested, we are in truth inching along to a "custodial state" in which some citizens are de facto inmates of an institution without walls (Murray 1988). Nevertheless, although affordable in principle, this "pay-them-off" solution is usually rejected as both contrary to our values of independence and, in the long run, impractical. Charles Murray (1992), for example, argues that unlimited generosity leaves untouched troublesome pathologies. Present-day crime-infested inner-city public housing exemplifies this imposed "helpfulness." The aim ought to be assisting people to upgrade themselves. As with improving health, empowerment has now been placed on the prescriptive options menu.

Between homelessness and poverty, the former seems more bounded, and we shall consider it first. Before examining proposals, a few preliminary points require attention. First, experts typically distinguish among target groups (see, e.g., Ellickson 1990; Tucker 1991). We can, for example, identify what are commonly nicknamed "street people." These disheveled souls, customarily seen panhandling in big cities, commonly suffer mental illness and/or alcoholism and often—if not usually—prefer shelter in doorways, abandoned cars or, in an extreme emergency, temporary social agency-supplied facilities. Rarely do they covet conventional housing.[7] Overwhelmingly, these are unattached males. Further up the social ladder are people who, for miscellaneous reasons, survive at the margins. Their lodging needs are driven by costs and opportunities—living with friends or relatives, for example, is preferable to renting. They utilize whatever is most affordable. Finally, we find those—often families—temporarily without adequate housing due to hapless circumstances: job loss or calamities such as fires or mechanical breakdowns.

Solutions for one clientele need not fit others (Ellickson 1990). At hand serviceable cheap hotels may not entice mentally disturbed street people, and under our legal system, they cannot be coerced into shelters unless endangering themselves or others. Those momentarily without accommodations can be easily assisted via short hotel stays. The middle group's predicament is perhaps the most troublesome, for they will often avail themselves of facilities intended for the other two, and more deserving, groups. After all, why rent if the government supplies lodging free? Thus, shelters for the truly wretched or the temporarily dispossessed often fill up with those minimizing housing costs. This demand may be virtually insatiable, and programs to alleviate homelessness inflate assistance seekers as bargain hunters opportunistically leave relatives and alight in shelters for the "homeless."[8] Moreover, people differ over the meaning of "adequate" housing. Physically sound housing may, nevertheless, be deemed inadequate if the surrounding neighborhood is dangerous, whereas people will pay hefty rents for dismal shelter if convenient. Some housing espousers, for example, demean minimal facilities as mere "warehouses" to store the poor (Fabricant 1988)

And, as with health care, empowerment hardly exhausts the menu of remedies. In particular, housing supply determinants often lie well beyond what a homeless person might possibly influence—zoning restrictions, interest rates, building codes, construction costs, physical space and innumerable other "structural" factors shaping availability. Despite radical rhetoric to the contrary, these regulations are not conscious "oppression of the poor," although harm may be the unintentional by-product. Hence, a law permitting the cheap conversion of commercial space to Spartan-type quarters would instantly flood the market with low-cost rooms. Similarly, anticrime efforts would release ample solid housing now currently "off limits." Ironically, the impetus for such relief need not come from "community activists" dedicated to uplifting the disadvantaged. Crass, selfish capitalists have long accommodated the poor dirt-cheap. And yesterday's reformist impulse has reduced the supply of cheap housing via rent control, tenant rights, high minimal standards, opposition to growth and similar well-intended though misguided nostrums.

How, then, can empowerment assist the homeless? One such solution, hardly unique in this literature's spirit, commences with an unflattering portrayal of American society. According to Yeich (1996), "Dramatic changes in the economy, the housing market, and the political system have transformed U.S. society and created growing inequality among its members. Today's society is characterized by a widening inequality among its members and social gap between rich and poor, and a lack of affordable housing for people in poverty" (111). In short, the homeless (a group undifferentiated) are victimized by larger political forces, and the cure is grassroots political activism.[9] Empowerment comes from oppressed people joining the Homeless Union, of which 23 now thrive in U.S. cities. Such action is to be guided by the now-familiar principles elucidated by Freire— deep analysis of obstacles, educating people on the plight's true nature (including undoing society's indoctrination) and then converting skills into political action.

The case study of remediating homelessness transpired in Lansing, Michigan, during the summer of 1990. The project began with uncovering a few homeless interested in creating a union. Membership soon expanded to approximately 350 members. The project's instigator was promptly asked to be the union's adviser, and with time, more advisers joined (dealing with specialized tasks such as fund-raising). Union activities included speaking to university gatherings, voting registration drives, testifying before the state legislature, organizing media demonstrations and similar politically oriented actions. Additionally, data on the Lansing homeless situation were collected and distributed to the homeless themselves. The Union became a tax-exempt, nonprofit organization with solid community support. The original investigator eventually left the group.

A principle Union activity was information sharing. As people discovered new facts and realized their common adversity, anger over societal conditions bubbled up. This anger, in turn, became the driving force behind demonstrations at legislative hearings when a newly elected conservative governor proposed welfare cutbacks. Other homeless joined the lecture circuit to elucidate their misfortune. Some became adept at securing media coverage. When the city proposed using a motel to ameliorate residence shortages, this too drew the Union's wrath and sparked an angry public protest (why this was unsatisfactory remains unclear).[10]

Whether these prodigious efforts resulted in one homeless person gaining shelter remains a mystery. As we noted, local motel rooms were disputatiously rejected. Conceivably, moreover, these demonstrations might have had generated a backlash, encouraging local officials to ship these malcontents elsewhere rather than deal with this tumult. Nor, despite an infatuation with research and education, has the problem's source been uncovered. No mention is provided of potentially pertinent technical factors such as converting industrial space into multiple single-room occupancy hotels. Political pressure to generate awareness was undoubtedly too diffuse and thus ineffective. Perhaps the zoning laws forbid high-density cheap housing, and this obstacle should have been attacked. Perhaps labor union contracts artificially inflated housing costs. The nature of the homeless population—drug addiction, criminality—might have made them unwelcome *and with good reason* in conventional facilities. Each explanation obliges a distinct political strategy. Clearly, the propounded goal is not housing; it is some vague "political change."

Empowerment similarly is advanced as the solution to homelessness, especially among women and children, in a study conducted by Albers and Paolini (1993). Again, those without housing are treated as a single entity and axiomatically confirmed as victims of exterior nefarious forces: economic conditions, greedy utilities, inadequate social welfare, deficient housing, lack of transportation or meager health care. Yet, ironically, despite these debilitating systemic impersonal factors, these victims are to be empowered to restore their self-mastery. And how are those confounded by their daily responsibilities to seize control, surmounting the treacherous designs of uncaring bureaucrats or greedy gas and electric executives?

The answer is to empower the social service agencies to supply indispensable services. In Lansing, Michigan, the homeless served as foot soldiers battling the political system; here they helped aggrandize welfare agencies and the University of Nevada's School of Social Work. Under the university's auspices, varied agencies addressing homelessness piecemeal now coordinate their efforts. It is empowerment on behalf, not empowerment individually. And much was done on their behalf. Thanks to foundation funding, 42 converted motel rooms were obtained. Program performance—for example, scheduling convenient day care services—was sharpened by interagency consultation. University of Nevada students canvassed agencies (not the homeless) regarding improved services delivery. Legal assistance, homemaker service, health care, job training and, predictably, housing were judged priorities. The collection of information about the homeless was systematized, and planning efficiency was increased. Parents and children were empowered through early childhood and adult education outreach interventions (all initiated and run by the agencies themselves).

This conflating of agency empowerment with "enhanced patron autonomy" is not inherently evil or harmful notwithstanding the deception.[11] After all, perhaps concealment effectively aids the troubled requiring assistance. It is surely a time-honored technique. Perchance wiser heads quietly concluded that to truly empower these homeless folk would only exacerbate their ruin (particularly given the lures of Nevada). Empowerment rhetoric was thus a benign cover, not too different than parents dispensing medicine as "candy." And since we do know that—unlike the Lansing experience—new housing was provided, maybe these energetic bureaucrats are to be commended.

A quite distinct approach to empowering the homeless offers no particular tangible program but instead seeks to reformulate the problem's definition (Cohen and Thompson 1992). The objects of this uplifting venture are the so-called mentally impaired homeless, a clientele traditionally receiving highly paternalistic treatment (including hospitalization and heavy medication). According to the authors, a close research literature reading will show this distinction between the merely homeless versus the mentally ill homeless to be "largely illusory." In their expert judgment, the disorders attributed to those classified as mentally ill essentially result from sociopolitical forces impinging upon all homeless. Rejected is the more familiar explanation pointing to the deinstitutionalization of mental hospital inmates during the late 1960s and early 1970s. In a nutshell, the popular psychiatric and public stereotype of the psychotic huddling in the doorway disdaining assistance is grossly unrealistic.

If this distinction is inappropriate, how can empowerment secure housing? The answer comes from altering the rendering of services. Traditional pathology-based invention, no matter how well intentioned, only humiliates, engenders resentment and is thus resisted. Proffered traditional treatment, moreover, is insensitive to "the desires, experiences, and social world of the homeless in psychiatric distress." (819). Since it is assumed that clean, safe shelter is preferred, failure must lie with would-be benefactors. Inappropriate therapy must be replaced by one more attuned to the environment, the individual and collective strengths of these homeless while upholding their rights and privileges. Stigmatizing them as "mentally ill" is especially troublesome, for these homeless often reject the psychotic label and will rebuff those who disagree. Ultimately, these unfortunate people must secure "the legal, political, therapeutic, and economic means necessary to construct and maintain a secure niche within the community" (830).

Concretely, this means reorienting psychiatric encounters to make them less paternalistic, less disease focused and more attuned to increased empowerment. The model is system-level outreach to the hapless, akin to those suffering from cataclysmic events—flood victims or war refugees, for example. Even the construction of larger-scale communities for this group is conceivable. And, predictably, psychiatrists must join with other specialists to champion the homeless cause, especially convincing legislatures on the importance of more social welfare aid. Equally critical is to proclaim the interrelationships between these personal traumas and larger sociopolitical inequalities. Hopefully, according to these advocates, a grand professional lead coalition of the homeless and indigent will bring about improved health care, an end to poverty and greater community development.

This espousal, needless to say, merely expresses earnest hope. It reasons that if (1) the mentally homeless can be reclassified away from the stigmatized psychotic label, (2) therapists will therefore modify treatment accordingly, and (3) if vital resources are mobilized via a homeless-expert coalition, the problem is remediable. At core is the belief in the potency of labeling to shape reality—calling something different will, indeed, alter substance. To wit, characterizing a disoriented, unkempt, delusional alcohol-addicted person unable to make reasonable choices as "virtually normal" commences the path to uplift. Again, to sound a repetitious note, this is a Huculean task absent any demonstrable promise. Surely psychiatrists en masse cannot be compelled to modify therapeutic approaches, and this "new" therapy may be no more successful than the old. And, yet again, empowerment is interpreted as soliciting yet more welfare services sans any hint of individual autonomy. This is not to argue that Cohen and Thompson's prescription will not convey relief—anything is, after all, possible—rather, this is a rather curious vision of self-determination.

Our final foray here is particularly important for the light it sheds on disentangling complex organization aims. Based on extensive open-ended interviews with savvy New York City agency housing administrators, Michael Fabricant (1988) offers a now-familiar catalog of advice. Most fundamentally, the hierarchical, bureaucratic and impersonal treatment afforded the homeless must be supplanted by client empowerment. Warm hospitality, not cold interrogation, should greet shelter visitors. Regarding the client's self-worth, his or her values are to be validated, not demeaned. Artificial barriers between professionals and those they serve must also be eliminated. Those in need are to reject self-blame and acquire authentic authority in program implementation. Discussions of shared predicaments are integral. Equally predictably, when necessary, the homeless must effectively mobilize politically to secure their rights.

Distinctive to this tale is agency intention to actually create housing. This constitutes a major shift. Essential housing market participants—real estate developers, banks and state offices—are now being seriously involved with welfare agencies. Although details are not forthcoming in this account, progress will undoubtedly involve many highly technical matters, for example, securing zoning variances. How these negotiations will be integrated into a setting in which the homeless themselves have been energized into new-found authority is a daunting dilemma. It is quite likely, however, that many decisions will have to be "sold" to the homeless rather than decided by them. It is inconceivable, for example, that mayors will acquiesce to cheap shelters situated in residential neighborhoods. Nor will banks be indifferent to repayment, and this insisted-upon prudence may well raise costs beyond what many homeless define as "reasonable." Flattering the homeless by acceding to their demands may not impress a zoning commission worried over loitering. No matter how much the homeless are empowered in meal selection or influencing staff appointments, building houses will surely bring a collision with intractable outside forces unsway-able to appeals to rhetoric. Such matters are easily slighted when singing the praises of empowerment, but they are, alas, inescapable.

Even more so than homelessness, antipoverty efforts have drawn multi-tudinous proposed solutions and untold billions of dollars. Without exag-geration, entire libraries of treatises catalog this effort. Yet seemingly intractable problems still remain. And in recent years, as the massive bu-reaucratic nostrums have struck out, empowerment advocates have ap-pealed for their turn at bat. Given the exhaustion of past "surefire" remedies, this novel scheme has predictably attracted adherents. Chapter 6 will examine its more top-down incarnation, namely, government-sponsored "empowerment zones" extending tax incentives and similar legal changes. Here we assess far more modest versions trusting on the personal involvement among empowerment devotees.

Joan W. DiLeonardi (1993) reports an intervention dealing with one aspect of poverty, namely, chronic child neglect. This is a severe problem affecting millions and is, unfortunately, interwoven with multiple con-founding disorders—drug abuse, family isolation, dismal education—that have often defeated conventional intervention efforts. Thanks to funding from the National Center on Child Abuse and Neglect, part of the U.S. Department of Health and Human Services, six specific demonstration pro-grams were created centering on poor families with neglected children. Ef-forts took place in divergent settings, from Iowa to Alaska, dealt with various ethnic clienteles and were administered by diverse agencies—tra-ditional state run, private charities, and a Social Work School–affiliated agency. All participating families had severe problems including numerous run-ins with state agencies monitoring child abuse and neglect.

Each project zeroed in on feelings of hopelessness and despair charac-terizing these families. The goal was to build on family strength and par-ticipation to facilitate empowered families. Depending on circumstances and resources, the at-risk family treatment emphasized group work and the assistance of multiple professionals, paraprofessionals and volunteers. Fam-ilies in need were abundant; agencies were flooded with requests for help. Careful evaluations of family behavior and physical circumstances were done both before and after the projected commenced. The empowerment portion of the enterprise was implemented largely through group work in which family members themselves determined their issue agendas. Profes-sionals would assist if requested but not direct in goal obtainment. On occasion, volunteers visited homes to help with housecleaning, budgeting, arranging medical appointments, transportation and similar everyday tasks. Emotional support and friendship were also given by these outsiders. In one instance, free day care was provided so at-risk parents could attend schools or job training.

Overall, the six projects suggested success over their 18-month (average) term. Based on assessments conducted during the intervention, about two-thirds of all families made progress as measured by the Childhood Levels of Living Scale instrument. Anecdotal evidence confirms improvements in family socialization, household tidiness and child discipline. No doubt, many families greatly appreciated the child care, educational opportunities and the assistance provided by volunteers. Nevertheless, whether such intervention—regardless of success—might be properly judged "empowerment" is another issue. The evidence here would suggest otherwise. After all, it is the agency, not parents, who have defined "good" child rearing. Perhaps cultures exist in which indifference is the valid norm or household clutter is morally acceptable. Equally important, what is being depicted is traditional social welfare assistance with a vengeance, not training for independence. At most, as far as can be ascertained, empowerment existed only to the extent that parental opinions were given a little extra attention in professional lead groups. An empowerment element, perhaps, but certainly not the genuine article.

A second exemplar of utilizing empowerment to uplift the needy similarly focuses on assisting low socioeconomic families (Trivette, Dunst and Hamby 1996). The research question was straightforward and scientific: Does participation in an empowerment-oriented assistance program improve over what can be accomplished in interventions without this philosophy? Put a little differently, did those families experiencing "empowerment treatment" gain a greater sense of personal control and then use this newfound feeling to obtain needed supports and resources? This is, potentially, a critical issue given the unfortunate frequency of those assisted by conventional means to develop even greater dependency.

The tested technique to facilitate betterment is called the "family-centered" model of assistance. It stands in contrast to other therapies that provide troubled families with firmer professional direction. This approach "view[s] professionals as instruments of families, and intervene[s] in ways that are individualized, flexible, and responsive." Moreover, "[h]elp seekers are viewed as having existing capabilities as well as the capacity to become more competent, and help-giver practices aim to strengthen functioning and optimally empower people as part of their involvement in these kinds of human service programs" (275). The specific study participants were 107 mothers of preschool-aged children involved (mainly voluntarily) in three distinct human services programs. Each of these interventions, for example, assisting the distressed with health care, reflected varied degrees of permissible family independence (as ascertained by expert judges). In the case of the greatest autonomy, families had pivotal responsibilities over how services were to be sought and utilized. Elsewhere the choices were far more constrained.

Information on the impact of these autonomy levels came from a mailed questionnaire. Orientation toward empowerment was operationally defined by answers to multiple questions, for example, questions about how people's capacities were perceived, whether steps were taken to gain knowledge and opinions regarding client-perceived control. Treatment group differences were then subject to complex statistical analysis. The hypothesis that those who had received family-centered programs were affected by this orientation was confirmed. Specifically, "families participating in human services programs deemed family-centered assessed the helping practices of staff from those programs as more consistent with the empowering philosophy compared to families participating in other kinds of human service programs" (288). The empowering treatment also seemingly encouraged family beliefs that they exercised greater resource control.

Leaving aside quibbles with the uneducated completing complex mailed questionnaires about perceptions rather than discernible behavior, a remarkable message shared with other social service–related empowerment celebrations is conveyed: "Empowerment" means skilled utilizations of professional ministrations. The overwhelmed indigent mother is thus no different from a savvy consumer—one must appreciate where to shop and get superior service. The "product" here, however, is welfare agency assistance. This formulation is not predetermined—one could just calculate how many clients escaped agency dependency and lived happily ever after. These studies must unconsciously assume permanent, unalterable client dependency. Empowerment is just making the best of this sorry situation. Given that professional livelihoods depend on such permanence, perhaps this assumption is to be expected. Perhaps financially profitable codependency is an apt characterization.

A further variation is EMPOWER (Encouraging Making Poverty Obsolete Welfare Reform), a church-based Rochester, New York, organization (Ingram 1988). Consistent with the principles of empowerment, nearly all leaders are themselves welfare recipients or former recipients. In 1987 it had a $30,000 budget and engaged in sundry activities from running a food bank to direct political action. Philosophically, it loathes traditional welfare services. As Robert Ingram, EMPOWER's founder put it, "Welfare recipients and their friends should look upon the welfare department as an adversary. As the institution is evil, all associated with it—welfare administrators, caseworkers, and all others—should be regarded as adversaries" (11). Moreover, it is plain, in Ingram's opinion, that the system reprehensibly harms its alleged beneficiaries. Words like "cruel" and "capricious" are used to describe it.

Nevertheless, despite this animus toward welfare bureaucracies, the goal is exclusively to extract increased favors from these tightfisted, uncaring, disrespectful pencil pushers. To be sure, organization members are taught skills, the facility of extraction: how to request attention, how to badger state officials. To repeat, empowerment is *not* escaping dependency; it is improving dependency via adroit harassment. Consider EMPOWER's chief goals: (1) Make it easier to contact the social services department by telephone and reduce operator rudeness; (2) increase rent allowances; and (3) exchange the existing health care provider for one more accessible. Activities were thus directed *solely* to modifying these policies. For example, to rid themselves of the disliked health care organization, petitions were circulated, and various pressures were put on the state legislature.

No doubt, to those in dire straits, easy telephone contact with those supplying life's necessities is critical, as is the nearness of medical attention. These are not trivial concerns, and outrage at being rebuffed is predictable. Goal worthiness is not the issue here, however. The proper end of empowerment, it would seem, should be freedom from the government's dole. Ironically, ensuring a more efficient dole only makes dependency more comfortable and, perhaps ultimately, inescapable. The narrative could be relabeled "Improving Paternalism." Perhaps the reverse objective is more worthy—make social welfare exceptionally unpleasant and inconvenient. Rather than treat recipients with respect, heap humiliation on them so as to prompt a swift exit from subservience. Stigma is to be an asset, not a liability.

CONCLUSIONS

Our brief excursion into this terrain surely reveals a paradox. On the one hand, we expose a thriving academic industry (together with their helping profession allies) of enthusiastic devotees. It is almost as if a sudden scientific breakthrough has transpired—once arduous predicaments will now succumb to the empowerment cure. If doubters are about, they remain silent in this published literature. Yet, approaching actual fulfillment, the promises evaporate. The attention to well-grounded theory, an essential precondition to future progress, is often haphazard. Whether those traits associated with empowerment can be transferred to the disadvantaged remains underexplored. A similar vagueness informs the pleas for political action. If the standards of medical research were applied, nearly everything would still be in the preliminary laboratory stage. That some, notably the faith in politics and self-esteem, have energetic followings hardly establishes worthiness. One recalls the Middle Ages when sensible people swore that plagues were God's punishment for wickedness and that self-flagellation was the cure.

As we proceed to concrete applications, the costs of shoddy theorizing proliferate (though with exceptions noted below). And this is not a selective, worst-example tour. To be sure, the jury is still out, and progress may eventually arrive, and applications elsewhere might succeed, but the record here is meager. The indisposed allegedly empowered are seldom uplifted, whereas the exhorted homeless remain without shelter. Only fervent true believers fantasize that empowering the insolvent will bring middle material comforts. Success is "accomplished" by substituting minor goals—often activity in and of itself—for true purpose; "failure" scarcely exists in this literature. The rhetoric of self-determination is ceaselessly transmuted into bargaining instructions for government handouts.[12] Shades of John Gay's *The Beggars' Opera* whereby children were expertly tutored in panhandling skills.

This incongruity of energetic activity and the sparse outcomes are numerous, profound and troublesome. Four points need expression here. First, an inescapable moral culpability infuses this giving of demonstrable bad or uncertain advice. These practitioners are no different from doctors attending to the sick: Recipients are misfortunate people, not laboratory rats. Telling ignorant Chinese peasant women that better health requires photographing their deplorable condition scarcely constitutes inconsequential academic foolishness. Quackery has its aftermath. Chinese officials obviously know this misery well, and documentation will not bring relief. The Ford Foundation money could have been far better allocated elsewhere. Ditto for all the time spent imparting political activism skills—perhaps learning a marketable competence is wiser.

Second, the possibility that at least some predicaments are unsolvable via empowerment is unspeakable. Not a single rejection from the empowerment club appears. Are we really to believe that the gravely mentally impaired can direct their medical treatment? Let us not confuse, say, attentiveness to dietary wants with a capacity for distressful choices. Perhaps some abusive mothers need children removed permanently, not be authorized by experts to pursue selfishness. Disillusionment with bureaucratic professionalism is certainly fathomable and, in some instances, appropriate. Nevertheless, one cannot conclude that since paternalism-infused remediation is imperfect, its opposite will flourish. It is said that perfection is the enemy of the good, and our tour suggests wisdom in this adage.

Three, and most ironically, the best case for empowerment comes when we move away from ventures steeped in academic theorizing. Orthodox empowerment adherents routinely belittle and condemn tersely this conception of self-determination as "futile," "inauthentic" or "conservative." What we have in mind are "self-help" or bootstrapping projects relying on ordinary people, bereft of fancy social science theory and academic guidance, pooling their resources and tackling small-scale obstacles. Such empowerment is commonplace—everyday thousands assemble and do things for themselves. If *empowerment* is defined accordingly, then the real issue is not whether it works—it surely does—but its precise application.

Robert L. Woodson, a leading proponent of this modest approach, depicts several such successes: finding adoptive homes for black children, promoting high-caliber inner-city education and ridding housing projects of crime (Woodson 1987). Typically, the uplifting occurs when community residents spontaneously begin to help those around them. Nothing fancy, just a kindly reaching out by neighbors. The project will often snowball, and only with growth is additional funding solicited. Goals are plain-Jane modest, not a grandiose transformation of an oppressive society. Pragmatism supplies the theory. Outside experts play little or no role. These humdrum undertakings are, alas, totally invisible in the academic-based literature.

Finally, a flavor permeates this academically defined empowerment chorus insinuating that ever more calamities await America, and professionally supplied empowerment may be our last great hope. Reading only these pessimistic, almost desperate citation-rich accounts, one hears of crises everywhere—hoards of homeless wandering about, the indigent falling deeper into despair and rampant diseases. This doomsday vision is, of course, grossly inaccurate—wretchedness is neither ubiquitous or on the upswing. Moreover, our disorders—AIDS, teenage pregnancy, dismal schooling, to name but a few—continue to receive intensive attention. Documenting rude agency telephone operators or psychotics availing themselves of abandoned cars as sleeping quarters reveals only a small portion of the story. Nearly all the relevant statistics—unemployment levels, life expectancy, expenditures for social services and education—do not foretell collapse.

More important, the empowerment nostrum is hardly the last hope. If anything, the academically flavored versions belong well down the remedy menu; they may even be contributing to the problem. Nearly every quandary now receiving the empowerment treatment has been ameliorated in the past, long before the empowerment appellation appeared. Reading any social history unveils familiar tales—cities overrun with vagabonds, homeless children, dismal health among the poor crowded into atrocious housing, armies of unemployed lacking hope, mental asylums overflowing with the deranged, rampant hunger and alcoholism and uncontrolled crime. Yet even without modern medicine and social science, amazing progress transpired. Epidemics of illegitimacy and crime have come and gone. Effective solutions were imposed, often with a heavy moralistic hand, from the regulation of alcohol to voluntary charities insisting that the wretched embrace diligence (see, e.g., Himmelfarb 1994, Ch. 1). A canvass of capable remedies to uplift the downtrodden would not detect empowerment. It is absolutely bizarre to abandon proven solutions in favor of speculative novelties launched by armchair academics.

NOTES

1. The fusing of "learning" with "learning about oppression" seems commonplace among educators proselytizing empowerment. Irwin, for example, defines empowered students as "persons who believe in themselves and their capacity to act. They understand systems of domination and work to transform oppressive practices

in society" (Irwin 1996, 13). A concern for writing or mathematics is, by contrast, seemingly lacking in this notion of self-determination.

2. An intriguing extension of this reasoning links improved black health care, specifically dealing with AIDS, to affirmative action in higher education. One analyst (Spigner 1989–1990) alleges that the solution to the AIDS epidemic among blacks lies in recruiting more blacks to research and professional medicine. Since African Americans are currently underrepresented here, continued affirmative action will bestow enhanced health to the black community.

3. This contradiction between preaching "take matters into your own hands" and preaching "you are the helpless victim of the system" seems to have escaped scholarly attention. Indeed, one devotee in listing empowerment's key ingredients as "reduce self-blame" followed immediately by "assume personal responsibility." How this circle is to be squared in never explicated (Gutierrez 1990, 150).

4. This autonomy to pursue unhealthy indulgences is a serious yet underexplored conundrum in the empowerment literature. Consider, for example, the fact that doctors are less likely to tell black women to stop smoking and drinking during pregnancy ("Study Finds Racial Disparity in Warning to the Pregnant" 1994). This is judged troublesome. Yet would stern admonitions violate the dictates of self-determination? Perhaps this silence by doctors reflects respect of the power of these women to make their own, and presumably intelligent, choices. After all, coercion would be paternalism. Then how do we assess a South Carolina program that coerced pregnant black women via threats of jail or involuntary enrollment in a drug program to be drug free? This, too, is troublesome (Hilts 1994) Which of these two alternatives is most consistent with the precepts of empowerment?

5. As is typical, no data on success are provided. This is particularly surprising here, given the involvement of so many health professionals. Again, effort is equated with outcome.

6. The rebellion against top-down professional advice is an oft-mentioned theme in empowerment exhortations. In one overview of a conference on health empowerment, a reoccurring call was for patients to take charge of their treatment. To be rejected was a model of health care that insisted on compliance with "predetermined standards of behavior and ignore[d] the full context of the lives of the poor and people of color" (Merzel 1991, 5). One might also speculate that this sentiment reflects a more general aversion to science and rationality occasionally evidenced in this literature.

7. Predictably, failures in enticing the homeless into shelters is a topic hidden from view. One notable exception is a report by Heather MacDonald on an outreach program in New York City's Time Square area. In 1994 local businesspeople received $2.5 million in funding and together with six local social service agencies launched a massive assistance program. Facilities also offered food, showers and medical attention with no strings attached. One year and $700,000 later, after 1,511 "contacts" with homeless loitering on the streets, 15 people had agreed to stay overnight in a shelter. Only 2 had agreed to accept regular housing, and 200 still wander about Times Square. Moreover, this experience of disdained outreach seems to be typical (MacDonald 1997).

8. It is also true that as government subsidizes housing, private providers leave the industry, creating yet more clients for the subsidized facilities (Tucker 1991). Private cheap lodgings—"flop houses," "flea bag hotels" in slang terminology—are

also the frequent targets of urban reform movements, given that they commonly attract unsavory types.

9. Infusing most of the empowerment rhetoric regarding homelessness is an almost antique, nineteenth-century vision of society in which capitalists relentlessly exploit the proletariat, driving the very poor on to the street (Lee 1991). Just why businesspeople want their downtowns filled with derelicts soaking up tax money and reducing property values is unstated. If anything, the desire to rehabilitate shoddy neighborhoods via urban renewal has inadvertently contributed to the proliferation of panhandlers and vagrants. Serious paradoxes abide here, and homeless advocates seem uninterested in them.

10. In extreme cases this empowerment of the homeless has taken on a provocative "street theater" flavor. One empowerment activist, for example, created "tent cities" in public parks and in front of the United Nations. How such publicity has improved the life of those lacking shelter remains unclear (Ferguson 1990).

11. In all fairness to the authors, their definition of *empowerment* is technically compatible with uses in the literature—notions of empowering organizations qua organizations. Nevertheless, not only is this unashamed top-down style inconsistent with the underlying *spirit* of empowerment, but on numerous occasions, the opportunity to consult directly with clients on their needs was easily bypassed.

12. How this plainer-than-day contradiction escapes attention remains a fascinating question. Only a single article—Grace (1991)—frankly explores this intriguing matter. Significantly, in an academic atmosphere where end-of-article bibliographies on empowerment have much in common, this essay remains unknown.

5

Empowered Education

Of all the domains applying empowerment remedies, none exceeds education. Pertinent books and essays overwhelm even the most prodigious appetites. Entering *empowerment* into ERIC, the computerized education database, yields precisely 2,900 entries from 1966 to 1997. Among pedagogical bandwagons, this ranks among all-time favorites. Scarcely any self-doubting pervades, no yearning for the preempowerment days when American education excelled. That "old-fashioned" answers might still prove valuable seems unthinkable; the quest is entirely for a *new*, almost entirely untried solution—empowerment. One education professor intoned, "I truly believe that the movement to improve schools through empowerment may be the last chance in many of our lifetimes to make schools institutions that are worthy of public confidence and professional respect" (Glickman 1990, 69).

Fervid devotion to an allegedly miraclelike cure is predictable. One more prodigious foundation report is unnecessary to confirm America's doleful scholastic accomplishment. We yearly spend billions and receive less and less for our efforts, particularly in inner-city, largely minority schools where physical security often overshadows instruction. Talk of "dumbed-down" education is ubiquitous. Seemingly every office seeker promises relief, whereas comparisons of dismal academic performance vis-à-vis other nations are commonplace. Plainly, our scholastic woes go beyond resource adequacy; it is *how* we direct our efforts, and into this dismay, empowerment disciples have en masse rushed in to supply the answers.

Although the empowerment chorus is deafening, it is—expectedly—not of a single tune. A cacophony emanates of every remedial idea imaginable, many inherently contradictory, all portrayed as empowerment. No sooner are teachers told "empowerment means concentrating on education" than, a few sentences later, they are advised to become involved in multiple outside activities to secure empowerment (Landsmann 1988). One sympathetic advocate even depicted this enterprise as "cuckoo-like," given this odd amalgam of secondhand theories (Troyna 1994). Equally foreseen, numerous prescriptions constitute heartfelt fantasies, whereas others are clichés masquerading as detailed blueprints. Yet all must be taken seriously. Canvassing only those hardheaded proposals steeped in scientific rigor supplies a too-diminutive menu. More significant, schemes dismissable as unworthy are the very candidates ebulliently welcomed as saviors. Such ironies are to be expected as one corrective after the next falls short of its lofty promise.

A BRIEF OVERVIEW

The best way to tackle this voluminous literature is to survey key questions, and we begin with the "Who?" question. Clearly, "education" is a wide-ranging collection of constituencies, and each is, in principle, capable of further empowerment. Thus, to say "the cure is empowerment" is silent on *who* receives this sought-after prize. Dozens of potential candidates would surely volunteer. Might this be the pupils themselves? Parents? Teachers and/or administrators? One study celebrates the empowerment of school bus drivers (Allen 1997). Perhaps empowerment is a medicine only dispensable to the hapless—ethnic/racial group members struggling to master unfamiliar subjects, myriad disability sufferers, or academic underachievers. It is hard to imagine any constituency unable to legitimately demand greater self-determination. Yet to empower everyone is, it would seem, nonsensical.

Imbedded in this "Who?" dilemma is the competence quandary. Surely not everyone craving enhanced authority could profit. Imagine "F" students revamping their examinations to gain self-mastery. Yet some allege that even the academically troubled must "take charge of" their own learning at the expense of teacher authority (Gruber and Trickett 1987). Are fans of schoolmaster capacitation willing to allow *any* teacher greater reign? Even those barely literate or pedagogically inept?[1] Conceivably, a wrongheaded empowered teacher *could* do wonders by showering pupils with bogus honors to inflate self-esteem. Should we cede control to crackpot parents? It is surely arguable that performance assessment might be appropriate prior to upgrading power. And who possess final sovereignty? Parents? Education professors? Such dilemmas are all too easily escaped when advancing untried vague ideas.

Equally plausible, aggrandizing today's teachers and bureaucrats rewards those responsible for our catastrophes. Listless students can hardly be *commanded* into proficiency by struggling teachers suddenly made almighty. Nor, for that matter, is it self-evident that empowerment can be bestowed giftlike to those mired in passivity (Clarke [1990] discusses this paradox). Such optimism presupposes that necessary knowledge is both available and easily implemented *only* if those in charge were enabled. More persuasive is that today's educational establishment, judging by outcomes, is not power deprived but largely incompetent. Helplessness is but a permanent convenient excuse. Empowerment clamors serve as defenses protecting ineptitude against a justifiably fed-up public. Current professionals should be *de*powered or fired altogether and replaced by new recruits. Why elevate failed generals and their lieutenants?

Empowerment's bestowment may well exist beyond the schoolhouse. Pleas for greater attentiveness to university experts as the ultimate solution despite their distance from day-to-day instruction are commonplace. Education unions are also anxious to secure greater control; others would banish them from schools altogether, also in empowerment's name. What about the taxpayers or businesspeople insisting that schools produce skilled, dutiful employees? Similarly, education has long been favored by disadvantaged groups to lift themselves upward economically. Not only does this betterment entail inculcating vocationally useful talents; the education "industry" itself is a rich source of jobs and contracts. And to recall past chapter descriptions, education can bestow legitimacy on collective traits ("validation of people's values" in this parlance). For some, no doubt, renaming a school after a prominent group hero or including group history into the curriculum constitutes empowerment, regardless of classroom leaning.

This "Who?" is not as simple as nominating from a list of worthies. Much depends on how one envisions educational politics. Conceivably, the process might unleash a torrent of disharmony. Empowerment can range from peaceful cooperation to bitterly carving up the spoils. For example, a familiar theme in overcoming our deficiencies is to enhance teacher authority as an inaugural step in capacitating all others. That is, once teachers gain command, the uplift will *peacefully* extend ever outward, beginning with their students and, eventually, ameliorating the entire community. Others, of course, commence elsewhere—perhaps allowing communities to dictate content and pedagogy. Recent parent-led revolts against education establishment–favored techniques—notably, whole word spelling or the "new math"—illustrate this possibility. A handful might even contend that pupils themselves are to be awarded ascendancy to lead the charge toward excellence. All visions assume dutiful cooperation with the freshly empowered.

A contrasting scenario sees this process not as a "Who will expertly lead the way?" question but as a zero-sum battle. Aims within education—professional goal attainment, money, prestige, power or ideology, to cite but a few—are, typically, disguised behind high-sounding rhetoric. Given these prizes, education soon succumbs to squabbling. Empowerment now becomes only a public relations gambit as teachers confront school boards, parents, state legislators and federal bureaucrats (and untold others) to govern resources. Business leaders selfishly wanting schools to impart arithmetic skills collide with ethnic group leaders pursuing cultural pride sans numerical knowledge. Parents may covet school vouchers, and this will surely draw rebuke from most professionals. Each faction, naturally, utilizes empowerment's vocabulary for its trendy advantage. Those initially helpless are not troops bringing up the rear; they are potential enemies to be conquered and then brought under benign domination. Thus, for instance, teachers might under empowerment's banner enlist once misdirected tax-resisting parents into the teacher-dominated PTA to secure augmented school funding. The upshot of this zero-sum empowerment might, alas, be gridlock—inaction—as all sides relentlessly jockey for position.

The rhetoric-surrounding turf battles can take on bizarre twists as disputes escalate. One theme permeating authority-sharing demands is that this promotes democracy by example to students and reinforces democratic society more generally. Yet often paralleling this love of democracy is a sturdy belief in the superiority of expert, professional advice when confronting elected representatives. Education specialists almost never impute good-hearted motives to state legislatures alarmed over failing schools. They may exhibit condescending, nearly contemptuous attitudes toward ordinary people who "suddenly" intrude into professional domains, particularly if this intervention has politically conservative overtone. One's territory (and ideology) must be protected. To one University of Wisconsin professor, "In these times of conservative resurgence, supporting a greater role for communities in their schools makes schools vulnerable to the wishes and desires of those who seek to force antidemocratic beliefs into the public schools" (Zeichner 1991, 364).[2] The author then goes on to welcome community participation in school affairs, but only to the extent that this involvement is "good." A more accurate depiction of this contrivance is "guided democracy" as once employed in Third World nations where educated elites "guided" the unsophisticated.

Nor does a consensus surround proper ends. Nearly every trait traditionally rectified by education is, someplace, to be gained. Occasionally the campaign is nothing more than altering administrative procedures, granting more decentralization or removing unwelcome meddlers. The aim might be vague "happiness" or "contentment" apart from demonstrable feats. One expert's goal was creating "organic intellectuals"—students combining school knowledge with understanding all the forces shaping schools (Shannon 1990). Even signifying "skill and proficiency" is inconclusive given distinct imputations of these terms. For some "skill" is narrow technical mastery—excelling in geometry or higher SAT scores, for example. An entirely different "skill" might be preparation of "democratic citizenry" or discerning the dominant culture's oppressive impact on group self-regard.

Romanish (1993b) speaks of giving students their "democratic voice." Nonintellectual objectives are also commonplace—building "self-confidence" or "social skills." (see, e.g., Renihan and Renihan 1995). There are administrators whose empowerment restores classroom decorum; yet others praise this formula as a hopeful methodology for imparting liveliness to stifling atmospheres. Some, reminiscent of those professionals depicted previously, identify enhanced self-mastery with extracting government largess. Almost any wondrous outcome can be aligned with heightened self-determination. Empowerment for one person trying to assist the disabled might be compelling schools to regard them as conventional students; for another, the term implies distinctive helpfulness.

Furthermore, enhanced education itself need not be the ultimate aim. A New Orleans plan envisioned updated schools as conduits for neighborhood improvement—locals for day care facilities and the like; learning was secondary (Miron 1995). For radical advocates, schools are but "agitprop" (to use an old Marxist term) instruments to transform society, whether by overthrowing oppressive capitalism (see, e.g., Brosio 1990; and most esp. Giroux 1988) or ending racism, sexism and homophobia. One education professor has labeled such radical instruction "critical literacy" (Shannon 1990). Zeichner (1991) links teacher empowerment to addressing the crises of our economy, society and political order. Egalitarianism, "social justice" and attacks on "privilege" also loom large as goals (Sprague [1992] tours this "liberation pedagogy"). To be empowered means escaping the hegemonic stifling status quo. Mundane issues—skill development, orderliness, professional attainment—are nearly irrelevant stepping-stones, not final objectives.

The instrumentalities to accomplish this aim also overflow—nearly every tool in the educator's arsenal is conscripted in this good-sounding cause. Parents increasingly interpret empowerment as deserting schools altogether in favor of home schooling. A handful stress artfully applied political pressure as empowerment (Clift 1991; Reed 1991). Technology fans see computers, interactive videos and the Internet as key allies defeating helplessness (e.g., Cooley 1997; Sandvick and Nauman 1991). Just as assuredly, others condemn technological infatuations as expensive "depowering" distractions (Callister and Dunne 1992). Experts occupying a seriously different vantage point proclaim the subjective virtues of self-discovery and learning to acquire one's own unique "voice" (see, e.g., McKinney and Fry 1994; Prawat 1991). Art and music may also claim their place in this campaign (Powell 1997). Of course, stuck-in-the-mud traditionalists will wryly intone that the rigorous study of the classics, including mastering ancient languages, is the proven path to empowerment.

Multiculturalistic pathways are especially prominent as ethnic and racial group advocates assert that only laudatory self-study engenders proficiency (e.g., McKinney and Fry 1994). Implied is that bored students will flourish if study enhances self-worth. Far more than a few historical exemplars or cosmetic textbook alterations are required, however. Says one expert, "Black history will be politically empowering, however, only if it encourages group solidarity, emphasizes collective goals, reveals the conflictive elements of black history vis-à-vis whites, and inculcates organizational competence among black students" (Merelman 1993, 336). Needless to say, using history to inspire can easily drift into propaganda or even deceit, hardly the purpose of education as generally understood.[3]

An especially noteworthy and seldom broached empowerment dilemma concerns limits. Power, after all, is boundless, and its quest may well become intoxicating. In principle, all society impinges upon the school and thus affects educational empowerment. School budgets are huge and thus draw the watchfulness of multiple interests, from construction contractors to the textbook industry. One teacher empowerment promoter frankly acknowledges this when he notes that many instructional obstacles reside beyond classrooms, and no amount of within-classroom control can remediate these quandaries (Romanish 1993b). Thus, might an empowered teacher proscribe expensive medical therapy to disruptive mentally ill students? Might these teachers direct book publishers on text design? What is the role of the school board in confronting a fully empowered classroom teacher demanding that taxes be raised?

This problem's seriousness cannot be overstated, and perhaps this explains its neglect. Plainly, expanding one's authority incurs new obligations and the need for fresh expertise, and this readily undermines traditional responsibilities. Recall Chapter 2's discussion praising the division of labor: Accomplishment comes from being focused, not dissipating energy by meddling everywhere.[4] More fundamental, *fully* empowering *any* participant in the educational process is both impossible and, at a more practical level, invites collisions with other legitimate interests. Deeply rooted notions of legal accountability impose restraints—budgets cannot be spent capriciously.[5] Even parents favoring enhanced teacher authority would object if this supremacy were utilized to impose loathsome moral values or racial discrimination. Conversely, teachers' glorifying parental enablement would be outraged, should parents dictate their private lives. In short, rhetoric aside, boundaries everywhere are inescapable and are built in to our system of limited, decentralized government. Education is immersed in multiple layers of government, untold bureaucracies, courts, regulatory agencies and unions, and each, properly, jealously guards its domains. Cooperation, not command, almost always governs. Any claim of final supremacy subverts the very fabric of the political order. *All* empowerments are thus limited, and to allege that success requires just one more measure of control is futile; success *must* come in the context of constrained power.

The final query is the most fundamental: A priori, why should empowerment work? Past success is obviously not the recommendation, for if it had transpired, our morass would be long gone. Surely hegemony, sagacity and accomplishment are not inexorably bound together: Absolute dictators regularly bring cataclysm due to their stupidity. Nor would anybody contend that empowerment prima facie is absolutely guaranteed; so let us brush aside all resistance and immediately impose the wonder drug. Surprisingly, theoretical underpinnings are quite casual, often but alleged "common sense." As our health and homelessness self-sufficiency nostrums reviews showed, hope repeatedly trumps harsh reality.

Self-interest, predictably, often justifies. For example, since parents unquestionably want the foremost education for their children, empowering them via vouchers (or comparable mechanisms) will assuredly coerce schools to perform. Pupils likewise crave learning but, alas, are obstructed. Similarly, teachers deeply love imparting knowledge, so empowering them allows fulfillment of this compelling desire. Empowerment merely becomes "impediment removal." Needless to say, taking all oratory at face value, everybody stridently wants the best, and removing all the encumbrances will—according to these believers—naturally bring forth progress. Unfortunately, huge gaps separate wanting and getting. The marketplace abounds with poor decision making, bankrupt "sure things," and we cannot expect greater know-how here. Harm can also be self-inflicted. Parents may foolishly favor athletics over mathematics, and teachers may guilelessly pursue disastrous stratagems if allowed free reign. If self-interest always worked as claimed, we'd have Utopia.

A quite different justification fixates on promised liberating benefits. For one ebullient administrator, "Empowered individuals feel 'alive' and are 'living' in the organization, can make significant differences, learn and grow; and become part of a 'community' with a common purpose" (Lagana 1989, 20). Another pledges that empowered educators "will work harder and smarter on behalf of their clients, students and their parents" (Glickman 1990, 69). Nothing is said, of course, about the enervating strains of heightened responsibility. A variant is that empowerment, by allowing teachers ample autonomy, will slow the flight of talented instructors from classrooms while making teaching more attractive (Carnegie Forum 1986). After all, capable employees hardly want to slavishly heed rules beyond reach or be compelled to follow ineffective strategies. And certainly students will be galvanized when guiding their own learning experiences (see, e.g., Wade 1997). Yet another expert counsels that if people can make their choices, as opposed to being directed, this newfound responsibility will certainly propel children to growth (Glaser 1996).

This "bring newfound dynamism" and variants are seductive, yet a fatal flaw is hidden: Zestfully "doing one's own thing" may, alas, not secure proficiency. Contentment and accomplishment differ. Math-hating teachers would surely be "alive" if they could justifiably dodge arithmetic. Empowered students may rush to school, hungry for "knowledge," if only athletics awaited them. Schooling, for all participants, is customarily painful, unpleasant and tedious; it is not a Disneyworld dedicated to unhindered enjoyment. The path to empowerment typically lies through drudgery. Abolishing the costs of risk taking in the name of personal autonomy invites irresponsibility.[6] That teachers may feel unjustly put upon to teach foolishness is understandable, and they surely can argue their case. But instruction is not a matter of liking or feeling imposed upon: It is a matter of imparting knowledge.

These, then, highlight the complicated theory-related issues infusing educational empowerment. Our more detailed review focuses on proposal worthiness, particularly confirmed accomplishment (if any). Scientific drug testing remains our model: The introduction of empowerment (somehow defined) should eventuate educational improvement (somehow defined). Although seemingly straightforward, this evaluative task is deceptively troublesome. For one, disciples are not above mislabeling or shading the outcomes to exaggerate claims. An empowerment "success" may not correspond to ordinary denotations of success. One New York City grade school mathematics teacher, for example, has depicted a philosophy in which math enhancement means open discussions of feelings about math, negotiations regarding correct solutions and a rejection of the "Eurocentric" methods. Accomplishment criteria also mandated uniform expertise across ethnic groups. Measuring calculating ability fell well down the agenda (Zolkower 1995). This substitution of aims is hardly unique: Amorphous, subjective states easily replace test performance in empowerment's name.

Empowerment rhetoric may also disguise traditional remedies cloaked in fashionable jargon. If school discipline improves after intensive rule enforcement, can we score a victory for modern "empowerment" if this tactic was artfully labeled "empowering" (see, e.g., Borelli 1997)? More generally, do we equate empowerment with showering schools with material resources via lavishly funded "demonstration projects"? Or, must some unique, nonmaterial feature be present—a reshifting of authority, perhaps—for the endeavor to qualify as efficacious? Disentangling one element from a medley of reforms is daunting. And claims of power sharing or redistribution are often unverifiable, told entirely from one perspective in situations rife with dispute.

Even more troublesome is the evaluative time frame. The 1960s massive Great Society remediation efforts showed, alas, that induced improvements can evaporate. To wit, Head Start, an extensive, well-funded intervention program to assist youngsters, ultimately lost its promising impact, a fact unknowable when data were initially analyzed (see, for example, Herrnstein and Murray 1994, 403–404). Even more pedestrian "crash course" interventions often lose their gains after a few months (Jensen 1973, 90–91). Equally relevant, sustaining prodigious assistance is not always feasible, and once the aid is removed, matters can deteriorate to "normal." This goes beyond funding—prodding the slothful may suffice, provided the beneficiary stays in school, but eventually, he or she joins the real world unsupervised. Hectoring parents into assisting their children may work wonders, but parental enthusiasm may wane once prodding ceases.[7] There is also the predicament of programs enjoying initial success falling into less-committed hands with a corresponding decline in effectiveness. Superhuman efforts to ensure progress cannot be expected forever. All in all, and our review of obstacles is but cursory, empowerment intervention efforts recommend considerable caution against premature celebrations. The problems to be solved are serious and long term, so equating a momentary blip of improvement with triumph is only a self-inflicted illusion.

EMPOWERED EDUCATION

Explicating thousands of empowerment musings is unfeasible.[8] We instead selectively concentrate on major themes embedded in one key slice of this colossal exhortation: the *why* and *how* certain "players" in education should be empowered. Our stand is one of a naïve but tough-mined outsider seeking to correct deficiencies. Before us parade sundry pleaders insisting that they be empowered. We appraise their cases, examining their logic and evidence and—critically—demand proof. Lurking in the background is the realization that American education has periodically recovered from grave calamities, and empowerment vocabulary was notably absent from the prescriptive menu. Likewise, flourishing educational systems worldwide thrive sans this oratory. Thus, to advance a novel cure in lieu of demonstrated restoratives requires convincing evidence. We shall review the claims of four prominent visitors to our Court of Proposed Solutions: students, teachers, parents themselves and entire schools.[9]

Empowering Students

The phrase *empowered students* suggests sundry possibilities. For traditionalists, its positive meaning evokes highly erudite, motivated students. Laggards would be pushed harder, and expectations would be demanding. Armed with the powers of reason, skill in mathematics, a firm grasp of history, philosophy and similar fields, these scholars every day conquer new challenges. One might append more modern facility, such as computer literacy. Being empowered could also include virtues such as courage, tenacity and self-discipline. This is classic liberal education—instruction for a free person compelled to navigate life's exacting choices (the opposite being vocational education). The negative version might be chaotic schools—inmates running the asylum—lacking learning. Here, for example, teachers are intimidated into rewarding the slothful. Genuinely empowering these students (in the prior meaning) would be to remove their domination and restore it to superiors capable of guiding youngsters to authentic accomplishment.

Not unexpectedly, this tough-minded vista draws *zero* acclaim from empowerment adherents. Perhaps someplace this traditional idea prevails, but our search fails to find it. Some of the traditional mechanism promoting mastery—tracking, grading, respect for authority, strict rules—are even depicted as absolutely "depowering" (Irwin 1996). The negative traditional version is more often idealized. If a single term infuses this call, it is *liberation*. Ubiquitously coloring exhortations is the assumption that traditional, conventional skill-intensive instruction is the *very enemy* to be overthrown. The honored tales of immigrants—notably Jews and Asians—marching upward through classical skill acquisition never, apparently, crosses anybody's mind. Instead, education is exclusively a vehicle for "social change," with free-thinking students the advanced infantry in the imminent transformation.

This "liberationist" sentiment demands that walls separating teaching and student, even in early grades, be abolished. In this pedagogy, teachers do not impart learning into their captive charges; they become collaborators, true partners seeking insight. Philosophically, radical egalitarianism triumphs. Yes, teachers may be older, more experienced and know more facts, but this certainly does not bestow a privileged status permitting the imposition of learning. Yonemura (1986) writing in the prestigious *Harvard Education Review* invokes an apparent consensual view when she asserts, "I have seen that children *and* teachers learn best when they are viewed as people rather than locked into *pupil roles* or *teacher roles* and are thus freed to bring themselves and their views to the classroom world. Teachers free to be themselves are not threatened by children; they move with, not against, the energy released when children find their own answers" (475; italics in original). Here students themselves, by drawing on their inner resources, guide edification. The idea that children are "empty vessels" is soundly rejected. Children are even active participants in parent-teacher conferences.

The heightened attention to the emotional, subjective dimension of education is similarly pervasive. Irwin (1996) proclaims the litany of this prescription: In addition to thinking, there is intuition, love, honesty, sensing and caring (294). The empowered student is, moreover, to be cured of racism and discrimination. Explicitly rejected is the traditional hierarchical, rationalistic setting in which hard-nosed learning proceeds via teacher explication (Brunson and Vogt 1996). The prospect of rote learning is almost terrorizing. In place of projecting images of strength, "coolness" and calmness, teachers are to encourage trust and the heartfelt expression of feelings (technically labeled "holistic pedagogy"). Particularly important is that everyone feels confident in self-expression without fear of judgment or rejection. Students are held responsible for their own learning; teachers can only facilitate, adapting to student needs, not instruct in the traditional sense. The key is "personal growth" rather than acquiring traditional erudition. A commitment to people, institutions and experience is a paramount precondition for true empowerment. Discussing the wonders of traditional science and mathematics, philosophy or English literature is off the agenda.

Consider one modest exemplar—a Group Dynamics and Leadership course offered by two empowerment experts (Brunson and Vogt 1996). The centerpiece of this instruction is dividing students into groups, randomly selecting group leaders and then having these student leaders motivate group members to drink buttermilk. Self-selected strategies varied from bribery to persuasion and deception. Learning derived from discussing this activity. Class discussions addressed ethical choices, the role of leadership plus the larger sociopolitical consequences of this exercise. It is this chatty discourse—not imparting any "formal" facts—that constitutes empowerment. According to organizers, "When learners experience concepts and issues in this manner they become empowered because they realize the learning activity was unique for them in that context. Such a realization is powerful because it makes *their* views, insights and knowings valid (77; italics in original). In discussing the virtues of this approach, what is stressed is the drawing previously buried, unexamined thoughts and feelings to the surface. Uncovering the preexisting constitutes personal growth, the primary learning objective.

This liberating of students from "imposed" can be pushed even further. For scholars such as Roger I. Simon and untold others, education is fundamentally about creating a better world, a form of "cultural politics," not conveying venerable facts (Simon 1987). Schooling, thus grasped, becomes the means to "the realization of a variety of differentiated human capacities; rather than denying, diluting or distorting these capacities" (372). Success is "a just and compassionate community," not higher SAT scores.[10] Not unexpectedly, the traditional school missions of inculcating "traditional values" and "character development" are singled out for special opprobrium insofar as these aims impose a preexisting social order. Indeed, those traditionalists insisting on this "narrow" definition must be held morally accountable for the damage they impose! Moreover, this liberation hardly ceases with schooling—it is to extend outward, transforming all society via the redistribution of material rewards. Classrooms serve as the initial point of attack to uplift the marginalized.

And how does this radical enterprise proceed? First, the new curriculum must give expression to students' own cultural "voice." The precise nature of this voice and how it is to be discovered is unclear. Second, the entire enterprise must be tied to a moral vision—a *what for?* With zero analysis of competing aims (e.g., promoting economic growth), the objective is announced: a just and compassionate society. Fortunately, however, this vague prescription is immediately followed by two concrete empowered education examples. The first is explicitly attuned to the cultural voices of his pupils, notably their infatuation with professional wrestling. This is, explicitly, a pedagogy whereby Hulk Hogan and Andre the Giant supplant Shakespeare and Dickens. Hulk Hogan in particular focuses moral education. Even math is now taught in the context of professional wrestling (just how is unclear). A second concrete example is a high school program whereby students can spend up to two thirds of their time employed. But this is not mere on-the-job learning; it is an opportunity to challenge communal historical and social definitions of the work environment. Rather than learn tasks, students instead inquire why this duty exists and whose purpose it serves; "fitting" into a vocation is a defect here.

Another "empowered education" illustration comes from a college course designed to fight campus racism (Ellsworth 1989). This offering emerged from responses to a fraternity displaying racial insensitivity at a party. It explicitly and enthusiastically employed empowerment pedagogy to achieve its antiracist aims. At the outset, campus racism was assumed—the course delved only into its operation. Equally explicit was the project's intent at challenging the endemic "business-as-usual" racist atmosphere. The instructor's radicalism, commitment to social justice, antihomophobia and subversion of authoritarianism are all explicit. Given that all of this transpired at the liberally oriented University of Wisconsin–Madison, the course enjoyed full administrative support and enrollees were likely sympathetic, this endeavor surely tests empowerment pedagogy.

Students reflected varied racial/ethnic backgrounds, and all agreed that campus racism needed remediation. What then befell this expedition to conquer racism via empowerment? A precise answer is unclear, given the account's effusive jargon-filled, meandering turgid style, but the bottom line seems "not much" other than unanticipated difficulties. The attentiveness to multiple voices, bestowing inherent validity on every caprice, this deference to student feeling, yielded a cacophony of conflicts. Voices of the oppressed, moreover, often could not all be coaxed forth despite frequent enticements and promises of safety.

The hoped-for dialogues on repression never materialized, and white males habitually dominated class discussions. Unity collapsed as like-minded students often coalesced separately. The postmortem suggested that trust and personal commitment had fallen short. Nevertheless, these dilemmas aside, groups of freshly empowered students did strike out at the "business-as-usual" racism with two "street theater" campus demonstrations and letters to various university publications. Regarding classroom learning, subsequent behavior change, defeating racism or overall impact, no answers are given. In fact, response to these queries are not even sought: It is the effort, properly vocabularized, that counted as student empowerment regardless of outcome.

An entirely different situation occurs where empowerment is applied to the disadvantaged. Affluent university students squandering class time rehearsing the liturgy of oppression hardly debilitates: This is but a minor detour to future accomplishment. Ditto for comfortable middle-class students deducing math from Andre the Giant. But if such empowerment were inflicted on the poor, the consequences are far graver. Here a worthy education may be the sole exit; failing to acquire basic skills and steady habits ordains permanent indigence. Thus, higher standards of accountability are necessary, for failure can be devastating.

Touring this empowerment literature, alas, does not inspire optimism. The navigation of impediments becomes a celebration of these debilitating obstacles. Cummins's (1986) *Harvard Education Review* essay is typical in the strident rejection of traditional education as the path toward attainment. Now, it is the relationship between the culture of the disadvantaged and society at large that must be altered, not pupil deficiencies. Indeed, the very idea of a pupil deficit is rejected. In a nutshell, teachers must cater to the preexisting inclinations of students and adjacent community. Empowerment is the authority to impose one's own culture, rather than being dictated to by outsiders. It is this absence of schools that are sensitive to minority culture imposition, in his estimation, that explains inferior minority student academic performance.

How can schools educate via attending to indigenous cultures? The answer, in principle, is straightforward. First, school programs must reflect minority student language and culture. Gone is venerating conventional English and "white" values; instruction must also reflect unique "learning styles" of the disadvantaged. Second, the community itself must actively guide educational policy. If parents are apathetic, an extra effort must be made, and this involvement must be "genuine" (undefined), not the familiar co-optation. Third, school must motivate students to generate self-knowledge. The relationship between teacher and pupils is one of dialogue, not top-down imposition. Children will set their own learning objectives. Finally, school professionals will become advocates of these children, not critics dwelling on their alleged deficiencies. Student contributions will be affirmed rather than treated as evidence of pathology.

The theory is then demonstrated utilizing a California preschool program where Spanish is the dominant language. The object here was to raise readiness for future education (measured objectively). Thanks to an intensive immersion in Spanish language and culture coupled with energetic parental involvement, school readiness test scores rose to levels comparable to English-only speakers. Overall, the results announced a culturally attuned pedagogy success. Left unsaid was the obvious: The ticket to advancement in the United States requires learning English, not Spanish. To slight English at the expense of Spanish is undoubtedly a liability since all subsequent schooling will be almost entirely English based. These students, despite their test outcomes, will pay huge penalties upon joining the "real world."

This educationally "soft," "culture-sensitive" version of empowerment is commonplace when applied to troubled minorities. Consider a science program—Science, Technology, and Society (STS)—directed toward enhancing urban students' science knowledge (Waks 1991). The empowerment of disadvantaged youngsters is explicit, and the project is university based and has corralled wide government and expert support. The project's mission statement is steeped in the necessities of everyone—even the poor—being science literate. Are pupils, then, to learn math and logic, the power of the experimental method and knack for observation and the laws of motion? If not Boyle's Law, at least the logic of scientific inquiry? Again, empowerment is transmuted into making learning easy, fun and "relevant" with an encrypted deeper ideological message.

The STS program has eight explicit, overarching goals in constructing science education; *none embody traditional science*. Taken together, they stress social responsibility, diversity of viewpoints and implications of science. The closest approximation of science mastery is the eighth criteria, an item added after the project was developed: "*Science confidence*—The material must use the STS linkage to foster learners' confidence in handling and understanding at least one (limited) science area, and/or their handling or using some quantification as a basis of judgments in the STS area" (196). When the conventional scientific language does surface, it is but a single sentence on application in urban life (e.g., fast-food restaurants). There is also an explicit attentiveness to STS promoting democracy and an equality of knowledge. And not unexpectedly, the older hierarchical relationships between teacher and pupils must be replaced by egalitarian models, and student "deficiencies" are no longer personal adversities but instead disorders of much larger "social dynamics." Indeed, the problem is not even teaching science; it is "*how to win their hearts and minds*" (197; italics in original).

The ideological baggage is hardly hidden, no small accomplishment given the subject. While suggested topics are often perfectly neutral—for example, urban architecture—several partake of a decidedly liberal flavor. Suggested exemplars proffered in curriculum guidelines include the closing of an urban hospital (assumedly a bad action), abortion, the multicultural-laden multiple scientific contributions of African Americans and technology in pre-Columbian and African civilizations. Messages are also conveyed regarding the biological unity of all races and the cultural character of food and drug use. Surprisingly, science lessons are to address "new techniques in manufacturing illicit drugs and drug apparatuses" (200). Let us be clear regarding this instruction: The fault lies in this education's vacuous content, not the real-world examples. Science is being "dumbed-down," and in some perverse twist of logic, this is labeled "empowering."

A similar tale informs the "empowered math" directed toward poor, inner-city students (Zolkower 1995). That learning mathematics can be wearisome, drill-intensive and often frustrating is obvious. Yet this is often a necessary and unavoidable price to pay for vital skill. Perhaps it compares with physical training: Lifting weights and wind sprints are seldom fun, but if done arduously, the rewards are substantial. One can easily imagine empowerment being the strenuous attainment of proficiency—teachers push their reluctant charges with carrots and sticks to help them reach once unthinkable mastery. After years of misery, the power arrives, and resentment turns to heartfelt thanks. Now they can enjoy for decades the fruits of their early torment.

This hardly exhausts the possibilities. Zolkower recounts the essence of the new empowered math. According to this doctrine, problem solving must be balanced with inclusiveness and the requirement that learning be fun. Indeed, instruction is to create "mathematical communicators," not "mechanical rule followers." Even finding the right answer is secondary to feeling good about one's ability and togetherness. Going further, the traditional instructional approach is rejected for its hierarchical character, its reinforcement of dominant authority relationships. Good math requires a "deeper understanding," not mere learning of concepts; more attention to daily relevance, not arbitrary ideas; student-constructed knowledge to replace transmitted learning; and democracy supplanting authoritarianism. Predictably, according to this philosophy, the "Eurocentric" math is out, replaced by multicultural arithmetic.

The teller of this tale concludes, alas, that this "new" math approach comes up short. Students are often confused, teachers are unsure of outcomes and classrooms are beset by disorder. Might this be a warning to restore traditional methods? Hardly. Instead, according to this teacher, "what is necessary is perhaps not so much a reform at the level of the math text but, rather, a radical transformation of pedagogical practices and of the broader social and economic contexts in which these practices are embodied" (154). In other words, if a little radicalism fails, keep upping the dosage until it works. Perhaps private property should be expropriated in the name of empowering these children to learn their sums.

Needless to say, our brief tour depicts a "dumbed-down" education as pupil empowerment. This is a prescription for *dependency*. This link was well understood by Antonio Gramsci, a patron saint of today's Left, who argued that the true path to power was through traditional academic diligence (see Hirsch 1996, Ch. 6, on this point). Study after study confuses pleasing students and capacitating them. The avoidance of drudgery will extract a huge price when these youngsters seek employment. The college bound will, no doubt, go right to remedial classes in fourth-rate schools.

Self-indulgence, discovering one's "own" knowledge and flattery are more like tickets to welfare programs than attainment. For those exclusively depending on schools for advancement, this damage is devastating. This irony is, of course, a familiar assessment, quite similar to our conclusions in the previous chapter. The true beneficiaries are perhaps the inept teachers who easily escape the challenges of genuine education. It is, after all, far easier to empower students by mindlessly discussing their unique understandings of odd shapes than teaching geometry. We can only surmise that whatever one might label these efforts—"fun education," "culturally sensitive education" or the like—to apply the term *empowerment* is a misnomer.

Nor is this flattering of deficiencies preordained. History is replete with examples of rigorous schools educating the very poor and thereby making escape possible. Immigrant group after group has found the classical curriculum far more appealing than "science appreciation." In 1884 English philanthropists founded Toynbee Hall to serve London's poor (and this poverty far exceed today's destitution). Along with practical courses (sewing and nursing) were classes on Greek, Latin, Hebrew, French, music (Bach, Händel, etc.), chemistry, European history and English literature. For recreation, visiting distinguished authors and scholars lectured on contemporary economic and social issues. By all accounts, the enterprise was a great success (Himmelfarb 1995, 154–155). Many of today's colleges, no doubt, have yet to reach this exalted academic level.

Empowering Teachers

To empower teachers conjures up multiple possibilities. One might, for example, imagine teachers as economic sovereigns dictating salaries, hours and responsibilities. Or teachers may be revered as cultural icons shaping our civilization or embodying virtues worth emulating. Nevertheless, while such fanciful interpretations are feasible, *teaching* is inescapably embedded in this concept; genuine empowerment *must* mean imparting knowledge.[11] The prerequisites—ability to impose discipline, patience, street savvy, own knowledge, patience, empathy, creativity—are endless, but these are not in and of themselves empowerment. A teacher may draw a handsome salary or dominate the school board, but this economic and political power should not be equated with educational empowerment. An "empowered teacher" who failed to educate is oxymoronic.

It follows that to empower teachers is to facilitate instruction. Power is entirely instrumental, and the end is learning. If disorderly students hinder instruction, the teacher can remove disrupters. If teachers are ill-prepared scholastically, they must retool or be fired. Improvements cannot be open-ended justifications for endless aggrandizing. A luxurious lounge will gladden teachers, and obtaining it may evidence power, but it would be bizarre to assert that this prize automatically empowers *teachers*. An empowered *employee* is a more apt depiction.

Three themes are dogmatically repeated in the call for teacher empowerment. Of these, none exceeds involvement in school decision making. This ubiquitous participatory covers a multitude of interventions (Mertens and Yarger 1988; Romanish 1993a; Irwin [1996, Ch. 4] offers an overview). Argued is that education will improve if teachers receive "greater say" over hiring, the curriculum, working conditions, school administration (from discipline rules to physical maintenance) and relation with outside groups such as parents, school boards or universities. Greater union involvement is also sometimes appended. In a nutshell, the traditional hierarchical bureaucratic structure is to be flattened. This expanded role need not be formalized. One overview (Sprague 1992) suggests that through passive resistance, if not obstruction, teachers can impose their views. That is, unwise top-down directives can be ignored or manipulated, meetings can be avoided and, occasionally, test results can be faked. Teachers "rule" in reality but not in name.

Examples abound of drawing of teachers into wider educational governance. In one California school district, for example, teachers directly controlled over a $1 million curriculum and staff development fund, helped decide classroom assignments, formulated student discipline procedures and assessed professional performances. Teachers were even consulted on budgets and school priorities. Significantly, a notable increase in pupil learning and other indicators of school performance occurred (Sickler 1988). Dade County, Florida, and Rochester, New York, programs have garnered extensive attention for their teacher engagement in educational administration. Here governance is by "management team" and "partnership" (see, e.g., Maeroff 1988a; Rist 1989).

This definition stressing consulting can be interpreted as virtual classroom sovereignty. Again, an infatuation with flattering self-knowledge: It is the teacher—not principals or parents—that decides learning content. In some instances, this is merely flexibility to meet arduous instructional challenges (Duffy [1992] uses "venturesome" and "idiosyncratic" to characterize empowered instruction). In other cases, however, this empowerment resembles a license to impose one's own Weltanschauung, even against opposing communal values. As one professor opined, "Empowerment is about liberation. This is as true for teachers as it is for women and people of color in political arenas" (Romanish 1993b, 57). A Columbia University education professor gives a slightly different twist: "[T]eachers should be empowered because teaching is a moral activity" (Bolin 1989, 82). Does this mean instruction in the traditional moral virtues, for example, honesty? Scarcely. For Bolin (and others) this "moral education" is not imparting values found "elsewhere." No precise list governs proscribed ends, nor can there be. Rather, teachers are to attend to vague cultural differences and an equally amorphous "democracy." For principals to insist, for example, that discipline be imposed upon those whose "culture" welcomes chaos undermines authentic teacher empowerment. This spirit is further echoed by another education professor (Zeichner 1991) who easily equates teacher empowerment with carte blanche authority to overthrow traditional Western, white Eurocentric, hierarchical curriculums with their nefarious emphasis on objective tests.

A second pervasive theme is enhanced knowledge. The logic here is that the ignorant cannot impart knowledge—erudite teachers may not enlighten, but without subject mastery, learning is impossible. Improved proficiency in the abstract can take varied paths, but not all enjoy equal popularity here. One fairly obvious—and undoubtedly most critical—mode *not* enthusiastically embraced is strict academic certification conditions: that is, raise admission standards to teaching programs, abolish content-free "Mickey Mouse" pedagogy courses, impose stiff postcollege examinations and regularly require retesting. In short, given its importance, govern teaching as one carefully certifies doctors or lawyers.

Instead, promoters of enhanced expertise routinely call for *upgrading* those already employed. Ample intellectual talent and drive are presupposed; it merely has to be perfected. These techniques include after-school in-service programs, college courses, special summer programs, specialized teacher centers, multidisciplinary team curriculum development, specialized clinics and classes about teaching taught by teachers themselves (Maeroff 1988b). IBM, together with the National Education Association, has even entered this empowerment quest by linking teachers to community colleges via computers (Sandvick and Nauman 1991). That significant numbers might be *beyond* remediation, regardless of effort, innovative technique or incentives, is taboo. Moreover, absent is a concern for measuring improvement; participation is equated with betterment. One assessment, not unexpectedly, judged this newfound educational "upgrading" worthy insofar as teachers afterward "felt better about themselves." Further study is also appreciated for making teachers feel "important" and encouraging self-confidence (Maeroff 1988a). Perchance the barriers to firing incompetents or strict entrance requirements bolster this half-a-loaf mentality.

The third element in teacher empowerment is heightened status. That teachers are poorly regarded is accepted by educators, and empowerment will remedy this defect. Said one expert, "There will be no empowerment while teachers feel small and insignificant because they are doing a job that they think is not adequately appreciated by those outside the schools" (Maeroff 1988a, 474). And why are teachers not regarded as doctors or university professors? The reasons are plain: It is a largely feminine occupation, salaries are middling, the task requires modest ability and job authority is constrained (Sprague 1992). We might also add that prestige seldom comes to those perceived as incompetent. The underlying logic is that while schools are now performing poorly, empowered teachers can improve learning; therefore, betterment requires raising teacher status.

Enhanced status can be pursued in many ways, and the status hierarchy is hardly fixed. Doctors were once far subordinate to warriors in prestige. How is reputation to be augmented? This quest is both arduous and paradox laden. If "feminine vocations" (e.g., nursing) will always be inferior to "masculine jobs," then the solution is to masculinize primary and secondary teaching, as is commonplace abroad. Needless to say, gender hiring restrictions violate antidiscrimination laws and are unethical. Or if ignorance breeds mediocre status, impose stringent exams to weed out the ill-equipped. When teachers pass CPA-like tests, their prestige will soar. We have already touched upon the nonworkability of this remedy. Or mimicking professional sports, abolish tenure and keep hiring and firing until achieving excellence. Again, this is totally unrealistic, given the unionization of education, and fails to address fresh recruit quality.

What quietly underlies status enhancement schemes is simple: money (see, e.g., Maeroff 1988b, Ch. 2; Rist 1989; Sickler 1988). When teachers earn hefty wages, their prestige will grow; they will be empowered. On its face, this "pay-more-and-excellence-will-arrive" argument is plausible. Surely higher salaries will theoretically draw more talented recruits, help retain the accomplished and, hopefully, energize the merely dutiful. Perhaps the transformation of medicine is the model.

Unfortunately, a huge chasm separates abstract argument and results. Most plainly, given that wages constitute the largest portion of the education budget, the necessary raises require massive increases in taxes or corresponding budget cuts elsewhere. In 1994, for example, nearly 2 million public school teachers earned an average of $36,500. Raises of $30,000 each would add nearly $60 billion to the education budget, most of it to local property taxes (*U.S. Statistical Abstract* 1996–1997; tables 256, 257). This is unlikely, especially given past history of ineffectual increased spending. This argument may have been conceivable in the optimistic 1960s, but it will not fly in the skeptical 1990s, even if correct. No political constituency outside of the education establishment favors this massive spending boost.

A second perplexity is that nearly all of this increase will go to those already in place, not new "superteachers." To repeat an earlier point: This stratagem rewards failure. Moreover, imagine the outrage if newly certified "expert" novices were paid, say, $75,000, whereas experienced senior faculty received $37,000? Unions would never accept wildly discrepant two-tier systems. Efforts in this direction have, predictably, proven acrimonious and troublesome (see, e.g., Mertens and Yarger 1988). And this massive investment rests wholly on the *promise* of educational enhancement. The relationship between teacher pay and learning is hardly self-evident, and evidence shows no straightforward connections (Ballou and Podgursky

1997). Perchance the problems are unsolvable, regardless of the pay, or are far too complex to be addressed by mechanically raising salaries. Country evidence also abounds. Catholic schools, for example, for decades turned out well-trained graduates while paying paltry salaries. Even prestigious private schools with splendid accomplishment records do not have to pay prestigious remuneration.

The teacher empowerment clamor plainly rests on hope. Bits and pieces of evidence offer some faint optimism, but even when first steps are taken, problems quickly surface (see, e.g., Mertons and Yarger 1988). For teachers to think they possess answers does not guarantee success. Everybody may think themselves an expert from the outside looking in. Despite some plausible arguments, no new "miracle cure" has been discovered. Obviously, teachers would benefit from greater dominance—controlling one's job and the extra benefits would surely be joyously welcomed. And a long record proclaims the rewards of permitting schoolmasters unchallenged classroom respect and autonomy. Empowerment *can* work, but abstract principles are not the issue here. It is teacher empowerment *as advanced by its contemporary prophets that we have found wanting.* Our verdict is one of "not demonstrated."

Marching today's instructors off to endless seminars, giving them a curriculum voice or boosting their incomes cannot guarantee learning. It is also not clear whether classroom teachers really want the responsibilities demanded by those outside the classroom. Several teacher surveys suggest that (1) many teachers accept present arrangements and (2) a gap separates desiring more power and a willingness to use it (Duke and Gansneder 1990). Moreover, not even the most fully empowered teacher can excel if he or she knows little, confronts hostile students and heeds idiotic pedagogical doctrines. Equally relevant, what might usefully restore academic excellence—tough discipline, no-nonsense grading, arduous drill, among multiple proven remedies—quickly invites intense opposition (see Bernstein 1994, Ch. 8). The all-powerful, draconian teacher will probably be wildly unpopular both inside and outside the classroom, regardless of success. Again, better employment conditions do not mean better education.

Empowering Parents

Of all the "players" in education, it is the empowering of parents that raises the most difficult questions. An especially troublesome paradox informs the issue. On the one hand, parents are sovereigns in education. As voters they possess the ultimate clout both directly—deciding taxes, electing school boards—and indirectly—choosing public officials with power over schools. Their willingness to pay profoundly shapes education. The dissatisfied "vote with their feet"—leave the district or send their offspring to private schools. Parental outrage over instruction or classroom behavior is a potent political force. Equally important, parents qua parents shape schools' performance by the values imparted to their children. Even the most ambitious teacher is constrained by parental boundaries. "Home life"—everything from tolerating truancy to favoring reading over the TV— is surely a critical variable in the educational equation.

Nevertheless, this immense, irreducible authority scarcely dictates outcomes. Many parents simply are generally indifferent to schooling. A few might even tolerate illiteracy; others gladly welcome "free" day care. Even if attentive, citizens often defer to educational experts on matters properly in parental hands, for example, moral training. That professional educators are often better organized and can claim certified expertise also undermine parental power. And while home life may be the critical ingredient in educational success, this need not be a deliberate choice. Severe obstacles abound in molding their children regardless of one's aims. The frustration of parents in propelling their children toward academic attainment is notorious.

The upshot of this situation is an oddity: Parents already *are* empowered—perhaps supremely so—although this authority may not be exercised regularly or adroitly. This even applies for dismal educational attainment; parent empowerment does not *require* scholastic excellence. Surely, many repudiate education, and for them to be fully empowered, this means wretched schooling is a "success." For teachers to impose excellence on parents not wishing it is, perhaps, teacher, though not parental, empowerment. The question is, then, How can this potential parental empowerment be made more effective? The model is one of consumer choice—allow the market (here schools) to satisfy consumer demand. Put more concretely, schools must determine what parents want, good or bad, and then seek to satisfy it. This is the inescapable core meaning of "parental empowerment." To be sure, educators possess every right to plead vigorously their own perspectives, but their aims cannot be substituted for parental objectives.

As with all empowerment schemes, multifarious paths abound. Several political devices would afford parents ample control—binding policy and spending referendums, regular election of all education administrators and legally powerful specialized citizen oversight boards are obvious choices. If "knowledge is power," one might also add mechanisms for honestly keeping parents updated, reports akin to corporation stockholder reports supplemented by outside detailed audits (including student performance). Parents may also be given greater access to schools, opportunities to monitor teaching, just as they might attend a choral performance. Most evidently, of course, are those mechanisms providing parents nearly total choice in education—vouchers and charter schools, even home schooling. Here, control over tax dollars blends education with the commercial market. Logically, students might even be permitted to escape public education altogether, as is done for the Amish past the eighth grade. To repeat, the issue here is *not* attaining scholastic excellence, although untold parents will prefer this aim (just as others covet champion football teams). The goal is to fully translate, for better or worse, potential parental sovereignty into actual power.

As one peruses this professional educator–dominated research literature, we find a rather constrained, one-sided interpretation of parental empowerment. Not surprisingly, admonitions for dissatisfied "customers" to escape public education are rare. Imagine citizen rejection of tax increases being celebrated as "genuine empowerment"? No experts announce that "competition is healthy" or that "consumer choice" is empowerment. This mighty chorus demanding autonomy exists well outside this literature.[12] Nor is there much attention to education's political context—the use of elections to impose accountability or shifting of legal authority to those outside "the system." At core, when educators speak of "empowering parents" they advise drawing parents into the realm of the professionally administered school. An entire issue of *Phi Delta Kappan* was devoted to parental involvement in schools, and despite a parade of innovative suggestions to bring parents into the schools, genuine political control escaped notice (see Epstein 1991 for a summary). This "taking charge" might more honestly be portrayed as "playing a role" in the school's smooth operation. That parental sovereignty might *oppose* goals formulated by educators is inconceivable; parent empowerment derives from reinforcing the public school mission.

Case studies of this "empowerment = parental involvement" abound, and although each has their local idiosyncrasies, their outlines are quiet similar (see, e.g., Dunlap 1996; Jackson and Cooper 1989; Wells 1997). Consider one such study as typical, a complex multischool California effort involving Spanish-speaking parents and children (Delgado-Gaitan 1991). The forces discouraging involvement in school activity are hardly unique here—language differences, a clash of cultures, unfamiliarity with local customs, social class divisions, plus the demands of arduous employment. Given these impediments and the long record of school failures in this quest, how was parental empowerment to be accomplished?

The schools here made a major effort to engage parents. Multiple formal opportunities—teacher-parent conferences, open houses, an "on-site" council with parent representation—were implemented. Bilingualism was the norm, and administrators actively sought parental input about larger issues, including budgets and curriculum. These conventional programs generally drew heavy participation and usefully addressed varied issues, for example, a student's difficulty in mastering English. Supplementing these school-instigated efforts, two state programs for Hispanic students with an attendant staff also facilitated extensive parental participation. Here the emphasis was on instructing parents to assist their children—the importance of reading stories, for instance—plus advice on disturbances such as alcoholism and drugs.

A third outreach element was a group initiated by Spanish-speaking parents themselves, *Comite de Padres Latinos* (COPLA), to both enhance parental mobilization and tackle larger controversies (significantly, the group's leaders were all local education employees). COPLA met regularly and its discussions touched on broader topics, for example, stereotypes, and also served as a support group. Its members tutored more recent immigrants on schools and politics more generally. Tensions between the school and parents were not unknown but were seldom divisive and were always amicably resolved. After a year of all these varied efforts, all parties generally viewed these undertakings as successful, thanks in large part to considerable hard work and state program assistance.

By any yardstick, this and the many other parental involvement programs are worthy and often successful academically (see, e.g., Griffith 1996). The issue is not one of worthiness; it is of empowerment properly understood. Surely parents who consult with teachers or chide principals for woeful performance have gained a measure of influence. And, no doubt, this influence may translate into desired outcomes—getting their child into a special program, for example. Yet if we examine this participation against the backdrop of citizen political control, such consultation, no matter how beneficial, is but a consolation prize. The basic framework remains in the hands of professional educators: They are always "in charge." Parents here are not deciding consequential policy; they more closely resemble a clientele being solicited for their opinions to fine-tune customer satisfaction.[13] Truly momentous choices—personnel, educational philosophy, administrative organization—are de facto off the agenda. Let us not confuse heightened appreciation of school management plus a dollop of attentiveness with genuine power.

To appreciate this conflation of consultative relationships with empowerment, imagine if parents took their sovereignty seriously. Suppose they insisted upon tough corporal punishment and severe suspensions to quiet troublemakers or that bilingual instruction should be abolished altogether as hindering economic progress? What if they demanded teachers have college degrees in the subjects they taught? Or that money squandered on incessant teacher workshops be reallocated to longer school years? No doubt, professional reaction would be intensely negative, and parent participation would quickly become a forum in which "enlightened" professionals tutored "misinformed" parents. If pushed, educators would invoke the camouflage of "expertise" or "supportive research" or just obscure everything in jargon. If these matters were placed on a referendum, it is unlikely that these "pro-empowerment" teachers would remain neutral and defer to the outcome. In short, deference to public desires is quite distinct from inviting parents to discuss their child's academic progress.

Empowering Schools

As with all other notions of empowerment, "empowered schools" is hardly self-explanatory despite its fashionableness. Not all denotations imply academic achievement. One might imagine powerful schools—institutions of appreciable political influence perhaps due to the lofty positions of their graduates or the prestige surrounding faculty pronouncements. Harvard University embodies this notion. Or schools may have a huge economic cloud from budgets or retirement funds (the California higher education retirement system is a major stock market player). Alternatively, institutions, as cultural models, may shape society's contours. It has long been said, for example, that English "public schools" (e.g., Easton) enjoyed this "power." A less exalted interpretation focuses on administrative capacity. Here school leaders command: Everyone—even the slothful—dutifully behave, learn their lessons and embrace school norms, and parents respectfully assist this mission. Finally, empowerment may conjure up visions of unfettered independence—the school is beholden only to itself. The institution can safely ignore laws, academic standards, financial limitations or whatever else might hinder whim. This might result in education marvels or disasters; this wholly depends on how this autonomy is exercised.

What, then, emerges from accounts of "empowered schools"? Of all the myriad possibilities, the infatuation with decentralization dominates. A "strong" school is one in which power is diffused. The most elaborate, detailed scheme is offered in *The Self-Directed School: Empowering the Stakeholders* (McIntire and Fessenden 1994). It commences by acknowledging our crisis—the terrible academic performance of American students (1). A facile parallel is then drawn between education and business histories. To wit, post–World War II American business prospered, but in the 1980s it lost ground to foreign competition due to shoddy products and inferior service. And how did business recover? By ridding itself of its cumbersome, top-down bureaucratic organization is the answer (no analysis is presented on this point). Once employees became more involved and communications flowed both ways, commercial vitality exploded. And, it is alleged, this lesson is equally applicable to schools: Triumph will come from flattening the hierarchy and giving a voice to all. Deterioration flows from poor management, and what is needed is pervasive collaboration and teamwork. In a phrase, "a Community of Stakeholders" (7).

The school's traditional leadership structure must give way to wider sharing of authority among all participants, from teachers to principals to school boards to citizens groups and everyone in between. And why should this egalitarian system outperform its top-down rivals? The answers are "obvious": School stakeholders are the most involved, the most committed, efforts will be collaborative and this produces enthusiasm and productivity. In a nutshell, tinkering with the organizational chart—replacing "management" with cooperation—brings academic adeptness. Moreover, there is no single precise blueprint for success; each school must discover its own solution (Ch. 1).

Page after page depicts this newly empowered Utopia. When perplexities do arise, they are glibly sidestepped. For example, the daunting obstacle of sufficient competence is "solved" when the school board and superintendent prepare a detailed, comprehensive policy manual (47). The obvious conflict between this micromanagement style and egalitarianism go unmentioned. The collision of interests is "resolved" by counseling yet more cooperation (46). The complete sharing of all information is proclaimed regardless of privacy principles and legally required confidentially (50). As for necessary training levels for this self-directed school, the answer is "sufficient" (95). The most strenuous problems crippling untold schools are "always" conquerable by trusting partnership. This is a make-believe world of eternal harmony. And not a single example from a real school or situation surfaces; everything is hypothetical.

Noteworthy is the compete inattention to academic outcomes; only process is judged important. The metaphor of the United States retaking world educational leadership, as it regained industrial prominence, quickly disappears. The ultimate goal, it would appear, is cloaking soft-headed egalitarian communalism in the trendy empowerment mantle. As such, this exercise illustrates just how easily the empowerment rhetoric can be captured for purposes irrelevant to academics. No doubt, a sermon calling for the exact opposite—organizing schools along military lines run by autocratic drill sergeants—could also claim the empowerment label.

Does the power-sharing recipe become more fruitful when applied concretely? Two examples will suffice. Carl Glickman (1990) presents himself as a cautious, experienced educator well versed with constraining realities. In his opinion, this partnership philosophy will produce because it will "free up" enormous energy—responsibility breeds accomplishment. He recounts a University of Georgia–assisted project involving 5 schools all embracing this promise of decentralized power. All schools have large numbers of disadvantaged students, and none are well-off financially. In addition, 25 other schools were enlisted in a similar project of assisting schools develop more egalitarian governance. The amount of resources committed to this enterprise seems substantial. Progress was monitored over a several-year period, including academic performance and dropout rate.

Does this hard-nosed decentralizing empowerment succeed? Hard—perhaps impossible—to tell. A handful, 4 of 29 cases, displayed bona fide academic progress. No claim is made that they are typical, although this is implied. It is also asserted that according to outside evaluations the impact on students has been "positive" and "significant" (in what sense is unstated). More telling than obscurity of outcomes is that all these accomplishments were associated with bestowing ample new school resources—

accelerated language tutorials, staff development activities, more individual attention to students, extra services for parents and students and similar costly intervention. To properly evaluate decentralization's net impact, all these compounding factors must be statistically extracted, and this is not evidenced. Thus, empowerment may have no independent consequences. A more apt conclusion is that if you are generous to many schools, some improve. The "how" and the "why"—key questions—remain mysterious.

The second concrete example comes from inner-city schools in Toledo, Ohio, with a familiar litany of troubles associated with teaching the disadvantaged (Kretovics, Farber and Armaline 1991). Again, to empower the school, those within it were given freer reign. And like similar remedies, this decentralization was complemented with extensive outside assistance. With University of Toledo experts and volunteers, a new curriculum was developed, schedules were rearranged, class size was reduced, additional teacher training was provided, students received more individualized attention, parental participation increased (a separate "parent coordinator" was hired) and lavish field trips were organized. A "family atmosphere" was created by keeping the same teachers and students across grades. Test scores generally increased, though progress was not uniform, and the academic gap between these students and those in other schools remains.

Again, an uncertain verdict regarding empowerment's benefit. Organizational structure changes are confounded with a multitude of circumstances conceivably upgrading achievement. Possibly, identical advantages allocated to authoritarian schools could have yielded the same—even better—outcomes. Alas, no attempt was made to disentangle these critical relationships. It is even possible that all this autonomy worked contrary to the positive impact of increased resources.

No inquiry into "empowered schools" would be complete without at least broaching the race issue. It is no exaggeration to say that the dismal academic performance of African-Americans students, often compounded with gang violence and drug abuse, is one of the instigating forces in this push toward school empowerment. In a sense, empowerment is the latest in a long line of proposed, and unsuccessful, solutions to this vexing problem. Perhaps what racial integration was to the 1950s, opulent buildings and equalized expenditure levels were to the 1960s and 1970s and Afrocentric education was to the 1980s, empowerment is to the 1990s. It is hoped, seldom with any supportive evidence, that giving black pupils, teachers, administrators and parents a powerful voice in school affairs will unleash the energy and knowledge necessary to overcome obstacles.

It is far too early, of course, to offer definitive conclusions, but much points in the direction of failure. Bits and pieces of anecdotal evidence— "tales from the front"—suggest that dispersing power widely among constituencies with profoundly different understandings of education and divergent goals is more likely to yield divisive antagonism sans academic improvement than productive, creative synergy. Diana Tittle (1995; Bernstein 1994, Ch. 8, recounts very similar incidents) presents an unusually forthright account of one such well-funded, well-intentioned experiment—the restructuring of Cleveland Heights High School, a racially mixed, middle-class suburban institution with a past record of academic excellence but with current sharp black-white differences in academic mastery. Here, in the late 1980s, teachers were awarded fresh new power, trained for leadership, eventually supplemented with outside grants, to reinvent an ideal school, one that would surely overcome the notable racial gap in academic performance. Freed from red tape and authorized with newfound budgetary power, the virtues of teacher empowerment would be demonstrated.

Despite the best of intentions, the project failed in both its educational objectives—eliminating racial differences in attainment—and in its administrative goals. Many of the reasons are deeply rooted, perhaps unchangeable, and predictable. Teachers are hardly a unified group, and differences over pedagogy, grading policy, protecting "turf" and job security issues can easily hinder consensus building. On more than one occasion, discussion over everything from academics to representation in governance would ramble on endlessly without closure. Nor are differences in personality and style among key figures solved by exhortations. Moreover, central figures periodically changed jobs or retired, and this altered philosophical directions. Clashes over race-related issues, often emotionally tinged, further undermined common purpose (teachers, like students, self-segregated voluntarily). These race-related issues grew more volatile as the school became increasingly black, eventually escalating into calls for a comprehensive Afrocentric curriculum and filling administrative positions with blacks as a matter of right. Inevitably, racial animosities instigated complaints with the federal government and investigation of alleged bias. The teachers' union was also outraged over innumerable proposed changes and, at one point, confiscated student schedules to block the reduction in class periods (Ch. 7). Union opposition was almost a constant theme during this restructuring effort. Proposals advanced by "study teams" frequently were grandiose wish lists incompatible with fiscal feasibility and political reality. White teachers in particular frequently resented coerced racial sensitivity training.

The academic side of the problem was approached cosmetically. The commonplace explanation for dreary black academic performance was "low expectation," an explanation that has *never* withstood scientific scrutiny (Jensen 1973, Ch. 14). Since ability groupings only highlighted racial differences in academic proficiency, they were almost entirely abolished. Similar academic ability divisions among courses were also labeled as "racist" and virtually eliminated. Meanwhile, the school was "improved" by adding a flagpole, a spruced-up lobby and a public sign announcing the

school's virtues (Tittle 1995, Epilogue). Meanwhile, area gang conflicts escalated and entered the school itself, while school violence and vandalism
soon drew police visits. The principal would now occasionally "congratu-
late" students for having "a good week" over the school's PA system. The
reform impetus petered out while disciplinary problems continued unabated. Most important, academic test scores did not increase over the five
years of all this good-intentioned turmoil.

If anyone displayed empowerment during this period, these were the parents who desired a first-rate education for their children. Some "voted with
their feet" and simply moved to communities with better schools (including
several Cleveland Heights teachers and administrators). Others stayed put
and enrolled their offspring in private schools. Many local people without
school-aged children showed their displeasure by voting down proposed
tax increases designed to pour even more money into this collapsing empowerment experiment. Untold others anxious to move to a good environment simply scratched Cleveland Heights off the list of possibilities. As the
area changed its demographic character, the cycle of mounting problems
coupled with diminishing resources only intensified.

Plainly, "empowered school" in these studies is but a synonym for ordinary decentralization surrounded with some preachy admonitions for
"partnership" and "trust." The evidence of improvement is spotty, and
perhaps more important, there is scarcely any effort to apply rigorous tests
or to take a hardheaded look at underlying theory. The "empowerment
project" far more closely resembles a religious faith by definition immune
to empirical examination. Clichés have been hardened into dogma. The
"logic" informing these efforts is little more than "If people have a stake,
they will perform better." Although a grain of truth may reside in this
dictum, it is only a minute piece of the picture. Faddishness seems to be
running rampant. Obstacles such as granting power to incompetents, engendering ceaseless conflict by fractured authority, expanding the size of
decision-making bodies and opening up sensitive quarrels to scrutiny are
blissfully ignored. Even worse, this insistence on freewheeling autonomy,
occasionally accompanied with a desire for riskless innovation, can easily
be interpreted as a retreat from accomplishment. After all, with everybody
legitimately "doing their own thing," how are we to hold anybody accountable? Empowerment thus becomes a license to fail.

CONCLUSIONS

Our trek began by noting empowerment's advancement as the great mar-
vel for the ills of American education. The results depicted here offer meager encouragement. The triumphs are rare, are seldom unambiguous and
may not survive. Some interventions—especially those downplaying traditional learning—may well worsen matters. Of course, as with all shortfalls,

excuses are plentiful: More time is needed, programs were not properly implemented, funds are insufficient, commitments are inadequate, enemies practice sabotage, society is unfair and so forth. Perhaps this litany is partially correct, but the problems, quite likely, run far deeper. Even under ideal circumstances, with ample cooperation and funding, these empowerment-based remedies are troublesome. Perchance even fatal.

To retell a familiar tale, theoretical foundations, regardless of rendition, are typically flimsy, almost nonexistent. Spinning out vocabulary is conflated with fashioning sturdy theory. A favorite methodology is to contrast a wondrous Utopian vision with grim reality to "prove" the value for the former (also see, e.g., Renihan and Renihan 1995; Shanker 1990). Educators today confront formidable hurdles, and those seeking solutions are armed with slogans disguised as "theory" to wage the battle.[14] How is reading to be taught by "attending to the child's unique culture"? Why should teachers' views of educational aims outrank those of parents? What is so magical about decentralization? Every question in the educational enterprise is tough, and yet nebulous answers are glibly offered without a second thought. As is common in this literature, preaching to the choir has disastrous consequences. Nobody seems inclined to challenge dubious fads marketed as wisdom. Who will aver: "Why give incompetents unchecked classroom authority? Who will wrestle (besides Hulk Hogan) with all the contradictions of celebrating student control over their own educational programs? In short, serious derelictions of intellectual duty abound. Like the students they admire, educators have made serious work empty "fun."

An embarrassing disdain for academic accomplishment deeply infuses this enterprise. Empowerment may connote many things, but the "knowledge is power" axiom remains far distant. Teaching children to read, write and do mathematics is inevitably secondary to goals enacting some eccentric "good society" or instilling self-esteem. It is entirely possible to discuss school accomplishment in detail while avoiding academics altogether (Stein 1996). The very idea of intellectual superiority and subordination may smack of dreaded elitism (Duffy 1994). Our negative assessments of American education's academic commitment is hardly unique (Kramer [1991] offers a grim tour of our education schools). Moreover, attempts to undo this orientation seem doomed. Even allegedly tough teacher certification tests becomes subverted by the education establishment. In one recent attempt—the National Board for Professional Teaching Standards—not only were these tests voluntary, but academic content was overwhelmed by subjective "soft" criteria ("caring," for example) that will hardly exclude incompetents (Buday and Kelly 1996).

Academic diligence is not the only labor escaped. Our educational system faces multiple, often embarrassing contradictions, and these, too, are slighted. The empowerment infatuation easily allows safe, trendy escapist denial. That "true" empowerment may be forever unobtainable makes it even more attractive as a permanent excuse. Perhaps educators resemble those unsuspecting souls buying endless "miracle diet" schemes, all promising immense but effortless weight loss. Failure only breeds desperation and even more gullibility for gimmicks. We want high achievement, but not if this obliges parental diligence or foregone recreation. We prefer academically qualified teachers, but not if strict examinations fail too many minority candidates. Awarding easy "I have an honor roll student at . . ." bumper stickers beats arduous, tedious labor. Why restore the tough discipline imperative for learning if this invites parental protest and litigation? There is an element of quackery here. One can easily imagine a late-night TV commercial—"Boost your school's performance painlessly and cheaply by taking just two empowerment pills once a week! Experts all agree, the best thing since sliced bread!" Thousands, no doubt, would phone in immediately.

This rush to embrace faulty novelty is especially depressing in light of available solutions. Empowerment is *not* our last desperate hope. Charter schools have shown promising results (Nathan 1996), and the "tried and true" can still work. Thomas Sowell's (1986, Ch. 2) approach is to examine what actually works, not what might perform according to seductive slogans. He examines black schools—six high schools and two elementary schools—producing outstanding academic achievement. The schools vary in student body talents, location, guiding philosophy, religious affiliation and physical setting. Despite differences, all share a deep commitment to academic excellence and traditional "law and order." Teachers are revered individuals, not "partners," and expectations of scholastic accomplishment are high. Practices anathema to empowerment devotees—tracking, corporal punishment, testing objective knowledge, religious education—are often standard. Many attend to black cultural pride, but nowhere does this pride overwhelm academics. In sum, these are truly empowered schools, although most empowerment prophets would expel them from the congregation.

Our final point here pertains to political ideology. If one surveys where the empowerment chorus resides in our political landscape, it is clear that it dwells on the Left. Given the close alignment of the educational establishment with the Democratic Party's liberal wing, this is anticipated. The preeminence of state-run schools is unquestioned—almost any privatization is heresy. It is axiomatic that more expensive Washington intervention—programs for every ill imaginable—are the preferred solution. Attacks on so-called traditional education—European history and literature, Western culture, science and mathematics—are endemic. The "enemies" of education are usually right-wing extremists, religious fundamentalists or Ronald Reagan. The contemporary cultural Left also gets in its licks with assaults on rationality, objectivity, the notion of transcendent knowledge, hierarchy of moral values and the superiority of reason over emotion. For good measure add all the praise for multiculturalism, diversity, liberation against oppression and the rest of the familiar agenda.

This exposé is *not* a criticism of comingling politics and education. That is not the point, and it would be foolish to insist on segregating one from the other. The point is that this uncompromising ideological devotion seriously subverts education. Forced to choose between achievement and politics, many educators opt for the later. This is clearly wrong: Educational achievement is what empowerment here is supposed to accomplish. If educators wish to pursue politics, they have every right to do so; what is destructive is when they relentlessly advance ill-conceived nostrums *within the school* whose only real utility is their conformity to ideological precepts. Perhaps a parallel can be drawn to Soviet economists clinging to Marxism even if it brings mass starvation. To be blunt, millions of children are being miseducated to flatter political sensibilities. And this is hardly predetermined—history overflows with proven remedies. It would be far more noble if an expert said, "I favor radical egalitarianism, but to push treating pupils and teachers as equals violates my responsibilities as an educator." If the conflict between the educator's personal political beliefs and his or her professional responsibility was unbridgeable, he or she should honorably resign or change politics. To draw a salary while dispensing nonsense is dishonest. Again, it is not the politics that is at issue; it is the failure to see beyond political dogma and concentrate on education that is the flaw.

NOTES

1. The "blind leading the blind" problem is undoubtedly obscured by publication requirements—absolute nonsense is rejected or cleaned up editorially. This "upgrading" becomes apparent when unedited convention papers are examined. Here one can witness garbled syntax, confusions galore and a fondness for empty rhetoric (see, e.g., Lockett 1994). One can only imagine the mischief caused when these "empowerers" are set loose upon the unsophisticated.

2. This conflation of "conservative" with "antidemocratic" is not unusual. The concrete examples of "antidemocratic tendencies" used in Zeichner's discussion— aversion regarding teaching about homosexuality or a desire for religious displays on school grounds—have *nothing* to do with democracy, as this term is generally understood. Elsewhere the author denotes standardized tests and ability grouping as "antidemocratic." Needless to say, such confusion might be used as evidence to disqualify this authority to participate in the public education debates until they complete remedial political science classes.

3. Multicultural empowerment fans always assume that group celebration must occur in *public* schools. They cannot imagine private academies (or after-school instruction, as in Sunday schools) accomplishing this goal, a strategy that rejects dependency on public funding. Perhaps these prophets are hardwired into subservience to the state despite all contrary rhetoric.

4. Empowerment enterprises often portray teachers so busy being empowered

that classroom presence declines. The guiding assumption is that solutions must be "discovered" by all participants at workshops, conferences and retreats. Readily available off-the-shelf proven remedies are inapplicable. Similarly, students are off on their own largely unsupervised projects. Perhaps this escape from drudgery partly explains empowerment's lure (for one such project, see Tuthill and Seidel 1987).

5. Complaints against "bureaucratic constraint" are endemic in empowerment calls, yet there is seldom any awareness why these "bad" practices exist. That the craving for "liberation" collides with accountability seems beyond comprehension (see, e.g., Clift 1991).

6. This notion of "freedom from consequences" is occasionally conflated with encouraging "innovation" in the education literature (see, e.g., Lagana 1989). Why "innovation" is reflexively considered better than "traditional" raises an odd question: Why prefer the untried to the proven? More important, it would seem that instructing that all actions have consequences would be of the utmost importance in instilling competence, or else one hardly learns from mistakes.

7. Empowerment via bribery may sound oxymoronic, but in a New Orleans empowerment project, parents were actually paid for attending parent-teacher conferences and if their children performed well academically (Miron 1995). One can only imagine the results if this funding stopped.

8. Sampling this vast literature is no simple task. As common in the empowerment literature generally, a scholarly "core," as evidenced by frequently positive mention, seems totally absent. Despite bountiful citations, overlap is rare; "classics" are apparently nonexistent. Our selection strategy must be somewhat idiosyncratic but we limit ourselves to materials published in traditional scholarly outlets (where some review process has transpired) and those that display the variety of this endeavor.

9. This list hardly exhausts would-be power seekers. Omitted are unions, professional consultants, education professors, government bureaucrats, various political interest groups and religious organizations. A full portrait of this clamor will fill books.

10. Simon, as is commonplace in this field, has a flair for obscurity (e.g., "the transformation of the relations between human capacity and social form," 373). We must therefore add the caveat that our interpretation may be an inaccurate "translation" of what is actually intended.

11. This literature assumes that learning is *always* possible. Conceivably, no amount of empowerment or intervention of any kind will succeed in some circumstances. Schools cannot always work miracles. But the *hope* of progress usefully serves to justify an endless parade of demands.

12. The voucher movement is largely centered in conservative-oriented think tanks and ad hoc citizen organization. It has its own newspaper—*School Reform News*—published by the Heartland Institute. In the March 1998 issue, 54 supporting organizations were listed favoring this form of parental empowerment.

13. Also note that the once unchallenged superiority of family over school is being undermined as educators increasingly see themselves as specialists authorized to intervene in family matters. Much of this is absolutely benign—for example, preventing child abuse. Nevertheless, an increasing tendency exists for educators to conceive of the family-school nexus as a broad, two-way street. Thus, bringing

parents into the school permits the schools to shape parents as well as vice versa (see, e.g., Coleman 1997).

14. The familiar scientific process of challenging novelties and thereby accumulating valid knowledge in tiny increments seems totally absent in education research. Vagaries follows vagaries with scant attention to critical details. Critical assessments are exceedingly rare (though see Pogrow [1996] for one well-done critique).

6

Community Empowerment

Our empowerment journey thus far has visited sundry settings, from mental health clinics to classrooms. All these ventures, as befitting the grassroots-laden empowerment philosophy, were of modest size. Some were barely shoestring operations dependent on heartfelt enthusiasm with modest goals, for example, shelter for the neighborhood homeless. Public officials may have played a role in these undertakings, but government itself was not central. Our focus now shifts dramatically and investigates the opposite possibility: empowerment as a government activity. Our principal focus will be on empowering flowing out of Washington directed at communities. In particular, one national law—the Empowerment Act of 1993—defines this effort. Simply put, can the trillion-dollar-a-year operation with millions of employees and untold complex regulations infuse vitality to once mori-bund, economically depressed communities? The theoretical and practical problems embedded in this grand social engineering enterprise are stagger-ing. We cannot promise definitive answers, for the jury is still out, but we can take a hard look at multibillion-dollar assistance programs draped in empowerment's mantle.

We shall also examine alternatives to this federal government version of community empowerment—cities independently, with modest Washington assistance, attempting to empower their citizens. This ongoing practice is easily obscured by the high-profile lure of billions allocated to overcome dependency. Here goals are much more reachable, largely providing ordi-nary folk a voice at city hall, not curing complex pathologies. Lessons from these modest endeavors will, hopefully, provide some guidance when public officials announce crash empowerment programs to uplift the economically downtrodden.

GOVERNMENT AND EMPOWERMENT ABSTRACTLY

At one level the concept of government collides with empowerment. Civil society entails substantial disempowerment—one cannot take the neighbor's property or mindlessly pursue hedonism. All government stifles as the lengthy criminal codes attest. Indubitably, the vision of life without government interference still fascinates those believing themselves trapped by unauthorized taxes and oppressive laws. A few outcasts probably live together in the wild and define themselves as genuinely empowered. Nevertheless, it is incontestable that abolishing government hardly empowers. A state of nature does not deliver supreme self-determination. The neighbors could take your property, too. It is no contradiction to say that by surrendering hypothetical power we gain authentic power as a community. Without government, to quote Hobbes's familiar dictum, life would be solitary, nasty, brutish and short.

It is the navigation of details, striking balances, that is critical; government is both depowering and empowering. Not all regimes capacitate; historically most have not. Without police, for example, visiting friends may be impossible, yet a too-vigorous magistrate may likewise bring reclusiveness. In fact, it is often argued that the federal government, perhaps unintentionally, has long waged a campaign of *depowering* localities and their residents for uncertain gain. Policies such as mandatory school busing, urban renewal, scattered site public housing, antidiscrimination laws and similar well-intentioned intrusive policies affecting personal association have deprived communities of the ability to control their cohesive character. One might also add laws protecting criminals from direct communal retribution. Neighborhoods are hardly likely to feel empowered if children cannot attend nearby schools or if Washington insists on placing homes for the mentally disturbed nearby regardless of local preferences.

Nonetheless, although reasonable difference may transpire on details, our present political arrangement of limited, democratic governance is incredibly *potentially* empowering for nearly everyone. By surrendering some freedoms we gain immense *opportunities* for others. This distinction between granting empowerment and granting the potential for self-determination is critical. Laws may confer citizens the right to vote and shield this right, but this power may not be availed or employed foolishly. These potentially enabling circumstances are so taken for granted, so deeply ingrained as "natural," that they are seldom appreciated. Concerns, not surprisingly, center on deficiencies, not for what is already possessed. Taxes conspicuously deprive us of indulging our material desires, but tax revenues build local parks that enrich local life. Cataloging what facilitates communal enablement would fill pages—we can select our political leaders, enjoy private property, congregate unhindered, choose jobs without restriction, form new communities relatively easily, indulge our specialized consumer tastes and practice our religions freely, and so on and on. Although community's decline is today frequently lamented, mass society remains quite distant, and government protection remains an essential element in this survival.

Properly understood, then, the pursuit is for an incremental (and highly selective) increase in communal self-determinacy potential. The contemporary United States is wholly different from the former Soviet Union in which citizens were nearly entirely trapped in debilitating dependency. Even one's place of residence was often centrally dictated. When the federal government in the 1990s invokes "empowerment," it is talking about setting the stage for economically uplifting poorer citizens, principally inner-city residents, who seem mired in nearly permanent poverty and dependency. This is but a sliver of the total population. As a gardener would restore a wilted plant in an otherwise blooming field by watering and fertilizer, Washington is to abet the despairing unemployed to become economically energetic. More accurate phraseology might be "the *extension* of empowerment possibilities to those now without." Although the details and terminology have a unique flavor, this enterprise is hardly novel. Since its creation two centuries ago the national government has been helping to empower its citizens piecemeal, though this modern vocabulary was nowhere present. A sound economic system and effective policing are merely two illustrations of hundreds that could be offered. Today's enabling venture is but the latest installment in an unending effort.

GOVERNMENT AND EMPOWERMENT CONCRETELY

On August 10, 1993, President Clinton signed P.L. 103–66, generally called the Empowerment Act of 1993. The act's broad purpose was to forsake the mighty, intrusive "top-down" federal intervention schemes of the 1960s and instead use government's authority to help people assist themselves. The strategy was one of calculated enticements over a ten-year period to overcome enduring poverty, not outright gifts. One of the three primary goals was "achieving or maintaining economic self-support to prevent, reduce or eliminate dependency" (*Questions and Answers* 1995). "Bricks and mortar"—federally funded construction projects and similar "make-work" contrivances—were implicitly judged failures in attacking deep poverty. At least that was the official rhetoric. Various provisions, all reflecting divergent political constituencies and their attendant philosophies, provided a multitude of tools for this economic liberation. Central was the creation of nine specifically designated "empowerment zones" (six urban and three rural) targeted for the bulk of Washington's generosity and attention. Los Angeles and Cleveland were separately designated as "supplemental empowerment zones." Also authorized were 95 "enterprise communities" (65 urban, 30 rural) eligible for lesser forms of assistance.

The principal expediting mechanisms were consequential—$3.5 billion in tax incentives, $1 billion in social service grants to selected communities and various assurances of eliminating red tape and similar regulatory obstructions to progress ("Congress Votes" 1993, 422–423). Statutory mechanisms also permitted loan guarantees, tax-exempt bond financing and accelerated property depreciation (Berger 1997). Communities were given fairly wide latitude in administration. The partnership between capitalism and government was central. Overseeing this enterprise was the Community Enterprise Board—later renamed the Community Empowerment Board—headed by the vice president and including the heads of seventeen federal agencies, all committed to coordinating local empowerment while slicing through bureaucratic impediments. Day-to-day coordination for urban areas was to be provided by the specialists of the Urban EZ/EC Task Force.

In its more detailed provisos the Empowerment Act permitted dozens of enabling actions at the community level. Job creation was absolutely pivotal. Employers locating in these zones received tax credits for wages, equipment purchases and various training expenses if those employees worked and lived in the zones. Paralleling these financial lures were numerous social service–type programs to make communities more attractive and productive—encouraging home ownership, greater education (particularly to assist in self-sufficiency), intensive skill training, building shelters for the homeless, drug and alcohol treatment programs and after-school facilities for youngsters. The theme of local, not distant bureaucracy, became a celebrated mantra. A report on Detroit's experience, for example, reaffirms, "Individuals closest to the problem know best how to solve them—a bottom-up relationship between government and communities." A few lines later, to drive the point home: "Government must learn to interact with the community. It must reach out and involve local residents" ("EZ/EC Empowerment Zone Performance Report 1995–1996" n.d.).

This scheme was hardly unprecedented or a sudden impromptu gesture as a tactic for government to uplift impoverished localities. Ample opportunities existed for discussion and examination of state-level ventures. Impressed with a British plan developed under Prime Minister Margaret Thatcher, President Ronald Reagan had submitted (unsuccessfully) similar proposals to Congress during his administration.[1] From 1982 onward, at least some enterprise zone measure was introduced yearly in Congress (Katz 1993). A 1988 bill was passed by Congress authorizing 100 enterprise zones, but then Secretary of Housing and Urban Development Jack Kemp took no implementation action. A comparable 1992 enterprise zone authorization was vetoed by President George Bush after passing Congress. What altered matters greatly, setting the stage for the 1993 law, were the Los Angeles riots following the acquittal of the white police officers charged with beating Rodney King. The huge damages and loss of lives, as was true in the 1960s, pushed the national urban policy agenda to the forefront. Economic development, it was hoped, could cool the big-city powder kegs.

Paralleling these national legislative debates were concrete state actions. From the early 1980s onward, some 37 states had actually created—or in a other few cases, attempted to establish—empowerment zones that sought to unleash capitalism to remedy severe poverty. The projects ranged from a single town to the entire state and mixed tax incentives with loans and state-funded job training. In some instances, laws even permitted 100 percent cuts in local property taxes and substantial reductions in state sales taxes (Riposa 1996). In Los Angeles enterprise zone businesses received a 25 percent discount on their city utility bills (Fulton and Newman 1994). On the whole, these "laboratories" of empowerment yielded mixed, often uncertain results. They certainly did not produce economic miracles.[2] A New Jersey study found that cities awarded enterprise zones did not economically outperform those that had applied but were turned down (Boarnet and Bogart 1996). Jobs were created, particularly among small businesses, although many were low paying. More relevant, this state strategy apparently failed in precisely those areas where it was most imperative, for example, the largely impoverished black Watts area of Los Angeles, the scene of particularly inflamed rioting (Fulton and Newman 1994; Riposa [1996] summarizes these evaluation studies).

EVALUATING WASHINGTON'S EMPOWERMENT

Assessing any extensive federal program is tricky business—results surely vary by locality and time, while officials are not always forthcoming in their inadequacies. The issue of "how long is enough time to judge?" is also formidable. It may well take decades and innumerable dead-ends to address long-term poverty successfully. A degree of mishap occurs even in the most auspicious programs. Nevertheless, assessments are vital regardless of the obstacles, and we shall undertake two distinct types of evaluation of this imposing Washington design. The first is more theoretical, namely, examining the 1993 act in the context of empowerment theory broadly defined. The issue here is less of whether this government program assists, but whether the enterprise deserves the mantle of empowerment. Let us not forget a lesson from preceding chapters: Labeling something "empowerment" may disguise dependency. This may even be true if the remedy is genuinely worthwhile. The second evaluative tactic asks: What has this act done? Have thousands of people gained from this Washington assistance, even becoming genuinely empowered? Or is this undertaking yet one more dubious stratagem to be appended to a depressingly long list of help-the-destitute failures? Judged by other empowerment efforts to cure poverty (Chapter 4), we perhaps should not expect too much.

Empowerment?

From the outset, the Empowerment Act of 1993 has an uncertain relationship to citizen self-capacitation despite the explicit nomenclature.[3] Several empowerment-oriented conservatives immediately criticized it as a stealthy reincarnation of the failed 1960s Great Society in which passive citizens are showered with government handouts (Weber 1993). A decent case could be made that it merely rewarded numerous big-city Democratic mayors and was not a well-crafted instrument to alleviate poverty (Liebschutz 1995). This uncertainty lies at the very heart of the legislation. Consciously infusing the entire enterprise is the pursuit of *economic* betterment, principally the employment of residents in depressed areas. Jobs, not power, are being distributed. It is axiomatic to project to proponents that generating paychecks bestows enablement and that the federal government could merely smooth the path. Most critically, that these jobs were to be primarily created by community outsiders and *given* to worthy recipients is *not* judged incompatible with empowerment. Proposals were aired for additional aid to assist indigenous entrepreneurs, but this failed to make it into the final bill ("Congress Votes" 1993, 423).[4] The social service component—money for drug programs and education, for example—would primarily assist in creating a superior labor pool as a step toward economic vitality.

Although urban unrest quickly faded from public discourse after the bill's passage, this element is critical to grasping this effort and subsequent developments. At core, Washington is attempting two distinct—and perhaps contradictory—goals: Foster independence among the once helpless and simultaneously "domesticate" potential troublemakers with jobs (including program administration positions). Our inner-city resident is supposed to feel a sense of self-determination from employment, yet also realize that if he or she misbehaves, this benevolence might be withdrawn by those above. It is a delicate balance, to say the least. This duality can lead to ludicrous, convoluted rhetoric as politicians try to blend dependency and independence. In a 1996 Executive Order (13005) called "Empowerment Contracting," President Clinton asserted that the efficiency of federal procurement will be enhanced if designated federal agencies reach out to distressed-area firms for goods and services, even assisting inexpert would-be providers with incentives. Obviously, this policy promotes greater *inefficiency* by raising procurement costs. The order's real aim, plainly, is to channel funds to noncompetitive inner-city firms under the guise of "empowerment."

Although this economic goal may be commendable, it is, in and of itself, hardly identical to empowerment as the concept is generally utilized. There is certainly no logical nexus—millions hold decent jobs, and this toil offers no sense, real or imagined, of empowerment. If one insists that jobs bring money, and money engenders empowerment, creating jobs still does not add up to empowerment. By identical reasoning, those idlers receiving copious welfare payments are "empowered" since they, too, have ample disposable income. To conflate mere employment with "empowerment" is somewhat deceptive. Indeed, the unemployed on the dole are conceivably more empowered than those sweating in some exhausting low-paid factory job. At least these beneficiaries can leisurely spend their money or pursue unencumbered pastimes.

A degree of duplicity also surrounds this "cutting bureaucratic red tape." The conservative interpretation of empowerment depicted in Chapter 3 invokes this spirit—allowing citizens themselves, not Washington-based pencil pushers, to manage public housing, schools or whatever. And this temper (at least rhetorically) appeared to infuse the act, perhaps helping sell it to conservatives otherwise suspicious of mammoth federal intervention designs. Nevertheless, similarities in vocabulary aside, this "liberation from bothersome government" is not being delivered. In lieu of autonomy, citizens are to be capacitated in securing *more* federally administered assistance. Now, thanks to freshly appointed coordinators and overseers, local officials seeking subsidies will be less encumbered in obtaining yet more handouts. On a massive scale this approximates how many academic espousers defined empowerment—guiding the subservient to clamor for additional regime ministrations.

Does this benevolence advance genuine autonomy even modestly? Hardly. Even relaxing paperwork requirements still leaves mountains of guiding rules and statutes. Ironically, though failed past programs such as Model Cities and Urban Renewal were often criticized for "bad" centralization, this 1993 scheme actually involved *more* federal agencies while mandating *more* state agency fiduciary supervision. Local citizens are not mailed hefty checks and told "spend as best you can."[5] The 1993 legislation does *not* (and legally cannot) suspend the highly technical federal administrative procedures plus provisos protecting against discrimination, environmental impact, community consultation, fiscal accountability and untold additional constraints. Nor are states and localities anxious to grant exceptions to their statutes. Imagine if teenagers were hired at below minimum wage or unions were not permitted to organize a bootstrapping business? Perpetrators would be taken to court and convicted. As evidenced by written guidelines, this "easy access" to federal largess is wholly a high-sounding pledge. For example, one guide announces that Davis-Bacon Act requirements, a law requiring "prevailing wages" (de facto union scale wages) be paid on federally funded projects, is suspended for empowerment zone proposals. This will reduce labor costs substantially, if permitted. Yet a few sentences afterward, this relief is partially withdrawn—officials are told to "consult an attorney" when these empowerment undertakings involve several other (undefined) federal programs. Furthermore, since these activities cut across several federal and multiple state agencies adhering to uncounted laws, the act itself spawns a whole new body of interagency red tape.

In reading the 1993 act's details, the inescapable conclusion is that ordinary people, those theoretically targeted for relief from dependency, must become completely reliant on experts to navigate the often bewildering legalities of this "liberating" enactment. The shift in power is not from Washington-based agencies to ordinary people; it is from one set of mandarins to another. Even if all power were nominally ceded to locals, they would be paralyzed until they consulted experts. To be blunt, dependency is sonorously disguised, not eliminated. Imagine if inner-city residents inquire about promised affordable housing. They will be reassured that all is well. One Housing and Urban Development (HUD) "question and answer" handout makes this perfectly plain—it says so in "597.200(d)(12)(ii)(B)(3) and (g)(3), and 597.201(b)(8)" (Department of Housing and Urban Development 1994, 12). No guarantees exist that these university-educated expert administrators will know local conditions or even sympathize with their clients. They may well have their own professional standards and career goals.

Indeed, a prodigious dilemma confronts any federally run program targeting complex, often intractable, obstacles across diverse settings. As remedies becomes more expansive, involving education, the tax code, health care, crime, housing, public welfare and so on, bureaucratic intricacies multiply exponentially. Even building an unadorned recreation facility can be technically daunting if federal money is affected. Goals may also become contradictory as efforts in one direction collide with other stipulations. For example, hiring the truly needy may run afoul of national and state antidiscrimination statutes. Tough zoning laws easily impede local creativity in promoting tiny businesses. Faced with all these compliance entanglements, those to be empowered increasingly cede authority to outside experts capable of professional administration. This is inescapable. If local residents complained that "nothing is happening despite the promises," they would naturally (and properly) be enlightened that "the downtown lawyers are still negotiating the details." And should locals take matters in their own hands, they doubtless would violate multitudinous provisions and quickly be deprived of what is supposed to make them empowered.

There is also the nagging question of why conventional social service programs bestowed under empowerment's guise will outperform those now condemned as debilitating. Again, helpfulness is not the issue—the debate concerns facilitating self-capacity. For example, since the government supplies after-school programs, what propels parents to press their own agenda regarding child care? Or if they did want their own ideas implemented, will this be allowed? Surely all the promised assistance to the empowered will carry every mandatory "made-in-Washington" constricting guideline. What if parents want religious observances in their "own" day care facility? Or ignore expensive requirements regarding disabled access? It is more than slightly ironic that heavy-handed bureaucratic social service agencies will be financially rejuvenated as a result of this empowering.

A further incongruity is its potential redirection of energy away from independence toward remonstrating for lucrative financial handouts. Again, another unforeseen push in the direction of dependency, not autonomy: Seeking a pledged $100 million from Washington can outshine establishing new and uncertain businesses. Getting grants to concoct possibilities now crowds out actually creating tangible enterprises. This acrimony and new-found displaced energy to snare federal prizes are already quite visible as cities compete for "free money" (Mahtesian 1995). Manipulating expenditures for electoral advantage is also plain, and a decisiveness is hardly helped by inclusionary requirements. It's a bit much, for example, to expect seasoned politicians, ministers, business executives, planning professionals and community activists to concur easily on policy. In Baltimore and New York City intense jockeying occurred in drawing zone boundaries, and the final results commonly reflects political clout more than feasibility.[6] Similar turmoil infuses the selection of representatives to sundry community boards. In Atlanta and Chicago the mayor's office has quickly (and contentiously) come to dominate, whereas neighborhood groups have triumphed in other cities. Deep divisions also affect the balance between the social service function and economic development (Mahtesian 1995). Enormous efforts have also been sunk into devising administrative systems and regulations (Berger 1997). Perhaps this divisive politicking resembles the troubled student who spends months energetically devising a cheating scheme rather than allocating a few hours to studying. The would-be capitalist is replaced by the grant-getting entrepreneur as the local hero.

The confusion of top-down–generated employment with empowerment runs far deeper. To wit, benefits gained by government intervention—bribery, in plain language—may well be judged less "authentic" than those secured via open-market competition. Some might view the entire endeavor as but charity, a well-disguised paternalism with language calculated not to offend. Imagine a worker employed *only* because his or her employer is "paid" to hire this employee? This munificence is, of course, hardly unique to inner cities or economically depressed rural areas; "gift jobs" abound in family-run firms or in public agencies where employees are rewarded for off-job political services. Nineteenth-century England provided gainful employment to the indigent with poor houses and "outdoor relief" in which the destitute chopped wood or otherwise toiled for their upkeep. Nor should we condemn this "make-work" as immoral or wasteful. The "rubber shovel" Civilian Conservation Corps (CCC) of the Great Depression kept many from starvation, though it was often criticized for being ineffective.

It is the empowering element of this employment that draws out attention, not the benefits that accrue from job holding. The artificiality of this assistance furthers yet more dependency on the whims of the truly powerful. For one, such "manufactured" employment may well be quite precarious and depart once subsidies are withdrawn or more attractive employer bribes occur elsewhere (quite likely given legislative vagaries). Like a mysterious pagan god, the federal government capriciously giveth and taketh. The matter would be quite different, for example, if these newly hired workers possessed genuine skills in hot demand. In effect, the federal government is paying employers to tolerate worker deficiencies.

Nor do the assisting firms have much incentive to upgrade their new employees. Assuredly, many—perhaps most—fresh hires are "troubled" workers who have difficulty securing "real" employment even in booming times. Their failing may entail illiteracy, slothful work habits or even drug/alcohol addictions. Subsidized risk breeds turnover since these workers, at least initially, produce little relative to their overall costs (and these exceed salary). By law, employers are limited to a $3,000 tax write-off per employee, surely less than half of real wages. Thus, someone hired for, say, $12,000 only "costs" $9,000 yearly, but given their liabilities, this may be actual worth. At this proportion, the arrangement is a wash—the employer gets $9,000 worth of labor and, thanks to the subsidy, only pays $9,000. If, as is hoped, this employee becomes more valuable with experience, the subsidy becomes a business windfall.

This windfall motivates many enterprises to locate in the high-risk area. Without this "profit," why engage troubled employees when conventional ones are available elsewhere? (Unless, of course, employment is being granted pro bono publico.) But especially in light of the inherent shakiness of hiring in distressed localities, many subsidized workers will never exceed the break-even point (and the minimum wage sets the lowest possible wage). Given the ample pool of unemployed, little incentive exists to sink additional resources into this $9,000-a-year employee. Just keep hiring and firing until one discovers a few gems generating the sought-after windfall. This logic stands in sharp contrast to closely held family firms where powerful inducements exist to assist underperforming family members. The Lumpenproletariat—the very intervention targets—will likely receive only brief shots at security. To increase subsidies, moreover, might only encourage greater disregard for hiring rationality, thereby increasing turnover even further.

The economic logic of these empowerment zones also assumes business profitability. Why seek tax credits if an enterprise breaks even or loses money? With no profit, tax credits are worth zero. And many start-ups, the very firms essential to impoverished areas, may have to wait painful years before seeing profits. Outright cash grants would be the appropriate instrument to stimulate this commerce. It is no wonder, then, that struggling inner-city entrepreneurs are hardly celebrating about these down-the-road prizes (Stanfield 1993). It is equally questionable whether industries contracting low-skilled workers will find inner cities more attractive economically than locating overseas where wages are even cheaper and health-safety regulations nonexistent.

There is also the equity problem when this policy is to be evaluated broadly. Is this effort "fair" generally? Perhaps not. Temporarily accept the act's core premises: Worthy jobs mean empowerment, and all the social programs and financial enticements will execute as intended. That is, thanks to this 1993 law, once impoverished neighborhoods now boom. Does this portray a notable success for local empowerment? For the immediate beneficiaries, certainly. Yet it is entirely possible that this accomplishment comes at the expense of others. Given this job-holding-tinged empowerment definition, to enrich some can cheat others. Difficulties are merely shifted, not solved. Employment in one place means unemployment elsewhere, while businesses receiving government subsidies in downtown Chicago (a designated empowerment zone) drive into bankruptcy adjacent suburban enterprises lacking federal generosity. Whether this version of empowerment is a positive- or zero-sum phenomenon (or some mixture) is, of course, an empirical question. Nevertheless, in a highly competitive economy closely attuned to slight advantages, many firms may well behave as "gypsies," migrating from one bribe to another.[7]

The equity issue also pertains to suspending government rules to empower, for example, awarding a legally sanctioned advantage. The point does not concern legal exceptions per se—this is done routinely and legitimately, from zoning variances to special laws awarding tax breaks to favored industries. It can also be argued that such exceptions reflect power (e.g., the ethanol industry's escape from federal gasoline taxes). The issue is one of appraising empowerment when those ostensibly empowered can compete *only* under more forgiving regulations. Imagine, for example, a basketball league in which one team was exempted from normal rules. They might carry the ball rather than dribble or get five points, not two, for baskets. This generosity "equalizes" outcomes since the assisted team was a perpetual loser. Further suppose that this adjustment was successful, for the failure now becomes competitive.

The alteration may bring bountiful benefits—a more interesting game, an uplifting of spirits among once dreadful athletes and so on. Nevertheless, is this newfound betterment the genuine empowerment article? A more accurate term might be *pseudo-empowerment* or even *gift empowerment*. Although to causal outsiders and those experiencing the rewards, it might be indistinguishable from the real thing, this is deceptive. Rather, its very existence depends wholly on the generosity of distant, unaffected rule makers. This forthright characterization in no way hints of anything unsavory or illegal about this helpful intervention. Our discussion concerns nomenclature, not helpfulness.

A parallel obviously applies to the logic of empowerment zones. The older, now unfashionable social work language would deem this strategy grandiose "sheltered workshops." The more cynical might draw a parallel with Indian reservations in which tax code suspensions permit thousands of Native Americans to prosper from casinos and cheap cigarettes. Such policy even resembles the medieval practice of awarding contrived commercial monopolies to prominent families or strategic cities. This creating empowerment by allowing some to play by more charitable rules is, at best, a *precondition* to real empowerment.

Our final point is possibly the most difficult to unravel: the complex interaction between empowering individuals versus empowering communities. Federal action seems wholly ambivalent, and deep contradictions remain unresolved. On the one hand, talk streams forth about strengthening "communities" and "neighborhoods," and the economically vibrant immigrant urban enclaves often appear to be the implicit standard. Projects such as enhanced health care facilities are, moreover, typically justified for their communal benefits. It is hoped, for example, that Washington can play a midwife role in making the desolate, crime-ridden Watts resemble its cross-town thriving opposites such as "Little Saigon" or "Koreatown." In sum, the goal is uplifting *communities*, commencing by finding jobs for individuals.

This from-individuals-to-communities sequence rarely translates into concrete policy, however, and this may be inherently impossible. Everything is being directed at singular recipients, with community spillover merely a distant hope. The act's legal requirements—dire poverty levels within the zone, its size, placement within existing jurisdictions—combined with all the predictable battling over inclusion may well subvert the communal purpose. "Communities" (understood as a shared common view and experiences) and empowerment zones are unlikely to overlap. The former is "natural"; the latter is purely administrative. In Baltimore, for example, the zone covers seven square miles and cuts across settings as diverse as urban neighborhoods, collections of public housing projects and barren industrial areas (Berger 1997). No doubt, the incentive to round up as many people and businesses as possible into Washington's bounteousness has similar impacts in other heterogeneous cities. The legal maximum of 200,000 (about 50,000 in smaller cities) may seem trifling in an urban colossus, but this figure well exceeds "a cohesive neighborhood."

There is also a far more serious flaw in this conflation of community and individual. Calling a geographical territory a "community" does not certify it as such. The opposite may be more accurate: The attendant pathologies facilitating zone designation may permanently stifle any communal development. The talented have long left. Watering and fertilizing sterile soil cannot bring germination. Undoubtedly embedded in this empowerment zone scheme is the idea that federal largess will prime the pump, regardless of how terrible the human capital and physical conditions. The newly employed will "naturally" spawn other economic activity. That is, stores will appear, new housing will be erected, crime will vanish, professionals will flock to new clients and the once-dreary slum will bloom. The possibility that these slum dwellers reside there *precisely* because of their incurable incapacity escapes debate. All collections of people are by legislative fiat conveniently labeled "a community," and it is but a short step to imagine this community being transformed into a "normal community" just like all the other city residents.

EMPOWERMENT IN PRACTICE: ATLANTA AND DETROIT

Federally, empowerment zones have existed only briefly and every year bring changes and learning. They vary enormously in virtually every imaginable trait. Even the most fleeting overall assessment must be tentative. We can only offer a snapshot of two large projects—Atlanta and Detroit—that apparently define the range of accomplishment, Detroit being the claimed success and Atlanta being acknowledged among the troubled. Our task is to glimpse into these endeavors as empowerment exemplars and less as pure economic revitalization efforts. After all, economic prosperity can also be bestowed by simply dividing the millions targeted for uplift among the indigents. Flush with their new wealth, these consumers may feel empowered, and in a real sense, they are since they can now indulge their wants. Clearly, however, this "win the lottery" empowerment is not anybody's goal. Empowerment requires something more than an unanticipated bonanza.

Atlanta

The Atlanta Empowerment Zone came into existence on December 21, 1994, one of six urban areas to receive $100 million in cash grants plus $150 million in tax incentives to promote economic development. Its 9.3 square miles included 30 impoverished inner-city neighborhoods. Over half the 50,000 residents are below the poverty rate. The plan's objective is to build multiple "urban villages" serving economic growth focal points. All "villages" would encourage small businesses, and a few will be targeted for larger commercial enterprises. Other villages are assigned tourism and higher education. A major industrial park will incubate hi-tech industries and recycling. Finally, an investment center will extend inexpensive loans to budding entrepreneurs (Atlanta, Georgia Empowerment Zone n.d.).

Atlanta's political environment seemed generally conducive to this economic mobilization. A long history of business-civic cooperation exists, and the Atlanta area is home to numerous thriving large "civic-minded" corporations (Coca-Cola and Delta Airlines, among many others). The city is largely African American, and blacks have long dominated politically, minimizing the potential for divisive racial conflict. For decades, Atlantans lauded themselves as "the city too busy to hate." Neighborhood political involvement has also been well established, and this permitted Mayor Bill Campbell to quickly form a Community Empowerment Board (CEB) of 69 diverse citizens to represent individual neighborhoods. A cooperative planning process was soon implemented pulling together neighborhood residents, local business executives, municipal officials, nonprofit group representatives, academics and varied others. A specialized committee dealing with technical concerns was also formed.

Financial assurances have flowed from nonfederal governmental sources as well. The state agreed to supplement Washington's incentives with $2,500 annual job tax credits plus easing the issuance of revenue bonds. Also added is a $2 million revolving loan fund, while administrative fees for handling federal programs will be waived. Fulton County (in which the zone resides) has committed to invest heavily in health care within the enterprise zone. The city itself will supply $29 million additional to upgrade zone infrastructure. Various commercial taxes will be reduced, and tax-delinquent property will be transferred to community organizations. More general federal resources will likewise be directed to the zone, as well. The private sector has some $700 million in investment funds that could be allocated and expressed eagerness to assist. Plainly, there is no shortage of financial commitment (Atlanta, Georgia Empowerment Zone n.d.).

The goals are ambitious and far-reaching. Upward of 5,000 jobs plus 100 to 200 home-based businesses comprised the initial central economic goal. Paralleling this aim is the creation of a "livable community"—adequate housing for everyone, sharply reducing crime, upgrading of public infrastructure, reducing the school dropout rate, restoring the environment and enhanced social service intervention. Efforts at food cooperatives, communal gardens and beautifying parks were similarly part of this announced package. The themes of cooperation and partnership infused the project at every stage. Slogans such as "It takes a whole village to raise a child" or "community-based partnership" regularly pop up in dry bureaucratic missives.

The administrative means to achieve these ends are comprehensive and balance local citizen input and professional expertise. Overall governance will be in the hands of a seventeen-member executive board representing divergent interests. At least six members will be zone residents (one of whom will be its vice chair). All goals will be broken down into specific intermediate steps and priorities assigned with an emphasis on early, tangible accomplishment. Provisions are built in for monitoring, measuring and assessing progress against current statistical baselines. Thus, at each stage it will be possible to ask just how far progress has gone and what remains to be done.

What, then, has transpired with this well-funded, grandiose scheme? Between various state and nonprofit group reports, plus various newspaper accounts, the conclusion seems to be: not much besides waste. Consider first administrative performance—how well leaders technically do their jobs. In 1997 the Georgia Department of Community Affairs, the agency legally responsible for monitoring zone performance, found significant "areas of concern" (cited in Morse 1997). These included extravagant meals at luxury hotels, irregularities in compensation, using zone property for personal use, poor cash management and several instances of outright wastefulness (renting and paying for unused hotel rooms, for example). Indeed, this improvidence has meant that the ten-year administrative budget has been almost exhausted during the first three years. A steady stream of *Atlanta Constitution* stories tell of bloated paralyzed staffs more adroit at indulging themselves personally than stimulating economic development. In August 1997 nearly the entire zone administration was fired, effectively beginning the development process anew.

This infatuation with administrative overhead is especially striking in comparison to funding ongoing projects. This gap is sometimes artfully disguised by portraying intentions as actual ongoing activities. An August 1997 report by the nonpartisan Georgia Public Policy Foundation (Morse 1997) showed that after two and a half years, 6.7 percent of the money allocated for economic development had been spent; for housing the figure was 4.1 percent. Merely 0.8 percent of the funding for "creating safe and livable communities" had been depleted, whereas the figure for antipoverty effort was *zero*. Keep in mind that this is merely money spent, not documented accomplishment; even this spending perchance has had zero impact. Performance has been notably inadequate in job creation and training, the alleged centerpiece of the entire enterprise. Of all the funds utilized, nearly half were on administration. In other words, combining the various aid categories, over $100 million lies idle while well-paid executives hold lavish conferences on empowering the disadvantaged.

This performance becomes even more dismal when the original goals are examined—in 82 percent of all these intended programs, *zero* spent. In only 4 of 34 programs have the objectives been met, and some of these, for example, conducting a single survey or installing low-flush toilets, hardly dent poverty (Morse 1997). This picture does not improve if one simply examines steps toward accomplishment. Of 40 proposed programs, 32 percent were still waiting after two and a half years. *Nothing* had been accomplished here. Forty percent were behind schedule or existed solely in the planning stage. Not surprisingly, this record of nonaccomplishment has not enticed private businesses to contribute, and nothing from the private sector has been forthcoming.

This lack of genuine progress has predictably pressured zone administrators to invent "accomplishments" of dubious merit to silence critics. One such effort in particular illustrates an almost perverse tactic—thanks to the lure of financial enticements, a Rolls-Royce dealership relocated twelve miles from Roswell, Georgia, to the empowerment zone. So "impressive" was this accomplishment that it was announced by the mayor himself at a press conference featuring a handsome $159,000 Silver Dawn sedan. According to the mayor, "This is another one of our success stories" ("Empowerment Zone Takes Shape" 1997). Needless to say, the sales volume here—particularly to local residents—is unlikely to add much to the nearby economy, even more so since many dealership employees will reside elsewhere. In other instances the "accomplishment" was financially disproportionate to costs. A $48,100 grant to Morris Brown College to train workers to remove lead paint and asbestos from buildings produced just 14 certified workers (of 112 who began the program), a cost of $3,500 per student ("Empowerment Zone Audits Point to Mismanagement" 1997). In another case a suburban business was improperly lured to the enterprise zone ("Feds Say Empowerment Zone Deal Was Improper" 1997).

Explanations accurate and otherwise for Atlanta's sorry performance abound. City officials bitterly complain about excessive state and federal red tape and the daunting nature of the problem. To be fair, it may be unreasonable to expect rapid progress in attempting to solve severe problems that have long resisted equally energetic remedies. Yet these state and federal monitoring officials, in turn, can amply document mismanagement and poor decision making. The charge of excessive feeding at the public trough while ignoring legal responsibilities surely has abundant truth to it. Surprisingly, the oft-made complaint of "insufficient funds" is nowhere made. Tens of millions remain unspent and may remain unspent, given to a slow record of implementation.

Detroit

If the Atlanta experience is the disaster poster child of urban empowerment, Detroit is hailed as the great success (Bivens 1997). The Detroit zone of eighteen-plus square miles similarly covers a multitude of dreary neighborhoods with a largely impoverished population of 101,000. And as was true for Atlanta, this largely African-American city has long had black mayors, mitigating the likelihood of racial divisiveness. Yet similarities quickly disappear. Detroit begins its development quest with notable liabilities compared to Atlanta. Violent riots of the 1960s and 1970s left a bitter legacy, a terrible reputation and miles of destroyed housing that was never rebuilt. The enduring repute of America's "murder capital" hardly helps. More important, beginning in the 1960s Detroit's well-paying automobile factory jobs relocated to more modern plants in low-wage areas. As older, inefficient plans were abandoned, unemployment skyrocketed and became virtually permanent. Much of the middle class moved elsewhere, gravely weakening the city's tax base. The growing popularity of imports from the 1970s onward also pushed many of the remaining automobile jobs overseas. Even when new positions were added in the Detroit area, they were located in the suburbs, beyond the reach of city residents. In short, Detroit had much further to go than Atlanta.

In its overall goals and mixing of public and private, Detroit and Atlanta are quite comparable—the blend of jobs and improved quality of life all reached with ample community participation. Various Michigan and city agencies have also agreed to supplement Washington's assistance. On the private side, eight Detroit banks and two other financial institutions have agreed to fund $100 million a year for ten years (a $1 billion total) to assist residents and businesses ("EZ/EC Empowerment Zone Performance Report 1995–1996" n.d.). The Big Three automakers have endorsed the project from the beginning and have made huge financial commitments to reinvigorating Detroit's industrial rebirth.

Overseeing zone initiatives is the Empowerment Zone Development Corporation (EZDC), a quasi-public corporation directed by a 50-member diverse board, of which 60 percent are residents from zone neighborhoods. What sharply separates Detroit from Atlanta administratively is the domination of elected officials, particularly Detroit's high-profile mayor Dennis Archer, over zone operation. Initially, the EZDC, the Detroit City Council and the mayor were all to share equally in administration. A reworking of the statutes plus Archer's dynamism and talent quickly gave de facto supremacy to the mayor's office through the power to approve all relevant expenditures. Even the EZDC's advisory role is subject to approval by the mayor and city council. This authority transfer makes policy far more publicly accountable than in Atlanta where appointed bureaucrats basically decided weighty matters ("EZ/EC Empowerment Zone 1995–1996" n.d.).

Although "quality of life"—more social services, better police protection and so forth—has been given its due in Detroit, it is abundantly clear that attracting industry overshadows all else. Economic progress—restoring manufacturing jobs—is goal one, two and three, and stories emerge daily of new industries being established and promises of far more to come. This single-mindedness of purpose is critical. The funding and tax breaks for industry have gushed forth at a level undreamed of in Atlanta, and their impact has been momentous. Between 1994 and 1997, Detroit's unemployment fell by one third (Solomon and Dixon 1997). Most conspicuous in this infusion have been the actions of the major automakers. Promises have been delivered. Chrysler is constructing a $1 billion truck engine factory that will employ 1,000 workers (another $1.3 billion has been allocated to expand six other area plants). GM has begun multiple projects including a $900 million contract with a local company for car interiors employing 140 new workers; other GM contracts will create 500 more positions (Mulligan n.d.). Ford has similarly contracted with a local firm to package "knockdowns," kits of cars in part form to be shipped overseas, and this will produce 400 jobs (Hindes n.d.). These items are hardly exhaustive.

Possibly more impressive than the corporate megacommitments is the burgeoning of smaller enterprises rushing to join the prosperity. Predictably, most center around the auto industry as subcontractors or related suppliers. Besides providing jobs, they build the foundations of a business culture capable of tackling larger projects. These firms produce such humdrum items as mechanics' uniforms or car seats and bear names such as Piston Packaging, Ace-Tex Corporation, New Way Handling, O-J Transport Company, Munoz Machines, Jordan Oliver Building Systems and Lear and Bing. Entrepreneurs have even created microindustrial parks for startups, for example, the $12 million Hispanic Manufacturing Center housing four separate manufactures. Nonautomotive projects have also flourished. The Detroit Symphony Orchestra is constructing an $80 million performing arts complex, whereas the Detroit Medical Center has instituted a huge program to train residents in medial skills. A refurbished Tiger Stadium for the baseball team is also on the agenda (Mulligan).

Nonindustrial enterprises have also grown. A community health outreach effort in which especially trained residents fan out into their neighborhoods to educate on health matters is under way. Topics include such serious issues as HIV (human immunodeficiency virus), prenatal care and cervical cancer. Housing construction has also increased (1,000 units planned for rehabilitation) along with the building of libraries, day care facilities, retail centers and neighborhood information centers ("EZ/EC Best Practices" n.d.). More police have also been hired (as part of federal anticrime legislation), and the city's capacity to combat crime is being brought into the technological era. Several skill training programs have been implemented and directed toward a wide variety of targets ("EZ/EC Empowerment Zone Performance Report 1995–1996" n.d.).

To be sure, failures will plague any new endeavor. Among the flops were a $45 million Indy-style racetrack, various luxury condominium ventures, a golf course/residence project and a large-scale retail business (Dixon 1997). Nor has the multifaceted enterprise been wholly conflict free. From the beginning, differences surfaced over the composition of key committee and their authority. Representatives of religious organizations in particular have often felt excluded. In other cases, disputes arose between EZ officials and those from long-standing programs seeking inclusion. Overall, however, particularly in light of the huge sums involved, acrimony has been surprisingly minimal. The mayor in particular has worked tirelessly to smooth over conflicts and ensure cooperation ("Topics Causing Disagreement" n.d.).

The reasons for this success are bountiful. The consequences of adroit political leadership are unmistakable—Detroit administrators did a far superior job at every step. Focusing responsibility on the Detroit mayor's office—not some faceless agency—helped enormously. And rather than attack all problems helter-skelter, efforts were concentrated on what could be accomplished reasonably: industrial jobs. The unproductive issue of black-owned enterprises supplying the jobs also never surfaced, as it has elsewhere (see Lloyd 1994). The match between the tax incentives and the financial needs of the auto industry is likewise critical. The 1990s have favored the Big Three, and with multibillion-dollar profits, tax offsets are appreciated. It might have been a different picture, had Detroit's economy rested on insurance or entertainment, industries less dependent on these tax breaks. Add the increasing reliance of automobile manufacturers on outsourcing—contracting out hundreds of products and services is now cost-effective. Lastly, and seldom mentioned, is the tight labor market. Automobile plants elsewhere were simply running out of workers, even transporting them in from Detroit (Solomon and Dixon 1997). Had unemployment been high nationally, these outcomes might not be so favorable.

LESSONS FROM WASHINGTON'S EMPOWERMENT

These two snapshots tell only part of the story. From what can be gleaned thus far from other sources, most urban experiments fall in between Atlanta and Detroit, with perhaps most toward the Atlanta continua end if one looks past the undelivered promises.[8] Nevertheless, even with this limited peek at short-lived efforts, some lessons emerge. Most evidently, money and tax breaks in and of themselves cannot ensure fruition. If Atlanta tells us anything, it is that millions cannot overcome ineptitude unless one defines "empowerment" as capacity to rent deluxe hotel ballrooms for poverty conclaves. All the facile past excuses—insufficient funding, paucity of commitment, no autonomy—do not apply here, and the venture still failed (at least so far). Empowerment requires something beyond money and opportunity.

Second, letting private industry attempt to enrich poorer citizens seems a worthwhile government strategy. This element in the Empowerment Act strategy is correct, provided government is restrained and the incentives make sense at that specific setting. In effect, when Detroit mandated the Big Three to create jobs and offered suitable incentives, industry performed with a vengeance. With that job machine in place, local government can attend to civic details—promoting neighborhood shopping malls or expediting improved health care. Compare Atlanta's pie-in-the-sky proposed "hi-tech" industrial park with Chrysler fabricating truck engines. Ditto for trying to cultivate cottage industries with ill-defined markets versus encouraging minority-owned start-ups producing Dodge Minivan seats. Detroit's officials also knew that the manufacturers themselves—not contract-assigning bureaucrats—could efficiently train new employees. In short, city government can assist greatly, but it cannot autonomously *command* employment into existence.

Finally, returning to an earlier theme, how genuine is this article apart from granting consumer power or the psychological benefits of decent employment? To repeat, the personal economic windfall or enhanced self-perceptions are *not* the issues; the contention concerns "achieved" versus "granted" empowerment. A dispassionate observer might well conclude that even the successful Detroit model is barely the real McCoy—an economic downturn could make much of it quite precarious, and today's beneficiaries are virtually defenseless. Eventually, the subsidies must cease, and if profits become losses, tax incentives are pointless unless the entire enterprise could stand freely. Ultimately, much depends on conditions well beyond Mayor Archer's or even Washington's reach. Desperate Asian nations might well make American auto manufacturers incentive offers they cannot refuse.[9] Even cheaper imports may wipe out any advantage, regardless of tax breaks, of locating in Detroit. What will empowerment mean then?

There is an obvious trade-off here. When Detroit gets into bed with the Big Three, it gains bountiful employment but simultaneously invites heightened dependency. What is given can be taken back. Perhaps a parallel could be drawn with those U.S. farmers whose livelihood depended on generous subsidies. Nor are the car producers forever supreme; history tells us that no industry forever escapes disaster. Vicissitudes in oil prices, pollution requirements, consumer taste or popularity of alternative transportation can bring the demise of the car industry altogether. Faced with these changes, Detroit's wonderful tales will become memories of a past golden era. This would be far less true if the incentives were wholly irrelevant. In sum, this Detroit has, in a sense, become more empowered, but it would be a delusional error to interpret this new circumstance as hard-won independence. Much of it more like a gift that can disappear as quickly as it arrived.

CAN COMMUNITY EMPOWERMENT SUCCEED?

The picture thus far of massive federally inspired communal empowerment is murky. Intervention has accomplished something, although this "something" is seldom unequivocal empowerment. Administrative positions or "expensive uncertain gifts" may be more accurate. Nevertheless, it would be premature—even mistaken—to conclude that government-assisted community empowerment is oxymoronic. This particular Washington experiment is not exhaustive, and alternatives require exploration. Recall earlier argument about the complex relationship between aggrandizing government and empowered communities—the details are critical, and as we have witnessed, admirable intentions and ample resources easily go astray. Such circumstances pertain to the goals of empowerment, its settings and the capacities of participants. Despite the hopes of those desperate for solutions, no guaranteed simple formulas exist. There *are* success stories of community empowerment via government, but there are also innumerable failures in similar situations. These achievements, notably those that concentrated on "natural" neighborhoods (not locals defined exclusively by economic characteristics), now draw our attention.

Successful communal-government empowerment examples might be thought of as the product of a long, complex evolution (Naparstek 1976; Pecorella 1988). As in the evolvement of species, the saga entails numerous dead-ends resulting from fatal initial flaws or failure to adapt to changing environments. Accomplishment may be momentary, even accidental, often tied to a unique issue. Oftentimes success itself provides the insurmountable challenge: What is an insurgent neighborhood organization to do if it accomplishes its agenda? Raising ambitions may now invite defeat. Or a prominent leader might leave the neighborhood or die and the empowered group withers. And, to continue with this Darwinian metaphor, there is no assurance that today's achievement will survive forever. Sudden economic upheavals or a drastic new highly unpopular government edict might breathe new life in old forms once believed extinct.

Before turning to successful contemporary exemplars, consider the version of "community empowerment" that immediately preceded today's "model" that still colors public perceptions despite its transience. In fact, although it has largely vanished decades ago, and seldom attained its lofty goals, its seem irrepressible and easily furnishes a false baseline in evaluating current manifestations. This is the community *control* model tinged with radical separatism: the neighborhood, ordinarily defined along racial or ethnic boundaries, would command its territory as if it were a sovereign state (Altshuler [1970, Ch. 1] offers a more theoretical explication of this view). The participatory democracy version of empowerment depicted in Chapter 3 also captures this spirit (for an alluring example of this "urban village" idealism, see Morris and Hess 1975). It drew an odd amalgam of champions—radical blacks fascinated with "self-determination," white ethnics protecting turf from forced racial integration, technocratic bureaucrats intent on decreeing urban Utopias, university-based social engineering intellectuals, well-intentioned private foundations and young middle-class white would-be revolutionaries seeking liberation. These ventures, often run by community activists with minimal administrative acumen, were sporadically amply funded by federal antipoverty programs.

This parochial "all-power-to-the-people" crusade was highly ambitious. Virtually everything of local impact—the police, education, retail commerce, housing, welfare—was to be brought under community authority, not mere community influence. While some proponents made pragmatic arguments—disaggregation would heighten efficiency—more radical adherents envisioned this as the first step in a broader social upheaval (Kotler [1969] and Fisher [1994] offer overviews of this divergent crusade). For a brief historical moment, this was *the* empowerment plan in America, the "obvious" alternative to "failed" centralism.

COMMUNITY CONTROL 1960s STYLE

To appreciate this enticing though now outdated "control" version of community empowerment, consider an especially famed example—the late 1960s New York City schools "wars." While this complicated event is scarcely typical, it does usefully illustrate key ingredients of this once alluring paradigm. Some background.[10] The New York City education system in the early 1960s was fundamentally a top-down, centralized bureaucratic arrangement. Weighty power resided in the board of education, typically filled by "establishment types" who has passed muster with the mayor (who formally appointed them) and traditional "good government" civic groups. Day-to-day administration was the responsibility of the superintendent of education assisted by a sizable permanent bureaucracy, *the* formidable power in school politics. These careerists had extensive experience with the city's schools and rarely willingly surrendered power. On-site school executives, from principals to department chairs, were accountable to this central administration. Surrounding this formal structure were multiple influential organizations—associations of education professionals, a forceful teachers' union and sundry citywide parent-citizen associations. Nominally running the entire operation was the mayor, but by tradition plus the tight civil service merit system, mayors usually shunned school politics. Students and their parents were ordinarily passive clients, although a 1961 provision created 25 local citizen advisory school boards.

For decades reformers bewailed the system's armylike, authoritarian character, the seemingly endless collection of pencil pushers far removed from actual teaching, but the academic results were typically commendable. The city's public schools generally enjoyed superb scholastic reputations and produced distinguished graduates. Several high schools—Bronx Science, Brooklyn Tech, among others—rivaled the most prestigious private academies in excellence. This splendid reputation headed downhill rather abruptly in the 1960s. As New York City drew more disadvantaged citizens, usually black and Hispanic, schools by the dozens at all levels declined academically. Standardized test scores plummeted, graduation rates fell, school violence skyrocketed and legions of middle-class white parents and teachers fled altogether. Given the importance of education for upward economic mobility, this crisis was inescapable.

These scholastic difficulties might be attacked in sundry ways, but this particular curative direction led inexorably toward community control. Initially, racial integration had been welcomed as the solution, but this evaporated as whites en masse abandoned racially mixed schools. Integration itself was soon perceived by many blacks as an obstacle, not a panacea. Limited decentralization—black-run schools for black students—had already transpired in the mid-1960s, and now it came to the forefront as *the* solution. This push was greatly facilitated by an exploding militant black civil rights movements (frequently assisted by black ministers) deeply imbued with the ideology of self-determination ("Black Power"). It was energetically claimed, though with scant hard evidence, that "the community itself" was best suited to devising educational excellence. Put sharply, white middle-class principals could not educate impoverished blacks. Securing "a voice" in education now edged toward demanding implicit sovereignty. Further pressure came from the increasingly acrimonious black parent-white administrator confrontations, frequent school boycotts by dissatisfied blacks, well-publicized sit-ins and growing urban violence, often punctuated by rioting.

By 1967 the transfer of power from downtown professionals to the local community commenced in several poorer black school districts. Attempts were now made to formalize this power dispersion legally. Thanks to the active support of Mayor Lindsay and Ford Foundation monetary generosity, decentralization soon exploded. Locally dominated school boards soon controlled all personnel, even firing longtime administrators (this plainly involved racial factors). Community control was extended to lucrative school-related business contracts and classroom policy, for example, disciplining disruptive students. The surrounding political turmoil quickly escalated to the state level, becoming markedly bitter and racially tinged. In one particularly rancorous incident, city teachers (mainly white) went on strike against a (black) community-run district to protest the alleged firing of nineteen local teachers. Charges of anti-Semitism and black racism abounded (fired educators were often Jewish).

As this battle unfolded, and strikes and demonstrations escalated, it became increasingly clear that jobs and contracts lay at the heart of this empowerment campaign. On one side was the largely white "establishment" (including the teachers' union plus several other labor organizations) who depicted community control as a balkanizing formula doomed to educational failure. Many of the city's white middle class apparently concurred. For them, the key issues were upholding civil service merit, the sanctity of negotiated contracts and the primacy of trained education professionals. Eventually, these interests prevailed, and the state legislature significantly curtailed the legal power of community schools boards. Battling this "establishment" unsuccessfully was a coalition of ideologically driven community activists, worried black parents and a few who stood to gain financially from community control.

With 20–20 hindsight, it is easy to see why this community empowerment (and other related misadventures) was virtually doomed apart from the usual political obstacles (more generally, see Moynihan 1969). The entire enterprise rested on shaky hope—the "theory" that community control could solve deep problems and that local people possessed the correct answers. Belief in this argument was fervent, but this hardly makes it universally convincing. It is one thing to fight for something of proven value; it is quite another to confront opponents with untested, dubious propositions. After all, the "old system" has been academically successful for decades; perhaps the blame lay elsewhere. Indeed, community control soon became reduced to a rallying cry for jobs and contracts. The clamor for academic achievement almost disappeared; power to spend freely somebody else's tax dollars overshadowed all else. Finally, and no doubt most critical, this empowerment was decisively zero-sum. Black activities and their few allies now "took on" varied strong interests—unions, "good government" groups, education professionals and politicians allied with white middle-class voters, all of whom saw their tangible interests subverted by community control. The lesson regarding empowerment is simple: Divisive "dividing up the loot" community control may be the genuine empowerment article, but its chances of attainment are meager.[11]

CONTEMPORARY COMMUNITY EMPOWERMENT

Beginning in the 1970s a new empowerment "creature" emerged soon to supplant this confrontational "control" version. The emphasis shifted from parochial sovereignty to what is now called "administrative decentralization." In a nutshell, the right to "own" neighborhood economic resources was subordinated to participation in specific political decisions. This shift is critical—locals could not run area schools, but they could seriously discuss education policy with school administrators. The financial costs are petty, and these adjustments rarely require drastic legal alterations. Accommodations over differences are pragmatic and incremental. Undoubtedly crucial is its non-zero-sum character and the absence of transferred resources across localities. Compared to the grand rhetoric of 1960s-style community empowerment, its aims are unpretentious. It will certainly disappoint those envisioning empowerment as the launching pad for radical upheaval.

Certain key elements in this new arrangement often appear in differing combinations (Naparstek 1976). Most conspicuous is locating city agencies more adroitly—for example, placing the city's personnel branch office in areas of unemployment—or simply scattering municipal facilities such as fire and police stations widely. Services can likewise be combined into "one-stop" locations to match localities. In high jobless areas this might mean having adult vocational education offices adjacent to the city's personnel department. In wealthier areas the assortment will surely differ. Finally, several political outreach mechanisms are available, for example, periodic public meetings with municipal officials or more institutionalized procedures such as block associations. These arrangements both make recommendations and serve as informational conduits to residents. Terms like *feedback* and *greater effectiveness*, not *power*, infuse this effort.[12]

Make no mistake: These mechanisms only permit relatively minor policy adjustments; empowering citizens to *decide* weighty matters is not the aim. Citizen "power" comes from obtaining superior civic service or having one's voice heard directly. Potential pitfalls abound even within these moderate objectives (Naparstek 1976). It is possible, for instance, that outreach will not overcome deeply ingrained apathy even if bureaucracy has a "human face" by situating agencies in popular supermarkets. Furthermore, no amount of facilitated citizen-government contact will surmount citizen incompetence. Occasionally inviting the mayor for "mini town hall" gatherings is pointless if residents are inarticulate or suggest crackpot schemes. Nor is this system immune to top-down manipulation. The city's social worker could easily use this outreach to drum up business for justifiably underutilized services. Perhaps most seriously, there is always the possibility that humdrum activity will mutate in violent conflict as grand expectations are dashed by grim realities. Local storefront agencies may become inviting targets for the disgruntled.

The key question is, of course, What transpires in "real life"? Can neighborhood administrative decentralization stressing feedback and consultation actually empower citizens? Fortunately, one large-scale, in-depth late 1980s study, *The Rebirth of Urban Democracy* (Berry, Portnoy and Thomson 1993) has examined this attempt in five cities—Birmingham, Alabama; Dayton, Ohio; Portland, Oregon; St. Paul, Minnesota; and San Antonio, Texas.[13] Generally, residents were somewhat empowered if we accept the researchers' circumscribed political definition. The gulf between these efforts and the promised economic miracles of the 1993 Empowerment Act are enormous. Nor are there any claims of universal applicability to all cities far and wide. Imitations may well fail. Moreover, these five exemplars were only uncovered after an extensive search among hundreds of other candidates, and much of their success is rooted in purely local, nonreproducible conditions.

A notable element is the variety of institutional arrangements, mixing and matching varied ingredients. For example, Birmingham employs procedures "paralleling" the more formal political system. The city is divided into 95 neighborhoods, and each elects representatives at the polls every two years. These small divisions in turn are democratically represented in broader associations and these, ultimately, are given expression in a citywide Citizens Advisory Board. It is a method in which "officials" communicate with every residence via newsletters and actually confer with their neighbors in administering community block grants. Portland, Oregon, has a comparable arrangement of independent neighborhood associations topped off with seven District Coalition Boards (DCBs), each with its own budget and administrative staff representing the 90-plus neighborhoods in city agencies. These DCBs involve themselves in citywide affairs (e.g., crime) or more focused dealings (traffic congestion on one street). For Portland generally a single neighborhood-based organization attends to overall city planning, securing development grants while providing diversified services (e.g., mediating disputes) to individual localities. In San Antonio the Hispanic organization follows Catholic parish boundaries and stands outside the electoral system. It is also notable that this organization refuses any government funding. All cities, save San Antonio, supply paid, professional staffs to these organizations (Berry, Portnoy and Thomson 1993, Ch. 1).

The issue of staffing—how they are hired, their expertise and overall responsibility—is critical. With an adequate staff the entire system lapses into uncertain volunteerism while excessive professionalism can divide staff from local clients. In Birmingham all neighborhood administrators are hired by city hall, and their responsibilities are delineated by elected public officials. More common is substantial local autonomy over these administrators, with San Antonio groups having most control given financial independence (though staff size was tiny). Dayton employs a mixed system in which neighborhoods can hire but only from a pool defined by the city's personnel office. Employment details can depend on resource availability, a matter largely decided by the city itself. Hence, at least in principle, regular city government could disempower neighborhoods by sharply curtailing their funding.

Actual neighborhood-based group responsibilities predictably vary across and within cities over and above routine consulting with public officials. In several instances the neighborhood itself allocated federal money for nearby projects. The community organization, not the city bureaucracy, is typically "the place to go" when something local has to be accomplished. In Dayton, Ohio, these councils serve as administrative agencies handling miscellaneous city activities. Portland, Oregon's Office of Neighborhood Association defines itself as a strong localism upholder, a counterweight to officialdom, not city hall's administrative assistant. The St. Paul system is especially vigorous in alerting citizens to impending municipal action— nearly all upcoming legal actions, from the issuing of liquor licenses to changes in the zoning law, are announced to citizens via regular newsletters. St. Paul is also unusual in the city budget control it cedes to neighborhood groups, although this is not completely unique. Particularly in Birmingham and San Antonio, budgetary input has resulted in funds being allocated to long-neglected poorer areas.

On the whole, these mechanisms have not, despite dire contrary predictions, exacerbated turmoil. Activity is typically quiet and uneventful. Issues tackled have sometimes been disputatious—for example, drugs and the environment—but quarrels rarely enter the electoral arena. The political culture of this empowerment clearly favors cooperation over confrontation. In some instances, for example, in Birmingham, they have helped to bring blacks and whites nonviolently together for the humdrum tasks of governance. Perhaps these mechanisms serve as "early warning" systems to anticipate troubles before situations deteriorate. Equally relevant, participation tends to be high, and most people are generally satisfied. Particularly on problems immediately affecting neighborhoods—notably land use and future planning—citizen input has proven highly effective. To be sure, criticisms do surface, particularly regarding constraints on local community power or the unevenness of citizen input, but few critics judge these arrangements shams.

Triumphs do not reflect demography or wealth—the five cities vary considerably by affluence and other pertinent socioeconomic traits. Portland is virtually all white, Birmingham is majority African American and San Antonio has a largely Hispanic population. There are certainly no massive Washington-supplied financial incentives to mobilize the disadvantaged for community control (though Birmingham does receive notable federal support for its arrangement). Nor does variation in city government structure or economic prosperity make much impact, although durability seems more likely if arrangements are instituted prior to economic difficulties. Sources of accomplishment lie more in "human" factors than material resources. Especially important is a consensus that citizen participation is indispensable to civic life. The "us" versus "them" mentality, reinforced by deep racial or class divisions, so prominent in 1960s confrontations, is absent. This consensus was also often facilitated by popular elected leaders; empowerment was not an attack on city hall but a way of making city hall function better (Berry, Portnoy and Thomson 1993, Ch. 3).

Important details likewise proved relevant. Federal community development block grants provided modest monetary incentives to entice citizen policy involvement (these are trivial compared to those of the 1993 Empowerment Act). Basing representation on "natural" neighborhood divisions, not economically driven demarcations, was crucial. In several instances this delineation was done through door-to-door surveys and thoughtfully. Most neighborhood areas were small, usually between 2,000 and 5,000, and even at their very largest (16,000 in St. Paul), they barely compare with 50,000 to 200,000 empowerment zone populations. Face-to-face discussions were possible and did occur. That *every* part of the city was included also attenuated the "we" versus "them" mentality. Empowerment did not give one neighborhood an advantage over another, whereas ubiquity alleviated the fears of elected officials over burgeoning rival power centers. Efforts were always made to separate neighborhood empowerment from partisan politics—local associations did not become Democratic or Republican auxiliaries (this divorce was often formally mandated).

If we probe deeper into this communal empowerment, conclusions regarding its effectiveness are mixed and frequently cloudy, given the multitudinous conditions shaping civic activity. The overall conclusion might be *some* empowerment. Analyzing the source of issues emerging in civic life offers no evidence for a strong role for these neighborhood-based associations. Overwhelmingly, conventional players—city government itself, citizens groups—instigated new policies (Berry, Portnoy and Thomson 1993, Ch. 5). Neighborhood activists were not particularly adept at shaping the overall urban agenda. At best, these organizations and activists may cultivate diffuse environments conducive to placing items on the agenda or setting outer boundaries regarding feasibility. Given the constant need to monitor *old* issues and the limited resource base, this inattention to policy novelties is predictable. Developing fresh ideas for imaginative problems may well be an unaffordable luxury. At the broadest level, this neighborhood activism may facilitate elected leader attentiveness to citizens, but it hardly stands as a countervailing defining mechanism.

Nor does an examination of big-time controversial, potentially disruptive development projects give neighborhood power much credence. When such proposals, for example, a sprawling retail complex, a race track, a professional sports facility, were contemplated, neighborhood groups could express views (not always hostile, either) but were helpless to override choices made elsewhere (Berry, Portnoy and Thomson 1993, Ch. 6). Plans were occasionally defeated, but for reasons besides local citizen resistance. This is hardly surprising. The projects generally transcended neighborhood concerns, involving much wider issues, notably tax revenue and community jobs, and thus were decided via conventional channels. Even intense local opposition could not outweigh the lure of overall economic benefits. Significantly, corporate decisions to relocate major facilities elsewhere often rendered community empowerment moot (e.g., U.S. Steel abandoned Birmingham, so neighborhood groups had absolutely no say in its operation). This threat to go elsewhere undoubtedly serves to restrain communal forces. At best, local groups exercised control over smaller businesses needing citizen cooperation, for example, a proposed tavern operating near a residential area.

Perhaps the best case for communal empowerment occurs at the psychological level. On the whole, residents appreciate this access and trust it, particularly when compared to the alternatives. *Beliefs* in organizational effectiveness among both administrators and ordinary citizens were commonplace (Berry, Portnoy and Thomson 1993, Ch. 7). Participants felt more effective regarding government, enjoyed a greater sense of community and were more persuaded of government responsiveness. Empowerment likewise encouraged residents to be more trusting of local government, especially compared to their confidence in Washington. Activists were correspondingly more knowledgeable about municipal politics, suggesting an educative function for empowerment. Overall, the study concludes that this empowerment is "healthy" for a democratic citizenry (Berry, Portnoy and Thomson 1993, Ch. 11).

Assessments of this administrative decentralization as "empowerment" naturally depend on applicable standards. Undoubtedly, all these mechanisms bestow a modicum of neighborhood political clout. This is reinforced by "regular" democratic channels—the right to vote, the right to protest, the standing to take legal action, availability of interests groups and so on. Communal empowerment is thus adding yet one more potential citizen control tool to an already ample collection. At the margin it can help, although, as we have seen, it tends to be restricted when aimed at larger policy. The simple answer to our query is that community administrative decentralization *is* empowerment.

This "helps a little" answer is not the only reasonable response. The more pertinent question is, Compared to what? Communal participation requires time and energy, and documenting its wonders does not certify it the most formidable option. Indeed, the above analysis suggests generally modest payoffs over an unpretentious range of policy choices. Opportunity costs must be weighed. Much depends, and this choice cannot be resolved abstractly. To demonstrate a marginal increment cannot prescribe this tactic as most efficacious. It is conceivable, for example, that moving or pursuing one's goals nonpolitically may be a far superior empowerment technique. That is, why fight high taxes or terrible schools via organizing with one's neighbors? Better to dwell where taxes are low or schools perform better. If moving is not feasible, devote more effort to economic advancement to make taxes less burdensome and private schools more accessible. There is scarcely any problem on the community agenda that cannot be addressed outside of political channels, so *relative* advantage is the real issue.

One final point regarding communal empowerment concerns a conspicuous silence. The subject's scholarly literature abounds with ingenious scheme after scheme to bring influence to the disadvantaged. Nearly all have ultimately failed or underperformed. Yet if one rummages through urban histories, one possibility is much neglected—machine politics. Under such mayors as Richard Daley of Chicago, many neighborhoods (provided they were on the right side politically) were empowered: Their alderman or councilman delivered the goods because he or she knew that his or her electoral career depended upon it. Citizens gave their unwavering electoral endorsements, and the machine guaranteed access. If citizens experienced inadequate city services or crime, the alderman's local office would surely listen and, typically, take action. It was a system built on petty corruption, favoritism and bending of the rules, but it usually supplied those rewards now celebrated by advocates of communal empowerment.

This neglect of a proven remedy is expected. Urban "bosses" hardly endorsed the lofty and largely radical ambitions of today's empowerment devotees. The goals were boring—a clerical job downtown—and they catered to a prejudice-tinged parochialism. Locals were far more concerned about boisterous drunks ruining the park, not some sociological Utopian vision. Politics was profoundly conservative in the sense of not rocking the boat on honoring society's verities. For these "community empowerers" to talk of social justice or participatory democracy would have properly been judged nonsense by constituents. If one recalls the arguments of Chapter 2 about empowerment being co-opted for grander ideological purposes, this neglect should be anticipated. Old-style machine politics may have empowered ordinary citizens, but it totally excluded academic prophets. For academics, the self-determination brought about by the intervention of university-trained experts is far more authentic.

CONCLUSIONS

The push to empower communities seems irrepressible. Since the 1960s huge investments have been made with typically meager results. Some experiments probably engendered more damage than uplift. This urge to improve civic life is certainly commendable, and we cannot castigate the well intentioned. Bashing communal empowerment is not the goal, however. Our purpose is to clarify what is being attempted and its outcome. Recall our earlier contention—the debate is not community empowerment versus dependency; the real issue is a marginal increment over what already exists. Thanks to enormous freedoms, the vitality of democracy, the baseline is already extraordinarily high. Communities possess immense power, and the disgruntled can vote the scoundrels out, move or organize to alter conditions. That remedial efforts fail hardly evidences dependency. Surely we cannot claim that in a world of empowered communities all enterprises succeed. Voting for the losing candidate does not prove that elections are futile; empowerment cannot mean guaranteed victory. Cataloging all the failed efforts does not confirm a political crisis—it merely reveals that not everybody wins 100 percent of the time. Nor can we use the standard of thriving economic well-being as the test for empowerment. Such a Utopian standard guarantees a dismal appraisal of the status quo.

Again, to assist might be likened to doctors searching for the best medicine. Nobody avers that distressed communities are unworthy of assistance, but is empowerment the foremost cure? Can this prescription fashion "communities" out of desolate neighborhoods more akin to wastelands? Can hiring professional administrators and locating them nearby bring health and safety to urban jungles? Many answer yes, although they scarcely consider alternatives. Ideological infatuation seems, once again, to blind. Perhaps a more effective strategy would be to acknowledge deficiencies frankly and remediate those honestly. To wit, a slothful illiterate should mend his or her ways and enroll in school if steady employment is the aim, not be rescued by some bureaucratic deus ex machina. If the local city council fails to represent, must we create a shadow instrument to correct this deficiency? Why not get the elected official to do his or her job instead? Perhaps the clamor for "more empowerment" is a convenient (and deceitful) escape from more daunting labor—literacy or voting wisely in regular elections.

It is ironic that each communal empowerment incites hiring more bureaucrats and the issuance of more detailed directives. The model of government assembling the necessary resources, for example, enforcing laws and providing police protection, and then standing clear has apparently been superseded by the model of an expanding government benevolently *granting* empowerment. Big government empowerment, if you will. That is, like children, the hapless will be assisted by a multitude of others to perform adultlike tasks. Let us be clear: Absolutely nothing is improper with government assisting the disadvantaged; this is hardly the genuine empowerment article, however. Under our "new" empowerment, state employees will be forever standing by to keep you moving down the path toward perceived independence. If those officials fail, it is *they* who will be terminated for incompetence, and a fresh crew will be assigned the task. To confess that perhaps a state of benign dependency may be worthwhile is taboo.

This infatuation with applying flattering, though misleading, language is rarely cost free. Hiring professionals and the drawing up of elaborate plans cost millions, perhaps billions. Imagine, instead, a forthrightness in dealing with the hard-core inner-city unemployed. We might decide, for example, that steady work is intrinsically beneficial, but, alas, some are incapable of attaining this autonomously. One solution is to have private companies, generously compensated by tax dollars, create workshops for the uncompetitive. This is not novel—many religious groups create useful "charity work," and governments have long used this contrivance to fight economic downturns. The Detroit experience is not all that far removed from this model. Assuredly empowerment advocates may judge it "degrading dependency" and demand "training for autonomy" instead. Yet and this is critical, nothing is mandatory—those humiliated by their charitable employment could leave at any time and find "real" work. The stigma of handouts might even encourage attaining genuine independence.

The bottom line is advising caution in treating communal empowerment as the latest Holy Grail. Our canvass has depicted a momentous crusade marching off to battles dimly understood. To criticize means is not to attack worthy goals—nobody wants dreary slums or rotten neighborhoods. And, on occasion, empowerment seems to assist, and no doubt, many feel enriched by being immersed in its rhetoric. Perhaps we should be thankful for anything of value. Yet to insist on pushing this cure without looking elsewhere is a disservice to those we intend to help. As in visiting the doctor with some "embarrassing" disorder, if we want effective cures, we have to be honest.

NOTES

1. Today's enterprise zone may claim British ancestry, but the original English version entailed creation only in desolate, run-down industrial areas of a square mile or so. Almost all taxes within this area were to be abolished, not unreasonable given that hardly anyone lived there. The U.S. version, by contrast, attempts to include as many people as possible, while eliminating personal taxes is unthinkable.

2. The rhetoric boosting these schemes is silent on the proposition that interventions only reward the inept. If one assumes that eventually government will "solve" one's plight, regardless of culpability, then why make the extra effort or sacrifices? If government followed the utilitarian principle of the greatest good for the greatest number, it undoubtedly makes more sense to pour funds into the already successful as a means of facilitating development.

3. The jumbled nature of the act is reflected in its legislative history. In passed both houses of Congress with the slimmest of margins. It had originally been opposed by Black Caucus members who eventually became supporters after realizing that this was the best they could expect. Its underlying muddled philosophy is also revealed by the fact that it lacked a strong congressional champion. (Congressman Charles Rangel was its principal advocate, but he originally opposed the idea of tax-incentive assistance.) One analysis depicted its survival as a near miracle (Rubin, cited in Liebschutz 1995).

4. The idea of "jump-starting" inner-city development by incubating small businesses long precedes this empowerment legislation. Multiple programs from Small Business Administration loans to the Community Block Grant program have long existed. One might also add the various set-aside provisions of federal contracts designed to assist minority-owned enterprises. Given their limited success, the lack of enthusiasm for this type of empowerment was undoubtedly understandable.

5. The idea of simply giving federal money with few restrictions existed for many years as general revenue sharing. This once popular program would, of course, be much closer to empowerment properly understood, but it would fail to address the goal of disproportionately assisting certain favored constituencies.

6. One of the bitterest disputes in New York City involved the inclusion of Yankee Stadium. Although the Yankees are is one of the wealthiest sports franchises, constant threats by its owner to abandon the city prompted Mayor Rudolf Giuliani to insist on its being in the empowerment zone. Over strong objections from black political leaders, Yankee Stadium was incorporated.

7. Perhaps the best example of this predatory migration is professional sports teams. Here teams extort tax breaks and below-market rentals from cities anxious

to have the prestige of a professional franchise. Similar bidding wars have occurred in the location of auto manufacturing facilities.

8. An accurate overall assessment is daunting. Positive spins are routinely issued by government agencies, though these are often short on details. Given the agency's public commitment to "success," deficiencies are barely mentioned. A read of local newspapers often tells a somewhat different tale—frequent squabbling and few positive outcomes. Our position here is that if there were great successes, they would be loudly proclaimed.

9. A timely example is the Daimler-Chrysler merger. German auto executives may well be less sympathetic to pouring industrial jobs into Detroit. For them, unemployment at home may be more pressing.

10. Our account is drawn largely from the descriptions provided by Zimmerman (1972) and Gitell (1971), the latter being quite sympathetic to community control. The critical question of its ultimate effectiveness is, of course, unanswerable given the brevity of the experiment. Ironically, today's incarnation—charter schools and vouchers—is very much a conservative cause.

11. Although the full-blown "community control" movement may be moribund, the spirit still survives. Now, however, the focus is on specific economic entities such as housing projects or health care facilities. That is, tenants may run the building, but this is not a stepping-stone to gaining wider political control (see Handler [1996, Ch. 6] for a tour of this change).

12. Although administrative decentralization seems very much today's alternative to 1960s community control, it was tried in New York City in the early 1970s in an experiment called the Office of Neighborhood Government. Despite some minor "outreach" successes, the project was plagued by problems, largely having to do with conflicting goals, and was discontinued (see Barton 1977).

13. It should be noted that this design may skew results to the highly favorable. These five cities were selected from a possible list of 900 citizen participation programs, and the final selection criteria emphasized demonstrated policy impact (see Berry, Portnoy and Thomson 1993, Methodological Appendix, for details on this selection process).

7

Black Political Empowerment

Chapter 3 briefly outlined black empowerment, noting how African Americans frequently saw political control as the most advantageous path to remedy their plight. This stratagem is hardly the obscure idea concocted by ivory tower academics—it is fervently and widely embraced almost to the exclusion of competing alternatives. Empowerment via the public sector has also grown infectious, spilling well beyond African-American politics as divergent groups (Hispanics, Asian Americans, gays, women) embrace its seductive message. Prodigious hours are spent on registration drives in the hope that "vote power" will bring uplift. Measured by any imaginable standard, this "empowerment via politics" is a truly consequential idea. Chapter 3's analysis only touched on multiple underlying issues in this cosmology, for example, extraordinary confidence in government's remedial potency. Our tour departed with a sense of skepticism. Here we continue our exploration, digging deeper into this pervasive orientation both theoretically and empirically. As before, ours is an FDA-like inquiry: Is the empowerment remedy as safe and effective as claimed by its proponents?

At the outset, two important qualifications are necessary. The first concerns the overall relationship between black empowerment and black politics more generally. The second deals with evidence. Regarding the first, our portrait of "black empowerment" is *not* coterminous with all African Americans politics. We are not about to classify blacks by ideological inclinations, and equally important, this may be impossible given fluidity of circumstances and definitions. We simply contend that this empowerment viewpoint, already once reviewed in Chapter 3, enjoys a substantial black appeal.[1] It is *not* an eccentric vision found among a handful of obscure radicals. If anything, it dominates academic scholarship and public rhetoric.

The second point concerns research bias. Inquires in other domains (education, poverty, health) have generally been tentative, given the imperfections of evidence; scrutinizing black empowerment adds a peculiar problem beyond informational shortcomings. This subject is highly politicized, infused with strident ideological dogma from top to bottom, and dissent is rarely tolerated. Scholarship and public discourse both embrace the supposition that the plights of black Americans are incontestably rooted in white malice and that only wholesale societal transformation—including redistributing wealth—can heal. One leading black scholar explained: "The distinctive characteristic of black political life . . . is the subordination of blacks by whites and concomitant institutionalized belief that white domination is a function of the inherent superiority of whites" (Jones 1978, 92). Differences may transpire but *only* within the broad outlines of this guiding convention. To be sure, all analyses of civic life invite real-world pressure, so coercion is not unexpected. The compulsions here are usually severe, however; dissenters may risk physical harm, even death threats. To ask, for example, "Can black poverty be reduced by greater voting?" draws one toward awkward and often explosive subjects if one ventures beyond conventional platitudes. This enterprise is light years from, say, examining homelessness.

An especially noteworthy theme informing black empowerment permanently on the edge of public discourse concerns black violence, whether petty crime or riots. This complicated topic has only received scant research attention, and our scientific knowledge remains inconclusive (see, e.g., Kelly and Snyder 1980 for some of these issues). Quite likely, however, many African-American tangible gains rest on white fears of disgruntled blacks turning to violence, even randomly killing innocent whites. Recall how the 1992 Los Angeles riots pushed the 1993 Empowerment Zone Act toward passage. This singular appeasement gesture was hardly exceptional. As the few studies on this topic demonstrate, "cooling" black urban violence via government generosity has become reflexive, although generosity is often a drop in the proverbial bucket (Button 1978; Gale 1996). Whether all these government programs had the desired long-term ameliorative impact, apart from galvanizing a government response, is, of course, the key question rarely investigated. Conceivably, the billions in programs came to naught. No forthright discussion of black empowerment could evade this sensitive subject, yet our knowledge remains fragmentary.

Nevertheless, systematic analysis is both difficult, and bare reference engenders discomfort and avoidance. It is perverse to defend a strategy of killing innocent bystanders and looting Korean or Indian businesses as a legitimate, democratic means to influence government. No matter how deep one's sympathy with ghetto despair, compassion cannot transform murderous extortion into legitimate democratic politics. Nor can it be argued that inner-city blacks, like some brutally subjugated Third World people, lack alternatives. Our prosperity has long attracted millions of quickly employed immigrants. Tens of billions (if not trillions) have been committed to alleviate black problems. The United States remains fundamentally democratic, and peaceful avenues abound. Analysis thus faces a paradox: One principal empowerment mechanism (mass violence) will inevitably lie largely outside our canvass. Conceivably, all else, even elections, are mere sideshows compared to the ever-impending mass mayhem threat.

This passionate ideological orthodoxy greatly constrains research more generally. Merely broaching heretical possibilities, regardless of relevance or how carefully nuanced, is customarily taboo. It is not that nonconformists are punished by the thought-police; rather, their accounts go unpublished, especially in academic outlets. Gatekeeping here is strict and censorship largely self-imposed. Those disagreeing wisely invest their energy elsewhere or write for nonacademic audiences. In present political circumstances a "respectable" university researcher would not dare publicly hypothesize that personal deficiencies—shortsightedness, a weakness for self-indulgence, lack of ambition, for instance—might better explain black poverty than white oppression, and empowerment might therefore be directed toward self-mastery, not harassing government. To make unfaltering comparisons with other ethnic groups who faced equally severe obstacles before advancing economically would outrage. Those inclined in this direction, for example, Thomas Sowell in his many books, are silently excluded from this black empowerment enterprise. Quite mild criticism of black leaders, hinting at ineptitude, or expressing doubts about inflammatory tactics is equally *verboten*. Thus, to venture forth into the scholarship on black empowerment is to encounter only a partial picture: information is both incomplete, *and* what exists is slanted toward confirming oft-repeated catchphrases.

Our survey is divided into two sections. The first again explores several deeper theoretical and general quandaries informing this empowerment nostrum. No doubt, this probing may well engender discomfort among the faithful. This is to be anticipated—those in the midst of a sacred mission are disinclined toward doubt. Yet moving beyond cherished buzzwords as truth is essential for progress. Compendiums of failed movements, from Marxism to Prohibition, suffering from flimsy theoretical underpinnings are plentiful; it is entirely possible that black empowerment may eventually join that list of popular well-intentioned failures. Better to pose awkward questions now than continue bumbling down ineffective paths. Our second task reviews the empirical evidence regarding the impact of increased black political mobilization on black betterment. Three types of possible mobilization-induced improvements draw our attention: (1) gaining public office; (2) securing government employment; and (3) redistributing of tangible benefits.

THEORETICAL AND GENERAL ISSUES IN AFRICAN-AMERICAN EMPOWERMENT

Present-day black empowerment emerged from the eventful civil rights struggles commencing in the 1950s. Its passing goals were fairly specific and situationally determined—desegregating a local bus depot or upgrading a nearby school were typical. Tactics such as sit-ins or boycotts were similarly largely impromptu, depending on immediate situations. Some conditions, for example, the federal government being the "good guys," and the locals as a rule being the "bad guys," were historical happenstance. But as successes multiplied, ad hoc tactics evolved into an overriding vision transcending at-hand particulars. By the mid-1960s tactics had hardened into a creed. Only details might shift with changing fortunes. Today's black activist, perhaps subconsciously, inherits an immense legacy of precepts and strategies, all of which derive from successes decades back.

The primacy of politics for substantial transformation is central. Initially the goal was equality of access and freedom from discrimination. Within a decade, however, the agenda expanded to pressuring government to remedy momentous historical disadvantages across a boundless territory, from health care to education, from welfare to home ownership, and nearly everything in between. The span of this agenda, this replacement of legal equality with socioeconomic parity, is critical. That government could "cure" black community troubles, whether narcotics addiction or school truancy, was made axiomatic. Equally pivotal, government would act *only* if compelled or controlled by blacks themselves. Depending on white goodwill or self-help invited failure. Similarly, alliances with liberal whites were secondary to mobilizing apathetic lower-class blacks (Jennings 1992, Ch. 2). Political command will unlock everything. If black children are illiterate, government must build superior facilities and provide satisfactory textbooks, or whatever else was required. If necessary, blacks themselves might secure public control to guarantee results. Even faulty face-to-face interactions, for example, business-owner and customer dealings or employer and employee relationships, were correctable by coercive legal regulation. To repeat, vigorous benevolent state intervention is fundamental. Failure flowed from government's insufficiency, not black deficiency. Communal organizations—churches or fraternal clubs—were relevant only insofar as they facilitated pressure on government.

The magnitude of this hoped-for enterprise, measured by both the prizes sought and its scope, cannot be overemphasized. One black empowerment devotee, in rejecting the traditional piece-of-the-pie strategy for economic advancement, contended, "Black activists [now] seek to determine the size and flavor of the pie, as well as who the baker is and how the economic pie will be actually cut and shared" (Jennings 1992, 10). To be sure, some tasks—equitable distributions of civic services—are well within government's traditional domain. Yet others, for example, providing jobs for the out-of-work, are reachable though vexing. Many other objectives are far more overwhelming. Achieving educational proficiency among black children has proven exceptionally difficult even with huge material investments. Ditto for transforming slums into economically vibrant neighborhoods. One might also add ensuring safe, decent housing among those inclined toward drug-induced violence and property destruction or instilling a strong work ethic among the chronic unemployed. And this just begins the agenda. The problem of escalating demands is also noteworthy—today jobs, tomorrow executive positions, next week a share of ownership, and so on. It is not that these goals are inappropriate or too costly; rather, solutions may be unreachable by *any* democratic government, regardless of commitment or who controls it.

The agenda's grandness is equaled by its exceptional technical demands. As the Great Society shortcomings demonstrated, a fiscal lavishness is *not* the total solution. Even after studies piled upon studies, commission reports upon commission reports, vital questions remain unanswered. If we knew how to motivate indifferent students or keep youngsters off drugs, this would have been accomplished years ago. And recall the difficulty of stimulating entrepreneurial activity in the slums. The key message is that executing the black empowerment agenda requires knowledge exceedingly difficult to obtain. One surefire solution after another, for example, Head Start, scattered site housing, vocational job training, has failed. This is only compounded by democratic limits—we cannot replace parents with involuntary state nurseries. The most noble of intentions and open pocketbook and heartfelt exhortations are zero without this technical information.

Superficially, this Messiah-like government is alluring, well nigh intoxicating. After all, why fight inconclusive battles everywhere against more numerous foes: Capture the all-mighty nerve center once and for all, and government with its ample coercive resources will then conquer all. Nevertheless, at core it is a faulty or at least inappropriate prescription if pushed beyond modest goals. The failing is not an abstract deficiency, however. The defect derives from congruence between this approach in its most expansive embodiment and our guiding constitutional arrangements. To wit, black empowerment, thus understood, rests on a statist (almost totalitarian) model of government at odds with limited, fragmented governance. The hope is that government can command into existence what blacks autonomously cannot perform.[2] It would be more pertinent if society were despotically ruled by an omnipotent philosopher-king. In advancing this formidable notion of empowerment, blacks are asking government to accomplish tasks at the edge of, if not beyond, our traditional constitutional range of authority. It is the matchup between this vision and our enduring system that is troublesome.

CONSTITUTIONAL AND POLITICAL CONSTRAINTS

Consider how this empowerment conception collides with limited government. While government (notably Washington) has of late expanded its authority enormously, huge areas still remain off limits. The United States is not the Soviet Union where apparatchiks assigned jobs and apartments or meddled in religion. Government, despite its magisterial power, cannot tell people where to live, where they can shop, who they can befriend, how they can vote or what they can express in public. A judge might order the school integration and define racial balances minutely, but the most megalomaniac judge is helpless against anti-intellectual parents or those who enroll their children in private schools. Nor can government command all key economic decisions despite its ample regulatory power. Only under extreme conditions, for example, a wartime national emergency, can public officials treat citizens or businesspeople as medieval surfs. To expect to apply governmental authority well beyond its proper scope invites disappointment. At best, as we have seen in our empowerment zone analysis, government can offer modest inducements.

This absolutely elementary point regarding governmental limits is often forgotten. Unrealistic expectations abound.[3] One investigation of black mayors coming to power in three tiny Mississippi towns invoked the term "revolution" to depict this change (Morrison 1987, 1). Clearly, such terminology is more appropriate elsewhere. In studies of black mayors in cities such as East St. Louis, Illinois, or Gary, Indiana, for example, sympathetic analysts—like many ordinary citizens—bemoan that the capture of city hall cannot stem a city's economic deterioration (Nelson and Meranto 1977). That whites hostile to living in a black-dominated city can migrate elsewhere or withdraw from public life seemingly hints at an antiblack conspiracy. The subsequent tax revenue loss that subverts the newly elected black mayor's ambitious economic plans "confirms" this evildoing. To alter these (and innumerable other) fundamental freedoms from government compulsion, these cherished "givens" of political life, would require the imposition of totalitarianism.

It is easy to grasp why this protection afforded personal and economic freedom can be construed as evidence of racism among the less sophisticated. And indeed, such liberty may well be consciously directed to achieve antiblack objectives or at least purposes inconsistent with black aspirations. Nevertheless, at the risk of reaffirming the obvious, to guarantee black empowerment effectiveness under existent legal foundations radically attacks the constitutional order. It is a matter of weighing competing principles in securing the common good: Lesser advantages must be sacrificed for larger purposes. Imagine if a judge ordered untold white Gary, Indiana, residents to stay put and pay increased taxes so the freshly elected black mayor can now pave streets in black neighborhoods? And if these residents secretly fled, the sheriff would forcibly return them to face trial for unau-thorized relocation. What would happen if U.S. Steel (a former major Gary industry) were commanded to lose money? Clearly, under extreme condi-tions, these missives are feasible—white residents can be bribed to remain and U.S. Steel could also be subsidized or managed as a state-owned char-itable enterprise.

A second constitutional element often colliding with black empowerment is the principle of dispersed political power. As any college-level "Intro-duction to American National Government" course explains, the Founders feared concentrated authority. Security from tyranny, not efficiency, was the primary objective in fashioning government. As the United States is not the Soviet Union, we are also not a Third World nation of the unchallenged autocrat. Within the national government, power was to be dispersed across all three branches as well as between the center and constituent states. This diffusion continues down into the furthest political corners—the mightiest mayors must contend with city councils, independent com-missions, a multitude of state officials, civil service–protected bureaucracies and innumerable others all jealously guarding prerogatives. "Pluralism"—a hodgepodge of competing interests peacefully competing within a demo-cratic framework—well depicts our politics. Racial divisions only add yet one more cleavage to an already conflictual arrangement (Levine 1974, Ch. 3). Additionally, the more grandiose the agenda, the greater the number of competitors drawn to the fray. A mayor fantasizing himself king and an-nouncing grandiose unauthorized undertakings would soon be brought down to earth by numerous contending power centers. "Off Limits" and "Danger: Conflict Ahead" warnings are everywhere. Fragmentation of power is *not* a racist flaw; it is purposeful and essential and applies to everyone regardless of race. In principle, it can just as easily work to the *advantage* of African Americans.

Reinforcing this fragmenting of power is the frequency of free elections.[4] The most glorious electoral triumph is typically short-lived; elected officials with unusually long careers—Richard J. Daley of Chicago, Coleman Young of Detroit—remain rare exceptions, and sixteen years is hardly lifetime employment. Several high-profile black officials—Chicago's Harold Wash-ington and David Dinkins of New York City, Wilson Goode of Philadel-phia, to identify but a few—served only briefly. Not only is time limited, but electoral requirements themselves, from raising funds among the status quo minded to placating divergent constituencies, work to undermine ven-turesome schemes. Generous programs essential for empowerment may quickly evaporate as legislative balances shift. Elections facilitate *incremen-tal* changes, not abrupt transformations. If we desired aggrandized central power, we would install a monarchylike system, not periodic democratic elections. Again, both the dispersion of power and recurrent elections hinder accumulating sufficient power to impose the drastic reconstruction implied by black empowerment. It is *intentional* that elected officials (regardless of race) are bedeviled by adversaries everywhere, ensnarled in debilitating regulations, tormented from afar and otherwise thwarted.

Particularly pertinent are the constraints imposed by equal protection of the laws and other strictures limiting racially distinctive treatment. In a phrase, the rule of law, not of benign whim, governs. No matter how tragic black suffering, no matter how grievous past treatment, blacks cannot obtain legal exemptions to facilitate their path toward equality. Blacks officials, in a sense, are prisoners of the very legal system protecting their rights. Thus, white civil servants who resist ultimatums from elected black officials cannot be summarily terminated simply because blacks "have waited too long." Taxes cannot be freely boosted to feed inner-city malnourished children. When Newark, New Jersey's black mayor attempted to impose a 2 percent income tax on those working in Newark (mainly white suburbanites), the state legislature vetoed it (Keller 1978). Tedious forbidding procedures must be followed. Government grants to cities cannot be allocated, as one report advises, exclusively to cities with black mayors (Colburn 1973). A business that resists pleas to hire their "fair share" of African Americans cannot be expropriated because men and women are desperate. If threats to impose a fair share become overwhelming, the business can move or close altogether. Hypercritical newspapers cannot be silenced to assist black progress, although this might help immensely. All of this is transparent, but all too easily neglected in the rush to alleviate deplorable conditions.

These constrictive factors cumulate. Tales of black mayors, not surprisingly, reveal a familiar scenario. Part one details years of frustration, narrow defeats, followed, at last, by eventual victory by a resourceful charismatic leader. Part two recounts high initial expectations—jobs, newsprung social programs and refurbishment of impoverished black neighborhoods will now transpire. Temporarily, all goes well as blacks are appointed to top positions, projects are initiated and everyone savors the honeymoon. Part three tells of mounting disappointment as squabbling breeds paralysis, former allies fall out, coalitions disintegrate, past opponents openly counterattack, debt ceilings are reached and outside benefactors fail to deliver on pledged assistance. The local media becomes adversarial with headlines of corruption and ineptitude. Potential political rivals join critics tempting former supporters. Almost overnight, ordinary blacks complain of former heroes "selling out" to the power structure or failure to honor expensive promises. Handsome projects become mired in red tape, rejected tax increases and acrimony. To repeat, this is not an antiblack white "power structure" plot; this gridlock process inheres in our political order, and as such, it conspires against *anyone* enlisting politics as a vehicle to achieve grand schemes. Yet all of this disappointment with modest accomplishment, no matter how frequent, always seems to astonish black empowerment devotees.

A further point has less to do with constitutional constraints than navigating these frustrating barriers. U.S. politics is intrinsically complicated—one does not assemble a few soldiers, capture the capital, rule by decree and liquidate dissenters. A charismatic knack for rallying followers or painting vivid pictures of good and evil need not translate into requisite administrative accomplishment. Grand ambitions require talents for negotiation, compromise, and bridge building, and these must be blended with a knack for technical details and legal acumen. Recall Detroit's job creation success: Mayor Dennis Archer, unlike his Atlanta counterpart, adeptly organized competing interests to cooperate while navigating statutory impediments. Insulating one's private life from distracting scandal also helps. Of course, many, perhaps most, American politicians fail these tests. What is germane here is the relationship between the agenda's scope and requisite capacities: Ambitious agendas demand extraordinary talent.

The colossal size of the black political task requires commensurate skill, regardless of race. Galvanizing slogans are not enough. For blacks, acquiring this combination of expertise may be challenging.[5] This is not a uniquely black problem—no doubt, it is commonplace among groups starting at the bottom rungs. Experienced middle-class technocrats intimately acquainted with policy mechanics and simultaneously attractive to those further down the ladder are inevitably in short supply. They are hardly unknown; for example, Mayor Kurt Schmoke of Baltimore or ex-Mayor Tom Bradley of Los Angeles are two successful examples of this technocratic style. Training in the ministry or community organizations, familiar recruitment grounds for black leaders, scarcely provides ample technical expertise. One might also add that blacks with superb managerial skills often do far better in the private sector and dodge the perplexities of political strife. To repeat, providing exceptionally talented political leaders is not uniquely a "black problem," but it does become especially troublesome if one seeks sweeping change.

It is also true that the weak, factional character of black politics does not facilitate the lengthy apprenticeships so necessary for building a cadre of deft potential leaders. The old-fashioned urban machines in which blacks had their own "submachine" are long gone. Only rarely is there today an enduring black state or local organization in which the administratively competent patiently rise upward, all the while building an army of loyal supporters. The upshot is a truncated learning curve—the newly elected black official, usually most adroit at mobilizing supporters, arrives on the job with limited managerial acumen, a tentative following and soaring public expectations and may only be granted a few years to accomplish an enormous task while facing formidable opposition.

THE CALCULUS OF MOBILIZATION AND REWARDS

Utilizing politics to accomplish goals might be likened to any other goal-driven asset deployment. One selects from an array of possible outcomes and then applies the most advantageous means. So it is with black empowerment. Let us first consider a deceptively unadorned question: What are the goals of black empowerment? The consensual "Make life better for African Americans" only disguises some serious differences and unanswered questions. For one, blacks are hardly a unified group, and as honest differences quickly arise, concrete choices are confronted. "Black progress" can mean, variously, advancement for *all* African Americans (perhaps unevenly) or merely the uplift of those clustered at the bottom. Is the ultimate goal some absolute level of betterment or across-the-board parity with whites? Merely announcing that an action is "good for blacks" does not unquestionably certify its racial universality or establish precise end points.

Moreover, and this point cannot be overemphasized, divisions will only propagate with time as blacks move up the economic ladder and enter "new" occupations, thus becoming more "white" in their perspectives.[6] A small political conservatism movement is already emerging within the black community (see, e.g., Faryna, Stetson and Conti [1997] for a pointed rejoinder to this reliance on the state). Perhaps economic *superiority*, not merely equality, will be embraced by some blacks. Add the further problems if blacks attempt to form opportunistic coalitions with other disadvantaged groups who also have lofty, potentially conflicting ambitions. It would be far different if African Americans were isolated and undifferentiated; then a single policy would suffice. Paradoxically, attainment breeds growing perplexity in sustaining cohesion.

Accounts of this dilemma are commonplace, unavoidable in a pluralistic society, and send an inescapable message about black empowerment as a unified mass movement. A few brief illustrations of this "lose-lose" phenomenon must suffice. In the late 1960s, for example, Cleveland's black mayor, Carl Stokes, proposed constructing a large public housing project to be occupied by lower-class blacks within an established black middle-class neighborhood. The black city councilman representing middle-class black residents predictably went ballistic and quickly allied himself with white councilmen to block the project. No amount of "racial unity" rhetoric softened resistance and this acrimony ultimately squandered the mayor's legitimacy (Nelson and Meranto [1977, Ch. 10] offer an entire catalog of such incidents). A more recent example concerns the mass exodus of home-owning middle-class blacks from Washington, D.C.'s incredible civic corruption. Such flight not only weakens an already precarious tax base, but the abandoned areas quickly become crime-ridden slums. Here the desire for adequate municipal services, preserving home equity and other quality-of-life ingredients outranks supporting a black mayor

(Marion Barry) committed to assisting less fortunate blacks by channeling good-paying city jobs their way (Holmes and De Witt 1996). In fact, one black suburban county executive has waged a campaign to keep impecunious Washington blacks from relocating to the suburbs. Such intraracial conflicts are *inherent*.

Over and above these frictions is the multiplicity of distinctive aims amenable to black empowerment. "Economic uplift" is only part of the story. Despite its frequent repetition, its meaning is far from self-evident, and its pursuit is seldom straightforward. The road may lead everywhere and sometimes nowhere. The quest can be likened to a multifront war on a grand scale, and—as in military campaigns—tough choices are required regarding allocating resources to secure differing objectives. Victory in one domain may be "paid for" with defeat elsewhere. This dilemma is not, of course, limited to black empowerment: It is integral to all politics, although it may apply more forcefully where the mission is of a huge magnitude.

Consider the uncertain connection between economic prosperity and political control. Although the two aims are often conflated by black activists, especially those labeling American blacks a "colonial dependency," the two goals are quite separate. Postcolonial Africa makes this plain. The Detroit and Atlanta empowerment zone lessons are also enlightening here. Recall that Detroit's mayor, Dennis Archer, de facto handed over job creation to the white-controlled Big Three automobile manufacturers, and thousands of unemployed blacks were soon hired. The city had minimal say in plant location, production or job description. By contrast, Atlanta kept job creation "in-house," and its black-dominated bureaucracy micromanaged the task. The Atlanta results were dismal. To go one step further, black control may well *exacerbate* unemployment and squalor as anxious whites and white-run enterprises flee the city. The few dozen municipal positions gained by blacks, the handful of public works projects directed toward black neighborhoods and all the other successes might be well overshadowed by substantial losses. The 1960s vision of black power unleashing a cornucopia of benefits on the black populace in Gary, Indiana, East St. Louis, Illinois, Newark, New Jersey, and similar localities flush with pride over "black control" have largely disappointed. The 1960s upsurge in southern small-town black mayors similarly found little proof that this changing of the guard brought instant *nirvana*. At best, a few energetic local executives extracted some temporary largess from the federal government (Colburn 1973). Ironically, one description of empowerment in East St. Louis, Illinois, argued that the white-led machine's *effectiveness* in providing material benefits to blacks *hindered* black control (Nelson and Meranto 1977, Ch. 2; this pattern is not unusual). Blacks might in some circumstances be wise to hire outside white experts if economic uplift is the chief goal.

An especially difficult dilemma is disentangling psychological benefits from more material rewards. This tangible versus psychic problem, as Chapter 2 reviewed at length, is endemic to empowerment and often quite mischievous. Is black empowerment exclusively the procuring of humdrum material benefits, for example, a job, or must there be some accompanying inner gratification? Does one outweigh the other? Again, these payoffs need not coexist, and may be conflictual. Recall how feminist organizations occasionally launched high-sounding quixotic campaigns whose "real" benefit was principally self-gratification. Does a newly employed Detroit black feel empowered when Congress grants tax relief to a white-owned company to hire him or her? Would things be better if, by contrast, the black mayor independently devised the empowerment program and it was black administered, but the results were less successful?

These are incredibly vexing questions requiring enormous yet-to-be done research, and the evidence is surely preliminary. Yet its relevance for black empowerment is absolutely central: Material advancement is *un*likely to be self-gained if the empowerment crusade chases transient psychological gratification. The answer must be empirical, not logical. Evidential reservations aside, however, evidence points in the direction of conflicts between psychological and material empowerment, with the psychological often outweighing the material.

One body of evidence concerns the "style" of many blacks achieving political prominence. Over 30 years ago, James Q. Wilson observed the sharp contrast between nondescript black leaders who quietly "delivered the material goods" versus those whose flamboyant manner exclusively provided bountiful psychic gratification (Wilson 1960, Ch. 9). The latter, often understandably, boosted communal self-respect with their fiery condemnation of white domination and belligerent independence. Indeed, a scorn for deal making and a taste for provocative theatrics alienating potential allies only served to heighten black support. This is not to suggest conscious choices between two extremes at election time; rather, many blacks willingly accepted psychic satisfaction independent of material advancement. In its own way, "standing up to the [white] man" in the face of fierce pressure bestowed a genuine sense of empowerment.

This penchant for psychological rewards at the expense of material dividends is particularly manifest in the theatrical "individualistic" style of black politics. It is not that this high-profile method is somehow "bad"; rather, progress is necessarily limited if this charisma cannot be institutionalized into an enduring organization. Without this transformation, far too much depends on the ups and downs of whomever happens to catch the public eye with whatever issues are handy. Unfortunately for the long-term empowerment agenda, this "cult of the personality" has been ever present. Charismatic personalities were the mainstay of the early civil rights movement, and protest groups were virtually indistinguishable from their enterprising leader. Martin Luther King, Jr., Stokely Carmichael, Ralph

Abernathy and others are all remembered as strong personalities, not their bureaucratic legacy. More radical forces such as the Black Panthers were similarly more defined by strong attention-getting personalities—an Elridge Cleaver, H. Rap Brown, Huey Newton or Malcolm X—than dull but effective bureaucracies.

This "cult of the dynamic personality" shows no signs of waning. The many dozens of black organizations often constitute little more than an enterprising leader and a tiny following opportunistically hunting for galvanizing issues. Even Jesse Jackson's ill-fated 1984 quixotic presidential campaign was judged a "success" by one prominent black academic (Barker 1988). "Black political organization" still conjures up high-profile personalities—Jesse Jackson, Louis Farrakhan immediately come to mind—in contrast to the preeminence of powerful yet obscure behind-the-scene organizations. In fact, Louis Farrakhan has virtually become a "mainstream," well-regarded leader among blacks despite his avowed anti-Semitism, calls for separatism and bizarre views on many topics, including tales of alien abduction (Keiser 1997, vi). Washington's colorful Marion Barry had no problem winning black endorsement despite his infamous antics, terrible record and drug conviction. Indeed, the traditional mainstay bureaucratic black civil rights organizations, notably the NAACP (National Association for the Advancement of Colored People), bereft of a charismatic leader, seemingly drift into irrelevance and incapacity.

Paralleling this energetic individualism is a fascination with dramatic, often momentary events. Again, it is a matter of preferable method, not inherent virtue. The history of black mobilization is replete with well-publicized marches, voter registration drives, picketings, demonstrations, rallies, boycotts and similar riveting occurrences. Jesse Jackson has made a career of high-profile, highly personalized but transitory confrontations with innumerable white "power centers" such as Nike, Wall Street, Mitsubishi, Texaco, General Motors, various government agencies and untold others.[7] There is also an inclination toward disruptive confrontation, occasionally led by outlandish leaders like Al Sharpton, at the expense of longer-term organization infrastructure development or self-help projects. Oftentimes it is a petty incident, for example, a white police officer beating a black motorist, not an enduring structural condition, that triggers the turmoil. After a few days, all returns to normal. In many instances, the gesture itself, independent of any tangible outcome, is taken as proof of empowerment. Even clear accomplishments—swelling the voting rolls or business promises to hire more blacks—are often fleeting, if not largely symbolic, without sufficient follow-up. Justifications usually stress the psychological: "instilling pride," "bring attention to the cause" or "displaying our numbers." The famous 1963 Washington "We have a dream" rally organized by Martin Luther King and the more recent "Million Man March" typify this "feel-good" approach to empowerment. These emotional events, often with a festive flavor, seem commonplace everywhere blacks live.

A confirming insight into this superficial style is the neglect of well-researched, carefully examined solutions to African Americans problems. To be blunt, empty slogans ("Social Justice," "Fair Share") and older, generally exhausted solutions—forced integration, community control, racial quotas, business set-asides—remain the heart of the black empowerment agenda. Innovations, notably multicultural education or guaranteed black political representation, are of uncertain value.[8] Indeed, as Chapter 6 on educational empowerment argued, this flatter-the-student's-deficiency tactic may well engender educational disaster. Some agenda elements—Ebonics, Afrocentric historical interpretation, reparation demands, quotas in capital punishment and a separate black political party, in particular—are bizarre, often bringing ridicule. There is often an embarrassing casualness to economics and business details, as if solutions merely constituted willingness to spend for every black demand. That people might be reluctant to bear higher taxes apparently dumbfounds.[9] The formula appears to be equal parts of stressing black adversity, heaping scorn on whites (especially conservative politicians) for permitting this plight and implying the efficacy of government intervention as a law of nature (e.g., Nelson, Mosqueto and Meranto, 1984; Persons 1993). Relevant "white" solutions, for example, school vouchers, cracking down on crime or tougher welfare laws, typically receive short shrift or opposition. It is almost as if solutions must be "Made by Blacks" to be taken seriously. As the previous tour of black empowerment observed, many blacks seem absolutely convinced that government could "really" cure the problem only if it sincerely desired.[10]

This preference for psychic gratification over more material accomplishment surfaces in the quest for black legislative seats. To summarize a long story, a choice emerged in the mid-1980s regarding black legislative representation, especially in the U.S. House. That is, should district lines be drawn to maximize black victories, even if this could enhance Republican legislative strength more generally? Given that the GOP usually opposed policies favored by blacks, notably continued affirmative action, these newly acquired "black seats" might well be paid with less desirable legislative outcomes. Blacks would surrender *influence* across numerous Democratic districts represented by a white in exchange for dominating a scattering of districts. And given population size, the potential number of black legislators was circumscribed, never to be a controlling majority.

The choice was never in doubt: Black leaders (tacitly aided by Republicans) pushed for "minority-majority" electoral districts. Or at least did not object. Boundary lines were often manipulated in endless twists and turns, across hundreds of miles, to include as many black voters as necessary to guarantee an African-American legislator. Legal doctrines regarding apportionment were pushed to their breaking point. The end result was twofold. First, as welcomed by black leaders, and amply assisted by the Department of Justice, the black legislative contingent grew significantly. Second, many seats immediately fell into the Republican column with more likely to follow (Hill 1995). In effect, black political desires expedited 1994 Republican control of the House and other state legislatures. Now, reduced to a larger element in the House's Democratic minority, black legislators could passively watch as their cherished programs fell under GOP assault. In a nutshell, the symbolism of more elected blacks overrode more concrete influence.

This commentary regarding black political "style" is only intended to align it with its ambitious agenda. Judgment is technical, no different from evaluating any other ends-means relationships. Disparagement is not our intent: Democracy hardly proscribes a single path in exercising participatory rights. If people choose to vote by flipping coins, this is their prerogative. It is the congruence between tactics and intent that is noteworthy. The dilemma only emerges when charismatic personalities providing thrilling rhetoric are favored, and these leaders are then expected to fix incredibly complex problems requiring administrative and technical expertise. And if the results are meager, or smack too closely of collaborating with "the enemy," disappointment may encourage others, perhaps those inclined toward even grander promises, to step forth as alternatives. The bottom line, clearly, is not circumstances conducive to addressing nearly intractable problems.

Our two further points regarding the black empowerment efficacy are more hypothetical, although both have concrete applications. The first concerns the diminishing returns from purely political strategies in ameliorating severe, wide-ranging impediments. That the early civil rights movement was successful in many areas is unquestioned. The combination of direct action reinforced by government intervention greatly reduced racial segregation in public life and opened new economic opportunities. Still, it is equally obvious that continued progress is not assured as goals become more perplexing. Enacting legislation or securing a new Washington-funded program is not journey's end. Abolishing "colored only" drinking fountains is comparatively simple compared to ending a debilitating attraction to drugs or teaching indifferent youngsters arduous skills. The former can be executed relatively painlessly by government edict; the latter requires serious social engineering with uncertain guideposts. Yesterday's solution may well be today's dead end.

Several factors suggest a diminishing marginal return on a purely political strategy. For one, as the agenda shifts from the "obvious," for example, removing restrictive housing covenants, to the more ambitious, providing decent housing, goals become more zero-sum, expensive and technically complex. Conflict possibilities multiply, as do resistance points. "Racial equality" as a purely legal principle may psychologically enrage white racists, but the material resources transferred to implementation are relatively modest. When blacks receive appreciable material benefits at white expense, however, matters change drastically. Resistance here, and not necessarily on racial grounds, may be far more intense and progress less rapid. The growing battle over affirmative action is typical—"giving" jobs, college admissions, loans and government contracts to blacks means less for whites, many of whom have superior claims on these prizes. The movement to reverse affirmative action is well under way and has had some notable successes, as in the passage of California's Proposition 209 banning state preferential treatment plus several federal court decisions. Yet this resistance is exactly what black empowerment invites as it moves from legal mandates to economic redistribution.

The empowerment remedy, as articulated by its defenders, unfortunately seems to forget that blacks are a numerical minority. Richard Keiser, one of its more thoughtful advocates, defined *empowerment* as the reallocation of political power (Keiser 1997, 5). This means the capturing of high-status, consequential positions—being mayor or governor, for instance. Logically, if political power follows the contours of race, blacks can rightly expect to dominate only a tiny sliver of U.S. politics—a few cities, perhaps, but not much else. In places with substantial, though less than majority, black populations, empowerment is beyond reach. Given that solidly black areas (mainly small southern towns) have already achieved black empowerment, not much else remains to be conquered. The battle is over unless dramatic migratory and demographic transformations suddenly appear.

It is also true, as already suggested, that requisite capacity (knowledge, tenacity, political skill) becomes far more Herculean as goals become more ambitious. It is comparatively simple to ban state-required school segregation; it is quite another to ensure equality of educational outcomes. Slow progress is *not* a matter of white foot-dragging or selfishness. Technical solutions often lie beyond our grasp. Our remarkable effectiveness in some domains does not imply that anything is possible if we merely roll up our sleeves and work hard. As the "easy" goals are accomplished, it may be necessary to spend 100 times the money and energy to advance just slightly, and this may invite proportionate resistance.

A second hypothetical issue concerns a political strategy versus nonpolitical alternatives. This is a familiar controversy and goes back to the Booker T. Washington versus W.E.B. Du Bois debate, if not earlier. In modern economic language, the dilemma is one of opportunity costs: a day spent demonstrating on behalf of affirmative action vis-à-vis a day acquiring a vocational skill. More generally, every black empowerment agenda element can be accomplished *without* government intervention.[11] Calculating investment mixtures returns is strictly an empirical task, yet it seems that the maximum contribution of political pressure is now being reached. The civil rights legislative agenda is finished. Even under ideal political circumstances, with sympathetic public officials and judges, the marginal benefit of additional mobilization seems minuscule compared to the rewards of nonpolitical strategies. The expenses of organizing million-people demonstrations or rallying parents to boycott schools might be better allocated outside the public sphere.

This paltry comparative advantage of politics has repeatedly been argued by Thomas Sowell, a black economist skeptical of the civil rights agenda (Sowell 1984). For one, many ethnic groups, for example, Jews and Italians, have advanced economically while being political apathetic or even *excluded* from civic participation. One only has to look at Americans of Asian ancestry to see prosperity coexisting with near-total political indifference. Higher participation rates are far more likely to be consequences, not causes, of prosperity. More generally, no clear relationship connects political adroitness and economic attainment (Sowell 1984, 32). At most, only a few group leaders reap the tangible windfall of activism. In fact, groups with an entrepreneurial knack, for example, East Indians, Koreans, reluctantly enter politics given superior opportunities elsewhere. Political activism may even be a luxury for the already successful and an injurious distraction for the needy. Sudden surges of political activism have even invited ruin, for example, the late nineteenth-century impetuous nationalism of overseas Chinese and the post–World War I separatism of Sudeten Germans in Czechoslovakia (Sowell 1984, 33). It is fantasy to proclaim this economic gain-political mobilization nexus as gospel.

Taken together, this overall assessment of black empowerment does not portend confidence. Let us be clear: We are not counseling apathy, nor are we suggesting the wastefulness of past campaigns. Politics in the United States is always useful for accomplishing certain goals, and the splendid civil rights historical record speaks for itself. Our perspective is forward looking, focusing on what can be attained as the agenda ventures into more difficult, contentious domains. This is easily misinterpreted, given that we scrutinize approaches long celebrated as unquestioned faith. Let us now turn toward more empirical findings regarding black mobilization.

THE BENEFITS OF POLITICAL MOBILIZATION

Black political empowerment involves multitudinous weapons, from litigation to threats of urban unrest. Moreover, several relevant techniques, for example, securing the support of sympathetic whites or manipulating the mass media via false or exaggerated reports of hate crimes, are rarely broached in this context.[12] Equally important, the full impact of this crusade is barely understood. The scholarly literature on this immense topic remains incomplete, and as we observed, it is deeply colored by a constraining one-sided ideology. Conceivably, some of the induced change might be *negative*, for example, white firms fleeing overseas rather than face black demands. It is no exaggeration to say that this empowerment movement prospers as a matter of faith or habit. Nevertheless, caveats aside, it is possible to offer an empirically based evaluation from one vantage point, the utility of electoral mobilization across a variety of outcomes.

Let us add yet further qualifications. Although the electoral process may be the most visible feature of black empowerment, the two are hardly synonymous. Indeed, a few black activists express reservations about routine, humdrum office seeking, often seeing it as too accommodationist, if not a distraction from grander pursuits (e.g., Jennings 1992, Ch. 4). Moreover, electoral politics has an invisible side, so voting turnout and campaign victories—our principal window into black empowerment—can only reveal glimpses, particularly if blacks underutilize these more unseen resources. Such key activities as campaign donations or skilled insider deal-making are seldom discussed in the context of black empowerment. That blacks typically *request* government assistance for pledging their vote, not make lavish campaign contributions along with bloc voting, is a pertinent fact largely escaping scholarly attention. Yet it is undeniable that the black empowerment cosmology requires *some* electoral clout to be successful. Voting and winning office may not be sufficient, but success, it is believed, is unattainable without a winning electoral strategy. Our survey begins with achieving office and then progresses to securing more difficult economic benefits.

Gaining Office

Winning elected office is the first step on a long journey. Measured by the energy expended—all the personal and legislative struggles, the countering of white intimidation and legal actions against the biased electoral system—this constitutes an especially expensive first step. The raw numbers reveal ample returns. According to one estimate (Williams 1982), in 1965, when the federal Voting Rights Act was initially passed, fewer than 500 blacks held elected office nationwide. The rare national black officeholders often served as attention-getting novelties, for example, flamboyant New York City Congressman Adam Clayton Powell. The massive surge in black voting soon saw a notable upswing in officeholders. By 1970, Joint Center for Political Studies figures showed the number to be 1,469; ten years later, the number had reached 4,912 (cited in Williams 1982).

By the early 1990s, black electoral victories ceased being oddities. In 1993, the count had reached just above 8,000. This progress was perhaps most conspicuous in the U.S. House, where black delegation size had multiplied from a tiny handful in the 1960s to 17 in 1981 to 39 in 1995. Only slightly less prominent was the emergence of black mayors. Virtually every major United States city—New York, Chicago, Los Angeles, Washington, D.C., New Orleans, Denver, Philadelphia, Detroit, Atlanta, Baltimore, San

Francisco—has now seen a black mayor chosen. In 1993, the last available year of Joint Center available statistics, in cities of 50,000-plus population, 38 were headed by an African American (*Black Elected Officials* 1993, xxxiii). These totals, predictably, swell as one moves toward smaller towns and cities. As of January 1993, for example, 35 towns in Alabama had black mayors; there were 26 in Arkansas and 27 in North Carolina. All told, some 356 black mayors held office in 1993 (*Black Elected Officials* 1993, xxxiv). A less visible increase has transpired virtually across the board in state legislatures, law enforcement, education, municipal positions, judgeships, and wherever else elections are held.

If all these officials were assembled together, an impressive picture would emerge. Moreover, "the black vote" is undoubtedly a powerful force in politics at all levels, even when the possibility of electing a black is remote. It is inconceivable that national or state office seekers can ignore black voters. President Clinton has repeatedly acceded to black preferences, no doubt in response to his reliance on African-American votes. This surely constitutes a transformation of the first order. Black community leaders are now power brokers in innumerable cities and even key states such as California and New York. Nevertheless, although the black vote is surely a political factor in many circumstances, the stark statistics also reveal a less impressive picture. Shifting from "being an influence" to the more daunting black empowerment ingredient "holding actual power," these figures indicate only a tentative beachhead being captured.

Most evidently, all these numbers constitute only a tiny percentage of all U.S. elected officials—while blacks may comprise approximately 12 percent of the population, their share of offices in barely over 1 percent (*Black Elected Officials* 1993, xxiii). Despite their infatuation with elections, African Americans scarcely resemble the politically adroit Irish who once dominated civic life despite their smallish numbers. Equally apparent, the rate of increase has slowed dramatically from the early 1970s when blacks triumphed in black-dominated urban and rural areas. Moreover, many of these black victories have proven fleeting—notable victories in Chicago, Philadelphia, New York City and elsewhere were brief, whereas in other instances, such as Governor L. Douglas Wilder's election in Virginia, reelection was legally forbidden. Today, it is the black who repeatedly wins in an overwhelmingly nonblack area who is the attention-getting novelty. With all these "natural" gains now secure, electoral advancement is now *qualitatively* different. Gains must now come in localities where African Americans are less than a majority or can depend on benign manipulation of boundaries or voting procedures to "guarantee" successes not otherwise obtainable.

This necessary advancement into coalition politics will surely impede the black empowerment enterprise. A collision with Hispanic allies, a group that has often supplied the victory margin where blacks are less than a majority, is particularly likely. Although blacks and Hispanics often share similar policy agendas, the black quest for black officeholders may alienate this ally as the expanding Hispanic population similarly seeks the identical electoral prizes. This tension is already apparent in New York and Texas in the creation of legislative district boundaries (Tate 1993, 173). Mexican Americans, Puerto Ricans and other ambitious ethnic groups may not be content to be represented by blacks as did Jews and Italians were once satisfied with Irish or WASP (White Anglo Saxon Protestant) officeholders. Ironically, the idea of a grand minority coalition may come to haunt blacks as demands for one's "own" position multiply. At a minimum, gaining majorities in heterogeneous settings where "physical representation" is largely irrelevant may necessitate abandoning the strident empowerment agenda. Appeals for economic redistribution and grandiose government spending may only anger those preferring low taxes, efficient municipal services and law and order. Pushing a black victory in such circumstances may also be but a Pyrrhic victory if blacks become estranged from other groups. Recall how the sudden upsurge in black legislative seats resulting from racial gerrymandering created Republican victories in 1994, reducing the Democratic Party to a congressional minority.

Far less visible that these statistics is postelection *incorporation* of blacks into the policy-making process (Browning, Marshall and Tabb 1984, Ch. 1). Here blacks officials can actually make a concrete policy difference. This next step is absolutely fundamental if blacks are to advance beyond figurehead representation. After all, it may matter little if blacks gain the trappings of office if they are excluded from consequential decisions. Translating black votes into incorporation requires a knack for coalition building, knowing how to bargain, compromise and all the other critical details of political life. One must also have demography and larger political trends on one's side. Incorporation need not be proportional to absolute numbers, for a few particularly skilled individuals might well use their position to secure far more benefits than a much larger contingent of inept black officeholders.

Incorporation is hardly guaranteed by electoral politics. One study of ten California cities with significant black (and Hispanic) populations provides some important clues on this achievement. The researchers found that black population size, the prevalence of Democratic Party affiliation (meaning liberalism) among voters in general and electoral support among minority interests greatly facilitated black influence (Browning, Marshall and Tabb 1984, Ch. 1). White liberal support was essential. Needless to say, this fortuitous combination is hardly commonplace in U.S. politics. In several of these California cities, blacks simply failed to mobilize sufficiently or were successfully resisted by conservative whites. Indeed, the existence of enduring liberal white racial ideology amidst a large black population may well be exceptional, and unstable in the long run, particularly if racial divisions over "gut" emotional issues such as crime and education become contentious. The one city with the greatest incorporation—Berkeley—is hardly one's average American locality.

The dilemma of intraracial divisions is also relevant to translating off-iceholding into enduring power. A review of black electoral triumphs will surely show that the victory party does not end factionalism. If anything, the dearth of nonpolitical opportunities may only intensify infighting among blacks seeking the rewards of office. Nor is there any reason to suppose that middle- and lower-class African Americans will coalesce for the sake of "racial unity." Even if a city is wholly black dominated, it is never a kingdom unto itself—its governance is inevitably integrated into a network of agencies, boards and other authorities with ample legal power to obstruct. African Americans will *always* be a political minority, so to fashion an agenda as if blacks could freely command the political system is fantasy.

In sum, over the last three decades blacks have captured a multitude of political offices. Yet these gains also mask serious shortfalls. Periodic victories have not always translated into the control envisioned by black empowerment rhetoric. Disappointment seems commonplace, even when blacks absolutely dominate a particular city. Moreover, accomplishing the agenda, particularly its most ambitious elements, still very much requires white cooperation. This cooperation becomes increasingly problematic as the black agenda ventures into zero-sum, controversial issues. Electing a few more blacks to Congress or installing a mayor is only a small step whose diminutive character is easily obscured by the huge effort invested in this accomplishment.

Government Employment

The installation of one's followers into positions of civic power is a time-honored recipe in American politics. It has certainly been a key element in black empowerment. Black voters rightfully expect that with the capture of office, jobs at all levels, from lowly toll collectors to top administrative posts such as police chief, will flow. Equally important in the long run, the employment system itself will be made more "friendly" to blacks via abol-ishing racially biased testing, removing discrimination in promotions and otherwise making access to government employment a priority. And most consequentially, gaining these positions will facilitate advancing black goals beyond mere paychecks. Having a black education superintendent along with supporting black education professionals, for example, will, hopefully, give rise to superior schooling. Similarly, having a black social welfare agency head and black caseworkers means more favorable treatment of welfare clients. In a nutshell, black electoral victories will mean the "blackening" of bureaucracies, which, in turn, will bring the full rewards of possessing political power.

As with so many black empowerment ingredients, this reasoning seems irresistible. Yet not surprisingly, formidable obstacles are often neglected in the rush to equate electoral triumph with broader uplift. Most conspicuously, the available jobs awardable to the faithful may be economically inconsequential given the magnitude of the problem. The days of bountiful "spoils" for nearly everyone are long gone, thanks to ample civil service protection, unionization and the technical requirements of today's governance. Dispensing hundreds of jobs and promotions to the needy may reap enormous publicity, but this generosity will hardly dent massive unemployment. Additionally, many "urban jobs" are controlled by the state and various boards, well beyond the black electorate's reach. And, particularly in decent economic times, the hard-core unemployed, those unable to find private sector jobs, may not meet minimal qualifications for government work either (including having criminal records). After all, even toll collectors must figure change correctly, be honest and show up regularly. Hiring the hopelessly unqualified for "no-show" jobs merely to assist the desperate is scarcely a solution to serious unemployment. If this bloating of the bureaucracy strategy is pushed, as Washington's Mayor Barry discovered, financial bankruptcy is inevitable. Furthermore, what politics bestows, politics can remove. Filling the police department with black appointees may only be a brief interlude until the inevitable next power shift.

All these limitations pale, however, beside the dilemma of ensuring indispensable competence. Once again, the ends-mean congruence is basic. If black empowerment merely sought a dreary status quo, then so-so appointees are adequate. Mediocre public servants would merely mechanically follow precedent, and life would continue. But if black betterment is to transpire, if neighborhoods and schools are to thrive, the pedestrian is wholly unacceptable. If black children cannot read, why hire a complacent black chief education administrator? If police brutality and inefficiency are rampant, an extraordinary new police chief must be enlisted. Again, as is true in attracting capable black officials, talented black administrators are hardly everywhere and may enjoy ample private sector opportunities. Moreover, if race constitutes the sole hiring criterion, the necessary competence may be sacrificed. Although the topic is *never* raised in the context of black empowerment, ample empirical evidence indicates that hiring by race *diminishes* competency levels. This can be witnessed across several occupations—notably, law enforcement, teaching—critical to advancing the black empowerment agenda (ample data are summarized in Herrnstein and Murray 1994, Ch. 20). In short, accomplishment requires *both* hiring more blacks *and* upgrading the government workforce to solve problems perplexing predecessors.

Unfortunately, the linkage between black political victories, black government employment and subsequent black betterment remains murky. What does exist is ample (though often conflicting) analysis of the necessary (but not sufficient) first step in this journey—the connection between electoral triumphs and employment. Typical is Eisinger's (1982) analysis of 43 cities of 50,000+ with at least 10 percent black population. Data from two time periods (1973 and 1978) show, not unexpectedly, that the single most important determinant of black government employment is black population size. "Black cities" such as East St. Louis, Illinois, or Gary, Indiana, have largely black municipal workforces, top to bottom. Beyond this obvious factor, however, the employment-political power relationship is hardly overwhelming. Electing black city council members, for example, gives little boost to black employment. Having a black mayor *did* have a modest impact on employment levels, often via the establishment of affirmative action in hiring practices, particularly in hiring black professionals.

Other studies similarly confirm the importance of politics, although differences in samples and analytical technique yield divergent patterns. For example, Dye and Rennick (1981) focus on 42 cities of 25,000+ population also with a minimum of 10 percent black population for 1977. Contrary to Eisinger's findings, they report a relationship between black city council representation and government employment levels, including higher administrative positions. Again, black population size is key. Surprisingly, this employment gain seems independent of black income and education attainment—political representation and population are the overriding factors. This is true even among professional and administrative positions where the talent pool size might be consequential. Additional evidence for the key role of city council power, not the mayor's office, comes from Kerr and Mladenka's (1994) analysis of data from two groups of cities across two time periods. As before, the black population size is critical. However, at least in their assessment, black mayors cannot enhance black municipal employment; rather, if black employment is to expand, it will likely come about via the actions of top administrators who are influenced by the city council (though this, in turn, can be affected by the city council's legal authority). The same general points are made in Mladenka's (1989) 1984 study of 1,224 cities: Black election to the city council, not capturing the mayor's office, played the pivotal role in shifting government jobs to blacks. And, as before, sheer size of the black population, interacting with the structure of local government, had a notable impact on employment patterns.

Comparable broad findings come from the California ten-city study (Browning, Marshall and Tabb 1984, Ch. 5). Again, the overall size of the black population is powerfully related to black employment levels. Yet a more detailed statistical analysis suggests that sheer numbers were less consequential that adept political mobilization. In the 1960s this mobilization took the form of protests, although by the 1970s the battles were occurring within local government (incorporation). Hiring blacks in upper-echelon positions also followed the contours of political pressure. This transformation was far from automatic—much depended on factors such as federal and state legal pressure and how well local black leaders adapted to circumstances (e.g., redefining job test standards and coaching applicants). It was also true that shifts in government structure that made administration more "political," for example, a strong mayor versus a city manager, facilitated political pressure and thus ultimately resulted in hiring more blacks.

Other differences in research technique aside (see, e.g., Santoro 1995), there can be little doubt that politics *matters*. All things being equal, black political mobilization in cities with substantial black populations does deliver jobs. This conclusion does not, however, end the issue. The desirability of this accomplishment is not self-evident despite its easy assumption. And the matter is critical. Surely, administrative ineptitude knows no skin color—black-run bureaucracies are not axiomatically any more superior for blacks than agencies formally administered by whites. This relationship is merely *hope*, not a scientific law. Evidence hardly confirms the proposition that black appointees cure the problems facing black communities. A black police chief or black school superintendent typically faces the identical problems—or worse—than his or her white predecessor. The jury is still out on whether "Made by Blacks" remedies are superior. If blacks have the solutions to these daunting problems, they remain secret. Surely East St. Louis, Gary, Newark and other largely black cities have not been reborn. Indeed, much of the urban decline prior to black electoral victories continued unabated, perhaps even exacerbated as a result of race-based political appointments.

There is also the deeper (and equally neglected) issue of group betterment via government employment. Government employment may award some security and (perhaps) prestige, but it is limited as an engine of group advancement. It may be a group stepping-stone, not a permanent condition. This is especially true in good economic times when ample nongovernment opportunities exist. In poorer times, all the "extra" blacks hired might well be the first to be fired (Henderson and Preston 1984). The growing black middle-class reliance on public employment in particular may be fraught with danger as governments downsize and privatize.[13] To be sure, for many, a city job is a worthy attainment, but to treat public employment as if it were the collective Holy Grail invites frustration. To allege private sector employment as inferior due to deep-seated discrimination, sans any evidence, is preposterous (see, e.g., Fainstein and Fainstein 1996, 27; Keiser 1997, 6). If the Irish experience remains relevant, staffing public bureaucracies may provide steady work, but public service cannot bring eventual collective advancement. Recall Thomas Sowell's analysis of Jews and Asians, groups initially avoiding politics. They, unlike the Irish, prospered. Compared to the private sector, even well-paying civil careers seldom create community wealth and spin-off jobs. A small business owner may, in fact, enjoy more discretionary economic power than a $75,000-a-year city bureau chief. Perhaps only in corrupt nations can public officeholding translate into group advancement. To counsel blacks to focus on public employment and then celebrate successes as genuine empowerment, as is common in this academic literature, may be foolishness.

REDIRECTING GOVERNMENT BENEFITS

Rewarding supporters with tangible government benefits has long been customary in U.S. politics, whether better garbage pickup or multibillion-dollar defense contracts. This process, notably for black empowerment, can be deceptively complex and far from automatic. Much depends on goals and availability. Recall the tangible versus symbolic distinction and the potential middle- versus lower-class policy gap. Nor can harsh reality be infinitely manipulated. A great election victory may came to nothing if one's supporters want a new neighborhood school and funds are unavailable or educational jurisdiction lies elsewhere. Not every wish can be funded, and negotiating skill is often essential. There is no guarantee, regardless of race, that electoral skills will easily translate into proficiency at compensating one's followers.

Especially critical for the black empowerment agenda is the enterprise's inherent complexity. This simple point cannot be repeated too often and inheres in *all* comprehensive social engineering in a limited government democracy. At best, government might supply the means of accomplishment; it seldom can command the ends. To channel resources into the black community only sets the stage for betterment, and government outputs—funding, laws—may not produce the intended outcomes. Consider as typical the adequate housing issue. During the 1950s and 1960s, public housing construction for inner-city residents was a major black agenda item. Indeed, one of Mayor Hatch's notable successes in assuming power in Gary, Indiana was securing more federal housing assistance. This Washington-financed bricks-and-mortar strategy was a commonplace sign of accomplishment when blacks gained political ascendancy. Alas, decades later, many of these projects are now certified disasters, incubators of crime, drugs and family disorganization. Similar doubts now infect nearly all past victories, including the once sacred principle of public school integration. The fought-for principle of "color-blind" has become obsolete for many backs, replaced by the very opposite "color-sensitive" doctrine. Those who once bewailed white inspired "law and order" today bemoan rampant black-on-black crime. Munificent welfare payments to unwed mothers have likewise proven a mixed blessing; they may even be toxic to long-run black progress. Today's quest may be tomorrow's nightmare.

Equally pertinent is the ambiguity of "black benefit." Even the most learned economist can be overwhelmed here. For example, would increasing the minimum wage assist since many blacks are clustered in these lowly positions? Are cheap imports "good" for blacks in their role as consumers but "bad" for them as employees? Indeed, many cherished empowerment agenda objectives—tough antidiscrimination laws, set-asides, affirmative action—may ultimately become economic liabilities for blacks by raising the costs of economic dealings. Conceivably, lavish tax breaks for wealthy whites may instigate opulence, which, in turn, will bring high-paying ghetto jobs. More generally, it may be unwise to speak of policies that *exclusively* profit blacks and concentrate on actions beneficial for all citizens. Unfortunately, these issues are skipped over in black empowerment rhetoric.

A final complexity is disentangling the *casual* impact of enhanced black representation. That blacks achieve some power and that certain consequences then flow hardly "prove" black representation's impact. It is conceivable, for example, that power was assumed in the beginning of a recession, and mounting difficulties (or advancements in the case of boom times) were unrelated to politics. Outside economic forces aside, political actions elsewhere, well beyond local influence, may be decisive. Judicial rulings on affirmative action plans might greatly shape municipal hiring policy. Similarly, national budget surpluses may permit even the most inept city official to be a "genius" in extracting federal generosity. Relevant external forces must number in the hundreds. Moreover, many of the most important effects may become visible only years after the actual exercise of power. All in all, black officeholding can only be one of dozens of factors in a vast enterprise.

Analytical complexities notwithstanding, what is the actual record regarding the channeling of benefits via black electoral attainment? Consider first several straightforward "before-after" studies of blacks replacing whites in power. One such exemplar was Greene County, Alabama, an exceptionally poor area, which went from being white dominated to black dominated in merely two years during the early 1970s (Coombs et al. 1977; Perry 1980). One notable change was that the heightened sense of black pride increased the willingness of blacks to contact government over grievances. Law enforcement also became less abusive, and reports of police brutality toward blacks diminished (Perry 1980). Political tensions also cooled and gave way to an atmosphere of accommodation (though several whites did leave).

Material benefits flowed, as well. Compared to similar white-run counties, Greene enjoyed a sudden surge in government employment entirely due to Washington and private foundation money. The federal government also funded Greene's new (and successful) public housing project, upgraded health care, instituted Head Start and built a water system facility, among other social welfare projects (day care, hot meals, senior citizen transportation, etc.). A local clothing factory received a Defense Department contract. Nevertheless, the "trickle-down" of this outside generosity is ambiguous—economic gains occurred largely among farm owners and businesspeople, not ordinary wage earners. Private sector life, particularly in employment, did not alter much for local blacks. Attempts to lure outside businesses were likewise unsuccessful. Not even the local school could be desegregated despite black authority in the matter. When black students entered, whites enrolled their children in private academies (Perry 1980).

Overall, the long-term impact of this sudden outside financial generosity remains unclear. Its beneficial physical legacy—housing, water lines—is perhaps most conspicuous. However, the termination of government assistance in 1974–1975 ended most freshly created public sector jobs, and high black unemployment returned. The few middle-class blacks generally did better economically by keeping their government positions, whereas their poorer brethren only retained hopefulness (Perry 1980). More fundamentally, this government generosity cannot be reenacted everywhere without seriously changing political life. Thousands of "new" Greene counties not only would mean huge federal budget increases (and thus much higher taxes), but it would engender a nationwide dependency on Washington bureaucracy.[14]

Other studies paint similar portraits. James Button (1982) interviewed 56 black Florida elected municipal officials in 1974 (supplemented with interviews of white officials and objective indicators). All served in small, largely nonblack communities. Not unexpectedly, a common important role definition was expressing black needs within government and assisting in greater political mobilization (including helping blacks gain appointments to boards and commissions). When asked about assisting fellow blacks, enhanced municipal services, for example, paved streets, predominated, with larger issues such as employment and housing further down the list. In areas where blacks were a minority, knowledgeable whites confirmed that black officials helped race relations and offered blacks a useful avenue to settle problems. As in Greene County, gaining federal funds loomed large as a means of improving economic conditions. Efforts were far less successful in attracting private sector economic assistance.

Achievement was also limited in the public arena. Leaders' beliefs about these shortcoming offers notable insights into the empowerment quest. Lack of local revenue, particularly in areas with black majorities, was especially constraining. In other words, without vibrant business activity, tax revenue is paltry, and without this revenue, betterment cannot be jump-started. Lack of cooperation among fellow African Americans, cynical distrust and unrealistic expectations also figured prominently as a cause for dismal accomplishment. Interestingly, while the federal government was viewed as sympathetic, the required application of red tape and regulatory control were interpreted as severe obstacles. Resistance from white officials was also noteworthy, although outright threats were relatively rare.

An in-depth analysis of two southern cities—Durham, North Carolina, and Tuskegee, Alabama—during the rapid 1960s black voting increases confirms these patterns (Keech 1968, Chs. 4, 5). Black votes did influence election outcome but largely when one candidate was avowedly racist. Blacks did, however, secure local government representation. Moderate gains also occurred in law enforcement. Poor treatment from the police was barely an issue in both localities and remained so as blacks grew more important politically. Treatment by the courts (including jury service) changed for the better, for example, eliminating segregated courtroom seating, but the direct role of elections appeared minor.

The most tangible gains came in municipal services, although this was uneven and often required leadership exertion. In some instances, for example, enforcing ordinances about sub-standard housing, middle-class black political leaders seemed neglectful of poorer blacks. Nevertheless, progress occurred in several domains. When black Tuskegee voters became a majority, streets in black neighborhoods were soon paved or added to the paving plan. This was not done in Durham, however, no doubt because street surfacing required payments from residents. Ditto for garbage service—voting made a major difference in Tuskegee but not in Durham. Recreational facilities in both cities became formally integrated (though not necessarily de facto, owing to neighborhood segregation) and equitably distributed. Interestingly, black voting support for revenue bonds brought better recreation facilities (and a nearby fire station in Durham). Finally, blacks in both towns (though more dramatically in Tuskegee) now clearly influenced appointments to various boards and city jobs, including positions once "off limits" to blacks. Progress in Durham was less sharp, in part, because notable employment steps had occurred prior to the upswing in black voting.

Political mobilization also played a private sector role. Businesses and employment access was significantly enhanced. Tuskegee blacks successfully passed ordinances forbidding racial discrimination in both hiring and public businesses. The same aims were achieved in Durham, although here the threat of public disruptions, even violence, encouraged the mayor to work with local businesses to eliminate racial bias in hiring and public facilities such as restaurants and theaters. Much of this progress resulted from the looming pressure of federal intervention to enforce federal anti-discrimination laws plus white acceptance of the inevitable.

Nevertheless, in his overall assessment of political pressure, Keech recognizes its limits (Ch. 6). Black leaders periodically failed to exploit advantages or were greatly restrained by their numerical minority status. In both cities decisions in such pertinent areas as housing and employment were well beyond political influence. Nor can the legacy of past discrimination be quickly reversed by a handful of election triumphs. Most centrally, political action has not equalized underlying socioeconomic conditions. Blacks still remain concentrated near the bottom economically and socially. The vote or raucous demonstrations have only resulted in eliminating the worst abuses and biases. As a tool for ending poverty or promoting easy relationships across racial lines, it is far less effective.

The last study here is Karnig and Welch's (1980) highly sophisticated overtime study of 264 cities of 25,000+ population with at least a 10 percent black population. Their question is whether black representation made a difference over a six-year period in four general budgetary areas: social welfare (health care, housing, etc.), protective services (police and fire), amenities (parks, etc.) and physical facilities (streets, sewers, etc.). The most prominent initial finding is that cities with high levels of black representation did over time increase both total expenditures and those for social welfare (Ch. 6). No such increases occurred in the areas of protective services and amenities. Interestingly, cities enjoying the greatest levels of black representation spent the least on physical improvements. Also, and consistent with other studies, having blacks in power drew more federal financial support.

This picture is somewhat misleading, however, given all the other factors that could conceivably affect these relationships (e.g., city per capita income, education levels). When various statistical controls and adjustments are introduced, the net impact of black electoral gain diminishes, although this varies by policy area and where black influence is centered. It is still the case, for example, that under black mayors social service expenditures rose, but black representation on city councils showed a more uncertain, and often insignificant, impact. In many instances, it appears that this increase in social welfare spending was "paid for" by lesser attention to physical improvements, for example, streets repair, sanitation and so on. It is worth noting, however, that hospital expenditures did grow rapidly when black mayors took office.

Taking all these findings and technical complexities into account, the bottom-line message appears generally consistent with previous assessment: Politics helps, particularly in municipal services such as better sewers or fire protection, but do not expect dramatic uplifts. As James Button (1989) concluded in his multicommunity examination of progress, "On the whole, southern blacks have achieved marked gains in the political arena in most communities, but improvements in the economic and social sectors have been more difficult and less apparent" (207). Even the best of intentions cannot overcome monumental fiscal and political limits; one must often settle for far less than half a loaf. Notable gaps separate the promises of black empowerment from reality. This modest conclusion, moreover, has been confirmed in other studies under differing circumstances and with varied techniques (among others, see Bullock 1975; Campbell and Feagin, 1975; Wirt 1970). And equally important, this translation is hardly automatic and may be temporary as coalitions unravel and economic conditions shift. To place one's faith exclusively in political action is, indeed, to rely on a slender reed. Yet this circumspection is seldom fully absorbed.

The limits of the political solution are not altered if we examine this nexus at a more macrolevel. That is, is the post-1950s black socioeconomic progress generally explainable by massive black investments in political mobilization and resultant government legal intervention? As professional economists will quickly note, this is a hugely vexing question. Recall that covariation of uplift and mobilization does not prove causality. Yet one careful review of this exceedingly technical economic literature concludes, this politics-begets-uplift argument is highly questionable (Donohue and Heckman 1989). It even flies in the face of much conventional economic wisdom, for example, that basic economic forces can be so easily overridden. The connection *may* be correct, it *may* be widely believed by blacks, but it nevertheless remains a long way from a demonstrated fact.

To appreciate fully the complexity of this politics–economic betterment link, evaluate it in the context of other equation elements. For example, in the early stages of the civil rights struggle-long before the government's full powers were mobilized by blacks and their allies—sizable southern black migration northward produced a notable income jump. Chicago was better than rural Mississippi, regardless of political activism or apathy, although this difference would eventually narrow, thanks to federal law and southern industrialization. In fact, black income soared in the late 1960s and early 1970s, well before vigorous bureaucratic enforcement of civil rights laws or affirmative action. When the full measure of government efforts to re-mediate black inequality did eventually kick in, black income gaps relative to white earnings plateaued (Donohue and Heckman 1989, 8). To be sure, some of black advancement may be indirectly politically created—for example, politics channeled more money toward black education, and this brought better-paying jobs years later. There are also contrary macroforces that easily overshadow an occasional political conquest—the movement of manufacturing jobs overseas, the mechanization of agriculture and the changing technical demands on the workforce, to note but a few. For the 1990s one might also append severe labor shortages amidst immense prosperity that makes racial generosity affordable and sensible. All in all, we can only once again reaffirm the weakness of the "empowerment breeds economic progress" argument. It is simply not proven, and at best, the impact is marginal.[15]

CONCLUSIONS

Our tour has covered extensive territory, but much remains unexplored, particularly the impact of nonelectoral stratagems. We have concentrated on black empowerment's shortcomings but these should not obscure its accomplishments. Without exaggeration, black empowerment comprises one of the most energetic, labor-intensive and resource costly campaigns in American history. Its triumphs are bountiful—numerous civil rights laws, dozens of bureaucratic enforcement agencies, thousands of hard-won electoral positions, tens of thousands of government jobs and resource shifts toward African Americans. Black progress in the private sector has likewise been enormous. A visitor from the 1940s would be absolutely amazed by all the gains.

Although these accomplishments would fill a book, the agenda demands an entire library of such books. The results have been modest when calculated against the colossal investment and the end goals. If notable examples to the contrary exist, if black officials have worked wonders, these exemplars remain hidden. Even the most fervent empowerment devotees concede that the racial equality journey has advanced only a few preliminary steps. Of course, rapid progress may soon occur, and the prodigious energy devoted to political mobilization will bear fruit. Yet all in all, disappointment would have to be the verdict from a disinterested outsider. To repeat, advancement was greatest initially when tasks were more manageable. As zero-sum, resource-intensive and technically daunting quests grew more appropriate, progress has slowed substantially. In some domains, government-mandated affirmative action, for example, the empowerment agenda is now on the defensive.

The less-than-wondrous results of the black empowerment strategy, although quite discernible, are seldom voiced, and if voiced, then ignored. Indeed, facing disappointments, advocates retell the message even more enthusiastically. The issue is not effort and devotion: The enterprise itself is deeply flawed. These are momentous defects, not details. Our analysis has highlighted only a few: the conflation between political power and economic gain, the tacit belief that only blacks can solve black problems, overreliance on state authority, inattention to demography, exaggerating the marginal benefit of political activism, the difference between psychological and tangible rewards, the neglect of nonpolitical alternatives and indifference to the technical fine points of social engineering. Of course, such shortcomings are hardly unique to black empowerment theorizing. In varying degrees, they plague other empowerment visions as well. But, given the problem's seriousness, they are more consequential here.

This discord between the advice pervading the academic scholarship and the less-than-outstanding outcomes raises awkward issues. Millions of blacks rightfully seeking betterment are engaging in a grand crusade egged on by dozens of black professors enjoying comfortable employment who should know better (see Lowenstein 1981 for these doubts years back). Professors and their allies take little risk when they pronounce (falsely) that capturing government will bring the Promised Day. Their careers suffer not one iota when they intone that school boycotts or abolishing unflattering standardized tests will deliver African-American educational empowerment.

In fact, their professional life may prosper as they publish yet one more diatribe damming "the white power structure" and demanding quixotic campaigns. One can only be reminded of Atlanta's bureaucrats lavishly dining in the Ritz-Carlton to ponder poverty. In a sense, these advisers are empowered, not their less-well-compensated followers. To resurrect a metaphor from Chapter 2, if this were a traditional doctor-patient relationship, the patient might well change physicians or file malpractice charges. To be sure, the patient is hardly resisting questionable counsel while many enjoy the prospect of easy shortcuts; yet the burden on those "who should know better" is inescapable.

Over and above this ill-suited advice, and recipients wasting efforts better invested elsewhere, the larger political damage must be reckoned. The black empowerment agenda has an uneasy relationship with traditional democratic, pluralistic politics, and this may become deeply troublesome as progress drags (Parks 1997). In some cases, this tension is openly recognized as its devotees invoke sweeping, though vague, anticapitalist schemes to bring black uplift (e.g., Nelson and Meranto 1977, Ch. 11). More common, however, are hints of potential totalitarianism: a predilection for government expansion, a hankering for bureaucratic decree-based control and a willingness to ignore legal requirements to achieve nebulous "racial justice." Imagine if a few fiery black leaders were given carte blanche to revise our political system to maximize African-American "progress." This Utopia might well resemble a grim dictatorship of the black proletariat compete with expropriated property and mammoth bureaucracies ruled by whim. One might also add a troubling affection for conspiratorial explanations sans facts—everything from AIDS being a white plot to transforming the slightest police incident into "proof" of a forthcoming white racist police state (D'Souza [1995, Ch. 12] offers a compendium of this paranoia, even among respectable black leaders).[16] If black leaders fail, it "surely" must be some hidden racist white business cabal or right-wing politicians. It seems "self-evident" that racial antagonism lies behind all white action unless whites accede to every imaginable black demand.

Lastly, the agenda's inattention to political history and technical detail borders on the anti-intellectual. Ideology, empty slogans and wishful thinking easily triumph. Our enshrined constitutional principles, for example, dispersion of power, limited government, seemingly exist as racist impediments to progress. Immensely complex issues—housing, education, crime— are often reduced to moralistic yet vacuous rallying cries. Elementary economic principles—notions of trade-off, marginal costs, fungibility of resources—are similarly absent from discourse. Talk of "economic limitations" by whites often is construed as a lame excuse. These deficiencies of knowledge are hardly dismissable among those who wish to govern wisely.

Let us conclude on an optimistic note. If there is such a hope, it is that many blacks, thanks to burgeoning private sector opportunities, will abandon their ill-fated infatuation with politics as The Mother of All Solutions. They will surely vote, make campaign contributions and otherwise be "good democratic citizens," but they will shun the hyperbolic political Pied Pipers. Instead, they will correctly grasp that political activity has its place, but in our society, it is a limited place, and this preserves liberty. They will understand, for example, that educational progress cannot be imposed via political fiat nor thousands of jobs invented by black officeholders. For them, not every malady hints a white plot, and some deficiencies are self-imposed. Promises of more government handouts will be viewed suspiciously, perhaps seen as continued dependency, despite attempts to disguise this largess with empowerment vocabulary. Of course, those shunning the empowerment crusade will be damned for "selfishness" and "abandoning" their less fortunate brethren. Yet, in the final analysis, like those freed from magical beliefs about deus ex machina miracle cures, it is they who will truly be empowered.

NOTES

1. A precise definition of *black empowerment* is perhaps impossible. *Impulse* is perhaps a more adept term. Only rarely do its advocates attempt such a formulation (e.g., Jennings 1992, 39–40). Even then, however, a gap can separate formal proclamations and more concrete manifestations—for example, Jennings links black empowerment to international issues, yet this never appears in black politics. Our approach is to focus on what appears in actual conflict, not abstract doctrine.

2. A reading of empowerment manifestos written for black audiences shows a penchant for "extractive" strategies—pressure on nonblack companies to "give" blacks benefits. Typically, an automobile manufacturer will be pressed to award dealerships to blacks or train blacks for jobs. The idea of black entrepreneurial activity scarcely is mentioned (see, e.g., Ayres-Williams 1997).

3. It is impossible to exaggerate these expectations. For example, the 1994 American Political Science Association presidential address of Lucius Barker, a distinguished professor at Stanford University, exclaimed that the Constitution "promised" "fair and equal opportunity for each person to develop to full potential, consistent with the clear recognition of the identity, worth, and respect that is due to every person by virtue of their status as human beings" (Barker 1994, 1). This is, to say the least, a most novel interpretation and one that is made without recourse to particulars.

4. Equally relevant is the winner-take-all, geographically based system. The need to win a majority within heterogeneous districts pushes candidates away from narrow group interests toward more encompassing consensual objectives. That strident racial radicals are disadvantaged by this system is predictable, perhaps even intentional. Yet again, this does not confirm the racist, repressive nature of the electoral system. The Klu Klux Klan would face the identical obstacles.

5. Yet one more daunting issue is "whose" knowledge will be applied to the empowerment quest. Increasingly, proposals are taking on racial casts. In education,

for example, Afrocentric approaches compete with traditional (read white) methods. This trend has clear political ramifications—imagine a black official who turned to "white" answers for such problems as schooling and welfare.

6. The divisions that can bedevil black politicians are seemingly boundless. In 1977 Ernest N. Morial was elected the first black mayor of New Orleans. Although he eventually became a certified black mayor, doubts always existed as to whether he was an authentic black, given his mixed ancestry and very light skin color. In fact, he was never accepted by black organizations as a friend until just prior to his election. And like so many others in the same situation, his leadership was often criticized by ordinary blacks as too beholden to white business interests (see Schexnider [1982] for a more complete account of Morial's tribulations).

7. Jackson's wide appeal among blacks, even academics, confirms the power of rhetorically adroit cheering serving as "leadership." His statements to black audiences (Jackson 1996, for example) are almost entirely bereft of specific proposals beyond "get out and vote." Dealing with crime and jobs is merely a matter of catchy slogans.

8. The gap between rhetoric and technique is easily seen in discussions of electing more blacks. Analysis of alternative electoral systems, for example, cumulative voting, proportional representation, as well as structural electoral features, for example, registration, inevitably takes a backseat to simplistic sloganeering. This is, alas, typical across other policy domains.

9. For example, Jennings (1992) seems unable to separate the concepts of "pro-growth" and "fiscal austerity" (40). More generally, critical issues such as interest rates, municipal securities, tax assessments, land-use law and similar technical matters seem well beyond the domain of empowerment activists. That assisting business interests would also aid lower-class blacks seems definitionally false in this literature. It is not surprising that their heartfelt but naive schemes receive short attention from "downtown" technocrats.

10. This fervent hope is sometimes called "The moon and the ghetto" argument. That being, if the government can send a man to the moon, it surely can fix up the ghetto. It is also worth repeating that this faith in white-dominated government and an infatuation with black-designed solutions are inherently contradictory.

11. This axiomatic reliance on government, especially the national government, as opposed to the nongovernmental path taken by various immigrant groups, is *never* seriously addressed by black scholars. Writing in 1982, Charles V. Hamilton, a distinguished black scholar at Columbia University, glibly justifies this reliance on the grounds that "[t]here is no private sector expanding economy" (Hamilton 1982, xx). He assumes that all other groups were lucky enough to arrive in the midst of a booming economy. Moreover, the post-1982 boom times have not weakened this reliance on government one iota. Another justification that periodically surfaces is that white racism is far worse than anything faced by other ethnic groups (see, e.g., Jennings 1992, 25). No analysis then follows of the problems experienced by the Irish or the Chinese; truth here is apparently self-evident. Lieberson (1981) suggests the root difference being the ease by which other immigrants obtained the franchise (383). But this assumes the intimate connection between politics and economic progress, a debatable relationship. Ironically, some black activists now blame electoral success as the culprit in emasculating blacks in their quest for genuine progress (see Jennings 1992, 105–107). Marguerite Ross Barnett (1982) offers

a medley of unsupported explanations, from the "all the others came during boom times" to, predictably, racism, the slavery legacy, the exploitative economic conditions faced by blacks and ease of political access for other ethnic groups. Interestingly, more recent black immigrants to the United States have faired exceptionally well at the very same time that native-born blacks are allegedly mired in economic stagnation (see Sowell 1981, 220).

12. Hoaxes as hate crimes apparently play a role in black empowerment, although again, as in threats of black violence, the subject is taboo. While some tales may be concocted by disturbed individuals, it is also true that black leaders are hardly reluctant to take advantage of positive public reaction. A detailed compilation of these frauds is presented in Wilcox (1994).

13. This expanding reliance on government employment (see Fainstein and Fainstein 1996 for a summary) may help explain the new found clamor for "less government." This impulse is not entirely racist. The woeful condition of Washington, D.C.'s public schools despite a huge expensive bureaucracy is hardly an isolated example. The bottom line is merely that public employment is not a sinecure.

14. This does not end the Greene County tale. In 1984 this newfound domination by older civil rights–oriented blacks came to an end. The impetus was a fresh coalition of younger, better-educated blacks and whites, angered by favoritism, bloated payrolls, dismal health conditions, and gross fiscal mismanagement. Ironically, the newly built grayhound track's revenues only seemed to contribute to the administrative ineptitude (see Edds 1987, Ch. 9 for a full account).

15. Herrnstein and Murray (1994, Ch. 20) make a different argument with a similar outcome: Blacks have long reached economic equality with whites within comparable intelligence levels. The inequality is due to the different distributions of intelligence. Thus, to insist on pushing more blacks into high-income professions will mean promoting the less qualified.

16. The resourcefulness involved in concocting bogus "explanations" for black problems is well demonstrated in how many blacks view the black middle-class exodus from Washington, D.C. For decades, it was alleged—with zero evidence—that pushing blacks out of Washington was part of "The Plan." Needless to say, this paranoia may well detract from facing serious problems (see Fisher 1997 for details on "The Plan").

8

Conclusion:
The Wages of Empowerment

This has been an extended and highly varied tour of an eminently simple term: *empowerment*. The journey has taken us from arcane theoretical complexities to real-world homeless shelters and multibillion-dollar projects to uplift entire cities. All ideological sites have been visited, and untold fanciful designs have been examined. Measured by the prodigious number of citations, little has escaped attention (and much remains uncited). What lessons, then, emerge regarding this ever-popular cure for our myriad deficiencies? Recall our scholarly FDA-like mission to assess worthiness. Assembling an evaluation is no small task, but it is indispensable. Our overarching conclusions should not, however, be taken as praise or condemnation for everything under empowerment's banner. With *thousands* of projects availing themselves of this label, exhaustiveness remains impossible. Ours is merely a high-altitude reconnaissance photo of prominent features. It is not an encouraging portrayal despite the effusive optimism shown by practitioners.

Most evidently, "empowerment" masks a bewildering collection of conflicting ideas, plans and goals, so one must wonder if the term has now lost meaningfulness. Nearly every possible program can, with some doctoring, claim to cure a malady via empowering. Chapter 3's trek across the ideological spectrum only highlights. The term risks becoming a marketing ploy designed to "sell" proposals by wrapping them in fashionable garb. Not all appellations conform to commonsense understandings of self-determination. Disturbingly, as Chapter 4 revealed, several nostrums aim at deepening dependency on government services, its ostensible opposite intent. This contradictory meaning abounds among African Americans: One is empowered by forcing, via political action, government to deliver goods—health care, jobs, housing—that plainly can be obtained nongovernmentally. Yet others promise uplifts entirely psychological in nature, divorced from tangible accomplishment. The "empowerment as feeling better" pervades feminist writings as well as among those championing racial/ethnic group uplift. Educational professionals periodically borrow the idea to enhance vocational status via salary increases or grander administrative titles. Chapter 6's empowerment zone exploration showed how personal empowerment can be easily transformed into wasteful bureaucracy playacting as the job-producing Messiah. If the concept signifies nearly everything to a multitude who share little in common, then its utility is nearly nothing.

Our analysis has seemingly been obsessed with the internal shortcomings of these exhortations. Relentlessly, we dissect loose vocabulary, sloppy reasoning and poorly articulated implications. A sizable portion of this literature, in our opinion, is but heartfelt speech making, not vigilant scholarship. "Theorizing" efforts can lapse into strident (and inaccurate) denunciations of the status quo. This was notably true for black empowerment—scores of difficult perplexities were skipped over in the rush to pressure a government believed to be negligent. Some conceptions reject rational inquiry itself in empowerment's name. Disquiet about these theoretical shortcomings is virtually nonexistent among the prophets. Our faultfinding—some might say bashing—is not unfair nitpicking; we are performing a responsibility that should have been discharged by advocates themselves. A dereliction of duty has transpired. Imagine if our subject were a powerful drug: It would never be brought to market without intensive examination and diligent pre-testing. Given that real human beings receive these defective remedies, harmfulness goes beyond inept scholarship. To be blunt, if these disciples were held to the standards of scientific medicine, most would be stripped of their professional status.

This inattention to tough-minded theorizing is deceptively serious. With conceptual foundations in disarray, progress will occur only through happenstance. Chapter 2 raised numerous qualms regarding this alleged panacea—for example, the equality among various empowerments, individual versus collective advancement and the tensions between self-determination and sustaining a democratic society. These inhere in the subject, yet all are neglected as one reads through this voluminous literature. At best, a brief mention occurs sans solution. Predictably, when advocates strive to assist the helpless, the lack of foresight becomes apparent. Despite the abundant invocations of "theory," our storehouse is nearly empty.

A political naïveté is ubiquitous. That ivory tower cloistered academics should confuse elementary politics is understandable, but if they are going to render counsel, brushing up is required. Simplistic appreciations of "power" are especially notable. Listening to these "experts" one would surmise that one "gets" power much like one acquires groceries. All the existent intricacies are pushed aside in favor of exhortations. Complexities of formal rules or resource utilization are blithely resolved by blurting out, "Get organized." Ditto for "democracy," for it is applied almost casually to all that is "good," while "bad things" become "antidemocratic." An inattention to momentous legal issues similarly abounds. It would seem that battling for the homeless solely demands commitment, not knowledge of the hundreds of pertinent ordinances. Recall the black empowerment complete inattention to the idea of limited government. "Getting out the vote" becomes a near-miracle cure for untold maladies.

Compounding these inadequacies are admonitions tempting a harsh collision course with reality. The scene recalls World War I trench warfare whereby entire armies were senselessly hurled to their deaths against impregnable positions. Here, too, the charge of malpractice arises since these invitations to failure are unnecessary. This is especially relevant for political mobilization pleas as the great cure-all. Relentlessly, the downtrodden are inveighed to organize and harass the powerful. The long-shot odds of victory are never discussed. The idea of independently creating wealth or acquiring knowledge autonomously is taken less seriously. It is seductive advice, cleverly draped in the finery of democracy, grassroots activism and similar buzzwords. Yet all the "fine-print" limitations and disclaimers are conveniently absent. Unsophisticated conscripts seldom demand proof or guarantees. It is easy advice for all parties: Marching and rallying are surely more fun (and therapeutic) than daunting activities such as gaining literacy or the habit of punctuality.

Indeed, a debilitating escapist flavor often imbues the quest for autonomy. Rather than confront difficult situations, for example, improving health care for indigent rural women, action is transmuted into consciousness-raising discussion. Acquiring exacting academic facility is made secondary to enjoyment or indulging weaknesses. When parents and legislators demand student proficiency, educators deflect the legitimate intrusion with empowerment alarms. Over and over, the traditional *and proven* virtues of determination, hard work, prudence, temperance and resourcefulness give way to clamors for gifts. One might guess that if empowerment experts ruled, the unemployed would exclusively hector government for jobs rather than learn skills. Being bothersome has been raised up to a hallowed principle. This movement thus resembles magical rituals whereby almighty gods are beseeched to bestow a good harvest. In a nutshell, the quest is for shortcuts.

Moreover, all too often counsel is Utopian. Cost and counterreaction issues elude empowerment devotees. Everything seems to be merely a matter of mobilizing the troops for guaranteed triumph. Perhaps it is blissfully presumed that if the helpless rise up, the once dominant will quickly capitulate. Unfortunately, capturing schools under self-determination's banner to impose fabricated history or a mathematics with no correct answer is not the final conquest. Those who object to this bogus education may abandon these schools and, eventually, defund public education. The empowering triumph will be but momentary, and this is surely foreseeable. Pouring billions into troubled urban empowerment zones cannot last forever. Wasteful projects are not bulletproof. What then happens to those bureaucrats when the well runs dry? Will another ill-conceived fad be embraced to find employment? What awaits those black mayors who rode into office with grand expectations when they face reelection?

Our dreary appraisal of this gospel hardly condemns its prophets to roast in hell. Most advocates indubitably sincerely believe that *the* answer is now discovered. Evil motivation is not entirely our worry; facile embrace sans deep reflection is the disheartening and perhaps incurable sin. With unanimity everywhere, the consensus soon becomes blinding. Scholarly journals and books function as convocations of the faithful, and controversy concerns mere detail with troubling deeper questions banished. To demur, to offer, for example, benevolent paternalism as the cure, invites swift marginalization. A black who criticizes the latest Jesse Jackson extraction scheme is a brave soul. The upshot, predictably, is a leniency toward fiction. That this suffocating conformity occurs in university environments dedicated to enhancing "diversity" is certainly ironic. Perhaps a similar indifference informs Washington's generosity—empowerment zones are small potatoes in trillion-dollar budgets, so why look closely at their performance?

If there is a more serious condemnation of those preaching empowerment's revelations, it is that this counsel is frequently disingenuous. This is especially relevant for the academic side of the project. Perhaps the most minor of these sins is that personal goals have been mingled with more lofty ambition. The offense is—to be magnanimous—one of confusion, not intentional harm. As one plows through endless treatises hunting insights, the inescapable conclusion is that gaining professional advancement constitutes the endeavor's primary purpose. Researchers, not the homeless family or lackadaisical student, secure empowerment via the building of well-compensated records. Providing the right bountiful citations outranks offering tips for enhancing people's lives. The goal, it would seem, is to be on the academic cutting edge, and exhorting "old-fashioned" nostrums invites rebuke. Disputes are far more likely to concern competing paradigms than unraveling the harsh dilemmas faced by the needy. This conflation of professional careerism and assisting the disadvantaged is hardly new, of course. The Great Society remunerated thousands of academics while intended beneficiaries often languished. Nor is this compensation criminal— professors, too, must eat. But it is surely a hoax that will understandably result in frustration, if not resentment.

A parallel personal opportunism infects the infatuation with political mobilization among African-American political leaders. This is not to argue that civic participation is a sham; it clearly is not. It is a valuable corrective tool, but like all tools, its application is finite. To insist otherwise, especially after exposing contrary evidence, raises suspicion regarding motives. Leaving psychoanalytic inquiry aside, it is clear that elected black officials masterfully gain by this strategy, far more than those who put them into office. The prizes of officeholding are sizable—handsome salaries, perquisites, prestige—while the profit for individual voters is less tangible after an early rush of benefits. Plausibly, mobilization efforts redirected toward other enterprises, for example, accumulating private business venture capital, would assist more. Yet perhaps seduced by the glory of electoral triumph, empowerment via political action becomes hardened into sacred dogma.

More serious sins, however, are the covert ideological agendas lurking behind multiple schemes pushed forward as plain-Jane helpfulness. Let us be clear: All uplift designs are ultimately rooted in some ideology, some conception of how "the system" works and how it can eventually perform. Distilling an ideological-free prescription is unattainable. Our point concerns *deceptively* promoting radical transformations. Informing students that they will "be empowered" by foregoing conventional learning and instead questioning all authority is duplicitous. The opposite is true: These uninformed "questioning" students will be condemned to a cynicism without accomplishment. Try telling a prospective employer that while one reads ineptly, one can nevertheless brilliantly expose hidden workplace hierarchies. The same is true when blacks are told that their failure at pluralistic politics now means that the entire system must be drastically overhauled.

The opportunity costs of this empowerment chase are huge. The objects of effort—poverty, ill health, dismal education, substance abuse, despair, depressing slums and almost all else—have all been remediated before. Dozens of times. Society is *not* facing a fresh AIDS-like virus epidemic demanding wholly original solutions. Conventional interventions will suffice, properly applied. How to apply empowerment to repair our calamities is not the issue; the prior question is whether empowerment *improves* over the off-the-shelf remedies in our arsenal. Those who sally forth to assist the homeless, for example, should weigh their counsel to march on city hall against proven alternatives, and these could range from religious devotion to "tough love" strict regimentation. The slothful student might be better served by stern punishment, not flattering his or her deficiencies as "culturally valid." Time spent organizing school boycotts on behalf of powerless inner-city students might better be allocated to tutoring. Housing project residents terrorized by violence might seek empowerment by giving the police freer reign.

This disdain for tried-and-true treatments in favor of risky novelties raises troubling questions beyond self-aggrandizing or stealthy ideological proselytizing. Is there some madness about? To put this matter into sharp relief: Why would a knowledgeable academic condemn the teaching of factual information to black students and the inculcation of classroom discipline as "depowering" (Merelman 1993, among others)? What explains the infatuation with telling people with histories of inept decision making that they can *really* run their lives successfully if only given a chance? What drove the Ford Foundation to endorse improving health conditions by teaching desperately poor women to take pictures of the obvious? The list of silly ventures is immense. Surely the counterarguments are not unfathomable. Are these experts privy to powerful knowledge unknown generally? One can only speculate as to why intelligent people proffer persistent bad advice.

Such optimism is even more remarkable when empowerment's successes are tallied. As chapter after chapter recounted in detail, the record hardly impresses. Successful exemplars such as Detroit's job creation program are, alas, rare. An enormous effort is expended for meager results. Many devotees barely seem to care—power seems to be the end, not the means, and even hinting at rewards is impertinent. This paucity of documented payoff is true whether the enterprise is personal—poverty, homelessness—or more grand—improving education or eliminating economic inequality across racial lines. Moreover, much of what is claimed as an achievement is of questionable value. Pumping millions of dollars into the Atlanta empowerment zone to fund a Rolls-Royce dealership hardly constitutes sparking newfound economic self-sufficiency. Giving teachers greater authority counts for naught if they are clueless on applying this newfound clout. At best, the jury remains deliberating on various projects, although reasons to be hopeful remain few. If empowerment were a drug, the FDA would remove it from the marketplace, and perhaps the Federal Trade Commission would sue its prophets for false advertising. Had only a fraction of the time spent writing articles or agitating been spent on traditional charity, the benefits would be immense.

And this paucity of improvement hardly inspires heightened diligence. If this enterprise were modeled on the Manhattan Project, these supposed revelations would largely have been junked years ago. Researchers would honestly confess that this didn't work, that it didn't do much good, and plans require endless sharpening. Blind alleys would abound, and occasional small successes would receive unwavering critical scrutiny. Those getting it wrong would be dismissed. After all, there are millions of people in distress. Progress would, predictably, be tedious, uncertain and frustrating. Needless to say, this hardheaded style hardly pervades this literature. The term *failure* is almost unspeakable, and irrelevant, discredited theories are cherished as valued family heirlooms. That the calamities continue unresolved hardly alarms; indeed, their continuances justify yet more ill-conceived forays bringing personal rewards and opportunities to propagate radical ideologies.

This is *not* to assert that *empowerment* is a sham. A more accurate assessment might be that the term has been expropriated well beyond its intended use. Everyday, no doubt, it works wonders and it deserves recommendation for many of our ills. And successes have been noted (Olasky 1992; Woodson 1987). There are modest efforts everywhere that have commendable records applying this cure. It is the distinction between the spontaneous empowerment activities occurring everywhere and the academic-inspired schemes endlessly reported in the disciplinary literature that is fundamental. This distinction should not be obscured by our pessimistic evaluation. We have no quarrels with community organizers instructing the unemployed how to read or the church volunteers tutoring young mothers about child care. Such traditional assistance, regardless of labels, is to be celebrated. The target of our indignation are those hundreds of self-designated empowerment experts occupying academic or professional positions. There is also a false infatuation with democracy infusing this empowerment clamor. Peppered about are assertions that self-determination and democracy go hand-in-hand. How this occurs is never spelled out. It is surely plausible that fully empowering innumerable now-passive interests will engender chaos, not dutiful citizen deliberation. Gridlock is equally foreseeable if power is widely dispersed. Worse, the sirens of empowerment may raise expectations to great heights, and the inevitable disappointments may engender a liking for more totalitarian solutions. As one ponders this often made association, one might well conclude that "democracy" is drawn into this picture for the prestige it conveys. Thus, to claim that democracy is to be served by empowerment is akin to an advertisement proclaiming "Endorsed by admired sports hero." If there is some evidence that enhancing empowerment shores up our faltering democracy, we cannot find it. Again, an element of disingenuousness prevails.

Our final points address moral, not empirical, issues. These overshadow particular outcomes and go unmentioned when advocates gear up to assist the helpless or bestow Washington's money, yet they transcend the entire enterprise. The first concerns the construction of a society elevating power to great heights. Leaving aside feasibility, do we sincerely wish a Hobbesian realm where everything is reducible to battles for supremacy? It is the *imperative* to gain empowerment that attracts our attention. Surely, it is bizarre to contend that a modern society requires people to seek hegemony and this will improve their lives. Are blacks forever mired in "colonial dependency" if African Americans do not gain their "fair share" of elected offices? *Dependency* is inevitable; cooperation is the norm, and only a tiny sliver of control is possible. Even billionaires will confess a degree of helplessness before market forces, government regulation or uncontrollable international economic forces. Only the unsophisticated impute absolute mastery to those above.

It is the unreflective, ceaseless quest for this illusion, particularly among those vulnerable to seductive suggestion, that is so pernicious. This is not to recommend subservience as the cure de jour. The homeless are not to be dispatched to monasteries for lives of quiet meditation. It is a matter of balance, proportions, the aligning of power with other, perhaps superior aims. For example, students who wish to succeed should obey their teachers, and teachers wanting to hold their positions have an obligation to attend to parental desires. Parents, in turn, have inescapable duties to their children. Advice from those that have accomplished something worthy is not to be easily rejected in the name of an incontestable self-determination. This is not so much a matter of perfecting our condition; it is a matter of sustaining civil society. Empowerment has its treasured place, but as with all potent medicine, overdoses are injurious. In pharmacology parlance, toxicity is in the dosage. There has to be some moment when the empowerment's most ardent fan, as a matter of moral obligation, says, "Patiently follow wise conventional counsel." Refusal to acknowledge the full array of remedies, to insist upon one regardless of circumstances, is the sin of pride, the very worst of the Seven Deadly Sins.

The easy insistence on power as the cure breeds insatiable appetites. A parallel can be drawn with the pursuit of pleasure: Left unchecked, it becomes rapacious hedonism. Capturing the entire city government will surely bring rewards, but such ascendancy cannot command all that is desired. Nor will teacher domination of the entire school system work magic on uninspired students unless these teachers have some yet undiscovered educational elixir. Ceding authority to the mentally ill is no guarantee of betterment, and faced with disappointment, they will surely demand even more to escape their illness. Impediments will *always* exist, no matter how successful the campaign. Recall our tale from Chapter 2 about tenants gaining control of their housing project—this is but one step on an endless journey. Ditto for African Americans gaining a foothold in municipal government. Down deep, to raise up empowerment as the great cure-all invites futility. Rather than attend to what is necessary, the quest is misdirected to securing yet one more dollop of power.

This insatiable quest affects democracy, at least our understanding of it. Democratic conflict rests on special moral sensibilities. Conflict is endemic and healthy, but it must be bounded. Democracy requires disputes be ended and defeats accepted. To subordinate loyalty, obedience, compromise, deference and trust to "taking control over one's existence" invites the twin evils of anarchy and dictatorship. After all, why should contestants stop with half a loaf, a small voice or a minor role? Is it not true that a little more effort will defeat one's adversaries and bring gratification? Perhaps if the array of techniques were expanded a bit, maybe a little violence here and there, the long-sought victory would materialize. Why settle for one's present lot; enter the battle, and the rewards will assuredly come. Again, it is a matter of degree, restraining the quest for control, that is essential.

And what about those energized by the siren of empowerment unable to manage? Surely, nearly everyone, most of the time, is unfit to decide autonomously matters of consequence. Empowerment is not inherently virtuous; seeking inappropriate control can be ruinous. Inescapable limits of ability and resources hinder the quest for superiority in human relations. It is folly to inspire pupils to dictate their own learning. Advising the disadvantaged that their self-inflicted misfortune can be remediated via collective political action only deepens their dependency. If corporations freely flee inner cities, it may be more fruitful to inquire why than to concoct huge bribes to secure their return. The Doctors of Empowerment have not taken a Hippocratic oath, but they cannot escape the moral responsibility of giving counsel wisely to those often knowing little. The evasion of responsibility is especially notable when the prescription's ineffectiveness is clear.

These moral quandaries are, alas, typically neglected by those wishing betterment. To be repulsed by human misery is commendable. And we all have obligations to assist, if possible. But no matter how laudable our intentions, no matter how pressing the calamities before our eyes, helpfulness carries its own responsibilities. Making the effort, in and of itself, carries no weight. To recommend empowerment simply because it conforms with one's own career needs, generates some prestige-bestowing publications or assists some ideological passions debases the very idea of helpfulness; it is selfishness.

THE FUTURE?

It is always possible, of course, that our pessimism is misplaced. Perhaps we depict only the first tentative steps, the initial fumbling prior to genuine progress. After all, modern science took centuries to mature. Empowerment theorizing is still in its infancy stage. Decades hence those reprimanded here may well be celebrated as Venerated Founders laying the foundation of wondrous progress. Our disapproval, by contrast, will be long forgotten as reactionary and mean-spirited. Anything is, after all, possible.

Again, hope trumps reality. The reasons why the multiple versions of empowerment depicted here will fail to deliver as promised are numerous and clear. The theoretical garble infecting the enterprise will surely choke any project, and surprisingly, devotees seldom attend to this deficiency. Hidden radical agendas endlessly corrupt, and again this does not seem especially troubling. An inattentiveness of critical detail is yet another plague. The catalog could continue, but if one reason had to be selected as the leading culprit, it would be the disconnection between advice and consequences. Today's prophets of empowerment do not live the results; necessity, it is said, is the mother of invention, and there is no necessity here. The experiment is always with somebody else. Those university experts tinkering with inner-city schools seldom enroll their own children there. Professors of social work hardly ever depend on state bureaucracies for necessities. The Black Studies professor is not forced to hire employees imposed on him or her by community activists intoxicated with empowerment. It is easy to be irresponsible if one does not suffer the dismal outcome.

This is not a matter of sincerity—counselors hardly wish calamity. It is a matter of powerful incentives and knowledge. Empowerment prophets play to their own audiences: the academic world, professional camp followers and politicians eager to secure yet more boodle. Terrible recommendations are not disastrous, provided they follow the correct disciplinary form and conform to prevailing theoretical or political fashions. This puts the bread on the table, and we cannot expect otherwise. To escape this strong gravitational pull is tantamount to leaving the academy or, allegedly, abandoning the poor. Ditto for acquiring the knowledge that would make recommendations more realistic: Few university-based experts or federal bureaucrats relish a life among those whom they counsel. Perhaps if this occurred, the tune would change. One can only imagine the frustration of a middle-class political science professor consigned to living in squalor until political action brought relief. No doubt, after a few months, this strategy would be reevaluated.

If there is an upbeat message to be announced, it is that we should not quickly abandon our historical storehouse of proven remedies. We have lots of admirable solutions waiting to be applied. An attention-getting clamor for "new and different" is best left to commerce. The novel makes sense only after past cures have been exhausted and the situation demands a degree of risk. Even then, caution is advised, for it is easy to forget that the status quo, though imperfect, may far exceed what has been accomplished before. Outer limits exist regarding human improvement, and a thirst for tinkering can well bring disaster. It is not a question of relishing misery as preordained; it is a matter of carefully and honestly attending to what is possible. The glorification of empowerment as today's Messiah is but a harmful and totally unnecessary illusion. We can do better.

Bibliography

Ackelsberg, Martha A. 1988. "Communities, Resistance, and Women's Activism: Some Implications for a Democratic Polity." In *Women and the Politics of Empowerment*, ed. Ann Bookman and Sandra Morgan. Philadelphia: Temple University Press.

Aeppel, Timothy. 1997. "Not All Workers Find Idea of Empowerment as Neat as It Sounds." *Wall Street Journal*, September 8, A1, A14.

Albers, Eric C. and Nancy Paolini. 1993. "The Dual Face of Empowerment: A Model for Cooperative Resource Building." *Journal of Sociology and Social Welfare* 20:99–109.

Allen, J. D. 1997. "Who's Driving This Bus Anyway? Empowering Drivers." *School Business Affairs* 63:33–35.

Almeleh, Naomi, Steven Soifer, Naomi Gottlieg and Lorraine Gutierrez. 1993. "Women's Achievement of Empowerment through Activism in the Workplace." *Affilia* 8:26–39.

Altshuler, Alan S. 1970. *Community Control: The Black Demand for Participation in Large American Cities*. New York: Pegasus.

Atlanta, Georgia Empowerment Zone. n.d. http://www.ezec.gov/ezec/GA/atlanta.html

Ayres-Williams, Roz. 1997. "The New Rights Agenda." *Black Enterprise* 28:85–90.

Bachrach, Peter and Aryeh Botwinick. 1992. *Power and Empowerment: A Radical Theory of Participatory Democracy*. Philadelphia: Temple University Press.

Balcazar, Fredrico E., Tom Seekins, Stephen B. Fawcett and Bill L. Hopkins. 1990. "Empowering People with Physical Disabilities Through Advocacy Training Skills." *American Journal of Community Psychology* 18:281–296.

Ball, Jeffrey. 1997. "Feds Say Empowerment Zone Deal Was Improper." *Atlanta Constitution*, October 2, B4.

Ballou, Dale and Michael Podgursky. 1997. *Teacher Pay and Teacher Quality.* Kalamazoo, MI: W. E. Upjohn Institute for Employment Research.

Bandura, Albert. 1986. *Social Foundations of Thought and Action: A Social Cognitive Theory.* Englewood Cliffs, NJ: Prentice-Hall.

Barker, Lucius J. 1988. *Our Time Has Come.* Chicago: University of Illinois Press.

Barker, Lucius J. 1994. "Limits of Political Strategy: A Systematic View of the African American Experience." *American Political Science Review* 88:1–13.

Barnett, Marguerite Ross. 1982. "The Congressional Black Caucus: Illusions and Realities of Power." In *The New Black Politics: The Search for Political Power*, ed. Michael B. Preston, Lenneal J. Henderson, Jr. and Paul Puryear. New York: Longman.

Barton, Allan H. 1977. "What Has Been Learned from the New York City Neighborhood Government Experiment?" In *Decentralized City Government*, ed. Allan H. Barton, Norman I. Fainstein, Susan S. Fainstein, Nathalie S. Friedman, Stanley Heginbotham, Joel Koblentz, Theresa F. Rogers, John M. Boyle and Ronald Brumboch. Lexington, MA: Lexington Books.

Belcher, John R. and Rebecca L. Hegar. 1991. "Social Work and the Casualties of Capitalism: Empowering the Urban Poor." *Journal of Progressive Human Services* 2:39–53.

Berger, Peter L. and Richard John Neuhaus. 1996. "Mediating Structures and the Dilemmas of the Welfare State." In *To Empower People: From State to Civil Society*, ed. Peter L. Berger and Richard John Neuhaus. 2nd ed. Washington, DC: AEI Press.

Berger, Renee. 1997. "People, Power, Politics: An Assessment of the Federal Empowerment Zones." *Planning* 63:4–9.

Bernstein, Richard. 1994. *Dictatorship of Virtue: Multiculturalism and the Battle for America's Future.* New York: Knopf.

Berry, Jeffrey M., Kent E. Portnoy and Ken Thomson. 1993. *The Rebirth of Urban Democracy.* Washington, DC: The Brookings Institution.

Bertolote, Jose Manoel. 1993. "Empowering the Mental Health Patient." *World Health* 28–29.

Bivens, Larry. 1997. "Detroit's Empowerment Zone Earns Praise." *Detroit News*, March 7, A5.

Black, Naomi. 1989. *Social Feminism.* Ithaca, NY: Cornell University Press.

Black Elected Officials: A National Roster. 1993. 21st ed. Washington, DC: Joint Center for Political and Economic Studies.

Boarnet, Marlon G. and William T. Bogart. 1996. "Enterprise Zones and Employment Evidence from New Jersey." *Journal of Urban Economics* 40:198–215.

Bobo, Lawrence and Frankin D. Gilliam. 1990. "Race, Sociopolitical Participation and Black Empowerment." *American Political Science Review* 84:377–394.

Bolin, Frances S. 1989. "Empowering Leadership." *Teachers College Record* 91: 81–96.

Borelli, Jan. 1997. "A Schoolwide Discipline Plan That Empowers Teachers and Gives Principals Time for Instructional Leadership." *NASSP-Bulletin* 81:68–75.

Bowser, Benjamin P., Mindy Thompson and Robert E. Fullilove. 1990. "African-American Youth and AIDS High-Risk Behavior: The Social Context and Barriers to Prevention." *Youth and Society* 27:54–66.

Boyce, William. 1993. "Evaluating Participation in Community Programs: An Empowerment Paradigm." *Canadian Journal of Program Evaluation* 8:89–102.
Braithwaite, Ronald L., Cynthia Bianchi and Sandra E. Taylor. 1994. "Ethnographic Approach to Community Organization and Health Empowerment." *Health Education Quarterly* 21:407–416.
Braithwaite, Ronald L. and Ngina Lythcott. 1989. "Community Empowerment as a Strategy for Health Promotion for Black and Other Minority Populations." *Journal of the American Medical Association* 261:282–283.
Brehm, Sharon S. 1988. "Feminist Issues in Intimate Relationships between Women and Men." In *Seeing Female: Social Role and Personal Lives*, ed. Sharon S. Brehm. Westport, CT: Greenwood Press.
Brosio, Richard A. 1990. "Teaching and Learning for Democratic Empowerment: A Critical Evaluation." *Educational Theory* 40:69–81.
Browning, Rufus, Dale Rogers Marshall and David H. Tabb. 1984. *Protest Is Not Enough: The Struggle of Blacks and Hispanics for Equality in Urban Politics.* Berkeley: University of California Press.
Brunson, Deborah A. and Judith F. Vogt. 1996. "Empowering Our Students and Ourselves: A Liberal Democratic Approach to the Communication Classroom." *Communication Education* 43:73–83.
Buday, Mary Catherine and James A. Kelly. 1996. "National Board Certification and the Teacher Profession's Commitment to Quality Assurance." *Phi Delta Kappan* 78:215–219.
Bullock, Charles S., III. 1975. "The Election of Blacks in the South: Preconditions and Consequences." *American Journal of Political Science* 19:727–739.
Button, James W. 1978. *Black Violence: Political Impact of the 1960s Riots.* Princeton, NJ: Princeton University Press.
Button, James, 1982. "Southern Black Elected Officials: Impact on Socioeconomic Change." *Review of Black Political Economy* 12:29–45.
Button, James W. 1989. *Blacks and Social Change: Impact of the Civil Rights Movement in Southern Communities.* Princeton, NJ: Princeton University Press.
Bystydzienski, Jill S. 1992. "Introduction." *Women Transforming Politics*, ed. Jill S. Bystydzienski. Bloomington and Indianapolis: Indiana University Press.
Callister, Thomas A., Jr. and Faith Dunne. 1992. "The Computer as Doorstop: Technology as Disempowerment." *Phi Delta Kappan* 74:324–329.
Campbell, David and Joe R. Feagin. 1975. "Black Politics in the South: A Descriptive Analysis." *Journal of Politics* 37:129–159.
Carnegie Forum on Education and the Economy. 1986. *A Nation Prepared: Teachers for the 21st Century.* New York: The Carnegie Corporation.
Clarke, Mark A. 1990. "Some Cautionary Observations on Liberation Education." *Language Arts* 67:388–398.
Clift, Renee T. 1991. "Teacher Education and Teaching: Empowerment for Whom? When?" *Teacher Educator* 27:14–23.
Coats, Dan, Gary J. Renzaglia and Marlowe C. Embree. 1983. "When Helping Backfires: Help and Helplessness." In *New Directions in Helping: Recipient Reactions to Aid*, ed. Jeffrey D. Fisher, Arnie Nadler and Bella M. DePaulo. Vol. 1. New York: Academic Press.

Cohen, Carl I., M.D. and Kenneth S. Thompson, M.D. 1992. "Homeless Mentally Ill or Mentally Ill Homeless?" *American Journal of Psychiatry* 149:816–823.

Colburn, Kenneth S. 1973. *Southern Black Mayors: Local Problems and Federal Responses*. Washington, DC: Joint Center for Political Studies.

Coleman, Mick. 1997. "Families and Schools: In Search of Common Ground." *Young Children* 52:14–21.

Collins, Patricia Hill. 1990. *Black Feminist Thought: Knowledge, Consciousness and the Politics of Empowerment*. Cambridge, MA: Urwin Hyman.

"Congress Votes to Create Enterprise Zones." 1993. *CQ Almanac* 49:422–423.

Cook, Terrence E. and Patrick M. Morgan. 1971. "An Introduction to Participatory Democracy." In *Participatory Democracy*, ed. Terrence E. Cook and Patrick M. Morgan. San Francisco: Canfield Press.

Cooley, Van E. 1997. "Technology: Building Success through Teacher Empowerment." *Educational Horizons* 75:73–77.

Coombs, David W., M. H. Alsikafi, C. Hobson Bryan and Irving I. Webber. 1977. "Black Political Control in Green County, Alabama." *Rural Sociology* 42: 398–406.

"Congress Votes to Create Enterprise Zones." 1993. *CQ Almanac XLIX*. Washington, DC: Congressional Quarterly.

Cruikshank, Barbara. 1993. "Revolutions Within: Self-government and Self-esteem." *Economy and Society* 22: 327–344.

Cummins, Jim. 1986. "Empowering Minority Students: A Framework for Intervention." *Harvard Education Review* 56:18–36.

Davis, L. 1964. "The Cost of Realism: Contemporary Restatement of Democracy." *Western Political Quarterly* 17:37–46.

Delgado-Gaitau, Concha. 1991. "Involving Parents in the Schools: A Process of Empowerment." *American Journal of Education* 100:20–46.

DeParle, J. and P. Appelbome. 1991. "Ideas to Help the Poor Abound, But a Consensus Is Wanting." *New York Times*, January 29, A1, A18.

Department of Housing and Urban Development (HUD). 1994. "About the Initiative." http://www.ezec/About/hudregs.html

Deutchman, Iva Ellen. 1991. "The Politics of Empowerment." *Women and Politics* 11:1–18.

DiLeonardo, Joan W. 1993. "Families in Poverty and Chronic Neglect of Children." *The Journal of Contemporary Human Services* 74:557–562.

Dixon, Jennifer. 1997. "Several Ventures Fail to Pan Out." *Detriot Free Press*, April 15. http://www.freep.com/news/econ/qffizz15.htm

Donohue, John J., III and James Heckman. 1989. "Continuous Versus Episodic Change: The Impact of Civil Rights Policy on Economic Status of Blacks." Working Paper 3894. Cambridge: National Bureau of Economics.

D'Sousa, Denesh. 1995. *The End of Racism: Principles for a Multicultural Society*. New York: Free Press.

Duffy, Gerald G. 1994. "Professional Development Schools and the Disempowerment of Teachers and Professors." *Phi Delta Kappan* 75:596–600.

Duffy, Gerald G. 1992. "Let's Free Teachers to Be Inspired." *Phi Delta Kappan* 73:442–447.

Duke, Daniel L. and Bruce Gansneder. 1990. "Teacher Empowerment: The View from the Classroom." *Educational Policy* 4:145–160.

Dunlop, Katherine N. 1996. "Supporting and Empowering Families through Co-operative Preschool Education." *Social Work in Education* 18:210–221.

Dunst, Carl J., Carol M. Trivette and Nancy Lapoint. 1992. "Towards Clarification of the Meaning and Key Elements of Empowerment." *Family Science Review* 5:111–130.

Dye, Thomas R. and James Rennick. 1981. "Political Power and City Jobs: Determinants of Minority Employment." *Social Science Quarterly* 62:475–486.

Edds, Margaret. 1987. *Free at Last: What Really Happened When Civil Rights Came to Southern Politics*. Bethesda, MD: Adler and Adler.

Eisinger, Peter K. 1982. "Black Employment in Municipal Jobs: The Impact of Black Political Power." *American Political Science Review* 76:380–392.

Ellickson, Robert C. 1990. "The Homelessness Muddle." *The Public Interest* 99: 45–60.

Ellsworth, Elizabeth. 1989. "Why Doesn't This Feel Empowering? Working Through the Repressive Myths of Critical Pedagogy." *Harvard Education Review* 59:297–324.

"Empowerment Zone Audits Point to Mismanagement." 1997. *Atlanta Constitution*, November 21, A1.

"Empowerment Zone Staff Being Slashed." 1997. *Atlanta Constitution*, August 20, A1.

"Empowerment Zone Takes Shape—First New Dealership Downtown in Decades: Rolls Royce and Bentleys Will Role Out for Sale in July, Joining the Effort at Inner-city Renewal." 1997. *Atlanta Constitution*, May 29.

Epstein, Joyce L. 1991. "Paths to Partnership: What We Can Learn from Federal, State, District, and School Initiatives." *Phi Delta Kappan* 72:345–349.

Evans, Estella Norwood. 1992. "Liberation Theology, Empowerment Theory and Social Work Practices with the Oppressed." *International Social Work* 35: 135–147.

"EZ/EC Best Practices." n.d. Detroit Empowerment Zone. http://www.hud.gov/cpd/ezec/ezecsucc.html

"EZ/EC Empowerment Zone Performance Report. 1995–1996." n.d. Detroit Empowerment Zone Executive Summary. http://hud.gov/cpd/ezec/demiperf.htm

Fabricant, Michael. 1988. "Empowering the Homeless." *Social Policy* 18:49–55.

Fainstein, Norman and Susan Fainstein. 1996. "Urban Regimes and Black Citizens: The Economic and Social Impacts of Black Political Incorporation in United States Cities." *International Journal of Urban and Regional Research* 20:22–37.

Faryna, Stan, Brad Stetson and Joseph G. Conti, eds. 1997. *Black and Right: The Bold New Voice of Black Conservatives in America*. Westport, CT: Praeger.

Faver, Catherine A. 1994. "Feminist Ideology and Strategies for Social Change: An Analysis of Social Movements." *Journal of Applied Social Sciences* 18:123–134.

Fawcett, Stephen B., Adrienne Paine-Andrews, Vincent T. Francisco, Jerry A. Schulz, Kimber P. Richter, Rhonda K. Lewis, Ella L. Williams, Kari J. Harris, Jannette Y. Berkely, Jacqueline L. Fisher and Christine M. Lopez. 1995. "Using Empowerment Theory in Collaborative Partnership for Community Health and Development." *American Journal of Community Psychology* 23: 677–697.

"Feds Say Empowerment Zone Deal Was Improper." 1997. *Atlanta Constitution*, October 22, B4.

Ferguson, Sarah. 1990. "Tent City Blues." *Mother Jones* 15:29–30.

Feste, Catherine and Robert M. Anderson. 1995. "Empowerment: From Philosophy to Practice." *Patient Education and Counseling* 26:139–144.

Fetterman, David. 1994. "Empowerment Evaluation." *Evaluation Practice* 15:1–15.

Fisher, Mary. 1997. "A Big White Lie?" *Washington Post*, July 31, B1.

Fisher, Robert. 1994. *Let the People Decide: Neighborhood Organizing in America*. Rev. ed. New York: Twayne Publishers.

Fulton, William and Morris Newman. 1994. "The Strange Career of Enterprise Zones." *Governing* 7:32–34.

Gale, Dennis E. 1996. *Understanding Urban Unrest: From Reverend King to Rodney King*. Thousand Oaks, CA: Sage.

Gelb, Joyce and Marian Lief Palley. 1982. *Women and Public Policies*. Princeton, NJ: Princeton University Press.

Gibbs, Jewlle Tayor and Dinna Fuery. 1994. "Mental Health and Well-Being of Black Women: Towards Strategies of Empowerment." *American Journal of Community Psychology* 22:559–582.

Ginsberg, Benjamin. 1982. *The Consequences of Consent: Elections, Citizen Control and Popular Acquiescence*. Reading, MA: Addison-Wesley.

Giroux, Henry A. 1988. "Literacy and the Pedagogy of Voice and Political Empowerment." *Educational Theory* 38:61–75.

Gittel, Marilyn. 1971. "Education: The Decentralization-Community Control Controversy." In *Race and Politics in New York City: Five Studies in Policy-Making*, ed. Jewel Bellah and Stephen M. David. New York: Praeger.

Glaser, William. 1996. "Then and Now: The Theory of Choice." *Earning* 25:20–22.

Glickman, Carl D. 1990. "Pushing School Reform to a New Edge: The Seven Ironies of School Empowerment." *Phi Delta Kappan* 72:63–75.

Grace, Victoria. 1991. "The Marketing of Empowerment and the Construction of the Health Consumer: A Critique of Health Promotion." *International Journal of Health Services* 21:329–343.

Graves, Earl G. 1996. "Wielding Real Power." *Black Enterprise* 26:9.

Green, Charles. 1985. *Elitism vs. Democracy in Community Organizations*. Bristol, IN: Wyndam Hall Press.

Green, Charles and Basil Wilson. 1989. *The Struggle for Black Empowerment in New York City: Beyond the Politics of Pigmentation*. New York: Praeger.

Griffith, James. 1996. "Relation of Parental Involvement, Empowerment, and School Traits to Student Academic Performance." *Journal of Educational Research* 90:33–41.

Gruber, Judith and Edison J. Trickett. 1987. "Can We Empower Others? The Paradox of Empowerment in the Governing of an Alternative Public School." *American Journal of Community Psychology* 15:353–371.

Gutierrez, Lorraine. 1990. "Working with Women of Color: An Empowerment Perspective." *Social Work* 35:149–153.

Hall, Melvin F. 1995. *Poor People's Social Movement Organizations: The Goal Is to Win*. Westport, CT: Praeger.

Hamilton, Charles V. 1982. "Preface." In *The New Black Politics: The Search for Political Power*, ed. Michael B. Preston, Lenneal J. Henderson, Jr. and Paul Puryear. New York: Longman.

Handler, Joel F. 1996. *Down from Bureaucracy: The Ambiguity of Privatization and Empowerment*. Princeton, NJ: Princeton University Press.

Hanks, Lawrence J. 1987. *The Struggle for Black Political Empowerment in Three Georgia Counties*. Knoxville: University of Tennessee Press.

Hatton, Barbara R. 1977. "Schools and Black Community Development: A Reassessment of Community Control." *Education and Urban Control* 9:215–233.

Henderson, Lenneal, Jr. and Michael B. Preston. 1984. "Blacks, Public Employment and Public Interest Theory." In *Contemporary Public Policy Perspectives and Black Americans: Issues in an Era of Retrenchment Politics*, ed. Mitchell F. Rice and Woodrow Jones, Jr. Westport, CT: Greenwood Press.

Herrnstein, Richard J. and Charles Murray. 1994. *The Bell Curve: Intelligence and Class Structure in American Life*. New York: Free Press.

Highsmith, Connie S. 1997. "HIV and Women: Using Empowerment as a Prevention Tool." *H&HC: Perspectives on Community* 18:6–9.

Hill, Kevin A. 1995. "Does the Creation of Majority Black Districts Aid Republicans? An Analysis of the 1992 Congressional Elections in Eight Southern States." *Journal of Politics* 57:384–401.

Hilts, Philp J. 1994. "Hospital Is Accused of Illegal Experiments." *New York Times*, January 21, A12.

Himmelfarb, Gertrude. 1994. *The De-Moralization of Society: From Victorian Virtues to Modern Values*. New York: Alfred A. Knopf.

Hindes, Martha. n.d. "Ford Unit Will Build Plant in Detroit for Contractor." www.rust.net/~workers/news/ford.htn

Hirsch, E. D., Jr. 1996. *The Schools We Need and Why We Don't Have Them*. New York: Doubleday.

Hoagland, Sarah. 1986. "Lesbian Ethics: Some Thoughts on Power in our Interpretations." *Lesbian Ethics* 2:5–32.

Holmes, Steven A. and Karen De Witt. 1996. "Black, Successful and Safe and Gone from Capital." *New York Times*, July 27, 1, 9.

Horowitz, Michael J. 1996. "Law and the Welfare State." In *To Empower People: From State to Civil Society*, ed. Peter L. Berger and Richard John Neuhaus. 2nd ed.Washington, DC: AEI Press.

Ingram, Robert. 1988. "EMPOWER." *Social Policy* 19:11–16.

Irwin, Judith W. 1996. *Empowering Ourselves and Transforming Schools: Educators Making a Difference*. Albany: State University of New York Press.

Jackson, Barbara L. 1989. "Parent Choice and Empowerment: New Role for Parents." *Urban Education* 24:263–286.

Jackson, Jesse. 1996. "It's Up to Us." *Essence* 27:71, 206, 207.

Jenkins, Susan. 1991. "Community Wellness: A Group Empowerment Model for Rural America." *Journal of Health Care for Poor and Underserved* 1:388–404.

Jennings, James 1992. *The Politics of Black Empowerment: The Transformation of Black Activism in Urban America*. Detroit, MI: Wayne State University Press.

Jensen, Arthur R. 1973. *Educability & Group Differences*. New York: Harper and Row.

Jones, Mack H. 1978. "Black Political Empowerment in Atlanta: Myth and Reality." *Annals of the American Academy of Political and Social Sciences* 439: 90–117.

Joyce, Michael J. and William A. Schambra. 1996. "A New Civic Life." In *To Empower People: From State to Civil Society*, ed. Peter L. Berger and Richard John Neuhaus. 2nd ed. Washington, DC: AEI Press.

Karnig, Albert K. and Susan Welch. 1980. *Black Representation and Urban Policy*. Chicago: University of Chicago Press.

Katz, Jeffrey L. 1993. "Enterprise Zones Struggle to Make Their Mark." *Congressional Quarterly Weekly Report* 51 (July 17):1880–1883.

Keech, William R. 1968. *The Impact of Negro Voting: The Role of the Vote in the Quest for Equality*. Chicago: Rand McNally.

Keiser, Richard A. 1993. "Explaining African-American Political Empowerment: Windy City Politics from 1900 to 1983." *Urban Affairs Quarterly* 29:84– 116.

Keiser, Richard A. 1997. *Subordination or Empowerment? African-American Leadership and the Struggle for Urban Political Power*. New York: Oxford University Press.

Keller, Edmond J. 1978. "The Impact of Black Mayors on Urban Policy." *Annals of the American Academy of Political and Social Sciences* 439:40–52.

Kelly, William R. and David Snyder. 1980. "Racial Violence and Socioeconomic Changes among Blacks in the United States." *Social Forces* 58:739–760.

Kerr, Brinck and Kenneth R. Mladenka. 1994. "Does Politics Matter? A Time Series Analysis of Minority Employment Patterns." *American Journal of Political Science* 38:918–943.

Kieffer, Charles H. 1984. "Citizen Empowerment: A Developmental Perspective." In *Studies in Empowerment: Steps towards Understanding and Action*, ed. Julian Rappaport, Carolyn Swift and Robert Hess. New York: Haworth Press.

Klein, Ethel. 1984. *Gender Politics: From Consciousness to Mass Politics*. Cambridge: Harvard University Press.

Knitzer, Jane. 1980. "Advocacy and Community Psychology." In *Community Psychology: Theoretical and Empirical Approaches*, ed. Margaret S. Gibbs, Juliana Rusic Lachenmeyer and Janet Sigal. New York: Gardner Press.

Kotler, Milton. 1969. *Neighborhood Government: The Local Foundation of Political Life*. Indianapolis, IN: Bobbs-Merrill.

Kotler, Milton. 1971. "Neighborhood Government." In *Participatory Democracy*, ed. Terrence E. Cook and Patrick M. Morgan. San Francisco: Canfield Press.

Kramer, Daniel C. 1972. *Participatory Democracy: Developing Ideals of the Political Left*. Cambridge: Schenkman Publishing.

Kramer, Rita. 1991. *Ed School Follies: The Miseducation of America's Teachers*. New York: Free Press.

Kretovics, Joseph, Kathleen Farber and William Armaline. 1991. "Reform from the

Bottom Up: Empowering Teachers to Transform Schools." *Phi Delta Kappan* 73:295–299.

Lagana, Joseph F. 1989. "Ready, Set, Empower! Superintendents Can Sow the Seeds for Growth." *The School Administrator* 46:20–22.

Landsmann, Leanna. 1988. "10 Resolutions for Teachers." *Phi Delta Kappan* 69: 373–376.

LaVeist, Thomas A. 1992. "The Political Empowerment and Health Status of African Americans: Mapping a New Territory." *American Journal of Sociology* 97: 1080–1095.

LaVeist, Thomas A. 1993. "Segregation, Poverty and Empowerment: Health Consequences for African Americans." *Milbank Quarterly* 71:41–64.

Lee, Judith A.B. 1991. "Empowerment Through Mutual Aid Groups: A Practice Grounded Conceptual Framework." *Groupwork* 4:5–21.

Lefcourt, Herbert M. 1966. "Internal versus External Control of Reinforcement: A Review." *Psychological Bulletin* 65:206–220.

Lefcourt, Herbert M. 1972. "Recent Developments in the Study of Locus of Control." In *Progress in Experimental Personality Research*, ed. Brendan A. Maher. Vol. 6. New York: Academic Press.

Lefkowitz, Mary. 1996. *Not Out of Africa*. New York: Basic Books.

Lenkowsky, Leslie. 1996. "Philanthropy and the Welfare State." In *To Empower People: From State to Civil Society*, ed. Peter L. Berger and Richard John Neuhaus. 2nd ed. Washington, DC: AEI Press.

Levine, Charles H. 1974. *Racial Conflict and the American Mayor: Power, Polarization, and Performance*. Lexington, MA: Lexington Books, D. C. Heath and Company.

Levin, Michael. 1997. *Why Race Matters: Race Differences and What They Mean*. Westport, CT: Praeger.

Levins, Richard. 1995. "Beyond Democracy: The Politics of Empowerment." In *Marxism in the Postmodern Age: Confronting the New World Order*, ed. Antonio Callari, Stephen Cullenberg and Carole Biewener. New York: Guilford Press.

Lieberson, Stanley. 1981. *A Piece of the Pie: Blacks and White Immigrants since 1880*. Berkeley: University of California Press.

Liebschutz, Sarah F. 1995. "Empowerment Zones and Enterprise Communities: Reinventing Federalism for Distressed Communities." *Publius: The Journal of Federalism* 25:117–132.

Lips, Hillary. 1981. *Women, Men and the Psychology of Power*. Englewood Cliffs, NJ: Prentice-Hall.

Lipset, Seymour Martin and Earl Raab. 1970. *The Politics of Unreason: Right-Wing Extremism in America, 1790–1970*. New York: Harper.

Lloyd, Fonda M. 1994. "Time of Live Up to the Hype." *Black Enterprise* 24:27.

Lockett, Gretchen C. 1994. "Empowerment in HBCU's and PBCU's: Developing Microcosms of the Beloved Community through the Re-Definition of Social Institutions and the Learning and Application of Values." Paper presented at the Annual Conference of the National Association for Equal Opportunity in Higher Education, Washington, DC, March 24.

Loury, Glenn C. 1987. "Making It All Happen." In *On the Road to Economic Reform: An Agenda for Black Progress*, ed. Robert L. Woodson. Washington, DC: Regnery Gateway.

Lowenstein, Gaither. 1981. "Black Elected and Appointed Officials: Black Mayors and the Urban Black Underclass." *Western Journal of Black Studies* 5:278–284.

MacDonald, Heather. 1997. "The Homeless Don't Need 'Outreach.' " *Wall Street Journal*, November 17, A14.

Maeroff, Gene I. 1988a. "A Blueprint for Empowering Teachers." *Phi Delta Kappan* 69:473–477.

Maeroff, Gene I. 1988b. *The Empowerment of Teachers: Overcoming the Crisis of Confidence*. New York: Teachers College Press.

Mahtesian, Charles. 1995. "Showdown on E-Z Street." *Governing* 9:36–41.

"Mayor Must Evolve with Zone" (editorial). 1997. *Atlanta Journal Constitution*, August 24.

McCartney, John T. 1992. *Black Power Ideologies: An Essay in African-American Political Thought*. Philadelphia: Temple University Press.

McClendon, Bruce W. 1993. "The Paradigm of Empowerment." *Journal of the American Planning Association* 59:145–147.

McClosky, Herbert and Alida Brill. 1988. *Dimensions of Tolerance: What Americans Believe about Civil Liberties*. New York: Russell Sage Foundation.

McIntire, Ronald G. and John T. Fessenden. 1994. *The Self-Directed School: Empowering the Stakeholders*. New York: Scholastic.

McKinney, Linda J. and Pamela G. Fry. 1994. "Personal Life Stories: A Strategy for Empowerment." *Social Studies and the Young Learner* 7:7–9.

McKnight, John L. 1985. "Health and Empowerment." *Canadian Journal of Public Health* 76:37–38.

McLaren, Peter. 1989. *Life in Schools: An Introduction to Critical Pedagogy in the Foundations of Education*. New York: Longman Press

McLean, Athena. 1995. "Empowerment and the Psychiatric Consumer/Ex-Patient Movement in the United States: Contradictions, Crisis and Change." *Social Science and Medicine* 40:1053–1071.

Merelman, Richard M. 1993. "Black History and Cultural Empowerment: A Case Study." *American Journal of Education* 101:331–358.

Mertens, Sally and Sam L. Yarger. 1988. "Teaching as a Profession: Leadership, Empowerment, and Involvement." *Journal of Teacher Education* 39:32–37.

Merzel, Cheryl. 1991. "Rethinking Empowerment." *Health/PAC Bulletin* 21:5–6.

Michels, Robert. 1915. *Political Parties: A Sociological Study of the Oligarchical Tendencies of Modern Democracy*. Trans. Eden Paul and Cedar Paul. London: Jarrtold and Sons.

Miron, Louis F. 1995. "Pushing the Boundaries of Urban School Reform: Linking Student Outcomes to Community Development." *Journal for a Just and Caring Education* 1:98–114.

Mladenka, Kenneth R. 1989. "Blacks and Hispanics in Urban Politics." *American Political Science Review* 83:165–191.

Mondros, Jacqueline B. and Scott M. Wilson. 1994. *Organizing for Power and Empowerment*. New York: Columbia University Press.

Morgan, Sandra. 1988. "It's the Whole Power of the City against Us: The Development of Political Consciousness in a Women's Health Care Coalition." In *Women and the Politics of Empowerment*, ed. Sandra Morgan and Ann Bookman. Philadelphia: Temple University Press.

Morgan, Sandra and Ann Bookman. 1988. "Rethinking Women and Politics: An Introductory Essay." In *Women and the Politics of Empowerment*, ed. Sandra Morgan and Ann Bookman. Philadelphia: Temple University Press.

Morris, Aldon. 1991. "Introduction: Education for Liberation." *Social Policy* 21: 2–6.

Morris, David and Karl Hess. 1975. *Neighborhood Power: The New Localism*. Boston: Beacon Press.

Morrison, Minion K. C. 1987. *Black Political Mobilization: Leadership, Power, and Mass Behavior*. Albany: State University of New York Press.

Morse, Steve. 1997. *Atlanta's $250 Million Empowerment Zone Mess: Big Promises Produce Few Results*. Atlanta: Georgia Public Policy Foundation. http://www.gppf.org/EZ.html

Moynihan, Daniel P. 1969. *Maximum Feasible Misunderstanding: Community Action in the War on Poverty*. New York: Free Press.

Mueller, John. 1988. "Trends in Political Tolerance." *Public Opinion Quarterly* 52:1–25.

Mulligan, Tom. "The Detroit Empowerment Zone." http://www.metroguide.com/~world/guide/feature/empower.shtml

Murray, Charles. 1984. *Losing Ground: American Social Policy 1950–1980*. New York: Basic Books

Murray, Charles. 1988. "The Coming of Custodial Democracy." *Commentary* 86: 19–24.

Murray, Charles. 1992. "Preface." In *The Tragedy of American Compassion*, by Marvin Olasky. Washington, DC: Regnery Gateway.

Naparstek, Arthur J. 1976. "Policy Options for Neighborhood Empowerment." *National Urban Policy Roundtable*: 73–91.

Nathan, Joe. 1996. "Possibilities, Problems, and Progress." *Phi Delta Kappan* 78: 18–22.

Nelson, William E., Jr. and Philip J. Meranto. 1977. *Electing Black Mayors: Political Action in the Black Community*. Columbus: Ohio State University Press.

Nelson, William E., Jr., Lawrence Mosqueto, and Philip Meranto. 1984. "Reaganomics and the Continuing Urban Crisis in the Black Community." In *Contemporary Public Policy Perspectives and Black Americans: Issues in an Era of Retrenchment Politics*, ed. Mitchell F. Rice and Woodrow Jones, Jr. Westport, CT: Greenwood Press.

Nessel, Linda. 1988. "A Coalition Approach to Enhance Youth Empowerment." *Social Policy* 19:25–27.

Olasky, Marvin. 1992. *The Tragedy of American Compassion*. Washington, DC: Regnery Gateway.

Olasky, Marvin. 1996. "The Corruption of Religious Charities." In *To Empower People: From State to Civil Society*, ed. Peter L. Berger and Richard John Neuhaus. 2nd ed. Washington, DC: AEI Press.

O'Leary, Ann. 1985. "Self-Efficacy and Health." *Behaviour Research and Therapy* 23:437–451.

Opels, Robyn. 1995. "Social Justice through Peace Education: Using Dance to Access the Affective Realm in the Non-Violent Curriculum." *Humanity & Society* 19: 85–94.

O'Sullivan, Michael J., Natalie Waugh and Wendy Espeland. 1984. "The Fort Mc-

Dowell Yavapai: From Pawns to Powerbrokers." In *Studies in Empowerment: Steps Towards Understanding and Action*, ed. Julian Rappaport, Carolyn Swift and Robert Hess. New York: Haworth Press.

Ozer, Elizabeth M. and Albert Bandura. 1990. "Mechanisms Governing Empowerment Effects: A Self-Efficacy Analysis." *Journal of Personality and Social Psychology* 58:472–486.

Parker, Frank R. 1990. *Black Votes Count: Political Empowerment in Mississippi after 1965*. Chapel Hill: University of North Carolina Press.

Parks, Ward. 1997. "Afro-Fascism on the Rise." In *The Race Card: White Guilt, Black Resentment, and the Assault on Truth and Justice*, ed. Peter Collier and David Horowitz. Rocklin, CA: Prima.

Parsons, Ruth J. 1991. "Empowerment: Purpose and Practice in Social Work." *Social Work with Groups* 14:7–21.

Pateman, Carole. 1970. *Participation and Democratic Theory*. Cambridge: Cambridge University Press.

Pecorella, Robert F. 1988. "Community Empowerment Revisited: Two Decades of Integrative Reform." *State and Local Government Review* 20:72–78.

Perkins, Douglas D. and Marc Zimmerman. 1995. "Empowerment Theory, Research and Application." *American Journal of Community Psychology* 23: 581–599.

Perry, Huey L. 1980. "The Socioeconomic Impact of Black Political Empowerment in a Rural Southern Locality." *Rural Sociology* 45:207–222.

Persons, Georgia. 1993. "Introduction." In *Dilemmas of Black Politics: Issues of Leadership and Strategy*, ed. Georgia A. Persons. New York: HarperCollins.

Pilisuk, Marc, JoAnn McAllister and Jack Rothman. 1996. "Coming Together for Action: The Challenge of Contemporary Grassroots Community Organizing." *Journal of Social Issues* 52:15–37.

Pogrow, Stanley. 1996. "Reforming the Wannabe Reformers: Why Education Reforms Almost Always End Up Making Things Worse." *Phi Delta Kappan* 77:656–663.

Powell, Mary Clare. 1997. "The Arts and the Inner Lives of Teachers." *Phi Delta Kappan* 78:50–53.

Prawat, Richard S. 1991. "Conversations with Self and Settings: A Framework for Thinking about Teacher Empowerment." *American Educational Research Journal* 28:737–757.

Prilleltensky, Isaac. 1994. "Empowerment in Mainstream Psychology: Legitimacy, Obstacles and Possibilities." *Canadian Psychology* 35:358–374.

Questions and Answers Concering the EZ/EC SSBG Grants. October 1, 1995. http://www.ezec.gov/about/ssbg.html#

Rabinowitz, Alan. 1990. *Social Change Philanthropy in America*. New York: Quorum Books.

Rappaport, Julian, Carolyn Swift and Robert Hess, eds. *Studies in Empowerment: Steps Towards Understanding and Action*. New York: Haworth Press.

Rappaport, Julian. 1977. *Community Psychology: Values, Research and Action*. New York: Holt, Rinehart and Winston.

Rappaport, Julian. 1984. "Studies in Empowerment: Introduction to the Issue." In *Studies in Empowerment: Steps towards Understanding and Action*, ed. Julian Rappaport, Carolyn Swift and Robert Hess. New York: Haworth Press.

Rappaport, Julian 1985. "The Power of Empowerment Language." *Social Policy* 16:15–21.

Reed, Joe. 1991. "Grass Roots School Governance in Chicago." *National Civic Review* 80:41–45.

Renihan, F. I. and P. J. Renihan. 1995. "Responsive High Schools: Structuring Success for the At-Risk Student." *High School Journal* 79:1–13.

Riessman, Frank. 1986. "The New Populism and the Empowerment Ethos." In *The New Populism: The Politics of Empowerment*, ed. Harry C. Boyte and Frank Reissman. Philadelphia: Temple University Press.

Riessman, Frank and Timothy Bey. 1992. "The Politics of Self-Help." *Social Policy* 23:28–38.

Riger, Stephanie. 1984. "Vehicles for Empowerment: The Case of Feminist Movement Organization." In *Studies in Empowerment: Steps Towards Understanding and Action*, ed. Julian Rappaport, Carolyn Swift and Robert Hess. New York: Haworth Press.

Riger, Stephenie. 1993. "What's Wrong with Empowerment?" *American Journal of Community Psychology* 21:279–292.

Riposa, Gerry. 1996. "From Enterprise Zones to Empowerment Zones: The Community Control of Urban Economic Development." *American Behavioral Scientist* 3:356–551.

Rist, Marilee C. 1989. "Here's What Empowerment Will Mean for Your Schools." *Executive Educator* 11:16–19.

Roberts, Paul Craig and Lawrence M. Stratton. 1997. *The New Color Line: How Quotas and Privilege Destroy Democracy*. Washington, DC: Regnery Publishing.

Romanish, Bruce. 1993a. "Teacher Empowerment as the Focus of School Restructuring." *School Community Journal* 3:47–60.

Romanish, Bruce. 1993b. "Teacher Empowerment: The Litmus Test of School Restructuring." *Social Science Record* 3:55–69.

Ryan, William. 1971. *Blaming the Victim*. New York: Random House.

Sacks, Karen Brodkin. 1988. "Gender and Grassroots Leadership." In *Women and the Politics of Empowerment*, ed. Sandra Morgan and Ann Bookman. Philadelphia: Temple University Press.

Safire, William. 1990. "Empowerment and Denouncement." *New York Times Magazine*, July 15, p. 12.

Sanchez, William and Olga Garriga. 1995. "Reality Therapy, Control Theory and Latino Activism: Towards Empowerment and Social Change." *Journal of Reality Therapy* 15:3–14.

Sandvick, Doris S. and Roberta W. Nauman. 1991. "Teacher Empowerment at Paul Norton Elementary School: In Progress." *Thresholds in Education* 17:22.

Santoro, Wayne A. 1995. "Black Politics and Employment Policies: The Determinants of Local Government Affirmative Action." *Social Science Quarterly* 76:794–808.

Schexnider, Alvin J. 1982. "Political Mobilization in the South: The Election of a Black Mayor in New Orleans." In *The New Black Politics: The Search for Political Power*, ed. Michael B. Preston, Lenneal J. Henderson, Jr. and Paul Puryear. New York: Longman.

Schuftan, Claudio. 1996. "The Community Development Dilemma: What Is Really Empowering?" *Community Development Journal* 31:260–264.

Shadish, William P., Jr. 1990. "Defining Excellence Criteria in Community Research." In *Researching Community Psychology: Issues of Theory and Method*, ed. Patrick Tolan, Christopher Keys, Fern Chertok and Leonard Jason. Washington, DC: American Psychological Association.

Shanker, Albert. 1990. "A Proposal for Using Incentives to Restructure Our Public Schools." *Phi Delta Kappan* 71:345–357.

Shannon, Patrick. 1990. "Re-Searching the Familiar." *Language Arts* 67:30–38.

Sickler, Joan L. 1988. "Teachers in Charge: Empowering the Professionals." *Phi Delta Kappan* 69:354–356, 376.

Simon, Barbara Levy. 1990. "Rethinking Empowerment." *Journal of Progressive Human Services* 1:27–39.

Simon, Roger I. 1987. "Empowerment as a Pedagogy of Possibility." *Language Arts* 64:370–382.

Skinner, Ellen A. 1995. *Perceived Control, Motivation, and Coping*. Thousand Oaks, CA: Sage.

Solomon, Barbara Bryant. 1976. *Black Empowerment: Social Work in Oppressed Communities*. New York: Columbia University Press.

Solomon, Deborah and Jennifer Dixon. 1997. "Investment Brings New Jobs." *Free Press*, April 17. http://www.freep.com/news/econ/qjobs17.htm

Sowell, Thomas. 1981. *Ethnic America: A History*. New York: Basic Books.

Sowell, Thomas. 1984. *Civil Rights: Rhetoric or Reality?* New York: William Morrow and Company.

Sowell, Thomas. 1986. *Education: Assumptions versus History*. Stanford: Hoover Institution Press.

Speer, Paul W. and Joseph Hughey. 1995. "Community Organizing: An Ecological Route to Empowerment and Power." *American Journal of Community Psychology* 23:729–748.

Speer, Paul W. and Joseph Hughey. 1996. "Mechanisms of Empowerment: Psychological Process for Members of Power-based Community Organizations." *Journal of Community and Applied Social Psychology* 6:177–187.

Spigner, Clarence. 1989–1990. "Sociology of AIDS within Black Communities: Theoretical Considerations." *International Quarterly of Health Education* 10:285–296.

Sprague, Jo. 1992. "Critical Perspectives on Teacher Empowerment." *Communication Education* 41:181–205.

Sprague, Joey. 1988. "The Other Side of the Banner: Towards a Feminization of Politics." In *Seeing Female: Social Role and Personal Lives*, ed. Sharon S. Brehm. New York: Greenwood Press.

Stacey, Margaret and Marion Price. 1981. *Women, Power, and Politics*. London: Travistock Publications.

Stanfield, Rochelle L. 1993. "The Ward Healers." *National Journal* 23:1344–1348.

Staples, Lee H. 1990. "Powerful Ideas About Empowerment." *Administration in Social Work* 14:29–42.

Statistical Abstract of the United States, 1996–1997. Washington, DC: U.S. Government Printing Office.

Stein, Bob. 1996. "O'Farrell Community School." *Phi Delta Kappan* 78:28–29.

Stevenson, Howard C., Jr. 1994. "The Psychology of Sexual Racism and AIDS: An Ongoing Saga of Distrust and the 'Sexual Other.' " *Journal of Black Studies* 25:62–80.

"Study Finds Racial Disparity in Warning to the Pregnant." 1994. *New York Times*, January 20, A16.

Swift, Carolyn. 1984. "Forward: Empowerment: An Antidote for Folly." In *Studies in Empowerment: Steps Towards Understanding and Action*, ed. Julian Rappaport, Carolyn Swift and Robert Hess. New York: Haworth Press.

Tate, Katherine. 1993. *From Protest to Politics: The New Black Voters in American Elections*. New York: Russell Sage Foundation.

Thayer, George. 1968. *The Farther Shores of Politics: The American Political Fringe Today*. 2nd ed. New York: Simon and Schuster.

Tittle, Diana. 1995. *Welcome to Heights High: The Crippling Politics of Restructuring America's Public Schools*. Columbus: Ohio State University Press.

"Topics Causing Disagreement ($597.200(d) (4)." Detroit Empowerment Zone Transition Office. http://www.detroit.freenet.org/Ezplan4.html

Topping, John C., Jr. 1982. "Empowerment: A Republican Alternative to Democratic Paternalism." *Ripon Forum* 18:8–9.

Trivette, Carol M., Carl J. Dunst and Deborah Hamby. 1996. "Characteristics and Consequences of Help-Giving Practices in Contrasting Human Services Programs." *American Journal of Community Psychology* 24:273–292.

Troyna, Barry. 1994. "Blind Faith? Empowerment and Educational Research." *International Studies in Sociology of Education* 4:3–24.

Tucker, William. 1991. "How Housing Regulations Cause Homelessness." *Public Interest* 102:78–88.

Tuthill, Doug et al. 1987. "An Ecological and School Specific Model of Student and Teacher Empowerment: The N.E.A.'s Master in Learning Project." Paper presented to the Annual Convention of the American Education Research Association, Washington, DC, April 23.

Wade, Ruth K. 1997. "Lifting a School's Spirit." *Educational Leadership* 54:34–36.

Waks, Leonard J. 1991. "Science, Technology, and Society Education for Urban Schools." *Journal of Negro Education* 60:195–202.

Wallerstein, Nina. 1992. "Powerlessness, Empowerment and Health: Implication for Health Promotion Programs." *American Journal of Health Promotion* 6: 197–205.

Wallerstein, Nina. 1993. "Empowerment and Health: The Theory and Practice of Community Change." *Community Development Journal* 28:218–227.

Wallerstein, Nina and Edward Bernstein. 1988. "Empowerment Education: Freire's Ideas Adapted to Health Education." *Health Education Quarterly* 15:379–394.

Wang, Caroline and Mary Ann Burris. 1994. "Empowerment through Photo Novella: Portraits of Participation." *Health Education Quarterly* 2:171–186.

Weber, Vin. 1993. "Empowering Clinton." *National Review* 45:22–23.

Weissberg, Robert. 1998. *Political Tolerance: Balancing Community and Diversity*. Thousand Oaks, CA: Sage.

Wells, Karen J. 1997. "Professional Development for Parents." *American School Board Journal* 184:38–39.

Wilcox, Laird. 1994. *Crying Wolf: Hate Crime Hoaxes in America*. Olathe, KS: Laird Wilcox Editorial Research Service.

Williams, Eddie N. 1982. "Black Political Progress in the 1970s." In *The New Black Politics: The Search for Political Power*, ed. Michael B. Preston, Lenneal J. Henderson, Jr. and Paul Puryear. New York: Longman.

Williams, Sharon E. and Dolores Finger Wright. 1992. "Empowerment: The Strength of Black Families Revisited." *Journal of Multicultural Social Work* 2:23–36.

Wilson, James Q. 1960. *Negro Politics: The Search for Leadership*. New York: Free Press.

Wirt, Fredrick M. 1970. *The Politics of Southern Equality: Law and Social Change in a Mississippi County*. Chicago: Aldine.

Wittig, Michele Andrisin. 1996. "An Introduction to Social Psychological Perspectives on Grassroots Organizing." *Journal of Social Issues* 52: 3–14.

Woodson, Robert L. 1987. *On the Road to Economic Reform: An Agenda for Black Progress*. Washington, DC: Regnery Gateway.

Woodson, Robert L., Sr. 1996. "Success Stories." In *To Empower People: From State to Civil Society*, ed. Peter L. Berger and Richard John Neuhaus. 2nd ed. Washington, DC: AEI Press.

Yeich, Susan. 1996. "Grassroots Organizing with Homeless People: A Participatory Research Approach." *Journal of Social Issues* 52:111–121.

Yonemura, Margaret. 1986. "Reflections on Teacher Empowerment and Teacher Education." *Harvard Education Review* 56:473–480.

Zeichner, Kenneth M. 1991. "Contradictions and Tensions in the Professionalization of Teaching and the Democratization of Schools." *Teachers College Record* 92:363–376.

Zimmerman, Joseph F. 1972. *The Federated City: Community Control in Large Cities*. New York: St. Martin's Press.

Zimmerman, Marc A. 1995. "Psychological Empowerment: Issues and Illustrations." *American Journal of Community Psychology* 23:581–599.

Zolkower, Betina. 1995. "Math Fictions: What Really Solves the Problem?" *Social Text* 43:133–162.

Index

About the Author

ROBERT WEISSBERG is Professor of Political Science at the University of Illinois, Urbana–Champaign. Professor Weissberg is the author or co-author/editor of numerous publications, including *Political Tolerance* and *Politics: A Handbook for Students*.